Henry
VIII

ABOUT THE AUTHOR

DAVID LOADES is Emeritus Professor of the University of Wales. He has written sixteen books on the Tudors including: *The Six Wives of Henry VIII*, *Elizabeth I*, *The Tudor Queens of England*, *Mary Tudor: A Life*, *The Chronicle of the Tudor Kings*, *The Chronicle of the Tudor Queens*, *The Reign of Mary Tudor*, *The Fighting Tudors*, *The Making of the Tudor Navy*, *The Tudor Queens*, *The Tudors for Dummies*, *The Cecils: Privilege & Power Behind the Throne*, *Intrigue & Treason: The Tudor Court, 1547-1558*, *Tudor Government*, *Henry VIII King & Court*, and *Henry VIII: Court, Church & Conflict*. He is currently writing a new biography of Thomas Cromwell, also for Amberley. He lives in Burford in Oxfordshire.

PRAISE FOR DAVID LOADES

The Six Wives of Henry VIII
'I warmly recommend this book' ALISON WEIR
'A very good book' *LITERARY REVIEW*
'Neither Starkey nor Weir has the assurance & command of Loades' SIMON HEFFER

Mary Tudor: A Life
'An excellent and sensitive biography' *THE OBSERVER*

Elizabeth I
'Succeeds in depicting her to us as a real woman'
LITERARY REVIEW
'Readable, searching and wise' *NEW STATESMAN*
'Everything a scholarly biography should be, and a good read too'
RICHARD REX, author of *The Tudors*

DAVID
LOADES

AMBERLEY

This edition first published 2013

Amberley Publishing
The Hill, Stroud
Gloucestershire, GL5 4EP

www.amberley-books.com

Copyright © David Loades 2011, 2013

British Library Cataloguing in Publication Data.
A catalogue record for this book is available from the British Library.

ISBN 978-1-4456-0704-7 paperback
ISBN 978-1-4456-0665-1 ebook

Typesetting and Origination by Amberley Publishing.
Printed in Great Britain.

CONTENTS

PREFACE

There are many books on Henry VIII; from learned works on different aspects of his reign to popular biographies. Some of these are based on original research, and some on what contemporaries chose to write about him. All reflect their authors' experiences both as historians and as writers. In that respect, this is no different. It reflects a lifetime spent working on the Tudors, and the writing of more books than I care to number. It also reflects many years of attending conferences and post-graduate seminars, on the Reformation and on Early Modern England. Latterly these have been in the History Faculty of the University of Oxford, and I am grateful to the Chairman of the Board, Professor Christopher Wickham and his staff for their hospitality. Gratitude is also due to those individuals, colleagues and students too numerous to name, with whom I have discussed Henry VIII and his problems over the years, and to my wife Judith, an unfailing source of inspiration.

It is now more than forty years since Jack Scarisbrick produced his magisterial biography, and it has stood the test of time, and of other scholarship, remarkably well. However, Amberley Publishing has now challenged me to make another attempt. I am less interested in the details of diplomacy than Jack was, largely because so much of it led to no tangible result, and although I am keenly aware of the importance of theology to Henry, I am less concerned with the contextual aspects of the Great Matter, which have been thoroughly explored by other scholars. My own work has been largely on the King's marriages, and on military developments, particularly the navy, and that will be obvious from the pages which follow. I have also been specifically guided by the work of others, most notably of Helen Miller, Mervyn James and, more recently, Eric Ives and George Bernard. In writing this book, it has struck me forcibly what an extraordinary person the King was, and how difficult it is to get inside the minds of renaissance men. Personal monarchy is, and has been for many years, alien to our political mindset. Preoccupied with democracy, we tend to forget how important it was for Henry VIII to build on the support of the gentry. Interest in his opponents has also detracted from our appreciation of just how much support he had, particularly towards the end of his reign. Henry thought of himself as enjoying a direct relationship with God, but he was also aware that God sometimes spoke through the people. I hope that I have succeeded in doing justice to this complex and compelling man.

David Loades
Burford, August 2010

INTRODUCTION:
THE HISTORIOGRAPHY OF A KING

Our King does not desire gold or silver, but virtue, glory, immortality ... (Lord Mountjoy, 1509)

Ricco, feroce et cupido di Gloria ... (Nicolo Machiavelli, 1513)

Both these very different observers noticed one outstanding characteristic of Henry VIII – his desire for glory, or reputation. It was as true in 1547 as it had been at the beginning of his reign, and was to enjoy a long and vigorous afterlife. Thanks largely to his own actions, he has remained one of the most fascinating of English kings, and speculation about his motives and his effectiveness is as vigorous today as it has ever been. Henry was passionately concerned about his own image, and thanks to his employment of Hans Holbein as his court painter, his magnificence and (largely spurious) self-assurance has communicated itself down the centuries.[1] He has been a hero and a villain; a lecherous tyrant and a constitutional monarch; 'bluff King Hal' and a serial wife-killer. The one thing that no serious student of the sixteenth century can do to Henry VIII is to ignore him.

The construction of his image began, not only in his own lifetime, but before he had even come to the throne. It was visual and ceremonial, and designed to support the dynasty through the creation of honours. In this Henry was preceded and at first overshadowed by his elder brother, Arthur, who in November 1489, when he was two years old, was borne in splendid state from Shene to London for his induction as Prince of Wales.[2] At the same time the infant prince was also created Earl of Chester and installed as a Knight of the Garter. Girls were less useful from this point of view, and the christening of Princess Margaret which occurred at the same time was a relatively low-key event. When Henry made his debut on 28 June 1491, he was, first and foremost, a symbol of that fertility which seemed to bless Henry VII and his Queen with the unmistakable marks of Divine favour.[3] Unlike Arthur, who had been Duke of Cornwall from birth, Henry did not automatically acquire any title, but offices were swiftly conferred upon him, long before he can have had any notion of their meaning, let alone discharged the duties in person. He became Warden of the Cinque Ports, Constable of Dover Castle and Earl Marshall before he was even out of his cradle, while in September 1494, at the age of three, he became Lord Lieutenant of Ireland. Just over a month later he was created Duke of York. This magnificent ceremony not only demonstrated the much publicised union of the Houses of York and Lancaster, it also stated in the clearest possible fashion that the previous Duke (Edward IV's second son) was dead, and that Perkin Warbeck, then claiming his persona, was a fraud.[4] In May 1495 Henry was also invested with the Order of the Garter. At the age of ten he played a prominent role in the marriage celebrations of his brother, but that was essentially in support of Arthur's image rather than his own. His next elevation was by necessity rather than choice, because Arthur died in April 1502, and on 18 February 1504 his brother succeeded him as Prince of Wales and Earl of Chester. The splendour of that occasion was somewhat marred by the circumstances which had deprived the aging king not only of his expected heir, but also of his queen. It represented an essential gesture of dynastic continuity.[5]

Apart from these rather notional positions, the adolescent Henry was kept carefully under wraps by his father. It was known in a general way that he was well educated, promised to be a fine specimen of a man, and had a boyish enthusiasm for war games, but as his father's health declined, the expectations which began to build were based on flimsy evidence of his character and capabilities. As soon as Henry VII was dead, they burst into flower, and Henry was shrewd enough to do everything in his power to encourage the magnificent image with which he had been presented.

At first his self-promotion was occasional, and limited in its appeal. Splendid ceremonies were held at court to mark the Church's seasons, the King's wedding and the birth of his heir.[6] Henry jousted, went Maying, and enjoyed innumerable banquets and masks. Some of these were put on for the benefit of foreign ambassadors, but always the King was the pivotal figure, his skill at the tilt and his magnificent costumes providing the raw material for innumerable gossipy letters. However, outside the range of the court, and perhaps the City of London, these displays were little known about or understood. What was understood was his appetite for war, and the recruitment of the army which he led to France with great fanfares in 1513 led to a wider understanding of his personality than a dozen court festivities. This was an opportunity not to be missed, and his magnificent entry into Tournai wrung the last ounce of advantage out of that not-very-splendid victory.[7] It was not his fault that his efforts, including the sending of the keys of the town as a trophy to his lady, were upstaged by his servant the Earl of Surrey, the victor of Flodden, who sent her James IV's bloodstained hauberk. Insofar as Henry features in the literature of the period, his appearances are allegorical or disguised. He appears in the title role of John Skelton's *Magnyfycence*, a piece now associated with the expulsion of the minions in 1519, in which role he is represented as a 'noble prince of might' who becomes ensnared by various Vices who succeed in joining his household. He casts off the restraint of wise and prudent councillors in favour of their riotous and irresponsible ways, until recalled to a sense of his duty by four Virtues, 'sad and sober' men to whom he is persuaded to listen.[8] This is an exaggerated but recognisable version of the events which led to the expulsion of Sir Nicholas Carew and Sir Francis Bryan, two 'Frenchified' jousting companions from the Privy Chamber. Several years later Edward Hall wrote that in May 1519:

... the kynges counsaill secretly communed together of the kynges gentlenes &
liberalitee to all persones: by which they perceived that certain young men in his
privie chamber, not regarding his estate nor degree, were so familier and homely
with hym ... that thei forgat themselves ...[9]

As a result, Henry entrusted the management of the situation to his
councillors, and they imported four 'ancient knights' into the Privy
Chamber to replace the minions, and the problem was solved. Whether
the King was really as compliant as this story suggests hardly matters
– 'magnificence' had justified his name and proved his worthiness, and
that was the point of Skelton's play.

John Skelton is best known for his satires attacking Wolsey, but even
they were backhanded ways of paying compliments to the King, who is
consistently represented as 'our moost royall Harry', the true type and
ideal of a royal ruler.[10] Until the late 1520s this kind of courtly flattery
was the most, and the least, that Henry could expect. He quarrelled
with his wife, took mistresses and begat a bastard, waged unsuccessful
war and tried to extract money from his subjects by underhand means,
but none of this was allowed to affect his chivalric image, which by
1527 had become seriously detached from reality. However, what
challenged his self-conceit fundamentally was his 'Great Matter' – his
desire to rid himself of Catherine of Aragon.[11] Once he was locked into
that struggle he could no longer expect a consensus of flattery to follow
his every move, and the historiography of his reign can truly be said
to begin. After a disappointing reaction to his public declaration of
his scruple of conscience, Henry could no longer deceive himself into
believing that whatever he did would be supported uncritically by his
subjects. Although his own propaganda team took the initiative and
issued tracts like *The Glasse of the Truth* in support of his position,
they also justified it in the carefully worded preambles to the relevant
statutes, and the King was well aware that he had a battle on his hands.[12]
Opposition works, usually printed abroad and written by responsible
men like John Fisher, concentrated upon attacking his policies rather
than his person, but popular opponents were often less scrupulous.

Elizabeth Barton predicted that he would lose his throne if he married Anne Boleyn, and others thought and gossiped to the same effect. Wild prophecies began to circulate, and the sinister word 'moldwarp' began to be uttered.[13] Henry overcame these seditious mutterings by well-directed coercion, and remained in control of his kingdom, but in Europe he acquired the reputation of a dangerous maverick. The King would probably not much have minded being accused of playing God by Martin Luther, if he had known about it, because he set no store by the reformer's opinions, theological or otherwise, but he was seriously riled by Reginald Pole's *Pro ecclesiasticae unitatis defensione*. This was ostensibly for his eyes only and constituted a thoughtful and intelligent attack, not only upon his policies since 1529, but also upon his personal integrity. It was published, probably without the author's knowledge, in Rome in 1536.[14]

Pro ... defensione was the first round in the creation of that 'black legend' of Henry VIII which thereafter dominated all those records of English events which emanated either from Catholic Europe or from the English Catholic community. One of the most vitriolic was Nicholas Sander's *De origine ac progressu schismaticis Anglicani*, published at Cologne in 1585, which attributed Henry's actions in the 1530s entirely to unbridled lust, both for Anne Boleyn and also for the wealth of the Church. This was a line also taken by Robert Parsons in his *Treatise of three conversions...* which was issued at St Omer in 1603.[15] Modern historians in the Catholic tradition have been far more judicious, not only because polemic no longer serves a useful purpose, but because the debate has broadened to embrace the King's whole style of government. Cardinal Gasquet in 1888, while not abandoning the lust and greed interpretation, was more concerned to set the events in context and to admit that there might have been some justification for the King's extreme reactions. In the twentieth century Philip Hughes, while pointing out that Henry had a tendency to alter the law to suit his own convenience, also proposed that there was much amiss with the late medieval Church, and particularly the monasteries, which invited the King's intervention.[16] This concession has been repudiated by more recent scholars, notably Jack Scarisbrick and Eamon Duffy, who have argued that the Church was in rude health and that Henry's success was primarily the result of his exercise of crude force. It was by executing dissenters on both sides of the confessional divide that the King enforced his will, using fear and intimidation as his principal weapons. Meanwhile, for historians of a Protestant persuasion the reformation was a change waiting to happen. Without denying the importance of the King's actions, they proposed a model of a Church corrupted from within by superstition and idolatry, a tottering edifice awaiting a decisive push. Unfortunately Henry's push had been anything but decisive, as they admitted.[17]

John Foxe, standing at the head of this tradition, was frankly puzzled by Henry, who seemed to blow both hot and cold on the reformers – often at the same time. When he repudiated the papal authority, reformed the calendar or introduced the English Bible, he was a Godly Prince, showing a proper regard for the spiritual welfare of his subjects. But when he passed the Act of Six Articles, imposing the mass, or burned John Lambert for heresy, he was a superstitious tyrant. Foxe solved this problem as best he could by claiming that Henry was gullible and easily led. It depended on whether he was listening to Cranmer and Thomas Cromwell or to Stephen Gardiner and the Duke of Norfolk:

> Thus while council was about him, and could be heard he did much good, so again when sinister and wicked councillors under subtle and crafty pretences had gotten ever the foot in, thrusting truth and verity out of the prince's ears, how much religion and all good things went prosperously forward before, so much on the contrary side all revoked backwards again …[18]

Henry's personality, no less than his council and his court, were thus caught up in the cosmic struggle of good and evil – the true Church against the false – which is the main theme of the *Acts and Monuments*. By the time that Gilbert Burnet and John Strype were writing in the late seventeenth and early eighteenth centuries, Foxe's eschatology was no longer in fashion, and Henry had become a sort of latter-day Joshua, a leader chosen by God who was nevertheless doomed not to see the promised land. His own image of himself as Solomon helped in this respect, because Solomon was not permitted to build the Temple, a task which was reserved for his successor David, an obvious allusion to the completion of the reformation under Edward.[19] Henry's role in the creation of the Church of England has been for generations the main focus for an understanding both of his personality and of his reign. That was the case for Geoffrey Dickens, writing after the Second World War, and for George Bernard in the early twenty-first century. Dickens was inclined to take Foxe's line, seeing the shifts in the King's position as a reflection of the influence of those about him, although he allowed a greater part for Henry's own uncertainties, as conservative instincts struggled with intellectual convictions. Dickens was concerned to demonstrate, as Foxe had been, that there was considerable support for Henry's actions among his subjects; a support which he was inclined to attribute to the early influence of Protestantism.[20] In this he was directly refuted by Christopher Haigh, who took the same line as Professors Scarisbrick and Duffy about the robust state of pre-reformation Catholicism. However, Dickens' thesis did have the advantage of offering a partial explanation for the relative lack of resistance to the King's policies – at least within the realm. For Professor Bernard, on the other hand, influences were beside the point. He argued at some length and with considerable erudition, that there were no inconsistencies to be explained. The King's position may have been idiosyncratic, and not have conformed to the models of Catholic and Protestant in which historians have dealt, but he was clear in his own mind where he wanted to be, and pursued his aim steadfastly.[21]

It is likely that this controversial view will herald a new round of more or less subtle interpretations of Henry's personality based on the events of the 1530s and on the emergence of his religious position. However, it must be remembered that he reigned for thirty-eight years, and did a great many other things apart from removing the Pope and imposing himself upon the English Church. There has always been a secular historiography, running alongside the religious one and interacting with it, but distinct in its priorities. Edward Hall's *Union of the Two Noble and Illustre Famelies of*

Lancastre and Yorke of 1548 follows on directly from the courtly writings of the early part of the reign.[22] Hall was a dramatic writer, and created heightened pictorial images of the splendours of the reign, so the reader gets dramatic images of Henry at play, Henry at war, and as a dispenser of justice. The magnificence of his court knew no equal. In describing the King's marriage to Catherine of Aragon (an event which he may have witnessed, being twelve at the time), he excels himself in his portrait of Henry himself:

> The features of his body, his goodly personage, his amiable visage, princely countenance, with the noble qualities of his royal estate, to every man known, needeth no rehersal, considering, that for lack of cunning, I cannot express the gifts of grace and of nature, that God hath endowed him withal. Yet partly to describe his apparel, it is to be noted, his grace wore in his uppermost apparel, a robe of crimson velvet, furred with ermines, his jacket or coat of raised gold, the placard embroidered with diamonds, rubies, emeralds, great pearls, and other rich stones, a great bauderic about his neck, of great balasses. The trapper of his horse, damask gold, with a deep pursell of ermines, his knights and esquires for his body in crimson velvet, and all the gentlemen, with other of his chapel, and all his officers and household servants, were apparelled in scarlet ...[23]

All this colour and opulence translates into qualities of moral and political superiority, so that the king can do no wrong. Henry thus emerges as the saviour of England, and the embodiment of its national pride and achievement. Hall invents freely; speeches, letters, and dramatic groupings of events, in a manner worthy of the humanist influences which were at work upon him. He interweaves narrative with dramatised scenes and dialogue, almost as if they were to be performed upon the stage. For example, in describing the pardon of the London apprentices after the Evil May Day riots in 1517 he explains how the prisoners were led through the streets, tied with ropes, amid the great mourning of their kinsfolk. Having executed thirteen of them out of hand by martial law, Henry is then persuaded by easy stages and the intervention of Queen Catherine to grant his gracious pardon to the rest.[24] He thus at once becomes both the just and severe judge and the merciful father of his people. Hall is entirely justified in calling that part of his work 'The Triumphaunt Reigne of Kyng Henry VIII', because the King emerges as wise, powerful and magnificent. He was right to repudiate Queen Catherine, and right to suppress dissent against the Royal Supremacy by whatever means were ready to hand. Without entering into difficult questions like consent, Hall represents his subject as a glorious king, and one whom his daughter Elizabeth might worthily try to imitate. In so doing he set the tone for generations of historians to follow – Grafton, Stow, and Holinshed; even the conservative John Leland, who lamented the fall of the abbeys, did not deny Henry his stature as a great king – although his work was not published until the eighteenth century.[25]

Shakespeare treated Henry VIII with kid gloves, as became the father of the incumbent ruler. The play which he wrote with John Fletcher was (like *King John*) mainly a piece of anti-Catholic polemic, in which Wolsey was the villain and Henry the hero, but it is not a memorable portrait, being notable mainly for its justification of the Royal Supremacy.[26]

Thereafter the King did not have a good press, as his bloodthirsty reputation gained the upper hand of his more positive achievements, and the gross Henry of 1546 overtook the attractive youth in the public imagination. The arbitrary enforcement of his will, notably against Anne Boleyn and Sir Thomas More, took precedence over more cautious appraisals of his use of the law and of Parliament, and he became a tyrant. A king who squandered the resources of his realm on pointless wars to feed his own ego, and who destroyed the Church to satisfy his craving for power. To J. A. Froude, writing in 1856, Henry was a king who did what he had to do to get rid of superstition and foreign interference, but that was already an old-fashioned point of view.[27] To the historians of the early twentieth century, and most notably to A. F. Pollard, Henry was a despot, who manipulated Parliament and public opinion in order to get his own way. He rode roughshod over the laws, executing anyone who displeased him, including his loyal servants Thomas More and Thomas Cromwell. He was a womaniser who repudiated two wives and executed two others, and who sought to distract attention from his egocentric activities at home by waging pointless and expensive foreign wars. The country which he left behind him was impoverished and deeply divided.[28] This orthodoxy was challenged in the early 1950s by Geoffrey Elton. In 1953 he wrote:

> There have been periods when the needs of 'good government' prevailed over the demands of 'free government', and of these the Tudor age was the most important. To speak of despotism and a reign of terror in sixteenth century England was easier for a generation which had not met these things at first hand; however, it remains true that it was a time when men were ready to be governed, and when order and peace seemed more important than principles and rights.[29]

The Tudors were not despots, and did not have the weapons of despotism. Instead he proposed a 'revolution in government' over which Henry VIII presided. Henry was, he argued, a man of cloudy but statesmanlike vision who realised the limitations of his own power. Deeply imbued with the idea of the supremacy of the law, he was a meticulous observer of its forms, and at no time acted arbitrarily. He also respected the legislative function of Parliament, and never attempted to create law *mero moto suo*, however pressing the circumstances. Faced with the real and urgent need for a male heir, and convinced of the unlawfulness of his first marriage, he took the only course open to him when curial politics denied him the annulment which he needed. It was Thomas Cromwell rather than the King who converted his aspirations into concrete political action, but Henry was willingly led into a position where his potential authority eclipsed that of any of his predecessors.[30] This authority he then defended ruthlessly, but no more ruthlessly than the circumstances demanded, and his subjects accepted it because the alternative was civil strife, and because he had convinced them of the need for obedience. His action against the Church was also justified by this vision of a unified state under a single ruler. The Church was the greatest of the medieval franchises, and the King was entirely right to regard the clergy as 'only half his subjects'. In bringing them under his effective rule he was taking one of the major steps needed for the creation of a modern state.[31] The abolition of the secular franchises, the reform of the financial administration and the reshaping of the council, were also further steps carried out by Cromwell in pursuit of Henry's less precisely articulated ideal. The egotism which drove the mature Henry was clearly visible in the young man who had executed Empson and Dudley out of hand and waged a vainglorious and unnecessary war against France from 1512 to 1514. Thereafter the King was always short of money, which he looked to his servants to supply. Wolsey let him down in that respect in 1525, and that marked the beginning of the end for their confidential relationship, but Cromwell succeeded triumphantly by persuading him to dissolve the monasteries. Henry was always in charge, but not in any immediate sense. As a young man he was more interested in his amusements, particularly masking and hunting, and as his athleticism faded in later life he became preoccupied with theology and with foreign policy.[32] Except for a few salient issues over which he felt it necessary to assert himself, such as the destruction of the Duke of Buckingham in 1521 and of Anne Boleyn and her followers in 1536, he was happy to leave the governance of the realm to others.

It was therefore Cromwell rather than the King who was the architect of the 'revolution in government' which saw the position of Parliament transformed from the medieval estates into a sovereign legislature, and patronage concentrated in the hands of the Lord Privy Seal. Administration was transformed from the personalised model of the later Middle Ages, when most power had been concentrated in the hands of the nobility and the royal household, into a more bureaucratic and 'modern' mode, focused in the offices of the King's leading servants, who were no longer primarily courtiers.[33] It was this change which led directly to the reform of the Privy Council, which instead of being a large and rather amorphous body of men, some of whom the King chose to consult much more regularly than others, became much more like a cabinet of senior office holders, who met regularly and transacted a defined body of business.[34] Elton's influence was immediate and overwhelming, thanks largely to his teaching position at Cambridge University and the large number of graduate students whom he supervised on 'constitutional' subjects. However, the 'revolution in government' was also controversial from the start. Medievalists like Gerald Harriss attacked the whole idea of radical change, proposing instead that the 1530s had merely seen a reversion to a Lancastrian style of government, as opposed to the more personalised style favoured by the House of York.[35] Although Harriss was prepared to concede that Henry had gone a step further than Richard II in repudiating the Pope's authority, he could not see any difference in principle between the Royal Supremacy and the Act of Praemunire of 1393.

Others followed Harriss with more or less vehemence, but it was one of Elton's own students who attacked the 'revolution', not on the basis of medieval precedent, but directly as an interpretation of the 1530s. It was, David Starkey argued, a mistake to see Cromwell's reforms in terms of bureaucracy. What he was doing was creating a personal empire in the King's service, concentrating administration in his own hands. The political focus, meanwhile, remained at the court, and particularly in the Privy Chamber.[36] This had the advantage of explaining why the centre of business shifted from the office of King's Secretary to that of Lord Privy Seal when Cromwell was promoted, and ultimately of accounting for Cromwell's own fall by invoking the political infighting of the court. Particularly after Cromwell's execution, control of the Privy Chamber, and with it of access to the King, becomes critical to an understanding of public events. This thesis also offered a more satisfactory explanation of the fact that the changes in the Privy Council did not take place until after Cromwell's fall. If they had been brought about by his own initiative, they could be expected to have taken place between 1536 and 1538. If, however, they were the King's idea and designed to reduce his minister's personal control, it would make perfect sense that the latter had dragged his feet over implementing them – so that they took full effect only after he had gone.[37] Although prepared to concede on points of emphasis, and to admit that he had neglected the court, on his main Cromwellian thesis Geoffrey Elton remained unrepentant, and twenty years later produced another revolutionary minister. Where he had previously presented a man of constitutional vision, well aware that he was creating a monarchy potentially limited by Parliament in a fashion that Henry simply did not understand, in *Reform and Renewal* (1973) Cromwell became a man of social and economic idealism, aiming to reshape the commonwealth by increasing the role of central government.[38] This thesis was in turn attacked, most notably by Penry Williams, who could see in the minister's actions no constructive vision, but rather a series of *ad hoc* responses to immediate crises. Elton again defended his position in a series of cogent articles. In all this debate, the King remained more a looming presence than an active protagonist, neither a despot nor a 'constitutional' monarch, but rather responding to domestic issues as he was prompted. He was, however, dominant, and his erratic interventions could never be accurately predicted. No one could take a decisive initiative without Henry's active consent, a point made more effectively by Elton's opponents than by Elton himself.[39] Eventually he did produce a more subtle and nuanced picture of Thomas Cromwell, but again Henry remains largely in the background.

Meanwhile, in 1968, another Elton pupil, Jack Scarisbrick, had published what still remains the definitive biography of the King. This he described as being neither a 'private life' nor a comprehensive study of the reign, but rather something in between. What emerges is a thoroughgoing account of Henry's achievements, not only his refashioning of the Church in his own image, but his restructuring (with Cromwell's help) of the governance of the realm, his creation of the English navy, and his self-created role in European diplomacy.[40] There he consistently punched above his weight and was taken seriously by both the major powers of the first half of the sixteenth century, France and the Empire. France he attacked three times without obvious provocation, winning (temporarily) no more than 'ungracious dogholes', but maintaining the image of a warrior upon which he relied for his influence. He was interested in ballistics, and with warlike ambitions in mind, transformed the English gunfounding industry.[41] He even fought a somewhat notional war against the Emperor from 1526 to 1529 in the interests of maintaining the balance of power which protected him, and thus made doubly sure that Charles V would oppose any move which he might make in Rome to secure the annulment of his marriage. Against Scotland, a lesser power whom he could be accused of bullying, he fought twice – and almost a third time. The first time he was not the aggressor, and was totally victorious, but the second occasion was unprovoked aggression, which resulted in a fierce and futile campaign for a union of the crowns.[42] On every occasion the King's motives for fighting were entirely personal, and expressed the interests of England only to the extent that he represented the realm. It was accepted at the time that war and peace were entirely matters for the King to decide, but when it came to paying for these adventures the Parliament had a legitimate interest, and what was said there did not always make comfortable hearing.

Henry spent money like water, not only on war but on his entertainments and most especially on his building programme. Sometimes this could be justified in terms of security, as with the south coast forts in 1539, and sometimes by the need for a residence in a particular place, as was the case with the palace of Bridewell, upon which work proceeded from 1515 to 1522. But for the most part it was to gratify the royal whim. Neither Oatlands nor Nonsuch nor St James' were really needed, but the King built restlessly to satisfy his craving for magnificence – a craving which inspired so many actions during his reign.[43] The king who emerges from this exhaustive study is first and foremost an egotist; a man determined to have his own way, and adept at convincing himself that that way was justified. When he was concentrating, his intelligence was formidable, and he had a miscellaneous range of accomplishments from fluent Latin to a mean hand on the lute. In the first half of his reign, his concentration wandered quite a lot, which gave the impression that his councillors – and particularly Cardinal Wolsey – were really running the country. This was a mistake, as no one knew better than Wolsey, because when the King chose to assert himself his grasp was formidable and his anger devastating. After Wolsey's fall there followed a period of some three years which earlier historians had dubbed 'the years without a policy'. Scarisbrick demonstrates that Henry did indeed have a policy, or rather a succession of policies, each of which was frustrated in turn, leaving him eventually with an option which he did not know how to implement.[44] Hence the importance of Thomas Cromwell, and here Professor Scarisbrick is inclined to follow Elton, at least part of the way. Henry knew where he wanted to go (and was morally convinced of his rectitude) but needed a 'ways and means' man to convert his aspirations into reality. When it came to dealing with the Church the King found his jurisdictional radicalism at odds with his sacramental conservatism. The humanist and the orthodox aspects of his upbringing coming into conflict for the first time. So we have a monarch arguing theology with the Pope, and convincing himself that he was a better Catholic than Clement VII. When it came to the point, he was able to shrug off his excommunication, and he carried the majority of his subjects with him because of the way in which he had succeeded in projecting himself as a great king who cared for his realm.[45]

Henry could be bounced into ruthless decisions if he felt that his will was being defied or deliberately evaded. He also had a streak of superstition in his make up, which made him sensitive to the prophecies of Elizabeth Barton, and persuaded him that his second wife was guilty of witchcraft. In spite of a protracted (and now somewhat dated) discussion of the theology of the divorce, and great deal of attention to foreign policy, the king who emerges from this study is a believable person – intelligent, arrogant and self-centred. He is vulnerable to criticism but at a somewhat impersonal level. It was left to Eric Ives in his two magisterial studies of Anne Boleyn (1986 and 2004) to bring out Henry's fragility at a more intimate level. He was, Ives argues, sexually insecure, which made him uniquely sensitive to Anne's thoughtless jibes of intermittent impotence. They were true, and Henry knew they were true, but they were completely at odds with his self-projection as a virile and masculine king.[46] He may well have believed the charges of witchcraft, because they offered a means of explaining this phenomenon which avoided reflection upon the King himself. The wicked woman could turn him on and off like a tap, and he had been too blind to see it! At first sight this thesis of insecurity does not fit with the image of magnificent self-assurance projected by Holbein, but upon further investigation they turn out to be two sides of the same coin. The chivalric bravado with which Henry entered the lists as a young man make good sense as a cover for one who knew his actual performance to be erratic. At first he seems to have had no difficulty in getting his wife pregnant on an annual basis, but by 1522 he had fathered only one bastard in spite of two lengthy liaisons, and perhaps other casual affairs that we know nothing about. Foreign ambassadors were always reporting his alleged 'amours', but these seem to have been no more that the conventional gestures of courtly love, and in fact Henry was nothing like the potent young man in whom he wanted his courtiers to believe.[47]

A similar insecurity, projected onto the more public arena of state affairs, may help to explain his ruthlessness when crossed. As Scarisbrick observes, not even those apparently most secure in the King's favour could be sure that expediency would not turn him against them. The fate of Thomas Cromwell was a stark warning. However, Diarmaid MacCulloch's work on Thomas Cranmer presents yet another Henry, one who on this occasion was loyal to his friend through thick and thin. There were good reasons why the King should have trusted his Archbishop, not least because of the unquestioning devotion with which Cranmer followed him. He could disagree with Henry in a manner which no one else could venture to do, and was excused attendance at the Parliament which passed the Act of Six Articles because the King knew that was repugnant to his conscience.[48] Since the contents of the Act reflect Henry's own conscience exactly, this reaction suggests a flexibility and tolerance which would not normally be associated with so touchy and explosive a ruler. One of the charges normally levelled against the King arises from just this type of inconsistency. Although it has long been recognised that Henry hated Lutherans and detested sacramentarians even more, the way in which he blew hot and cold on other aspects of the reform programme has long puzzled historians. As we have seen, John Foxe ascribed it to conflicting council, and

Scarisbrick is inclined to take the same view, but it is equally plausible to argue that the division was within the King's own mind. He authorised the English Bible, and insisted on its being set up in parish churches for 'all to read on that would', and then attempted to restrict such access to the gentry. Apparently he was alarmed by the manner in which it was being 'rhymed and jingled', as though he had never thought of such a possibility.[49] He apparently supported Cromwell's negotiations with Tyndale and Barnes, and made use of their arguments, but eventually had Barnes burned for heresy and passed the highly conservative Six Articles, which he then partly inhibited his bishops from enforcing.

In his latest attempt to resolve this conundrum, *The King's Reformation* (2005), George Bernard argues that the problem is more apparent than real. The King's religious position was always consistent, even before his Great Matter arrived to disturb the surface. He believed in the unity of the Church, and had even written in defence of the papacy as the upholder of that unity, but as a result of his experience in dealing with Clement VII he partly changed his mind. The papacy was a political office, like any other, and Clement was so highly politicised that he was forgetting his duty as a Father in God. Unless or until the office was purged of its corruptions and returned to its earlier purity, it would be better for the unity of the Church to be preserved by a consensus of Christian princes – like himself.[50] He was a Catholic king, and it was his responsibility to maintain the faith within his domains. This meant exercising his own judgement over issues in controversy, a judgement which he firmly believed would be informed by the Holy Spirit. He encouraged evangelicals because he believed their teaching to be in accordance with that of the early Church, but persecuted heretics because theirs was not. The apparent reaction of 1540–42 was in reality nothing of the kind; it was merely the reassertion in a public format of that sacramental doctrine to which Henry had always been loyal. Appearances of vacillation were deceptive, because the King had always steered a humanist course, getting rid of the 'abbey lubbers' upon whom Erasmus had poured such scorn, and bringing the clergy under control while continuing to have a healthy respect for their true vocation.[51] It was, and always had been, the prime responsibility of the clergy to minister to the spiritual needs of the people, not to concern themselves with offices, or property or profits. In imposing his own discipline upon them, he was recalling them to a true sense of their duties, undermining only their political pretensions. This is a Henry whose strength of purpose has not always been apparent to other historians, and is already leading to a fresh round of controversy, but it has at least the merit of contradicting that school of thought which sees the King as merely a weakling, confused in his mind and determined only to be obeyed in his own backyard.

Physically, Henry deteriorated in later life, as is only too apparent from the suits of armour made for him at different stages and of growing corpulence. A number of years ago Lacey Baldwin Smith argued that the savage moods to which he became prone in the 1540s were a direct result of that deterioration, and particularly of the pain which he suffered from ulcerated legs.[52] This disability had long been attributed to venereal disease, contracted in the course of a supposedly wild and promiscuous youth. However, such promiscuity was a myth, and Smith argued convincingly that the real cause of the ulcers which so troubled him was repeated falls in the lists and in the hunting field, which we know that he suffered as a young man. They seem to have baffled the skill of the best physicians in the land, and occasionally seem to have closed up, causing the sufferer exquisite pain, and causing rumours to circulate that the King was dying.[53] Henry was already overweight and eating too much by 1530, and the gradual change of lifestyle from athlete to couch potato, which took place between 1529 and 1539 has caused one of the most recent studies of the King – *The Virtuous Prince*, (2008) by David Starkey – to propose that there were really two Henrys, and that the brutal tyrant of the 1530s and 1540s was the result of the traumatising impact of the Great Matter upon an otherwise fairly amiable young man.[54] In spite of the wealth of detail with which the thesis is supported, this seems to be too simple an explanation of a very complex man, although it is possible that the second volume on the mature Henry (which has not yet appeared) will resolve that issue.

The most balanced summary of Henry's character to appear so far is that contributed by Eric Ives to the *Oxford Dictionary of National Biography*. Ives points out that much of the story of his reign is explained by the need to accommodate his particular vision of personal monarchy, which developed progressively in a number of stages throughout his life.[55] He continued to seek an answer to the question, what did it mean to be a king under God? In that search he drew on the thinking of a number of different people – Edward Fox, Thomas Cranmer, Anne Boleyn, and Thomas Cromwell in particular – and that seems to have given him the confidence to proceed as he did in and after 1533. Henry was incapable of original or radical thinking, but he was capable of radical action once he had been persuaded. However there was a sense in which all this confidence was a fraud, a mere public show upheld by falsity and deceit, because what it concealed was a gnawing self-doubt. It was the brief exposure of that self-doubt by the behaviour of Catherine Howard which caused such emotional storms at the end of 1541.[56] Like Smith, Ives sees the 1540s as a period of growing personal insecurity, not least because of his deteriorating health. As death approached, Henry took refuge in an increasingly bellicose self-righteousness. Not only, he observes, were the earlier changes road-tested after 1540, but 'the legacy of these years substantially determined the agenda for the next twenty', and in many ways he left an evil inheritance. His realm was in debt because of his wars, and deeply divided in religion, a division reflected in the in-fighting of the court over the last five years of his life. When he died at the not very advanced age of fifty-six, he left his kingdom to a child, and a vast quantity of personal possessions, which, when inventoried, amounted to some 20,000 items. Everything he had done was, or appeared to be, more than life sized. His appetite for money, food and women appeared to be insatiable. He was immensely greedy of power, and dealt savagely with anyone who challenged him. He defied the Pope, the Emperor and the King of France, and yet remained unsatisfied. His craving for glory turned in upon itself as his once-magnificent body decayed. However, his legacy was more than one of monumental selfishness, and his achievements outlasted his personality.

Neither Parliament nor the Church of England nor the navy would ever be the same again, and although it was Elizabeth's religious settlement rather than her father's which was to endure, that would not have been possible without his initiative. Jack Scarisbrick's conclusion, that 'rarely, if ever, have the unawareness and irresponsibility of a king proved more costly of material benefits to his people', is in need of a certain revision.[57]

The historiography of Henry VIII is therefore an ongoing operation, not merely for the learned but also for the population at large. It is embodied in articles, in books, and in film and television presentations. We have moved a long way from Gasquet and Pollard (to say nothing of John Foxe), just as we have moved on from *The Private Lives of Henry VIII* when Charles Laughton represented that self-indulgent monarch. For that very reason, we are in danger of reinventing Henry to suit the ideas of our own generation. He was, in his own mind, a very moral and upright man as well as the model of a Christian Prince, and we should beware of attributing those convictions to self-deception. To his subjects he was not a psychological dilemma, but he was a great and terrifying king, and however much we may wish to gloss our interpretation of his actions, that contemporary image should always be born in mind. 'Everybody loved him,' wrote Polydore Vergil of the young Henry, 'and their affection was not half hearted.'[58]

I

THE PRINCE, 1491–1509

The story of Henry VIII begins long before his birth. That he was the heir to the throne of England from 1502 to 1509 goes back to the strange story of his father's lineage. The older Henry was born in 1457, the only child of Edmund Tudor, Earl of Richmond, and of his young wife Margaret, the daughter of John Beaufort, Duke of Somerset.[1] Edmund owed his title to the fact that he was the acknowledged half-brother of King Henry VI, having been born of the union between Owen Tudor of Penmynydd and Catherine de Valois, the widow of King Henry V. Both the timing and circumstances of that union are obscure, but Henry VI had no difficulty in recognising it as a marriage, and consequently accepted Edmund as a kinsman. This meant that although Henry was born into the royal family, he had not the slightest claim upon the Crown of England. Had it not been for the Salic Law, he would have had a better claim to the throne of France. His mother, on the other hand was a granddaughter of John Beaufort, Marquis of Somerset and Dorset, and consequently a great granddaughter of John of Gaunt, the third son of King Edward III. Unfortunately John Beaufort had been born while his mother, Catherine Swynford, was still the Duke of Lancaster's mistress, before she became his third wife. Whereas that marriage had legitimated him in the canon law, such legitimacy did not extend to transmitting any claim to the throne – a possibility which was specifically blocked by Henry IV in Parliament.[2] It could be argued that Margaret was the great-great-granddaughter of Edward III, and that no human interference could affect the law of nature, but only by that rather far-fetched special pleading could she convey to her son any sort of claim to the throne. On the other hand, after the death of Prince Edward in 1471, he was the nearest thing to a male claimant that the House of Lancaster could produce, and die-hard Lancastrians such as the Earl of Oxford, recognised that claim. His uncle Jasper, the Earl of Pembroke, was senior to him, but Jasper could not pretend to possess the smallest quantity of English royal blood, and concentrated his attentions on the protection of his young nephew.

After the Lancastrian disaster at Tewkesbury in 1471, he took the fourteen-year-old Henry off to exile in Brittany, and reared him as best he could to be an English prince. Edward IV was understandably very keen to lay hands on the young exile, and tried repeatedly by diplomatic means to extract him from the protection of Duke Francis II.[3] Following Edward's deal with Louis XI at Picquigny in 1475 he almost succeeded by bogus professions of goodwill, but fortunately for Henry the Duke changed his mind at the last moment, and the exile was able to stay in his haven. There he might have remained and been forgotten if it had not been for the circumstances following the death of Edward IV in April 1483. By usurping his nephew's crown, Edward's younger brother, Richard of Gloucester, effectively split the Yorkist party down the middle. Having secured his position as King Richard III, he almost certainly arranged for the murder of his two nephews, Edward V and Richard of York, and drove many of Edward IV's most loyal supporters into the arms of Henry, who was now the only possible alternative.[4] Richard realised this as well, and immediately picked up Edward's diplomatic attempts to obtain his extradition. He might even have succeeded because Louis XI was pressing Duke Francis to acknowledge a feudal dependency, which the latter was resisting. By offering military assistance against the French, Richard might well have obtained his desire, but Louis died in August 1483 and the threat temporarily disappeared. However, within a couple of months Humphrey Stafford, Duke of Buckingham, had risen in rebellion against the new king and invited Henry of Richmond to participate in his movement.[5] In return he would recognise his claim to the throne. Behind this rebellion, and indeed in anticipation of it, lay a plot which seems to have originated with Margaret, Lady Stanley, Henry's mother. Seizing the opportunity presented by the Yorkist defections, she presented a plan to the Queen Dowager, Elizabeth Woodville, then in sanctuary at Westminster. Henry would undertake to marry one of her daughters in return for Woodville family support in his bid for the throne. Elizabeth responded positively, and Margaret thereupon sent her servant Hugh Conway to Henry in Brittany, armed with a good sum of money and an exhortation to him to go to Wales and take advantage of Buckingham's insurrection, which was by then under way.[6] Having already received messages from Buckingham, Henry perceived that there had been a dramatic turn in his fortunes, and succeeded in persuading Duke Francis to give him some (although probably not very much) support in his bid.

In spite of attracting some influential backers, Buckingham's revolt came to nothing. He was captured and beheaded, and Henry's intervention, which was in Kent rather than in Wales, was easily repulsed. The Acts of Attainder subsequently passed against the principals suggest a co-ordinated uprising on 18 October, but that is probably a convenient fiction. Henry's attempt appears to have taken place on 10 October, while Buckingham was captured at the end of the month and beheaded on 2 November. At first it might appear that the attainders of Henry, his mother and several leading supporters were the only outcome of this fiasco, but that would be far from the case. Fugitive dissidents, including John Morton, the Bishop of Ely, now began to declare for Henry in some numbers, and on Christmas Day, in Rennes Cathedral, he solemnly swore that, when he had entered into his inheritance, he would marry Elizabeth, the eldest daughter of the Queen Dowager.[7] He began to style himself 'king of England' and to speak of a 'return' to his rightful dominion. Meanwhile, on 22 February, no fewer than four bills of attainder became Acts, naming altogether over 100 people – 100 who now had nothing more to lose by throwing in their lot with Henry.[8] Richard was even more anxious to lay hands on one who was now an attainted traitor, but first he had to sort out his relations with Brittany. In this he was aided by the incapacity of Duke Francis and by the bad relations between Peter Landois, the effective head of government, and the Breton nobility, who resented him. Landois succumbed to Richard's blandishments and agreed to hand Henry over in return for the King's support against his enemies. John Morton, however, got wind of what was intended, and warned Henry in time. Early in October 1484 he escaped into France, where he was welcomed at court.[9] The Queen Dowager, disillusioned perhaps by Henry's failure to follow up his advantage, had meanwhile come to terms with the King, emerging from sanctuary and (presumably) annulling her promise in respect of her daughter's marriage. By the end of 1484 the indicators of Henry's fortunes were pointing in radically different directions. On the one hand, in spite of his welcome, Charles VIII's regency council was reluctant to back him; but on the other hand Richard's only son (another Prince Edward) had died about 9 April, leaving the King in a dynastic wilderness. This misfortune was aggravated by those sympathetic to Henry's cause, who muttered about Divine retribution, and also by the death of his queen, Anne Neville, which occurred in March 1485. So poor was Richard's public reputation by that time that he was forced to issue an official denial that he had poisoned her.

Anne of Beaujeu, who was effectively running the regency government of France, was determined to secure control over Britanny, a course which Duke Francis, when he recovered his health, continued to resist. He no longer had control over Henry Tudor to use as a bargaining counter, but nevertheless sought the aid of Richard III to resist this pressure. How much support might have been forthcoming if it had come to the point is not known, but the possibility persuaded the Regency Council to give Henry enough support to make a serious nuisance of himself. While it dithered and delayed, divided within itself and preoccupied with other matters, Henry's following continued to grow. Other dissident Yorkists joined him out of England, including Richard Fox, and the Earl of

Oxford broke out of Hammes Castle, where he was being held, and brought most of the garrison with him.[10] Such opportunities, however, do not prosper on inactivity, and it became imperative that Henry should do something. He had already sent messengers into England bearing regal letters, and had received some encouraging responses, particularly out of Wales, where Sir John Savage of Cheshire and the formidable Rhys ap Thomas were supposedly committed to his cause. Still he struggled, but eventually the Council gave him enough money to hire some ships and about 2,000 mercenaries. With this force, augmented by some 500 English exiles, he set out on 1 August 1585 to try his fortune in England. He landed at Milford Haven in Wales just before sunset on 7 August.[11]

Such a modest army should have occasioned King Richard no problems, but he led a deeply divided realm, a large part of which believed that he was accursed by God. He had hoped that the invaders would be defeated before they could emerge from Wales but in fact they encountered no serious opposition, and on the 12th Rhys ap Thomas honoured his pledge by joining Henry with a band which nearly doubled the size of his army. On the 15th he reached Shrewsbury in good heart and at the head of about 5,000 men. On about the 17th he made contact with the Stanleys, who had also promised their support, but that was not immediately forthcoming and what transpired in their discussions we do not know.[12] Meanwhile Richard, his councils clouded by uncertainty, had mobilised about 10,000 men at Nottingham, and on the 19th, following reports that his enemies were making for Lichfield, set out for Leicester to intercept them. Still uncertain of the Stanleys' loyalty and intentions, on 21 August he encountered Henry about two miles south of Market Bosworth. There is no reliable contemporary account of the battle which followed, but it seems that a part of the royal army did not engage, and that Richard, seeking to end matters at a stroke, endeavoured to take out his enemy in person.[13] When he became enmeshed in serious fighting, the Stanleys took him in the rear and he was defeated and killed. In the circumstances his death was as important as his defeat, because in the absence of a direct heir, he was the last of his line. Henry Tudor was proclaimed king upon the field of battle, and there was no one to gainsay his triumph.

Henry thus obtained the crown. He was twenty-seven years old, deeply experienced in the evasions and plottings of exile, but totally ignorant of how to run a kingdom. He was king by the Grace of God, and by virtue of his victory, but he was well aware that his hereditary claim was of the slightest. He consequently set out to build a government of reconciliation, giving many former Yorkists places on his council. He also took immediate steps to secure the person of Edward, Earl of Warwick, the nephew of the late King and his chief rival for the throne, who disappeared into the Tower.[14] Elizabeth, his intended bride, he restored to the custody of her mother, partly to await the dispensation which would be necessary for them to marry, and partly to gain a chance to get to know the nineteen-year-old, whom he had not seen since she was a small child. On 15 September writs were issued for a parliament to meet on 7 November, and the date of the coronation was fixed for Sunday, 30 October. On the 27th Henry solemnly processed to the Tower, and the following day bestowed the dukedom of Bedford upon his uncle Jasper, the guardian of his youth, and the earldoms of Derby and Devon upon Thomas Stanley and Edward Courtenay. On the 30th he went from the Tower to Westminster, accompanied by all the great and good of the realm, and was solemnly crowned and anointed by Thomas Bouchier, the aged Archbishop of Canterbury, who had already performed a similar office for both Edward IV and Richard III.[15] A magnificent banquet duly followed, but the jousts which should also have ensued were delayed for a week to enable the parliament to be opened on 7 November. This assembly immediately busied itself with all the formal business attendant upon a new reign, including the annulling and replacement of attainders, the voting of tonnage and poundage, and the registration of the King's title.[16] Just before it was prorogued on 10 December, the Speaker of the Commons, in the name of the whole Parliament, besought Henry to honour his promise and to marry Elizabeth of York.

The King intended to do no less; indeed the couple may actually have been sleeping together as early as Christmas. The wedding was fixed for

18 January, and by utilising the good offices of the Apostolic Delegate, the Bishop of Imola, a form of dispensation was issued on the 16th, although not confirmed by the Pope until 2 March. In its eventual form this drew attention to:

> ... the long and grievous variations, contentions and debates that hath been in this realm of England between the House of the Duke of Lancaster on the one part and the House of the Duke of York on the other party. [It continued] Willing all such divisions ... to be put apart ...[that the pope, by the counsel and consent of his College of cardinals] approveth, confirmeth and stablisheth the matrimony and conjunction made between the sovereign Lord King Henry the seventh of the House of Lancaster of the one party and the noble princess Elizabeth of the House of York of that other [party], with all their issue lawfully born between the same ...[17]

By 2 March Elizabeth was well and truly pregnant, and their first born son was delivered at Winchester on 16 September. They called him Arthur, and the choice of this somewhat unusual name has been the subject of much debate. The allusion to the mythical king of Britain seems unmistakable, but whether this was intended to draw attention to his role as a reconciler of factions, or to his Welsh ancestry remains uncertain.[18] What is certain is that for the next fifteen years, he was the apple of his father's eye. Duke of Cornwall from his birth, he was created Earl of Chester and Prince of Wales on 29 November 1489, when he was a little over three years old, to enable his father to resurrect the Prince's Council for the government of the Marches. This followed the precedent of 1471, and was placed at once under the Presidency of the Duke of Bedford, who was also Earl of Pembroke and a man of influence in Wales. Arthur was given his own establishment within the court, but it was funded from the revenues of the Duchy of Cornwall and his servants do not appear in the *King's Book* of household payments. His first nurse was called Katherine Gibbes, but beyond that we know little of his early upbringing, except that it would have been 'among the women', as was customary.[19] Henry and Elizabeth's marriage appears to have been a close and loving one. She was pregnant again by early 1489, and was delivered of her second child, a girl who was named Margaret, on the same day that Arthur was made Prince of Wales, an event which somewhat overshadowed Margaret's christening on the 30th. Although a girl was only of secondary use from a dynastic point of view, her appearance was taken as a sign of continued divine favour. By 1489 Henry was in any case more securely seated on his throne, having seen off the rather perfunctory rebellion of John Stafford at Easter 1486, and the more serious incursion of the pretender Lambert Simnel at Stoke in June 1487.[20] He had also successfully deployed his firstborn on the European marriage market. Taking advantage of the desire of Ferdinand and Isabella of Spain for support against France, on 27 March 1489 he signed the treaty of Medina del Campo, whereby Arthur was betrothed to their daughter Catherine (then aged four), and various guarantees of mutual support and recognition were made. The Tudors had now arrived among Europe's ruling families, and when the treaty was renewed a few years later, Catherine was referred to as the 'Princess of Wales', a title which she was apparently happy to grow up with.[21] By the end of 1490 Elizabeth was pregnant again, and on 28 June 1491 at Greenwich her second son was born, and christened Henry in honour of his father.

Unlike his brother, Henry was born without a title, and it was not to be until 1494 that the significant designation of Duke of York was conferred upon him. Many years later, in 1527, Richard Fox, who in 1491 had been Bishop of Bath and Wells, recalled christening him in the nearby church of the Observant Franciscans.[22] His wetnurse was called Anne Locke, who was the wife of Walter Locke, but no one remembered to reward her services until 1509. Like his brother he was given a modest establishment within the court, but nothing else is known about his early life. On 5 April 1493 the twenty-month-old child was granted the offices of Constable of Dover Castle and Lord Warden of the Cinque Ports. Described simply as the King's 'second son born', this was clearly a device to keep these offices in the hands of the Crown through the deputies who discharged the actual duties.[23] Not even the most optimistic councillor could have expected Henry to have the slightest awareness of these appointments. When the King went to France in October 1492, Arthur was similarly appointed 'Keeper of England', again an appointment which he was not expected to discharge in person. The Council, and particularly the Chancellor John Morton, governed the country during Henry's brief absence in 'remote parts'. It was not until the autumn of 1494 that Henry partly emerged from his brother's shadow. On 12 September he was appointed Lieutenant of Ireland during the King's pleasure, an appointment which he was expected to discharge through Sir Edward Poynings, who significantly became deputy by the same patent.[24] Poynings departed at once to Ireland, accompanied by a sizeable army, but young Henry remained at home. His appointment was merely a device to keep the Lieutenancy out of the hands of the 8th Earl of Kildare, who had blotted his copy book over the incursion of Lambert Simnel in 1487. About six weeks later, on 28 October, his grant of the constableship of Dover Castle was renewed, this time without the reservation 'during pleasure', and he was granted 'all the emoluments which Humphrey, late Duke of Gloucester, used to have'. Whether this made any difference to the scale of his housekeeping is not apparent.[25] Since his expenses were met entirely out of the King's Chamber, this was probably just a means of recycling money in the King's interest.

So far, he had been merely the King's second son, but on 1 November 1494 Henry VII decided to bring him to the attention of the court in much the same way as he had done with Arthur at a similar age. He was firstly to be dubbed a Knight of the Bath, and then to be created Duke of York. There was a double significance in this choice of title, because not only would it draw attention to the much vaunted reconciliation of York and Lancaster, and demonstrate the King's goodwill towards his wife's family, but it would also indicate that the previous holder of the title, his uncle Richard, was dead and that Perkin Warbeck, who had assumed his persona, was actually a fraud. There survives among the Cotton MSS in the British Library a very detailed account of the ceremonies and entertainments which accompanied these events, which makes clear just how seriously the King was taking them.[26] Henry, we are told:

> ... beying at his manoir of Wodestock determyned at Alhalowyn tide then foll[owing] to holde and kepe roially and solemply that fest in his palace of Westmynter, and at that fest to doube his ii de son knyght of the Bath and after to create hym duc of Yorc ...

No sooner was this decision made than a solemn tournament was proclaimed, wherein four 'gentlemen of the king' challenged all comers to run at the joust on 9 November, the prizes to be gold rings set with diamonds and rubies. So popular did this turn out to be that a second tournament had to be proclaimed to take place on 12 November, the challengers being six 'oder gentillmen'. Both were to be graced with the presence of the King and Queen, but the star attraction was to be 'thair redoubted lady and fairyste yong princesse, the eldest daughter to our souverayn lord the kyng' (then aged about five) who was to give out the prizes. On 28 October Henry and Elizabeth, accompanied by Margaret, the King's mother, arrived at Westminster from Richmond, and the following morning the younger Henry was brought in from Eltham through London, where he was received by the Mayor, the Aldermen and by all the crafts in their liveries, 'and so honnorably brought to Westmynster'. When the King dined in state on 30 October, the three-year-old Henry held the towel for his father's ablutions, although who guided him in that service is not recorded.

As night came on, the young Prince, and the thirty young noblemen who were to be dubbed with him, were led into the Parliament chamber where baths and beds had been prepared for them, Henry having been first signed with the cross by his father and blessed by his mother. While they were bathing, the King came into the Parliament Chamber and spoke briefly to each. They were then ceremonially dried and retreated to their beds for an undisclosed period of rest, after which they were vested in 'theyre heremites wede' and led off to the chapel. There they were supposed to keep vigil, but all that we are told is that they were refreshed with spices and confectionary, and it is reasonably certain that young Henry went to sleep.

In the morning, after mass and a suitable distribution of largesse, the potential knights were mounted, and rode through the palace to the Star Chamber, where the actual ceremony was to take place. In the case of Henry this was suitably elaborate and focused. The Duke of Buckingham placed the spur upon his right heel, and the Marquis of Dorset upon the left. The King then girded him with his sword and dubbed him knight. Presumably these symbols of his new status were then removed while the other knights were dubbed. At no point in the ceremony was there any recognition of the fact that the Prince was little more than an infant – and if he felt like crying for his mother or his nurse, no such weakness was recorded. With the other knights he then returned to the chapel and offered his sword on the altar, a feat for which he had suitable adult help. After that 'my said lord dined in his own chamber', because he could not be expected to partake of the rich meal which his fellow knights enjoyed. It would not have done for the star of the show to be sick![27] The following morning was the first of November and the King 'did on his robbes of astate roiall and crowned came into the parliament chambre', where he was awaited by all the nobles and prelates of England, led by the Cardinal Archbishop of Canterbury and the Duke of Bedford. Henry was then led in by the Marquis of Dorset and the Earl of Arundel, all clad in their 'robes of estate', the Prince having been provided with a miniature version for the occasion. After Garter King of Arms had read his patent of creation, 'there the kyng creatyd him duc of Yorc with the gyfft of thousand pond by yere', which would have been another notional recycling of royal revenue. They then processed to the chapel to give thanks in a solemn mass, and thence to yet another sumptuous banquet. This time, apparently, Henry did partake, and a generous largesse was cried in the hall in his name.

On 9 November followed the first of the advertised tournaments, also described in loving detail. John Peche, one of the King's gentlemen, was awarded the prize, apparently adjudicated by 'the kyng, the qwene, my ladie the kynges moder, and of all the ladies ...' who must have made up in goodwill what they lacked in chivalric expertise. Peche was led into the presence of Princess Margaret by two other damsels, and must have been immensely gratified by his success – particularly as the narrator thought that it was not entirely justified.[28] A second tournament was held on 11 November, when the Earl of Suffolk led the challengers and carried off the first prize, the other being awarded to Thomas Brandon. So great was the appetite of the aristocracy for this type of entertainment, moreover, that a third session was necessary. This was held on 13 November, and the prizes were awarded to the Earl of Essex and Sir Thomas Borough. It is tempting to think of the young Henry being so impressed by these feats of arms that he became determined to emulate them when he grew up, but he really was too young, all the adult ceremonies which he had endured notwithstanding. More probably that inspiration came from the jousts which accompanied the visit of the Archduke Philip in 1506, when he was fifteen and already accomplished in 'riding at the ring'.[29]

It might be thought that Henry's elevation to the dukedom of York would have been in a sense a 'coming of age', when he emerged from the shadow of his elder brother, but this seems not to have been the case. Arthur remained close to his father, while his sibling appears to have been cared for by his mother. David Starkey deduces from the similarity in their handwriting that she personally taught him his early letters, and although there is no conclusive evidence for this it is possible that she did.[30] The birth of Mary in 1496 made no difference to this close relationship, and when Elizabeth died in February 1503, the twelve-year-old Henry felt it keenly. As we have seen, his household was not always resident at court, but it was never far away and mutual visits were frequent. By this time he was funded out of the revenues of the Duchy of York, but its officers do not appear among his servants. A comprehensive list of the latter was drawn up in connection with the Queen's burial, but it is headed by John Redyng his treasurer, and the Duchy officers do not feature.[31] This list contains the names of 102 men and 13 women, and includes a schoolmaster (Mr Holt), a master to teach French (Giles Duwes) and a master at arms (Thomas Sympson). Five chaplains are named, a complete Chamber from Gentlemen Ushers to Footmen, and a full list of household departments. It was in fact a ducal establishment, and operated with full independence. The only time when the Duke of York features in the list of the King's payments is when a book was purchased for him at a cost of twenty shillings in 1495! [32]

As he began to grow up, the Prince would probably have known his own servants more intimately than his family, and when he reached the age of six or seven would have been placed under the care of a tutor. We are not sure who this was at first, and he may have shared the services of Bernard Andree, who was appointed to supervise Prince Arthur in 1496, although the five-year age gap between them means that it is unlikely that they actually shared lessons. The syllabus laid down for both of them was remarkably similar, but that was prescribed by the King rather than by the tutor. [33] It consisted mainly of classical Roman authors, but also embraced historians like Tacitus and, rather more unusually, the Vulgate Bible. Both boys were well read in the scriptures, and that was to remain with Henry throughout his life. If Andree was the Duke of York's first tutor then he was replaced in about 1497 by John Skelton, who certainly looked after the boy's learning until 1502. Like Andree, Skelton was a poet, and something of a self-publicist, who later claimed to have taught Henry his 'learning primordial', thereby implying that he was in charge from the start:

The honour of England I learned to spell
I gave him drink of the sugared well,
Of Helicon's waters crystalline,
Acquainting him with the muses nine ...[34]

By 1501, when he was fifteen, Arthur was extremely well read being familiar (more or less) with the works of Homer, Vergil, Ovid, Terence, Cicero, Thucidides, Caesar. Livy and Tacitus. Andree, who recorded this information, did not mention any medieval or modern authors, presumably because they were not considered respectable in such company, but since the Prince of Wales was being trained for the kingship, he must have been made familiar with some more recent examples of statecraft. Henry followed the same track, but since he was not expected to succeed to the throne, the statecraft may have been omitted in his case. Years later Lord Herbert of Cherbury expressed the opinion that the Duke of York's initial training was designed to fit him for high preferment in the Church. He appears to have derived this from Paolo Sarpi's *Historia del Concilio Tridentino*, which in turn took it from William Parron, Henry VII's favoured astrologer, but there is no contemporary evidence to suggest any such intention.[35] The thought of Henry VIII as Archbishop of Canterbury is an intriguing one, but unreal on all counts.

Meanwhile, as Arthur's marriage was renegotiated and confirmed in 1497 and 1499, Henry seems to have confined himself to the schoolroom. He was admitted to the Order of the Garter on 17 May 1495, but otherwise was not used about his father's business beyond the offices already conferred upon him.[36] He next emerges onto the public stage in the celebration of his brother's wedding, when he led the procession of welcome to Princess Catherine, and took a prominent part in the dancing which followed the wedding. He was already remarkably well grown for a ten-year-old, and his appearance attracted much favourable attention. This event also had the astrologers busy, predicting a long and fruitful life for both the principals, a mistake compounded by Parron, who also forecast that the Queen would live to be over eighty.[37] The events of the next two years were to prove them spectacularly wrong, which may explain why Henry, when he came to the throne, never had much faith in the self-styled 'science'. His development during these years of relative obscurity presents a number of problems. Someone trained him well in the rudiments of music and taught him to play a number of instruments. This is unlikely to have been Skelton, who is not known to have possessed the relevant skills. A 'Schoolmaster at pipes' was listed in 1503, but he is described only as 'William' and his identity is uncertain.[38] The Prince was also taught to ride, and must have begun to acquire those skills at tennis and shooting which, ten years later, were to be the subject of such awed comment. This may have been the responsibility of Sir Richard Guildford, the Controller of his father's household, or of his Master at Arms, but whoever was in charge of his musical and physical education did exceptionally good jobs. Ironically in 1501 Skelton wrote for his charge a *Speculum Principis*, despite the fact that he was not then heir to the throne. Although this was, in a sense, a conventional literary exercise, it also contained much advice which would only be relevant if he became king – to keep power in his own hands, not to trust servants overmuch, and to choose and cherish his own wife. All of which, as Jack Scarisbrick observed, was to be more honoured in the breach than the observance.[39] Then, in April 1502 Henry's whole life was turned upside down by the death of his brother Arthur. The Prince of Wales had been fifteen when he married Catherine, and was deemed to be of sufficient age to cohabit with his wife, then aged seventeen, the minimum canonical age being fourteen for males and twelve for females. They consequently began living together as man and wife, first at the Bishop of London's palace near St Pauls, and later at Ludlow in the Welsh Marches.[40] In spite of the brave figure which he had cut on his wedding day, Arthur was not in robust health, and seems to have contracted pneumonia in the draughty castle. In spite of the best efforts of his physicians, he left a seventeen-year-old widow and two devastated parents. He also left a brother whose prospects had suddenly been dramatically enhanced.

Thanks to an anonymous account, which may be contemporary, we know a good deal about how the King and Queen received the news of Arthur's death, but on his brother's reaction there is no comment.[41] Negotiations were already well advanced for a marriage between him and Louis XII's kinswoman, Margaret of Angouleme, then aged nine, presumably with the intention of keeping a foot in both camps. However, the disappearance of Arthur caused a rapid reappraisal of priorities.[42] The preservation of the Trastamara connection took precedence, and before the end of the year an agreement had been made with Ferdinand to transfer the widow from one brother to the other, a process which it was recognised would need a special dispensation. Ferdinand was equally anxious to maintain the connection, and although he had opened his campaign with a demand that the Princess be returned to Spain forthwith, that was clearly a bargaining position. The initial treaty was drawn up on 24 September 1502, although it was not finally signed until June of the following year.[43] Whether Henry either knew or cared that his name was being taken in vain in this manner we do not know. Catherine, when she had recovered somewhat from her traumatic loss, did know, and seems to have regarded the possibility with some enthusiasm. The Duke of York was a promising boy, and she was beginning to put down roots in England. Meanwhile, a further disaster had overtaken the royal family. Prince Edmund, born in 1499, had lived barely a year, and having been the proud father of three sons at the beginning of 1500, by the summer of 1502 Henry VII was reduced to one. As Elizabeth pointed out, they were still young enough to try again, and by the autumn of that year she was pregnant again.[44] However, she was thirty-six, and although there were no obvious complications the daughter born on 2 February 1503 lived only a few days. Worse still, the Queen failed to recover from her ordeal, and died in her turn on 11 February. The ministrations of Dr Hollysworth, sent for in haste from Kent by the King's commandment, had proved unavailing. She was buried at Westminster a few days later, with her sister Catherine, Lady Courtenay, as chief mourner.[45] Her husband, deeply distressed by her death, did not appear.

Life, nevertheless, had to go on, and it was not long before diplomats were looking at the King's widowhood, and speculating upon the prospect of his marrying again. Henry did nothing to discourage this, because it was to his advantage to keep his fellow rulers guessing, and he eventually sent a special commission to inspect the charms of the young Queen of Naples, Joanna, the niece of Ferdinand. The commissioners visited her at Valencia on 22 June 1505, and their report leaves little to the imagination, but he did nothing, and probably never intended to.[46] Meanwhile something had to be done to sort out the English succession. The Duke of York might be the King's only surviving son, but not everyone was convinced that he would succeed without dispute if Henry should follow his wife to an early grave. He followed his brother automatically as Duke of Cornwall, but it was not until 18 February 1504 that he was created Earl of Chester and Prince of Wales, making at least Henry VII's intentions abundantly clear. Unfortunately we have no such detailed description of these ceremonies as we have of those which accompanied his creation as Duke of York, and it seems likely that no tournament or other public celebration followed. This was a strictly political event, as is made clear from the Act of Recognition which was passed by the Parliament then sitting. This confirmed the young Henry 'to be now the King's heir apparent, Prince of Wales, Duke of Cornwall and earl of Chester', and annulled his creation as Duke of York.[47] The revenues of that Duchy now reverted to the Crown.

Then in November 1504 Queen Isabella of Castile died, and Ferdinand became likewise a widower. Whereas the death of Elizabeth had caused much private grief but little political disturbance, the death of Isabella gave her husband grief of a quite different kind. She had been Queen of Castile in her own right, and the union of the Crowns of Castile and Aragon had been purely personal. The couple's only son, Juan, had died in 1499, and Isabella's heir was not Ferdinand but their eldest daughter Juanna. Juanna was married to the Archduke Philip, the son of the Emperor Maximilian, and by 1504 the mother of two promising sons.[48] Philip consequently claimed the Crown matrimonial, and a strong party among the Castilian nobility backed him. Even if Ferdinand managed to fend off Philip and Juanna's claim on the grounds of his foreign birth (which he had every intention of doing), the next heir was still not himself, but his younger daughter, Catherine, the dowager Princess of Wales. It is therefore not surprising that the King of Aragon was anxious to keep his daughter in England, and for a while Henry was happy to oblige. During the summer of 1505 letters and embassies were exchanged, in which both monarchs referred in amiable fashion to 'the Princess of Wales', meaning not her dowager title but that which was about to be renewed by her marriage. It even appears that a date was fixed for the ceremony, or at least someone thought that it had been:

... forasmuch as everyday approacheth the time appointed of the marriage betwixt my Lord the Prince of Wales ... and the Lady Catherine, daughter unto the said noble king ... which time should be at the feast of St.John the Baptist [29 August] next coming, or thereabouts ...[49]

However, it was not to be, and the reason why probably lay in the treaty of Blois which Ferdinand signed with Louis XII in October 1505. It may well have been knowledge that such a treaty was impending which caused 29 August to pass unmarked. That treaty bound Ferdinand in marriage to the King of France's niece, Germaine de Foix, and signified that in the interest of securing Castile, the King of Aragon was prepared to end his long-running feud with his northern neighbour.[50] This naturally led Henry VII to reconsider his position, and caused him to enter a protest against the intended matrimony in the name of his son, who was now fourteen years old and canonically of age in such matters. This declared that he, the Prince of Wales, had not been consulted over the issue, and as far as he was concerned, the arrangement was null and void.[51] This caused understandable distress to Catherine, who was now apparently wanted in neither England nor Spain, and who was struggling on an inadequate allowance irregularly paid. Being a pious young woman, she took refuge in her religious observances, and convinced herself that, in spite of all the portents, that it was the will of God that she should marry the younger Henry. Rejection was probably not an expression of the Prince's true wishes, although whether he managed to convey that to Catherine is not known.

He was still for most practical purposes a schoolboy, and as such well thought of by no less an educationalist than Desiderius Erasmus. They had first encountered in 1499, during one of Erasmus' early visits to England, when (no doubt prompted by Skelton) the eight-year-old had challenged the distinguished visitor to produce 'something from his pen', a demand which caused the scholar three days of anxious toil.[52] Skelton's tour of duty came to an end in 1502, and he was replaced by John Holt, who was a protégé of that up-and-coming humanist and lawyer Thomas More, a change which David Starkey describes as 'stepping from the middle ages into the renaissance' – although that would not have been an opinion which appealed to John Skelton.[53] Holt died in 1504 and William Hone was appointed in his place. Hone, who was also later to tutor the Princess Mary, seems to have been responsible for the carefully crafted epistle which the Prince directed to Erasmus in 1506, a letter so sophisticated in its construction that its recipient was immediately suspicious. It was only when Lord Morley, who was Erasmus' English patron, testified to having seen a number of drafts of similar letters written to other people, complete with their modifications and corrections that the great man became convinced that Henry was indeed a scholar to be respected.[54] Hone deserves credit for having persuaded his pupil to write these epistles because all the indications are that the Prince was no keener on putting pen to paper then than he was to be later as king. As well as bringing a change of tutors, 1504 seems to have marked a change in Henry's lifestyle also. Although he retained his full household establishment, he became normally resident at court, and as became the Prince of Wales, came much more directly under his father's eye. It may have been Henry VII's intention to give his heir the benefit of his own experience but, if so, he went about it in rather an eccentric fashion. Whereas at the age of fifteen Arthur had been married and despatched to Ludlow, where he had at least nominal responsibility for the Council in the Marches, at the same age Henry was given neither a wife nor any degree of independence other than financial, where the revenues of Cornwall and Wales had replaced those of York. According to Gomez de Fuensalida, a Spanish envoy who arrived in England in 1508, and who was not the best informed or most observant of ambassadors, the Prince was kept in seclusion like a young girl. No one was allowed access to him, and he never spoke except in response to a question from his father.[55] Not only is this intrinsically improbable, but the King had his own reasons for wishing to keep Fuensalida away from Henry, because the envoy had been sent for the specific purpose of reviving the marriage project between him and Catherine which Henry VII had deliberately consigned to limbo. It is true that the King never gave his son the opportunity to exercise any political responsibility, but social seclusion of the kind described would have been virtually impossible in the crowded environment of the court. What does seem to be true is that Henry was becoming increasingly aware of his own dour and unpopular image, and was more than a little challenged by the magnificent and glorious young man that his son had grown into.

It is possible that it was the King's mother rather than Henry himself, who was responsible for her grandson's academic training.[56] Both Skelton and Hone were from her favoured university of Cambridge, and she certainly exercised great influence over her son. There were reports to that effect soon afterwards, but it is unlikely that Henry would have entrusted the training of his heir to anyone else, however favoured. Moreover, his grandmother would not have influenced the Prince's physical education, and it was that which attracted most attention at the time. Henry engaged a Spanish professional to teach his son how to play tennis, a game at which he soon excelled.[57] Other similar experts must have been behind his skill in archery, his strength at hurling the javelin, and his effectiveness as a jouster. The origin of this skill, which was to become so obvious in later life, is something of a mystery. He seems to have progressed from riding at the ring to tilting proper in about 1506, and by 1508 was spending many hours at Richmond exercising in this fashion. According to Fuensalida the King occasionally took time out to watch. But this was a strictly private activity, in which he presumably jousted with his instructors or with carefully chosen companions. We are told that he 'excelled all his opponents', but it is not obvious that he took part in any public tournaments,[58] indeed he seems to have chafed at being excluded from the courtly entertainments of that summer. In the *Iustes of May and June* (1507), the author noted the Prince's presence among the spectators and observed:

> Syth our prynce moost comly of stature
> Is desyrous to the moost knightly ure
> Of armes to whiche marcyall aventure
> Is his courage

Notwithstondynge his yonge and tender aege
He is moost comly of his parsonage
And as desirous to this ourage
As prynce may be ...[59]

At the age of sixteen, he clearly felt that his talents deserved more public recognition, and this may well have been partly to blame for the strained relationship which is hinted at in what followed. The old king had not merely frustrated his son's ambition to shine in the court, he had also prevented him from marrying the young woman he fancied. It is not surprising that when Henry VII died on 22 April 1509 the shrewd men who made up his council should have been willing to endorse the transformation of the royal image which the new reign in any case portended.

2

A RENAISSANCE KING, 1509–1511

As far as the political nation was concerned, the young king who succeeded in April 1509 was an unknown quantity. He had discharged no public duties, and expressed no opinion on affairs of state. His views on the state of Ireland, or the condition of the royal revenues were alike mysteries. He was a few weeks short of his eighteenth birthday, but no one suggested even the briefest minority, which meant that he was thrown into the role of monarch without any relevant preparation. Not surprisingly, the observers concentrated on what they could see, rather than on those things about which they must speculate. They celebrated his magnificent physique, and his youthful exuberance, contrasting these with the drab image of his father's last days, and in so doing did less than justice to Henry VII:

> Our clypsyd son nowe cleryd is from the clerke
> By harry our Kyng the flower of nateurs warke ...[1]

The old king had been in failing health for several years, and had taken refuge in caution and prudence, but he was still capable of putting on a good show when the circumstances required it as the jousts of 1507 and 1508 demonstrate. Henry had never been a glamorous figure, and as his anxiety over the succession became obsessive, it pushed him into a systematic policy of financial coercion which made him deeply unpopular with the aristocracy. This caused them, and their client writers to represent him as a rapacious miser – an image which stuck until the twentieth century.[2] He was in an institutional sense rapacious, but he was not mean, and in spite of his extreme caution in exposing his son to public scrutiny, the Prince of Wales was very much the man that his father had made him. It is even possible that his explosion upon the scene in the days following his father's death was calculated. Henry VII was very well aware that his son was very large, very athletic and very intelligent. He was bound to make a big impact on the court, and was equally certain to make his own policies. The less he was inhibited by his father, the better for all concerned. Edward Hall, although writing many years later, expressed the feeling of the time:

> Wonder it were to write of the lamentation that was made for this prince [Henry VII] amongst his servants, and other of the wisest sort, and the joy that was made for his death by such as were troubled by the rigour of his law; yet the toward hope which in all points approved in the young king did both repair and comfort the heavy hearts of those which had lost so wise and sage a prince; and did also put out of the minds of such as were relieved by the said king's death, all their old grudges and rumours, and confirmed their new joy by the new grant of his pardon ...[3]

This pardon was granted at once, before the end of April, and significantly excluded, along with 'the king's enemies' the De la Pole brothers, two of his late father's executors Sir Richard Empson and Edmund Dudley. These two had become notorious in the last days of the old regime as the King's fiscal enforcers. Using the Council Learned in the Law, over which Empson had presided, they had exacted large sums of money from those caught in the web of Henry's financial policies. This had made them many powerful enemies, not least within the King's Council.[4] These may well have included Archbishop Warham and Bishop Fox, because someone close to the King persuaded him almost at once to make a gesture by repudiating their work. Within days they had been arrested and conveyed to the Tower on charges of having raised forces to resist the succession. What they had almost certainly done was to gather (and possibly arm) their servants for their own protection, knowing perfectly well how many, and what powerful, enemies they had now that their defender was gone. This provided sufficient pretext for the King to order their arrest (without resistance) and to exclude them from his accession pardon. '... noble men grudged, mean men kicked, poor men lamented, and preachers openly at Paul's Cross and other places exclaimed, rebuked and detested ...'[5] Henry VIII could hardly have made a more timely or symbolic gesture of his determination to make a new start. Commissions were established to examine the enforcers and their work, which resulted not only in charges of malpractice against Empson and Dudley, but in many bonds being cancelled. Acting no doubt under a certain pressure, the late king's remaining executors 'made restitution of great sums of money, to many persons taken against good conscience to the said king's use ...'[6] Both the enforcers were indicted, and eventually executed, but their agents escaped more lightly:

> Soon after were apprehended divers called promoters belonging to Empson and Dudley. As Crosby, Page, Smith and divers others, as Derbie, Wright, Sympson and Stockton, of the which the most part wore paper and stood in the pillory ...[7]

It was all very public and visible.

Meanwhile the old king had lain in state in various locations before being transported to his interment in Westminster Abbey on 9 May. This ceremony was conducted with the utmost lavishness and decorum, and many thousands of yards of black cloth were issued to the courtiers and their servants for the occasion. The late king's officers duly broke their staves of office into his grave, but in the event most of them were reappointed.[8] The continuities between the old reign and the new were less apparent than the discontinuities, but were equally important. This was particularly true of the Council, where the Chancellor, Lord

Privy Seal and Treasurer all remained in post, and it was not for several years that the new king began to appoint his own men. This inevitably meant that there were certain tensions and disagreements, as the King tried to persuade his servants of the merits of his own chosen courses of action. There were no doubts about the desirability of removing Empson and Dudley, or of repudiating what they stood for, but over foreign policy there were quickly tensions. Henry, for reasons which must have been embedded in his education, was backward looking. Not only did he revel in the Burgundian-style chivalry which had dominated the courtly scene in the later fifteenth century, he also hankered after the glories of Agincourt.[9] He knew perfectly well that the quickest way for a young ruler to make an impact on the international scene was as a warrior, and the traditional enemies of the English were the Scots and the French. However, the King of Scots was his brother-in-law, and Scotland in any case was a minor power with whom his relations were for the time being amicable. So Henry began to think of renewing the Hundred Years War, although he would not have thought of it in those terms. He would press his claim to the Crown of France, a claim which had been dormant since 1453, but which had never been renounced. As early as 25 May 1509, just over a month into the reign, the Venetian ambassador reported that he was 'greatly inclined to take up arms against the French'.[10] His councillors were alarmed, but probably not greatly surprised, by this bellicosity. During the summer they set out to allay any anxiety which Louis XII may have been feeling, and wrote a letter in the King's name requesting the renewal of the established peace between the kingdoms. It is inconceivable that such a letter could have been sent without the King's consent, but entirely likely that he was not concentrating at the time. When Louis sent a special ambassador to acknowledge the courtesy, Henry exploded with wrath, claiming to know nothing about it. 'Who wrote this letter?' he demanded. 'I ask peace of the King of France, who dares not look me in the face, still less make war on me.' The ambassador was astonished – as well he might have been – and the council was no doubt embarrassed.[11] However, the King was not so adolescent that he did not realise the impossibility of attacking France on his own, and for the time being confined himself to making friendly noises to the Venetians, who were at that point being hard-pressed by the League of Cambrai, which embraced France, Spain and the Holy Roman Emperor. With Spain and France in alliance, Henry had no leverage to use against the latter, and good though his relations with Ferdinand were, he could not very well act without him. So in spite of his outburst, he took Ferdinand's advice, and pretended that he wanted to maintain his father's friendly relations with Louis. On 23 March 1510 an Anglo-French treaty was signed, embodying exactly those terms.[12]

Throughout the winter of 1509–10 the English court continued to send out contradictory messages. Formally there was amity, and any transactions involving the council were careful to preserve that façade, but privately the King continued to make warlike speeches, to hire gunfounders, and to respond sympathetically to Venetian pleas for help. On 7 December the Venetian ambassador thought that he had won. 'The king,' he wrote, 'will not delay hostilities. He intends to attack France.'[13] However, nothing happened. Maximilian and Ferdinand signed a new treaty on 12 December, and for the time being the League of Cambrai held together, inhibiting any action on Henry's part. It was not until the summer of 1510 that the League showed signs of breaking up, as Julius II decided that the French were a greater threat to the papal states than were the Venetians. It may have been some early signs of that break-up which caused Ferdinand to sign a new treaty with Henry on 24 May. This provided for both an offensive and defensive alliance, and virtually annulled the French treaty of two months earlier. Whether this represents the King asserting himself against the wishes of his council is uncertain, because the latter may well have seen it as just another step in the diplomatic dance whereby Henry kept his options open.[14] If the King was taking charge, then the Spanish ambassador Luis Caroz had not noticed. On the 29th he informed his master that 'all business is in the hands of the bishops of Durham [Thomas Ruthall] and Winchester [Richard Fox] …'[15] Again, no action followed, although Henry and Ferdinand, who was now his father-in-law, kept up an amiable correspondence.

Henry had married Catherine in June 1509. In spite of his repudiation of their prenuptial agreement in 1505, he had in a sense continued to regard her as his wife, and various schemes to marry him elsewhere had come to nothing. Whether, as he claimed, he was obeying the deathbed wishes of his father is uncertain. He was certainly with his father when he died, and it is unlikely that such an injunction would not have been heard by someone else, but it is possible.[16] Certainly his leading councillors seem to have known nothing about it, because only a few days later they were assuring Caroz that the King's options were open. Indeed, according to William Warham, marriage to Catherine was unlikely because of the doubts which had been raised about the lawfulness of the papal dispensation which was required for a man to marry his former sister-in-law. However, these doubts may have been in Warham's mind, because they were not in the King's. Barely had Caroz concluded his interview than he was summoned back to be informed that the royal marriage would indeed go ahead. The King had spoken, and all difficulties, whether over the dispensation or over the outstanding part of Catherine's dowry, were simply swept aside.[17] The Princess, who had struggled both personally and financially since 1505, until she had been rehabilitated by appointment as her father's special envoy in 1507, now felt entirely vindicated. Her brief as an envoy, of course, finished with the old king's death, but that had no time to make an impact before Henry made his announcement. Her difficulties, her work, and her faith in the eventual outcome were all now triumphantly vindicated. They were married at the Church of Observant Franciscans in Greenwich on 3 June, and everybody commented what a magnificent couple they made; Catherine, at twenty-four, was pretty and petite beside her splendid eighteen-year-old husband. In spite of her tactful words to her father about loving her husband for his sake, it was clearly a meeting of mutual desire, and that desire on his part was the reason why it had happened.[18]

Although no longer an accredited representative, Catherine's unique access to her husband meant that her father continued to correspond with her about matters of state. On 18 November he wrote confidentially that he had learned that the King 'wished to prevent the utter destruction of Venice' and was seeking a closer alliance with himself and Maximilian. The conclusion of that alliance should not be delayed, but meanwhile it was necessary that Henry should remain on good terms with the King of France, because 'he can afterwards easily find a pretext for quarrelling with him'. Not surprisingly he went on to emphasise that secrecy was necessary in all such dealings.[19] His daughter was suitably discreet. Indeed her letters to him contain few references to such matters, being filled with her own sense of joy and celebration. 'The news here,' she wrote, 'is that these kingdoms of your highness [*sic*] are in great peace, and entertain much love to the king my lord, and to me. Our time is spent in continual festival ...' Henry wrote in similar vein on 17 July, that since his coronation he had diverted himself with jousts, and that he would shortly go hunting, although he added that the purpose of this would be 'to view divers parts of his realm and to look into public affairs ...'[20] In fact it was to be the following year before he made his first progress. How important Catherine may have been in influencing her husband's foreign policy is difficult to say. She was undoubtedly an enthusiastic advocate of the Spanish alliance, but Henry hardly needed prodding in that direction. Not only were they now kindred, but Ferdinand was by far the most powerful ally available for any enterprise against France. Maximilian the Emperor (who was technically only King of the Romans because he had not been crowned) would no doubt have been willing, but his resources were so limited that his impact would have been minimal. The Archduke Charles was a child, and Juana, theoretically Queen of Castile, was mentally disturbed and under Ferdinand's tutelage. For serious business there was no alternative to the King of Spain, and he would bide his time, urging his daughter to restrain her husband's youthful enthusiasm until some suitable opportunity presented itself.

That opportunity began to appear in the summer of 1510, with the breakdown of the League of Cambrai. This, as we have seen, was on the initiative of the Pope, who began to put out feelers for the creation of a 'Holy League' with the intention of driving the French out of Italy.

Well aware of what was going on, Louis XII convened a Council of the French Church in the autumn of 1510, which expressed traditional Gallican sentiments as a means of putting pressure on Rome.[21] It did not work. Julius merely increased his diplomatic efforts, and relations between France and the papacy became increasingly hostile. So hostile indeed, that Louis took advantage of dissension within the College of Cardinals to convene a General Council of the Church to meet at Pisa in May 1511 for the purpose of deposing the pontiff. This was an act of open schism, and Julius responded with excommunication, which made little difference to the King, but served to cut France off, to some extent, from the rest of Christendom.[22] It soon became apparent that Louis' rash intention had played into Julius' hands, because he could now make his league Holy indeed, with something of the atmosphere of a crusade. Although disconcerted by the existence of the Anglo-French treaty of March, he quickly realised that this had been virtually annulled by Henry's subsequent agreement with Ferdinand, and he continued to woo the King of England with small gifts and flattering words during the winter of 1510–11, while he painstakingly put his coalition together. Eventually, on 4 October 1511 the Holy League came into existence, the original members being the Pope, Ferdinand and the Doge of Venice.[23] In spite of the Francophobe position taken up by Cardinal Bainbridge, Henry's representative in Rome, England was not an original signatory. Although the treaty was described as having been made 'with the full knowledge and participation' of the English King, he did not in fact become a member of the League until 13 November. Perhaps he still had conciliar opposition to overcome, although it would have been difficult for his senior advisers, most of whom were clergy, to object to following where the Pope had so obviously led. It was not until the end of April 1512 when Lancaster Herald finally arrived at the French court to deliver the formal declaration of war.[24]

Meanwhile, Henry had carried out two partial mobilisations. Early in 1511 Margaret of Savoy had requested the aid of 1,500 English archers against the Duke of Geuldres, who was making a nuisance of himself in the Netherlands, and:

The king tenderly regarding the request of so noble a Lady, and also because there was a communication hanging at that time of marriage between the young Prince Charles and the lady Mary his sister, gently granted her request and appointed Sir Edward Poynings, Knight of the Garter and Controller of his House ... to be lieutenant and conductor of the said 1500 archers ...[25]

The campaign was brief and successful, costing (as the chronicler noted) only 100 casualties. It had been a useful trial run for the larger expedition which was by then in prospect. A second venture, however, was conspicuously less fortunate. This was in response to a request from Ferdinand for 1,000 men to assist in an expedition which he was planning to North Africa. Lord Darcy was commissioned to raise this force, which he did largely at his own expense, and it duly set off from Plymouth in the middle of May 'with iiii ships royal', arriving at Cadiz on 1 June. The King received them 'very gently', but he had changed his mind. There would be no expedition to North Africa and the English were not needed.[26] Unfortunately Darcy decided that after two weeks cooped up in their ships, the least he could do was to allow his men a few days ashore. There some of them immediately became drunk and started causing mayhem in the locality. One of them molested a girl, and in the resulting brawl several lives were lost on both sides. It was altogether a very inauspicious demonstration. Darcy managed to get his discredited men back on board, and on 17 June sailed for home, not best pleased either with himself or with his reception.[27] He was also heavily out of pocket in spite of the grant of £1,000 which Henry made towards his expenses. However, as we shall see, the lessons which should have been learned about the behaviour of undisciplined soldiers on unfamiliar soil were not taken, and were to recur again in the following year, to say nothing of the shiftiness of Ferdinand.

These expeditions provided small exercises for the mobilisation of troops, but as Henry was only too keenly aware, there was more to making war than the raising of soldiers. The question of money was not an immediate problem because of the healthy state of the old king's revenue at the time of his death. It was later believed that

Henry VII left over a million pounds in cash, bonds and jewellery. A more modern estimate would be about £300,000, or the equivalent of two years income; but in any case it was sufficient for the King to be able to contemplate war without any financial anxieties – at least in the short run.[28] There was also the matter of ships and guns. Henry VII had started his reign by commissioning two large, state-of-the-art carracks, or war ships; not because he intended to make war, but as a power statement. Ten years later he had also caused a new dock to be excavated at Portsmouth, and had turned the harbour into an embryonic naval base. However, he had done nothing more, beyond replacing his half dozen or so smaller ships as need required. The *Regent* and the *Sovereign* had been kept in repair, and were still in service in 1509, and Robert Brygandyne was reappointed as Clerk, or Keeper of the King's Ships.[29] It is possible that two further capital ships, later named the *Mary Rose* and the *Peter Pomegranate*, had been laid down just before his death, but more likely that they were the immediate fruit of the new king's interest. They were launched in 1510, with every intention that they would be used, and the *Mary Rose*, which was equipped with gun ports for side-firing cannon, may well have been partly designed by the King himself.[30] Henry does not seem to have decided quite how he wanted to mobilise his ships for the war which he was intending. Probably his first thought was to take up whatever vessels he required in the traditional manner, building a temporary fleet around the nucleus of his own ships. In June 1511 Sir Edward Howard took two Scottish prizes, the *Lion* and the *Jenny Pirwin*, on the pretext that they were pirates, and both were added to the royal fleet, but it was not until 1512, with the war upon him, that the King changed his mind and decided to build up his own navy. A flurry of activity then followed, and nine ships were purchased and seven built within a year, transforming the nature of the royal fleet.[31] It is possible that the King was inspired in this change of heart by the development of Scottish naval power, symbolised by the launching of the *Great Michael* in October 1511, because he certainly had no desire to be upstaged by James IV.

Henry VII had not been much interested in the toys of war, but he had prudently built up his position early in the reign by acquiring an effective siege train. He had encouraged the establishment of at least one gun foundry in the Kentish Weald, and had imported Flemish and French gunners. However, his policy had been based upon considerations of his own security rather than his capacity to make war, and that was never going to be enough for his son. Henry VIII was almost obsessively interested in big guns, and as prince had attended at least one test firing, so it was always likely that his accession would see a major deployment of patronage. In 1509 he appointed one Humphrey Walter to be his Master Gunner, but that was to manage the guns which he already had, not to acquire more.[32] It was still not possible for the English forges to produce weapons of sufficient quality to satisfy the royal connoisseur, so they had to be imported from Malines. In 1510 Henry entered into an agreement with Hans Poppenreuyter to supply forty-eight guns of the finest quality, some of which were probably deployed on board the *Mary Rose*.[33] In 1511 he established a new forge at Hounsditch for the making of bronze cannon and set up an armoury, perhaps in emulation of the one established at about the same time by James IV at Linlithgow. Other foundries were also patronised and by 1515 the Tower armoury contained over 400 guns, some at least of English making. However it was not until the 1540s that the manufacture of cast-iron guns in this country began to catch up with the best Low Countries products.[34]

At first, however, it was neither the navy nor the artillery which caught the diplomatic limelight for the new king's benefit, but rather the spate of tournaments which followed his accession. Although the dominant arm in European warfare was no longer the heavily armoured knight, the role of such cavalry continued to be important, and arms was still the chosen profession of the nobleman. Henry was sufficiently old-fashioned in his outlook to take both these points seriously. Back in 1484, when he had published the *Booke of the Ordre of Chyvalry*, William Caxton had written:

> wold it plesyd oure souverayne lord that twyse or thryse in a yere or at the lest ones he wolde doe crye Iustes of pees to thende that everie knyghte shold havee

hors and harneys and also the use and crafte of a knyght and also tornaye one
against one or ii ageynst ii ... Thys wolde cause gentylmen to resort to thauncyent
customs of chyvalry to grete fame and renome. And also to be alwey redy to serve
theyr prynce when he shall calle them or have need ...[35]

As we have seen, the King was steeped in this chivalric tradition, and
believed that it was the vocation of every nobleman and gentleman
to fight. At this early stage of his reign, Henry's attitude towards the
aristocracy was in sharp contrast to his father's. The old king had been
deeply suspicious of claims to authority based on lineage, because they
based rank on ancestry rather than on service. He had no intention
of attacking the old nobility, but he did not favour them, preferring
to trust peers of his own creation like the Duke of Bedford (who was
also his uncle) or the Earl of Surrey. His chosen servants tended to be
knights, like Sir Reginald Bray, or clergy like John Morton. Henry VIII
suffered from no such inhibitions. There was no list of new creations
on his accession, because there was no need, but such early creations
as there were – Henry Stafford as Earl of Wiltshire (1510), William
Courtenay as Earl of Devon (1511), and Margaret Pole as Countess of
Salisbury (1513) – all came from established peerage families.[36] More
helpfully he reduced or cancelled most of the bonds which had placed
so many of them in the King's debt. Noblemen who were of a suitable
age and disposition were expected to repay these favours by appearing
in the King's revels, and most particularly in the jousts. These had
originally been 'war games' in the proper sense, wild melees covering
large tracts of country, in which ransoms had been taken, and serious
injuries inflicted. However, the impact of chivalric ideology in the early
thirteenth century had disciplined them into contests for honour and
a lady's favour, so that already by the fifteenth century they had been
reduced to the disciplined sports with which Henry was familiar.[37] They
took three forms: the tournament in which teams of contestants fought
on a delimited ground with rebated – that is blunted – weapons; the
barriers, in which dismounted knights fought with swords or poleaxes
across a central barrier; and the jousts proper. In the joust, which also

took place across a barrier, the objective of the mounted knight was to break his spear, ideally upon his opponent's helm, but more realistically upon his body. This was the most prestigious form of combat and the one in which gentlemen (the King included) were most anxious to excel.[38]

Although not without precedent, in the mid-fifteenth century the court of Burgundy had made the tournament into an art form. The combats themselves were governed by the strictest rules of engagement, and the participants were expected to observe a rigorous etiquette. They were also at the centre of theatrical and allegorical displays of the most lavish kind, in which banquets, dances and strange and fanciful entries all featured. The combatants would make their initial appearance in artificial castles, ships and woodland grottos, often in disguise as hermits or 'wild men', and the performances would conclude with a 'battle of the flowers' between the ladies and the gentlemen, followed by a dance. It was in this form that the 'feats of arms' accompanying Henry's creation as Duke of York had been cast, and similarly those which had been prepared for the nuptials of Arthur and Catherine in 1501.[39] Although similar 'feats' were sponsored in 1502, 1506 and 1508, the records are meagre and the allegorical element appears to be missing. By contrast the first tournament of the new reign, in honour of the joint coronation of the King and Queen, which took place in June 1509, was dramatic in the extreme. The theme was a debate (and combat) between the Knights of Pallas (wisdom, arms) and those of Diana (purity, letters), which was a renaissance trope. The combatants made their entries within a mountain, a castle, a forest and a park. The two-day event was characterised by speeches (an unusual feature) as well as by ritualised fighting, from which the Knights of Diana emerged victorious. Because of its sensitive proximity to the coronation, the King did not take part.[40] Even in this stylised form, the fighting was still dangerous, and it would not have done for the King's reign to have ended almost as soon as it had begun. Henry's enthusiasm for the tilt was not dimmed by having to sit this one out, but it seems that his council was opposed to the idea of him hazarding himself in this fashion. When he did appear for the first time, on 12 January 1510, he was 'secretly armed' and joined in the tournament incognito, which suggests some doubts behind the scenes. However, once he had distinguished himself in the lists, the King was revealed, 'to the great comfort of the people', as we are told.[41]

Once he had taken this step, Henry became a regular participant, and notably in the great tournament which was held at Westminster in February 1511 to celebrate the birth of his son and heir. An allegorical challenge came from four strange knights, passing under the names of Coeur Loyale, Valliant Desire, Bon Valour and Joyeuse Penser, who entered the lists in a huge pageant car made like a forest, and '… all the trees, herbes & floures of the same forrest were made of grene Velvet, grene Damaske and silk of divers colours …' which must have taken hours of patient toil to construct. When the pageant rested before the Queen, the 'foresters' who were accompanying it blew their horns 'and out issued the foresaid foure knyghtes, armed in all peces' to begin the jousts. The King was Coeur Loyale.[42] This tournament, which also featured Henry as one of the Nine Worthies, was the most expensive of any in the reign, with the exception of the Field of Cloth of Gold. It cost nearly £4,400, or about 9 per cent of the King's ordinary income. In spite of the death of the Prince who was so honoured, the May Day celebrations of the same year were almost equally ornate, featuring a 'shyppe under sayle' bearing a cargo of 'Renoune' which the King offered to purchase with his deeds of arms.[43] Just over a year later, in June 1512, another allegorical tournament was held, this being the last to be recorded before the outbreak of war:

first came in ladies all in red and white silke, set upon Coursers … after whom folowed a fountaine curiously made of Russet Sattin … [and] within the fountaine sat a knight armed at all peces … After followed a knight in a horse litter … When the fountaine came to the tilt, the ladies rode round aboute and so did the Fountaine and the knight within the litter … and when they came to the Tiltes ende, the twoo knights mounted on the two coursers abidyng all comers. The king was in the fountain and Sir Charles Brandon was in the litter. Then sodainly with great noyse of Trompettes, entered Sir Thomas Knyvet in a Castle of Cole black … and so he

and the erle of Essex, the lorde Howard and others ran their courses with the King
and Sir Charles Brandon, and ever the King brake the moste speres ...

The records show that Sir Thomas Knyvett won the prize for the
first day, but Henry got all the limelight.[44] After this extravaganza,
such pageantry seems to have been largely abandoned. Tournaments
continued to be held, and the King continued to take part – often in
disguise – but the fashion for allegorical fantasies seems to have
passed. This may have had something to do with the intrusion of
the realities of war, but is more likely connected with the rise of the
mask and other indoor entertainments, which offered more scope
for speech making, music, and fanciful dumb shows. Jousts, and
particularly the tourney proper, were not yet so far divorced from
the realities of warfare that they did not form a valuable training
ground for militarily minded gentlemen, and consequently featured
in the education of their sons.

In principal, humanism and chivalry should have been pulling
in opposite directions, and Erasmus was full of contempt for
the renaissance equivalent of the 'muddied oaf', but the King's
example appeared to bridge the gap. No one could have been more
ostentatiously devoted to the military code of honour which chivalry
represented, and yet, according to Lord Mountjoy, he was equally
ambitious to be seen as a patron of scholarship:

> The other day he said to me 'I wish I were more learned than I am'. 'That is not
> what we expect of your grace', I replied, 'but that you should foster and encourage
> learned men', 'Yea, surely' he said, 'for without them we should scarcely exist at
> all'. What more splendid saying could fall from the lips of a prince?[45]

In fact the cultural division between arms and letters may not have
been as great as it was made to appear, or has continued to appear
since. Diplomacy, for example, was conducted in both media. Latin
was the international language, and Henry spoke it fluently, however
ambassadors never ceased to be impressed when the monarch to whom

they were accredited spoke to them in their own vernacular, and the King had excellent French, and enough Italian to get by. He probably did not speak much Spanish, but for that purpose he could always rely upon his queen, who continued to form a channel of communication with Ferdinand independent of Luis Caroz – a circumstance which caused some confusion.[46] In addition to exchanging classical quotations with witty Italians, however, Henry was also out to impress them in a more physical sense. No special envoy could escape the tournament which would inevitably be provided in his honour, and the resident ambassadors were expected to attend as part of their regular duties. Their despatches were always carefully worded to include appreciation of the King's accomplishments in the lists, but the probability is that their praise was not feigned. Tilting was a part of their culture too, and sophisticated Venetians had rejoiced when twelve Italian champions had overcome their French opponents in 1495. It reduced the shame of not having stood up to Charles VIII's invasion! After having been treated to one such demonstration in May 1510, the Venetian ambassador had described Henry as 'courageous and very robust'.[47] The Romans had had military writers too, and as Richard Pace was to write in *De Fructu qui ex Doctrina Percipitur* (about 1517):

> Military training was also renowned amongst the ancients … [and] I'll say this much, speaking as a soldier who had sworn on Christ's words, that if you have to have wars, it is much better to settle them with the good sense of learning than with a sword.[48]

Although, as Pace admitted, the Schools were hostile to all wars, in practical terms fighting and learning could be brought together. Not only was the King both a soldier and a scholar, but the heralds, whose services were so essential to the 'feats of arms', were also men of learning. These were two sides of a royal image which deliberately set out to break new ground.

The young king was a man of remarkably varied accomplishments, and boundless energy. Apart from his classical training in Latin, he was later to show sufficient interest in Greek to engage Richard Croke to teach him – although how long that enthusiasm lasted we do not know. On the basis of his Bible reading, he believed himself to be a better theologian than he was, but his knowledge was still outstanding among contemporary princes. He was an apt student of mathematics, and interested in astronomy, geometry and cartography. He is suspected of having a hand in the design of the *Mary Rose*, and is known to have been the principal inspiration behind the *Great Galley*, which was launched in 1515. The origin of his friendship with Thomas More lay in shared intellectual interests. Sometimes, according to Roper's later *Life of Sir Thomas*, the King would take him into his private rooms:

> … and there … in matters of astronomy, geometry, divinity and such other faculties, some time in his worldly affairs to sit and confer with him and others, and other whiles would he in the night have him up to the leads [roof] and there to consider with him the diversities, courses, motions and operations of the stars and planets.[49]

The King was as avid for intellectual stimulus as he was for physical exercise, and he did not find that among his jousting companions. Above all, he was a talented and enthusiastic musician, who took his minstrels with him wherever he went; on progress, on campaign, even on hunting trips. Most of the evidence dates from later, but the 'king's musik' was noted for its excellence from the very beginning, and in 1516 he tempted the distinguished Venetian organist Dionisio Memo into his service. He played the lute and the virginals well, although he was less sure on the organ, and his greatest asset was his singing voice, which was strong and steady, although we do not know what his register was.[50] Later in the reign one of his favourite occupations was part singing with the Gentlemen of his Privy Chamber, and he seems to have written such songs, perhaps even while he was still prince. One of the earliest was 'Pastime with good company', which expresses the whole philosophy of the young Henry:

For my pastance,
Hunt, sing and dance,
My heart is set,
All goodly sport
To my comfort
Who shall me let?

The best I sue,
The worst eschew;
My mind shall be
Virtue to use;
Vice to refuse ...[51]

God, he was convinced, would be pleased with this lifestyle. Idleness was the devil's instrument, but in the midst of all this frenetic activity there was little reference to affairs of state. When he went on progress in 1510, he occupied himself 'in shooting, singing, dancing, wrestling, casting of the bar, playing at the recorders, flute and virginals ... and when he came to Woking, there he kept both jousts and tourneys' as Edward Hall recorded.[52] He also found time to set 'two godly masses', and to play at cards, tennis and dice, at which he got fleeced by divers 'crafty persons' until he saw their drift and sent them away. However, there was a serious side to all this frivolity. The King was showing himself to his people as the very model of a dashing renaissance prince, and they loved him for it.

The King and Queen undertook two progresses in these early days. In the summer of 1510 the court travelled through Hampshire and Dorset to Corfe Castle, Southampton and Salisbury, staying with several courtiers on the way: with William Sandys at The Vyne, and Robert Knollys at Rotherfield Grey, concluding at Woking in September, as we have seen. 'Beffore hym and some of counsayll' as they went, 'many of the commons shewid grevous byllis and complaints again dudly and Empson',[53] which seems to have settled his determination to deal with those offenders. It is hard to believe that these complaints were spontaneous, but they are a useful demonstration of the way in which a progress could be used. In January of the following year, before he even indulged in a tournament, Henry went off on his own to our Lady of Walsingham to give thanks for the birth of his son, and in order to demonstrate that they were both fully recovered from the trauma of his premature death, the whole court made another splendid progress in July. This time they went north, to Northampton, Leicester, Nottingham and Warwick, staying at Leicester Abbey and Nottingham Castle on the way.[54] By then Empson and Dudley had been disposed of, and if any other petitions were offered, they have escaped the record. Later in the reign, short progresses became annual events, but they seldom went as far afield. In these early days he was very much concerned to show himself to his people – sure enough that they would be pleased by what they saw. 1511 was also the time of Lord Darcy's ill-fated expedition to Cadiz, during which the council was constantly in session, and Henry was much exercised over the attitude of Ferdinand. The business of government and the preparations for war continued, and in the latter at least Henry, in spite of his amusements, played a full part.

Catherine, meanwhile, was struggling. She was pregnant within a few weeks of her marriage, which boded well for both parties, but in May 1510, at almost exactly the time when Henry signed his treaty with Ferdinand, she was delivered of a stillborn daughter. It was, as she wrote to her father, 'the will of God', and a fairly standard misfortune.[55] Within a month she was pregnant again, and after an apparently easy confinement, on New Year's Day 1511 was born the hoped-for prince. He was christened Henry and the rejoicings were thunderous, including the great tournament which we have already noticed. However, the nobles who had assembled for that great occasion remained to bury the child, who lived just six weeks. The news was a terrible blow to everyone, and most of all to his parents. Henry was so shattered that the ambassadors dared not even venture to offer their condolences, and Catherine took refuge in prayer.[56] Infant mortality, even in royal families, was appalling by modern standards. Henry VII and Elizabeth lost four of their eight children, and Isabella of Spain saw five either die at once or shortly after birth. However, this was no consolation to the bereaved couple, who mourned deeply. Henry recovered more quickly, and by the summer was disporting himself furiously on his progress, but Catherine kept herself in seclusion for some time, and from that may have arisen the circumstantial story of his first affair. In spite of his status as Ferdinand's ambassador, Luis Caroz was a marginal figure at court who filled his dispatches with trivial gossip. This situation he blamed on the influence of Catherine's confessor, Fray Diego Fernandez, who, he claimed, turned the Queen's – and consequently the King's – mind against him. Fray Diego interfered in all sorts of improper ways, and it would be better if he could be removed.[57] However, this perception was not the result of first-hand observation, but reflected the opinion of Diego's arch-enemy, Francesca de Carceres. Francesca had left Catherine's service not long before Henry VII's death in circumstances which point to a falling-out between them. The hostility, however, was apparently all on Catherine's side, and her former servant intrigued constantly for reinstatement. This she mistakenly chose to do by undermining Fray Diego.[58]

She also sought to undermine the King, and one of the stories which she fed to Caroz implied that the marriage was in difficulties. Henry was 'enamoured' of two married sisters of the Duke of Buckingham, Anne Hastings and Elizabeth Ratcliffe. Anne was being courted by Sir William Compton, an intimate of the King's who was, it was alleged, a stalking horse for Henry himself. Elizabeth told her brother what was going on and the latter caught Compton *in flagrante delicto*. He was furious, not only at such behaviour but also at the disparagement involved. Stafford ladies were no fit prey for the likes of Compton – or even Henry Tudor. The Duke made a scene, and Henry became equally angry at the insult to his favourite, and by implication to himself.[59] He insisted that Catherine should dismiss Elizabeth, who was a great favourite, from her service. She had no option but to comply, and a furious quarrel was followed by a sulky stand-off between the royal couple. How much truth there was in all this is uncertain. Its substance probably lay in a 'courtly love' flirtation, in which the King loved to indulge. These were relatively harmless games in which the gallants of the court pretended to be in love with the Queen's ladies. Bombarded with small gifts and with 'love tokens', the latter would respond with coy encouragement or simulated disdain. The whole idea was that the lady was virtuous and unattainable, and the 'winners' were those who kept up the pretence the longest and the most convincingly. These games had originated with the troubadors in the court of Eleanor of Aquitaine, and were intended to raise the status of women in the often uncouth environment of the medieval court.[60] By the early sixteenth century they were well entrenched in the courtly culture, and would not normally have raised any eyebrows at all. Perhaps Henry was unusually zealous, or perhaps the whole story was made up. Francesca did not regain her place in the Queen's service, and Catherine was not pregnant again until 1514, but there is no evidence to confirm a serious rupture between the two, and when Henry went to France in 1513 he left his wife as governor of the realm. He continued to show the greatest affection towards her in public, and she went on presiding at his 'feats of arms'. In spite of the normal habits of renaissance princes, it is highly unlikely that Anne Hastings was ever his mistress in any real sense. For the time being at least, he was well satisfied with his devoted wife, whose pious exercises and works of charity did much to augment his more flamboyant reputation. In 1512 God was still on the King's side.

3

THE KING AT WAR, 1511–1514

On 25 April 1512 Henry finally sent a herald to proclaim war against France. The King had been committed to such a course since adhering to the Holy League in the previous November, and the relevant decisions had been taken in council in January. The fleet had been mobilised, and was already at sea when this tardy declaration was made, so it can have come as no surprise to Louis, who had already ordered the mobilisation of his own fleet.[1] The English preparations, and indeed the council decision, were probably made easier by the fact that the King had at last identified an executive agent of his own, a man of remarkable competence and energy called Thomas Wolsey. Wolsey was a man of notoriously humble origins, his father, Robert, having been a prosperous Ipswich grazier. He had been born in about 1472, and having shown exceptional promise as a schoolboy, in 1483, at the age of about twelve, had matriculated at Magdalen College, Oxford, taking his BA in 1486. For the next fifteen years he had pursued an orthodox academic career, registering for the Master's degree, and becoming first Fellow, then Junior Bursar and finally Senior Bursar of his college. Having attracted the patronage of Thomas Grey, Marquis of Dorset, he acquired, in the normal fashion, several benefices which he did not visit. However, Dorset died and in 1501 he finally quitted Oxford for a chaplaincy in the household of Henry Deane, the Archbishop of

Canterbury.[2] He was clearly high in Deane's confidence, and became Chief Mourner at the Archbishop's funeral when he died in 1503, as well as being one of his executors. Although there is no record of the fact, he must have accompanied Deane to court, because his services were quickly engaged by Sir Richard Nanfan, who was a courtier in addition to being Treasurer of Calais. When Sir Richard also died in 1507, Wolsey was well established at court, and shortly after became a chaplain to the King. By the time that Henry died in 1509, he was a substantial churchman, being Dean of both Lincoln and Hereford, neither of which he visited, as far as is known. He was clearly something of a favourite, and when the King's health was in visible decline, in February and March, he was given the task of saying no fewer that 8,000 masses for the repose of Henry's soul. For these he was paid at the rate of 6*d* a mass, although it seems unlikely that he would have had the time to say them all himself.[3] He had also become friendly with the young Prince of Wales to whom, at the age of thirty-seven, he must have been something of an avuncular figure, and had made a very favourable impression upon the powerful Bishop of Winchester, Richard Fox.

John Edenham, who had been Henry VII's Almoner, was removed on 21 July, and replaced by Richard Hobbs. However, Hobbs died soon after, and on 8 November 1509 – probably at the instigation of Bishop Fox – Thomas Wolsey was appointed in his place.[4] Not very much is known about him at this stage of his career, but his duties soon transcended those of distributing the King's charity. In April 1510 he was appointed Registrar of the Order of the Garter, and at about the same time joined the royal council. He had replaced Thomas Ruthall, who was the King's secretary, in the Garter office, and had been identified by the young king, not only as a man of exceptional ability and energy, but one who would quite happily get on with the business of state while Henry went about his various amusements. He was in no position to reproach his master for neglecting his duties, but that is hardly the point. Unlike more senior councillors, he was quite prepared to encourage the King's lifestyle, because it gave him more scope to perform his own duties as he thought fit. As George Cavendish wrote many years later:

> ... so fast as the other counsellors advised the king to leave his pleasures and
> attend to the affairs of his realm, so busily did the almoner persuade him to the
> contrary, which delighted him much, and caused him to have the greater affection
> and love to the almoner.[5]

How far it would be fair to describe him as Henry's 'friend' at this stage
(or at any other stage) is debatable, but he was high in favour, and
in consequence was placed in charge of the logistics for the planned
summer campaigns, which meant mainly victualling. He seems not to
have been involved in preparing the fleet, for which the council dealt
directly with Robert Brygandyne, or in mustering the soldiers, which
was done by commission of array, but may well have been an agent in
the purchase of armour and weapons, for which the records are very
incomplete.

Two strikes were proposed. The first, led by Sir Edward Howard,
was to be against Brittany, and was to involve 18 ships and 3,000 men.
The second and more substantial effort would be for the recovery of
Guienne, and would be led by the Marquis of Dorset with 15,000 men.
Although Howard's enterprise involved landing in Brittany, his was
principally an 'army by sea', and its main purpose was to secure the
command of the Channel.[6] When Howard's instructions were issued on
7 April, they included the clause:

> After the fleet shall come to the sea, the Admiral shall take his course, if wind and
> weather will serve, towards the Trade, for the defence of the sea on that coast ...
> and from thence return, scouring the sea, to and fro, as the case shall require ...[7]

The following day he entered into indentures with the King for the
command of his ships and men, '... of which 1,750 shall be soldiers,
1,233 mariners and gunners', undertaking to serve for 10s a day. His
captains were to receive 18d a day 'except they be of the number of
the King's Spears, which shall be contented with their ordinary wages'.
These Spears were a select band of gentlemen, set up by the King in the
previous year as a kind of personal bodyguard, but they did not survive

the war, because of the costs involved.[8] Howard's ordinary soldiers, mariners and gunners were to be allowed 5s a month for wages, plus another 5s for victuals, although of course they did not receive the latter sums, which were paid direct to the Admiral. He was to be provisioned in the first instance for three months, at the end of which time he was to return to Southampton, there to make his musters and to receive 'new wages and victual money' for a further three months. Two crayers were to be provided for victualling while at sea, and coat and conduct money were to be paid to all the men recruited. The musters were held at Blackheath on 16 April, Howard took an oath in the presence of the King, and £6,000 was sent to John Dawtrey, the Customer of Southampton, for the first three months necessaries. About the end of the month, the Admiral set off on his cruise, and spent the next couple of weeks picking off fishing boats in the Channel while he awaited news of French naval preparations.[9] Louis seems to have been taken by surprise, because although he had been warned in early February that Henry was intent on war, and he had started taking precautions, things had gone quiet thereafter and his detailed intelligence seems to have been defective.[10] Consequently he had neither ships nor men prepared to meet the English threat when it came. This was very frustrating for Howard, who continued to take prizes, sometimes of dubious legitimacy. He returned to Portsmouth about the middle of May to collect the *Regent*, which was being added to his fleet, but saw no meaningful action until early June, when he was called upon to escort the Marquis of Dorset's 'army by land' until it reached the Bay of Biscay. This turned out to be unnecessary, because the French still did not have a power at sea, but having discharged his duty and desiring to give his soldiers some occupation, on 6 June he 'suddenly set his men on land' at Bertheaume Bay. Over the next two or three days he went inland about seven miles 'burning and wasting towns and villages' and meeting only light opposition. A few days later a second landing at Crozon was resisted with more determination – or at least a larger force – but having carried out a similar raid the admiral was able to draw off his force substantially unscathed.[11]

Hearing that there were 'ships of war at sea' he then coasted round to Normandy, but either the rumour was false or they did not want to encounter him, because he found nothing, and returned to lie off the English coast. At the end of July he met the King at Portsmouth, when Henry came visiting to see how his navy fared. Meanwhile the ponderous French naval machine was at last creaking into action. Starting about 20 June fourteen Norman and eight Breton ships had been fitted out and despatched to Brest, where they arrived about 3 or 4 August. Meanwhile Pregent de Bidoux had been instructed to bring some of his galleys round from the Mediterranean.[12] Hearing the good news that he was at last to have an enemy to fight, Howard quitted Portsmouth and arrived off Brest on 10 August. Again his appearance seems to have caused surprise, because the French ships were outside the harbour and entertaining guests to celebrate St Laurence's day. To the disgust of the English they quickly retreated to lie beneath the guns of the fortress, leaving only the 700-ton *Cordelière* to sustain the expected assault. The result was both disastrous and spectacular. She was grappled by the *Regent*, and fierce hand-to-hand fighting ensued. The English were (they later claimed) gaining the upper hand when, whether by accident or design, a fire started aboard the French vessel. With the two ships locked together, the fire soon spread, and when it reached the *Cordelière's* magazine, blew up with lethal consequences. Fewer than 200 of the 1,500 or so on the two ships escaped, and among the dead was Sir Thomas Knyvett, to whom Henry had given the command of the *Regent* as a special favour.[13] Unable to force his way into the harbour, Howard then again visited Bertheaume Bay, where he carried out some more raiding and considered his options. In spite of Wolsey's efforts, he was seriously short of supplies, and would not in any case be able to remain at sea for much longer. He had hoped for a quick and decisive strike against the French fleet, but that had eluded him, so he decided to return home by way of the coasts of Normandy and Picardy, capturing or burning as many French ships as he could on the way. The French fleet, holed up in Brest, made not the slightest attempt to stop him. When the English were safely out of the way, the

French Admiral, René de Clermont, (who had not covered himself with glory in this operation) moved his ships to Honfleur and Dieppe, where they were demobilised in late September.[14] Howard had by then been safely back at Southampton for nearly a month.

Somewhat paradoxically, Henry VIII seems to have been pleased with this inconclusive operation. This may be because Howard had exposed a streak of timidity in the French naval command, which he hoped to be able to exploit, or it may be because using his navy on its own, rather than in support of a land army, seemed to have been vindicated. It is possible that the King had been urging this tactical innovation upon his more conservative military advisers, and felt justified by the result. Certainly Howard was far more successful than Dorset, whose major operation had come to grief on the Franco-Spanish border. The object of this operation, as the English understood it, was a joint Anglo-Spanish attack upon Guienne for the purpose of restoring it to the Crown of England, the idea being that Dorset would make his landfall on the French side of the frontier, and that Ferdinand would provide logistical support in the form of horses, guns and tents.[15] The Marquis made a bad start by overshooting his target and landing on the Spanish side, near San Sebastian. However, none of the support which he had been expecting was anywhere to be seen, and when he moved to the frontier town of Fuenterrabia, it still did not materialise. Without tents, many of his men were forced to sleep in the open – and it rained. Moreover, without the promised food supplies they had to live off the country, and whereas that might have been acceptable in France as an act of war, it was not acceptable in Spain. Dorset, acting on instructions from Henry, was completely at odds with Ferdinand. In addition to what seems to have been a misunderstanding about tents and supplies, there was no consensus about tactics either.[16] Whether this was due to wilful obstinacy on the Marquis' part, or to double-dealing by the King is not entirely clear. Each side told its own story, but when Dorset proposed Bayonne (about thirty miles away) as a sensible starting point, his suggestion was refused. It looks very much as though Ferdinand never had any intention of campaigning in Guienne, and was using the English force simply as a distraction while he seized control of Navarre, which he proceeded to do during August. He instructed the English to join him in the latter campaign, probably knowing perfectly well that they would refuse.[17] Meanwhile, as Dorset was fed with duplicitous words, his forces were kept idle. Discipline inevitably became a problem, as Darcy's experience of the previous year had suggested that it would. His men got drunk, and being made ill by the unfamiliar diet, began to die of disease. By the end of August, morale was at rock-bottom.

What then happened is not entirely clear. According to the story told later, the men mutinied, and seized ships to take them back to England, carrying their captains with them. However, it is more likely that the only mutiny involved was that of the captains against Dorset. Taking advantage of the illness of their commander, they themselves organised the return; otherwise it is hard to see how so many ships could suddenly have become available. In so doing they crossed with orders from Henry that they were to obey Ferdinand's orders and join him in Navarre.[18] The King was as up to date as sixteenth-century communications could make him, but on this occasion he was too late, because only Dorset and a handful of men were left in Fuentarrabia when his letter arrived. When he recovered from his illness, the Marquis found himself stranded, and having taken the precaution of sending William Knight back to England to explain what had happened, returned on 30 October. He soon found himself being used as a scapegoat, because although Henry must have been suspicious of Ferdinand's conduct, he had no desire to fall out with him in the midst of a war. According to a report sent to the King of Spain on 19 November, Henry summoned the captains of the Guienne expedition, and in the presence of the ambassadors, asked them for an explanation of their conduct.[19] They pleaded mutiny, and laid the blame firmly on their commander, whereupon, the report continued, 'The Privy Council saw very clearly that the English were in the wrong, especially the Marquis ...' However, that was no doubt what the ambassadors were intended to believe. No action was taken, either against Dorset or any of his captains, and the whole episode was consigned to a resentful silence. For his part, Ferdinand used the episode to convince himself that the King of England was not in earnest about the war, and signed a truce with Louis on 1 April 1513.[20]

It is hard to know what the King of Spain did believe, because his correspondence with Henry and with his ambassadors elsewhere tell radically different stories. Henry was certainly in earnest, and his fleet was almost ready for the sea at the same moment that Ferdinand was signing his truce. However, he does seem to have decided to wage his own war, and not to be caught out again in specious joint projects which cost so much and achieved so little. On 5 April he renewed his treaty with the Pope and the Emperor, but does not seem to have been expecting either of them to make a major contribution.[21] Ferdinand was actually included in this treaty, in spite of his recent truce (which seems to have been unknown to the other signatories), and it was even suggested that he should make a further attack from the south, but the following month he was making secret overtures to Louis for a defensive alliance – which was certainly not known to either Henry or Maximilian.[22] Nothing came of this initiative, but that it should have been made casts an interesting light on the King of Spain's style of diplomacy, which was both opportunistic and deceitful. Meanwhile, apart from Howard's somewhat over-emphasised success in the Channel, Henry had gained neither honour nor territory for his efforts. 1513, he decided, would be different. He had bought or purchased a number of ships over the previous twelve months, and had about twenty-six in commission by March; of these twenty-three were designated to form Howard's fleet for the new season, together with five others which had been taken up in the traditional fashion. The navy was manned and equipped to sail, but still deficient in victuals. As Howard pointed out in his first report 'from the sea' on 22 March, he had only fifteen days' supply of biscuit and beer,[23] and thereafter his correspondence with Wolsey was punctuated with requests for more, and more reliable, supplies.

This time Louis was not taken by surprise. Although Pregent de Bidoux had arrived too late to influence the 1512 season, by March of the following year he was in Normandy with his galleys, equipped and ready for action. He had an independent command of six of these, and seems to have been intending a pre-emptive strike at the south of England. By 13 March he was at Brest, but the expected action did not ensue, partly on account of the bad weather, which made galleys particularly hazardous, but partly also (it would appear) from lack of provisions.[24] This time the two fleets were at sea almost simultaneously, but Sir Edward had only progressed as far as Plymouth by 5 April, while the French were still busy moving ships from Normandy to Brest. On the 11th Howard encountered them near St Mathews, fifteen in number, 'which, as soon as they spied us, fled like cowards' into the safety of Brest harbour. These were vessels in transit, and were presumably not equipped for fighting. At this stage the initiative clearly lay with the English, who not only blockaded Brest, but also succeeded in cutting off Pregent's galleys, which were forced to resort to St Malo to replenish their supplies. Admiral du Chillou (who had taken over from Clermont in January) was thus bottled up in port without the services of his most effective inshore vessels.[25]

Time, however, was not on Howard's side. His victuals were once again running low, and he needed a quick decisive action. Consequently he tried a frontal attack on the harbour, but these were perilous waters without local knowledge, and no sooner had he entered than one of his ships, which was probably the *Nicholas of Hampton*, struck full on a hidden reef and foundered. Warned by this mishap, Howard backed off and reconsidered his options. Over the next few days he landed parties both sides of Brest, but found the resistance tougher than he had anticipated, and was nowhere near strong enough to attack the town. Some victuallers reached him on the 19th, but these only gave him a few extra days at sea because, although welcome, the quantities involved were inadequate.[26] Then on the 22nd, Pregent's galleys suddenly reappeared on the scene, and attacked an outlying part of the English fleet, sinking one vessel and severely damaging another. This attack appears to have taken Howard by surprise, and led to a healthy fear of the galley's big guns, the forward-firing basilisks. However, being unable or unwilling to penetrate the blockade of Brest, Pregent then retired to Blancs Sablons Bay, where he drew up his ships in a defensive formation.[27] Howard now faced a dilemma. He still needed a quick action, and the galleys seemed to offer the only option. He appears to have considered landing 6,000 men to take them from the landward side, but did not eventually do so. Eventually, on 25 April he made the disastrous mistake of deciding to attack from the sea, using what shallow-draft boats he had available. These were the rowbarges and they were quite inadequate both in size and in numbers. In the face of relentless fire, both from the galleys and from the shore, Howard managed to get aboard Pregent's own ship, but he was inadequately supported, and being thrust over the side, was drowned.[28] The English drew off in confusion, having little other option in the face of such odds. They confirmed Howard's fate under flag of truce, but now lacking a leader and being seriously short of victuals, the council of captains decided to raise the blockade and return to Plymouth, which they duly did on 30 April.

Sir Edward had been one of the King's boon companions, and Henry was much grieved by his loss, even in such heroic circumstances. However, the first priority was to recover control over the fleet, and Howard's brother, Lord Thomas, was immediately despatched to Plymouth as Lord Admiral. There he spent the next month restoring discipline and re-victualling the fleet for a possible revenge attack.[29] The latter never came, partly because the King switched his priorities to his intended campaign in Artois, and partly because the French fleet returned to Honfleur and demobilised. Pregent's galleys remained, but they were out of action for several weeks on account of sickness among the rowers. The naval war was suspended and most of the ships switched to the traditional duty of escorting an 'army royal' to Calais. The council, we are told, were not at all keen on this campaign, and still less keen on Henry's intention to lead it in person, but the Queen was enthusiastic, perhaps seeing this as a means of fulfilling her husband's desire for military glory, but more likely as a demonstration of the continued 'love' between Henry and her father.[30] Commissions of array had been issued, and troops had already begun to assemble by the middle of March, when in his Good Friday sermon before the

King the Dean of St Paul's, John Colet, threw what could have been a spanner in the works. He preached against war in general, and against wars of ambition in particular. The effusion of Christian blood could not be justified by those who needed brotherly love as the gateway to heaven. Henry summoned Colet to a private interview, and the Dean's enemies sensed his undoing, but (rather surprisingly) nothing of the kind occurred. Either the King succeeded in convincing him that his intended campaign was defensive in its intention, or Colet decided that discretion was the better part of valour, but the two parted amicably and Henry was full of praise for the dean's learning.[31]

The King had already taken the precaution of getting a subsidy voted by Parliament, and on 4 November 1512, with a pretentious flourish, had announced how it was to be assessed. Emphasising the schismatic persistence of the French King, he went on:

> For reformation whereof, our said sovereign Lord the King, of his blessed and Godly disposition for the true faith ... hath prepared and ordained in all hasty speed to prepare and make ready as well by land as by water, divers and sundry great armies and navies for the intents ... beforesaid ...[32]

Wherefore every marquis, earl or countess was to contribute £4; every person with lands or goods valued at £40 or more, 20s; and so on down to the person with lands or goods valued between 40s and £10, who was to contribute 12d. In theory this taxation was comprehensive, and commissioners for its collection were appointed, but in practice it was disappointing. Thanks to exemptions and evasion, the yield fell far short of what had been intended, and eventually direct taxation covered less than a third of the £900,000 which the war was to cost. Meanwhile, having ready money available from his reserves, Henry was purchasing thousands of suits of armour, and a number of heavy guns, including the so-called 'twelve apostles'. Bows, arrows, bills and other weapons were assembled, and thanks to Wolsey's tireless efforts, draft horses, ships, beer and victuals – enough for an army of somewhere between 35,000 and 50,000 men.[33] Henry was not only in earnest, but he was also planning on a large scale. It would have been unthinkable for so vainglorious a monarch to have entrusted his host to any other commander. Quite apart from anything else the uncertainties of communication would have left it unresponsive to his wishes, and possibly pursuing different priorities. So the slight risk of death or injury to the King was set aside, and it was determined that Henry would indeed lead this army in person. His professional officers were dutiful, but unenthusiastic. In a brief dated 20 March 1512 – a year before – Julius II had stripped Louis XII of his title to the Kingdom of France, and conferred it upon the loyal Henry. The only drawback with this magnificent coup was that he would have to conquer it for himself.[34] Now, in the spring of 1513, he was ostentatiously preparing to do just that. Or so it was intended to appear. In fact the King knew perfectly well that even a victorious campaign would be insufficient unless it was supported by invasions on the part of at least some of his ostensible allies. Maximilian was showing some signs of willingness, but his resources were small and of Leo X and Ferdinand there was no sign.

It was therefore with high, but not unlimited expectations that transports were commissioned on 20 May, and the foreward under the command of George Talbot, Earl of Shrewsbury, about 12,000 strong, was shipped over to Calais on 6 June. Four days later the rearward, led by Charles Somerset, Lord Herbert followed suit, and a week or so later the middleward, which was the King's own responsibility, also crossed over. Henry himself joined them on 30 June.[35] At this stage the discipline and organisation of the army were excellent, each part moving out of its encampment near Calais in time for the next to arrive. By the time that Henry reached the town both the foreward and the afterward had moved out of the Pale in the direction of Thérouanne. There they stayed for about three weeks while the King busied himself in Calais, and with receiving embassies from the Emperor, whose co-operation was clearly going to be much smaller scale than he had hoped. This delay could have been a serious error of judgement on Henry's part, leaving his army divided and vulnerable, but in fact Louis had no force in the neighbourhood which would have been capable of taking on even half the English host, so his luck held. On 21 July the mainward eventually set off, and several days later joined the rest of the army before Thérouanne.[36] It would have been more logical for Henry to have attacked Boulogne, but Maximilian's envoys had presumably persuaded him that the Emperor's support would be conditional on his targeting a border town in which the latter had an interest. If such was the case, the promise was misleading, because when Maximilian turned up, it was with a small force offering to serve under the command, and at the expense, of the English. There was some skirmishing, but the march through Artois was generally unimpeded, apart from the fact that the French cut off and captured one of the twelve apostles, which had become bogged in a ditch.[37] This was just as well, because Henry's middleward contained about 12 per cent non-combatants, who were his personal and household servants. Unfamiliar with the realities of campaigning, and unwilling to undergo its rigours, the King had brought everything with him – a wardrobe with a staff of forty-nine, a chapel with 115, eight trumpeters and ten minstrels. None of these would have been present if the King had stayed at home, and they were undoubtedly a liability to an army in the field.[38] Every time the camp was pitched, the siting and erection of the King's elaborate tents took a disproportionate amount of time and effort, and one of the results was that the 'middle ward' moved only with excruciating slowness. By the time that Henry reached Thérouanne on 1 August, the siege had already been in progress for some time. Many of the siege guns were in place and some of the outlying houses had been demolished. The town had already rejected a summons to surrender, and was therefore a legitimate target for a sack if the besiegers gained the upper hand. The King's presence may have inspired his troops to feats of heroism, and he certainly busied himself enthusiastically about the laying of the additional guns which he had brought with him. Nevertheless objectively he made very little difference and several observers (from a safe distance) were deriding the ineffectual efforts of the English forces against what was, admittedly, a very strong fortress.[39]

The turning point came on 16 August when a force of French cavalry, escorting a wagon train, tried to get supplies into the besieged town. They were looking for evasion rather than a fight, but the English had superior intelligence and ambushed them in force. Realising that they were outnumbered, the French abandoned their wagons and fled. This skirmish at Bromy consequently became known as the 'battle of the spurs'.[40] As a military victory, it scarcely rated, but it did persuade the defenders of Thérouanne that they were unlikely to be relieved. Just over a week later, on 24 August, they surrendered. By this time Maximilian had arrived in the English camp with his flattering offer of service, and he and Henry made their ceremonial entry together. Satisfied with his achievement, three days later the King handed over the town to his ally. Maximilian had held Thérouanne briefly in 1479, and had a genuine strategic interest in the place, which was not the case as far as Henry was concerned. The Emperor expelled the inhabitants, and razed it to the ground – apart from the church.[41] What the King thought of this procedure we do not know. Flushed with victory, he had taken himself off to Lille where he spent three days of lavish celebrations in the company of the Regent. Henry may not have impressed his professional soldiers, but he certainly made an impact at Margaret's court, where his dancing and singing left a lasting impression – particularly on the ladies.[42] However, one 'ungracious doghole' did not make a victorious campaign, and during his absence (but acting on his orders) his army had moved on to the siege of Tournai. Tournai was not a border fortress but a prosperous commercial centre, and the burghers had been taking anxious council for some weeks about the possibility of an English attack. Should such an attack materialise, they wanted to be able to negotiate a surrender on favourable terms without appearing to be disloyal to Louis XII. They tried to use Margaret of Savoy as an intermediary, but Louis wrote insisting that their first loyalty was to him, and ordering the town to be put into a state of defence. Margaret urged neutrality, and Maximilian put in a counter claim to their allegiance, leaving the townsmen in an impossible dilemma.[43] Against a background of much internal controversy, the city authorities prepared for a siege, demolishing some of the houses in the suburbs which it was feared would give cover to an attacking army. By 20 September the English guns were hammering away at the town, demolishing the fortifications and silencing the answering cannonade. However, it was no part of Henry's intention to treat Tournai as Maximilian had treated Thérouanne, and the citizens' resistance arose more from divided councils than from determination. Consequently the bombardment was punctuated by truces, and eventually the burghers found an acceptable formula. If they surrendered to Henry as King of France, rather than to Maximilian, they could preserve their French allegiance and protect their commercial interests. A document to this effect was drawn up on the 23rd, giving all those citizens who refused their new allegiance twenty days to leave, taking their goods and chattels with them. This was signed and sealed the same day, and Brian Tuke, the Treasurer of the War, was able to write that Henry now had the 'opulent, strong, fair and extensive city of Tournai' at his obedience.[44]

The King made his ceremonial entry into the town on the 25th. It must have been a strange occasion because Henry and his nobles were dressed in their finest armour, and the city authorities put on a sumptuous welcome, but the majority of the citizens made their discontent clear by silence, and had to be dragooned into taking the oath of allegiance to their new Lord. Thomas Wolsey supervised the administration of this oath in the market place, but not even an ingratiating speech made on the King's behalf or his determined attempts to be affable could reconcile the majority to their new circumstances.[45] Fearful that this sullenness would take a more explicit form, Henry's servants made sure that he left before nightfall, and spent the night in his camp rather than in the town. Undaunted by this hostility, or perhaps thinking that a good show would convert the sceptics, Henry commanded that jousts should be held on 8 October, and in spite of the fact that it rained hard a goodly crowd turned out to see the show. Margaret of Savoy was the guest of honour, and the tilting (as usual) was accompanied by much feasting and dancing. Meanwhile the realities of managing his new acquisition had to be faced. Sir Edward Poynings was appointed governor, and he, with the assistance of Thomas Wolsey, who would shortly be given the revenues of the see of Tournai, got on with the business of establishing the garrison, and calling in all the weapons which had been issued to the citizens at the time of the siege.[46] On 13 October, the King left to return to England, and Poynings with his force of about 5,000 men was left to consolidate his position as best he could.

Catherine had been left as governor in England during the King's absence, and Henry, as a romantic gesture, had sent her the keys of Tournai, perhaps with a sly allusion to the fact that the town had called itself 'la pucelle'. Her position was no sinecure because the King was away upwards of three months, and during that time James IV of Scotland attempted to take advantage of Henry's absence. James had renewed his treaty with Louis XII in November 1512, and there was no love lost between the brothers-in-law, but James' gestures of naval assistance to France had been just that and nothing substantial had materialised.[47] However, when Henry went to France, and seemed committed to a longish stay there, the opportunity was too good to miss. Urged on by Louis, and ignoring warnings from Leo that he risked anathema by attacking a participant in the Holy War, on 11 August he sent a herald to the English camp outside Thérouanne with a formal declaration of war. Henry was disgusted, but there was not very much that he could do about it. Fortunately Catherine and her council were warned in advance that this was likely to happen, and had mustered an army in the north commanded by the Earl of Surrey, the most senior and experienced soldier not in France with the King.[48] By 13 August James had assembled some 40,000 men outside Edinburgh, the largest field army that Scotland had ever put forth, and at the beginning of September crossed the Tweed, taking and razing Norham castle on the way, and dug in on Flodden Edge, south-east of Coldstream.[49] The Earl of Surrey advanced against him, gathering forces as he came, and on 9 September the two armies made contact. James had about 30,000 men at this point, and Surrey substantially fewer, perhaps 15,000 to 20,000. It was a battle which the Scots should have won, because not only did they have an advantage in numbers, they also had superior artillery.

However, in a daring manoeuvre, Surrey bypassed the Scottish position and got his infantry between the Scots and the Tweed. This tempted the Scots from their strong position, and it seemed at first as though their tumultuous charge would carry the day. But the English stood firm, and in the resulting melee the advantage of the Scottish artillery was lost. It was the English archers which won the day, proving more effective at close quarters than the Scottish pikes. James, who had led the charge in person, was cut off and killed, and the hard-fought engagement turned into a rout.[50] The Scots left about 5,000 dead upon the field, including their King, exposing their realm to a long minority because James' son was barely a year old. It was a military and political disaster, because twelve earls and three bishops had also died upon the field, leaving the political leadership of Scotland in tatters for years to come. Surrey had moved fast – so fast indeed that his troops were alleged to be famished for lack of food – but his decisions both on and off the field had been vindicated, and he had won a victory besides which Henry's exploits in France paled into insignificance. Henry had sent Catherine French prisoners as well as keys, but she was able to send him the blood-stained hauberk of a king.[51] Henry was very much aware, however, that from the perspective of Rome, victories in France were more significant than ones obtained in Britain, and he made sure that news of his success was conveyed to Cardinal Bainbridge in the Curia. Bainbridge began to press for Leo to crown his master as King of France, but the Pope judged (rightly) that the war was very far from won, and the reward which he had promised was still to be earned.

With that in mind, Henry began to prepare for a new campaigning season. While he had been at Lille, before the fall of Tournai, he had agreed with the Emperor that their campaign should be renewed in 1514, not later than 1 June. At the same time a marriage was to be concluded between Henry's sister Mary (then aged eighteen) and the fourteen-year-old Archduke Charles, the Emperor's grandson.[52] Necessarily, but optimistically, Ferdinand of Spain was to be included in this agreement, his part being a new invasion of Guienne. To this, apparently, Ferdinand agreed in an absent-minded kind of way, because his thoughts were concentrated upon Italy and he had no intention of doing anything against France. Henry put most of his fleet on standby during the winter instead of discharging it, while Louis apparently did the same. Building work on the *Henry Grace à Dieu* continued, and the *Great Galley* was laid down. However, Julius II had died on 21 February 1513, and his successor Leo X was a man of a very different stamp. The war had developed a momentum of its own by then, but Leo was not anxious to pursue his predecessor's feud against the French, and began to press the combatants to settle.[53] Moreover the costs of the war were mounting alarmingly, and Ferdinand's intentions, as always, were uncertain. There was no sign of the military preparations which would have been expected if he had seriously been intending to invade Guienne, and in fact he signed another truce with Louis at the end of February. Henry ennobled his two war lords on 1 February, creating the Earl of Surrey Duke of Norfolk, and Charles Brandon, Viscount Lisle, Duke of Suffolk, but by March he was changing his mind, and signed a truce in his turn.[54] This was not quite the end of the fighting, because Pregent de Bidoux, apparently ignoring this development, launched a galley raid on Brighton in mid-April, burning down what was then a 'poor village', and taking what goods he could find. This provoked the Lord Admiral (by this time Earl of Surrey) into launching Sir John Wallop against the coast of Normandy, where he in turn burned several villages, and 'divers ships in the havens of Tréport and Etaples'.[55] Fortunately these actions did not lead to any general resumption of hostilities, and at the beginning of June Henry ordered a ceasefire, which was observed, in order to give the peace negotiations a chance. To encourage him in this, Leo sent him a sword and cap of maintenance in mid-May, with which he was invested in St Paul's Cathedral on the 21st. A little later another papal envoy arrived via France to add his voice to the papal pleas for peace, and Thomas Wolsey, by this time Bishop of Lincoln, was of the same mind.[56] By July the bargaining on both sides was getting hard, but early in August terms were agreed. Louis was to pay the arrears on the pension which Henry VII had received under the treaty of Etaples of 1492 – a substantial sum – and the Princess Mary, recently destined to wed with Charles, was now reassigned to the fifty-two-year-old Louis. She allegedly agreed to this arrangement only on the condition that she could have her own choice next time around, but in fact was probably tempted by the thought of being Queen of France. The peace was to endure until one year after the death of whichever of the signatories died first.[57]

Henry thus abandoned the warlike posture which he had consistently adopted since 1509, and which he had sustained as recently as January 1514. One of the main reasons for this *volte-face* was the fact that he now realised how his youthful enthusiasm had been taken advantage of. The Pope, the Emperor and the Venetians had all taken money off him in pursuit of their own interests. Maximilian and Margaret of Savoy had both exploited his gullibility for their respective purposes, and Ferdinand had betrayed his trust no fewer than three times. The latter, he now realised, had never had any intention of honouring the undertakings which he had made, or which had been made in his name. These latter betrayals left Henry feeling particularly angry, so much so that within weeks of the peace with France he was talking of entering into an alliance with Louis against Ferdinand. When the Duke of Suffolk went to France in October 1514 to witness Mary's marriage, he was empowered to raise this issue, which could have taken the form of English support for the recovery of Navarre, or, more fancifully, the pursuit of a claim to Castile on behalf of Catherine of Aragon, who was after all Isabella's daughter as well as Ferdinand's.[58] The French made polite, unenthusiastic responses to these suggestions. Having disburdened himself of war in the north, Louis was really interested only in Italy, and in any case he died on 1 January 1515, leaving the peace at risk and Anglo-French relations in mid-air. Nor was this the only relationship upon uncertain ground. It was widely believed at the time that the King's marriage had suffered from his falling out with Ferdinand, because Catherine was known to be a loyal daughter and deeply committed to the continuance of the alliance. However, before 1515 Henry's alleged 'amours' turn out to be insubstantial rumours based upon exchanges of gifts, or the part played by a particular damsel in some court festivity – in other words just the kind of developments which were associated with courtly love. The King's eye may have roved, but there is no evidence that it lit on any particular lady, and the Queen is known to have had another miscarriage in 1514.[59] Moreover, Catherine was too well skilled in the wifely arts to put her father's interests before her husband's in the event of their being any clash – as there clearly was by 1514. However, this falling-out clearly weakened her political influence, and that was also eroded by the rise of Thomas Wolsey.

As we have seen, 'Master Almoner' was high in favour by 1512, largely because of the skilful tactics which he employed in the King's service. Henry was both intelligent and well educated, but his concentration span was short and he easily became bored. Consequently it was a great relief to him to have found an extremely diligent and able man who was prepared to read and précis all the papers which reached his desk, and to offer him a brief and comprehensible list of options on every issue which required a decision. Wolsey may have adjusted these options occasionally to suit his own priorities, but Henry's complacency could not be taken for granted. He was occasionally and unpredictably astute, and this had to be taken into account.[60] Wolsey thus became, in a sense, the King's shortcut to statesmanship, and his own authority was greatly augmented. Although it did not make him popular, observant courtiers were quick to realise that securing the favour of Master Almoner was the quickest route to the royal bounty. For his part, when Henry needed a job doing, particularly a complex and demanding one, he knew where to look. It had not been Wolsey's fault that Dorset's Guienne campaign had been a fiasco, and he was naturally given the responsibility for the logistics of the King's major campaign in Artois in the summer of 1513. From an administrative point of view, this had been a triumph. The troops were both paid and victualled on time, with the result that excellent discipline had been maintained throughout, in spite of Henry's overblown household, and the cumberous slowness with which the main army had moved. It was right and proper that Wolsey should have been present at the royal entry to Tournai, and should have received a modest share of the plaudits which were so generously on offer.[61] Because he was a priest, the Almoner could also be rewarded with ecclesiastical benefices without becoming a drain on the royal resources – or at least not much. Wolsey loved luxury, and always claimed that an ostentatious lifestyle was necessary for the King's honour. As early as 1511 he was receiving £1,000 a year as a councillor for the expenses of his household, and at the beginning of 1514, before he became Bishop of Lincoln, an establishment of 160 people was costing some £2,000 a year to support.[62] In February 1513 he was provided to the Deanery of York, and when Henry took Tournai he attempted to promote his servant to the bishopric. This was blocked by the Pope in the interests of the French incumbent, but Wolsey got the revenues, which was probably what mattered to him. When Bishop Smith of Lincoln died in January 1514 he was promoted to that see, and translated to the archbishopric of York when Cardinal Bainbridge died in Rome in July of the same year.[63] The archbishopric was worth about £5,000 a year, but even that was barely sufficient to keep pace with Wolsey's rising pretensions. His power, however, was essentially that of a servant and broker of royal favour. It would be a mistake to see him as being in any sense 'in charge' of policy. As a churchman he was a thoroughgoing civilian, and temperamentally inclined to peace, but at first his duties required him to serve a policy of war, which he did with his customary efficiency. However, when the King's mind began to change early in 1514, and with the papacy also pressing for peace, he threw his weight onto that side of the debate, and became an active protagonist of the agreement which was reached in August.

There were also occasions when his dual standing as a royal servant and ecclesiastic became something of an embarrassment. Anti-clericalism was nothing like the problem which it is sometimes represented as being, but it did exist, and the Archbishop of Canterbury was well aware of it. When he called a provincial council in 1510, Warham had dwelt upon the hostility of the laity to the privileges of the Church, and must have been disconcerted when Dean Colet, in his opening sermon had laid the responsibility for that mainly at the feet of the clergy, because of their moral and constitutional laxity.[64] Bishop Fitzjames of London apparently contemplated proceeding against the Dean for heresy, but Colet's motivation was to encourage the clergy to be more worthy of their high calling, and that point was well taken by the majority of the prelates present. In 1512 an Act of Parliament had removed benefit of clergy from those in minor orders who committed murder or robbery with violence – a statute which was to stand to the next parliament – and in May 1514 Pope Leo X had promulgated a decree that no layman had jurisdiction over any clergy whatsoever; a declaration which promised direct confrontation.[65] The following year this led to a showdown in Parliament, when Abbot Richard Kidderminster declared that to extend the 1512 statute would be to fly in face of all laws, human and divine. When Henry Standish attempted to respond that a papal decree had no force in England, he was summoned before Convocation. Convocation was then accused of praemunire, and a monumental row threatened, involving the privileges of Parliament and the prerogative of the King. Wolsey was thus caught between a Church which believed that its liberties were in danger, and a king who believed that he had no superior on earth.[66] It required all his peace-making skills to patch up a compromise whereby Henry caused his servants in Parliament to drop the offending bill, and Convocation refrained from prosecuting Standish. Nobody, least of all Richard Fox, was satisfied, but at least a damaging quarrel had been averted.

Similar tactics had to be employed to defuse another simmering anti-clerical issue which came to a head at the same time, and which, although it did not directly impinge upon the royal authority, did impugn the jurisdiction of the King's officers. This arose from the death in the bishop's custody of one Richard Hunne, citizen and Merchant Taylor of London.[67] In March 1511 Hunne's infant son had died in the parish of St Mary Matfelon, Whitechapel. The rector, Thomas Dryffeld, demanded his winding sheet by way of a mortuary fee, and Hunne refused on the grounds that the sheet was his property, not the child's. The value of the sheet then became irrelevant, because an issue of principle had been raised, and in April 1512 Dryffeld instituted proceedings in the archdeacon's court at Lambeth. On 13 May the case was decided in his favour, whereupon Hunne, who was clearly a vexatious litigant, initiated two cases in King's Bench. In the first place he sued Henry Marshall, Dryffeld's curate for describing him as 'accursed' because the archdeacon had ruled against him, and secondly he accused Dryffeld and others of praemunire for taking him to court in the first place. What grounds he could have had for such a charge are not clear, but instead of allowing his case to run into the sand, Bishop Fitzjames decided to take a hand. In spite of an irreproachable personal reputation, Hunne was a man whose religious orthodoxy was suspect. He was arrested and his house was searched. A Wycliffite Bible and various other suspect or forbidden books were discovered, prompting charges of heresy. On Saturday 2 December 1514 he was taken to Fulham for examination by the bishop, and two days later was discovered hanging in his cell in the Lollard's Tower.[68] Having examined the evidence, the coroner's inquest decided that he could not have killed himself, and brought in a verdict of wilful murder against the bishop's Chancellor, Dr William Horsey, and two of his servants. Insofar as it can be reconstructed from conflicting accounts, the evidence was not as clear-cut as the inquest claimed, and the bishop at once cried foul. Charles Joseph, one of Horsey's servants, actually confessed to strangling Hunne, but as is often the case, his confession was unsafe as evidence for a variety of reasons.[69] The trio were duly indicted, but never brought to trial because Fitzjames managed to traduce the indictment, a process which convinced the citizens of London that they were guilty as charged. The bishop would have been well advised to leave this row to simmer down, but instead he felt bound to vindicate his jurisdiction, and had Hunne posthumously tried and convicted of heresy. He was probably guilty, but that was scarcely the point. By confiscating his property, and reducing his family to penury, the Church stood convicted of malice, and his fellow citizens were convinced that he had been 'made a heretic for suing a praemunire' – a perfect example of the kind of abuse which was frequently alleged.[70] The feud between the Londoners and their bishop, which had hitherto fed largely off tithe disputes, thus took off to a new level of intensity, and the King could be made a party by pointing out that both the coroner's inquest and the jurisdiction of King's Bench had been treated with contempt. This could hardly have come at a worse time for Wolsey, who was simultaneously struggling to contain the row in Parliament over benefit of clergy. Henry made no direct comment on either process, but he did promote Henry Standish to the bench of bishops in 1518.

During these years, Henry had been much concerned with war, and with his own efforts to make an impression on the international scene. His success had been modest, but the war which fizzled out so unsatisfactorily in the summer of 1514 had been immensely important in one respect. It had led to the establishment of the navy as a permanent fighting force. As we have seen, with war impending, the King had built up his fleet, until by the time the fighting finished he had over thirty ships of his own, of which seven had been purchased and nine built since 1512. His new flagship, the *Henry Grace à Dieu*, displaced 1,500 tons and had cost upwards of £8,000 to build. It was the most powerful warship afloat, and was equipped with the latest design of heavy gun, firing through gunports in the new style.[71] Most important, when the war came to an end, Henry did not dispose of most of these ships as his predecessors would have done, but rather retained them on a care-and-maintenance basis, anchored at Deptford and Portsmouth under the care of shipkeepers. His reason for doing this is unknown, but of course it made them easier to mobilise at short notice when the need arose, and may well have been connected with his fear (or hope) that the peace which he had recently signed would not last.[72] At the same time several of his smaller vessels were kept in commission and assigned the task of patrolling the Channel and the Western Approaches. Henry was taking his traditional duty to 'keep the seas' seriously, and had no intention of being taken by surprise. At the same time, his merchants were grateful for the additional protection which these patrols provided against the perpetual menace of piracy. It seems that this decision to build up the navy had been taken some time before, because new docks were constructed at Limehouse and at Erith in Kent in 1512 and 1513, and storehouses at Erith and Deptford. In the winter of 1512–13 no fewer than twelve ships were repaired at the Erith yard, and a new officer, the Clerk Controller, was appointed to supervise this work. John Hopton, who was appointed to that office, thereafter shared responsibility for the King's ships with the existing Clerk, Robert Brygandyne. Hopton looked after the ships in the Thames and the Medway, while Brygandyne supervised those at Portsmouth and Southampton.[73] A keeper of the storehouses was also appointed, and the position given to an experienced sea captain named William Gonson, who was to have a long and distinguished career as a naval administrator. What the navy was not given at this stage was any institutional structure or chain of command. Each of the officers answered and accounted separately to the King's Council, which meant for all practical purposes to Thomas Wolsey. There is no doubt that Henry made the relevant decisions affecting the navy himself, because it was a matter which deeply interested him, but the implementation of the policy he left (as usual) to his most effective servant.

By the end of 1514, Henry was no longer the callow youth of five years earlier. He knew that real warfare did not bear much resemblance to the chivalric games of which he was so fond, and he had learned something of the deceits and evasions which were involved in European diplomacy. Most important he no longer trusted his father-in-law, and that had caused questions to be asked about the soundness of his marriage. These were probably not justified at this stage, but Catherine had still not succeeded in producing a son who survived more than a few weeks – or indeed any living child at all. This was inevitably a source of anxiety. He had also been warned that relations with the Church could be problematic, because his Parliament was not happy with those clerical pretensions which the papacy was clearly determined to maintain. This was also not a major issue – yet – but might become so if a long-term solution was not found. The King's relations with his council had been eased by the rise of Wolsey, because the almoner enjoyed excellent relations with Richard Fox as well as with Henry, and the indications are that the latter was quite happy to hand over some of his responsibilities to so able a successor.[74] Wolsey's unique ability to read the King's mind, and to serve his interests efficiently, gave Henry a new façade of responsible judgement that was invaluable in dealing with his subjects, and particularly with the nobility. He also gave the King a scapegoat for the unpopular decisions which he was finding it necessary to make. By the time that he made peace with France, Henry was in control of his kingdom in a new sense. He had also spent his father's treasure and would in future have to come to terms with Parliament if he wished to pursue an adventurous foreign policy. The death of Louis XII, and the advent of Francis I in France, who was a man far too similar to Henry for comfort, promised interesting developments.

4

A PRINCE AT PEACE, 1514–1522

The signing of a treaty with Louis did not necessarily mean that Henry was determined to embark upon a period of retrenchment. When the Duke of Suffolk went to France in October 1514, ostensibly to witness Mary's marriage, he was entrusted with a secret mission to sound out Louis about the possibility of a meeting between the sovereigns in the spring of 1515, for the specific purpose of taking aggressive action against Ferdinand.[1] The King of France, with his eyes on Italy, was polite but unenthusiastic, as Suffolk reported to Henry on his return. In any case, all such plans were rendered nugatory by Louis' death on 1 January, an event attributed (quite unfairly) to his having married a nineteen-year-old bride. Now the Queen Dowager, Mary was left stranded, and plans for her future suddenly became urgent. Exactly what happened remains uncertain, because contemporaries told different stories. According to one version, Henry had promised his sister when she left for France that in the event of Louis' early demise, she would be free to marry Suffolk, who was high in the King's favour.[2] A different story claims that the King was mortally offended at Suffolk's effrontery in marrying her without his consent, and it took much work on Wolsey's part to assuage Henry's wrath. What does seem clear is that during the early weeks of 1515 Mary felt that she was being subjected to the unwelcome attentions of Francis and was anxious to escape, not only from that situation but from the kingdom. According to the first version, Francis encouraged her plan to marry Suffolk, because he did not want to see Henry deploying her in the international marriage market. He, at any rate, seems to have been under no illusions as to the Duke's intentions when he returned to France to escort the Queen home. 'My Lord of Suffolk,' he is alleged to have said, 'so it is that there is a great bruit in this my realm that you are come to marry with the Queen, your master's sister …' When Wolsey received this news, he responded that the King was well pleased with this arrangement, and conveyed his thanks to Francis for his goodwill.[3] The alternative story is that Suffolk had no such intention, and was sprung into bed by an enthusiastic Mary, which left him no option but to marry her, which he did with the utmost secrecy. The upshot was that they returned as man and wife, and Henry (whatever his real feelings) showed indignation and imposed financial penalties upon his friend.[4]

The truth seems to lie somewhere between these two tales. Henry had actually discussed such a match with Suffolk before he sent him on his second mission, so he was well aware of the possibility. However, he seems to have extracted from Brandon a promise that he would not do anything until after their return to England, so it was the latter's precipitate action and his broken promise which aroused the King's anger rather than the marriage itself. That would be quite consistent with Mary having seized the initiative, perhaps with the intention of fending off Francis rather than out of an overwhelming desire for Charles Brandon. It may also be that Henry's wrath was exaggerated by Wolsey, who was claiming the credit for having appeased it, and very likely that it was stimulated by Suffolk's enemies, the Howards. A number of quarrels erupted in the wake of this dispute, and it was not until Mary surrendered her French jewels and other possessions to her brother in March that he was satisfied.[5] While all this was going on, the offending couple remained in France, and it was not until 2 May, when Henry's good humour had been restored, that they returned to his warm welcome.

The financial settlement was reached on 11 May, and on the 13th the couple repeated their wedding vows in public at Greenwich. At a cost of about £19,000, Mary had bought peace with her brother and, presumably with her self-respect intact, resumed her role at court. By the summer of 1515, Suffolk was back in the tilt yard. Meanwhile, Henry and his ministers were at odds about relations with France. The King was inevitably suspicious of one whose ambitions and personality so closely resembled his own, and spoke ominously of Francis' 'ambitious mind and insatiable appetites'.[6] Nevertheless he was persuaded to renew his peace treaty with France, which was due to expire in January 1516, one year after Louis' death, and there was even some talk, inspired no doubt by Wolsey, of a meeting between the two monarchs. That did not happen, and over the next twelve months Henry's attitude increasingly prevailed.

One of the reasons for this was Francis' dabbling in the affairs of Scotland, where the widowed Margaret was struggling to control a country ridden with noble factions. In the wake of James IV's death, Louis had claimed a protectorate over the kingdom, and this claim he transmitted to his successor. Attempts by Henry to negotiate this away had failed, and it remained as a potential irritant after the peace treaty had been renewed. To give some substance to his claim, Francis permitted the return to Scotland in the early summer of 1515 of John Stuart, Duke of Albany. Albany, although a long-term resident in France was in fact a grandson of King James II, who had died in 1460, and was therefore the heir apparent to the Scottish throne. He wasted no time in increasing French influence in Scotland, and even went to the length of imprisoning Margaret in Stirling Castle, whence she eventually escaped into England.[7] Faced with this provocation, Henry forgot his recent animosity towards Ferdinand, and in October 1515 signed a fresh treaty with him, professing the warmest affection. If he needed any prodding in that direction, it was provided by the fact that Francis had further exposed Henry's diplomatic weakness by marching his army into Italy in defiance of any efforts to stop him, and had roundly defeated the Swiss at Marignano on 14 September. This victory not only secured his control of the Duchy of Milan, but knocked the stuffing out of Henry's anti-French coalition even before it had begun to form.[8] Angry at having his pretensions thus exposed, the King entered into fresh discussions with the Swiss, who were equally irked at their recent defeat, and with Maximilian for a joint invasion of France, and at the same time began to toy with the idea of war with Scotland in the spring of 1516. Richard Pace's negotiations with the Swiss, backed by a liberal supply of English cash, quickly bore fruit. They entered Italy in March, and Maximilian swiftly followed, pressing upon the defences of Milan. An incursion into southern France seemed imminent. Then the whole campaign fell apart, partly because the Emperor inexplicably abandoned it, and partly because the Swiss were demanding more money.[9] The money eventually arrived, but the Swiss nevertheless went home, leaving Pace to lament the lost opportunity. By the end of May the King had given up on his grand design. It seems that his council, and Wolsey in particular, had never supported him anyway, and a complex letter from Wolsey to Pace at this time supports such an interpretation. The latter was asked to persuade the Swiss to petition Henry to call off the invasion of France, and stick with the plan to recover Milan. The orthography of this letter strongly suggests a disagreement between the King and his chief minister, because Henry obviously remained committed to the Italian aspect of the proposed campaign, an aspect which Wolsey was constrained to back.[10] Meanwhile Ferdinand had died, and been succeeded in both kingdoms of Spain by his sixteen-year-old grandson, Charles of Ghent.

This development prompted Henry to revive his plan for an invasion, albeit on a rather longer time scale. The diplomatic plan was now for a coalition of England, the Empire, Spain, the papacy and the Swiss against Francis. Unfortunately no one else was as keen as the King of England. The Swiss might have been willing, at a price, but the Pope could not be persuaded, and Charles would not give a firm answer. However, what ostensibly wrecked the idea was the signature of the treaty of Noyon between Francis and Charles in August 1516.[11] Maximilian was slippery, and Wolsey thought that he could detect flaws in the treaty, so negotiations continued, but with diminishing chances of success. Characteristically, the Emperor signed with Henry in October a treaty which appeared to bind him to the new coalition but neither the Pope nor the Swiss were to be persuaded. Then Maximilian, tempted by French money, agreed to join the treaty of Noyon, to meet Francis and even to marry a French bride. By February 1517, Henry's hopes had finally and crashingly collapsed, and Wolsey wrote (moderately enough) that the Emperor 'doth play on both hands using the nature of a participle which taketh *partem a nomine et partem a verbo*'. Maximilian was quite unabashed, even renewing talk of a meeting with Henry, but Henry had had enough of attempts to form an aggressive alliance.[12] He returned to the charge early in 1517, but only to the extent of a defensive league, which was signed on 5 July. This had cost a lot of money, and was celebrated in London with great magnificence, perhaps because, for this more limited aim, the King had the full co-operation of his chancellor.

The treaty of Noyon, and particularly the Emperor's adherence to it, seems to have caused a good deal of confusion in English diplomatic circles. Thomas Spinelly, writing to Wolsey soon after it had been signed, believed that the terms were 'very favourable' to Charles, but Cuthbert Tunstall in a letter to the King dated 13 September, believed that no action would follow until Charles had been to Spain 'which will not be soon'.[13] Some thought the friendship feigned, and others believed that it would take no effect because of the youth of Francis' daughter, his intended bride. It was reported that the Estates of the Netherlands were upset at not having been consulted, and that the Council of Spain had refused ratification for the same reason. In spite of Spinelly's opinion, by November there seems to have been a conviction in London that the treaty endangered Charles' control of Navarre and Naples, and there were references to the 'detestable treaty'.[14] It was in any case partly invalidated by the death of the young French princess in March 1517, and was soon to be overtaken by Wolsey's fresh diplomatic offensive. Meanwhile, Margaret had returned to Scotland, and to her second husband, the Earl of Angus, on the understanding that she would play no part in the government of the country, which remained for the time being in the hands of the Duke of Albany and his friends.

Wolsey's diplomacy in 1518 was set up by Pope Leo X, who in 1517 had convened a conference of cardinals and ambassadors, which proposed an ambitious scheme for a new crusade, to be preceded by a universal peace in Europe. When he circulated this scheme to the monarchs for their comments, their response was tepid (and in the Emperor's case bizarre), but Leo was not discouraged, and in April 1518 sent out legates to stimulate support for his cause.[15] The emissary chosen for England was Lorenzo Campeggio, the Cardinal Protector. The King appeared to be reluctant, protesting that 'it was not the manner of this realm to admit legatos a latere', but he would consider the matter favourably if Wolsey was raised to the same status and joined in the mission. This demand, which almost certainly originated from Wolsey himself, was at length agreed to, and after some weeks of delay, Campeggio was allowed to cross the Channel. The Pope had taken the precaution, on 6 March, of proclaiming a five-year truce in Europe, and circumstances favoured him, because in spite of the dense web of diplomatic antagonisms, no war was actually in progress to test his authority.[16] This situation also favoured Wolsey's plan, which had nothing whatsoever to do with a crusade, a prospect which he regarded as a chimera. Consequently, when Campeggio eventually made his entry to London on 29 July, he was met by studied magnificence, and smooth words which had no substance, because Wolsey's own scheme was by that time nearing fruition. This involved no less than a complete diplomatic *volte-face*. Since 1515 Henry had been trying to curb French ambitions by forming leagues and alliances for that purpose using the threat, and even the fact, of force. Now he was to attempt the same goal by friendship and alliance. The objective remained the same, but the method was to be completely different; or to put it another way, Wolsey's agenda had eventually won the King's acceptance.[17] Leo's scheme for a universal peace was thus to be hijacked without reference to a crusade, in the interest of the prestige and honour of the King of England. It is probable that the basic idea had already taken shape in Wolsey's mind as early as January 1518, before there was any question of Campeggio's mission, but that it was that development which raised his ambitions from an Anglo-French entente to a universal peace. A treaty resolving all outstanding issues between England and France thus became a grand plan for the pacification of Europe.

By the end of September informal discussions had made sufficient progress to warrant a formal French embassy, and Wolsey wrote to the Pope, the Emperor and the King of Spain to explain what he was about.[18] The treaty which was signed by representatives of the two powers on 2 October thus allowed for the adhesion of all the major players, and over twenty lesser states from Scotland to Portugal. Detailed provisions were included for its implementation, providing for action to be taken against any potential aggressor, and most important, any existing treaty in conflict with it was to be annulled – thus theoretically putting paid to the treaty of Noyon.[19] In the short term, this move was spectacularly successful, all the major and nearly all the minor powers signing up to it within the eight months allowed. Henry's and Wolsey's reputations soared, and the King renewed his fantasies of 1515 about being the arbiter of Europe. The Pope, although realising how his own scheme had been frustrated, did not feel able to withhold his approval from so worthy a treaty. Ostensibly the peace of Europe was guaranteed for the foreseeable future. In the shadow of this grandiose agreement, a more mundane treaty was also signed between England and France on 4 October, which provided the substance underpinning the more general pacification. Tournai was to be returned to France, and the Princess Mary (then aged two and a half) was betrothed to the Dauphin, Francis, who was newly born. Henry had thus quietly paid a considerable price for his prestige, because Tournai, although very expensive to maintain, had been the main fruit of his last great war. Nevertheless he celebrated with a good grace, with a solemn high mass in St Paul's, and a great banquet which ended with a mumming in which the King himself and his sister Mary took part.[20] However reluctant he may have been at first to give up his warlike ambitions against Francis, by the time that the treaty of London was actually signed, he embraced it wholeheartedly.

While diplomacy occupied much of the King's attention, and still more of Wolsey's, domestic affairs proceeded more or less smoothly. Wolsey, Archbishop of York since August 1514, became in 1515 a cardinal on Henry's suggestion, and in December of the same year followed William Warham as Lord Chancellor. In that capacity he began at once to increase the King's equity jurisdiction by using the Council to plug the gaps which had appeared in the Common Law, and to administer justice to those who were considered capable of manipulating the normal courts in their favour.[21] It was during these years that his influence over the King probably reached its highest point, because Henry was still young, and still hankering after military glory, a yearning which Wolsey, with skill and great difficulty, succeeded in containing. There was plague in London, and an outbreak of the sweating sickness which caused the King to flee. The Cardinal, remaining at his post in the capital, succumbed to the illness, but recovered rapidly. In the summer of 1516 the court went on progress, getting as far as Corfe Castle in Dorset in late August, and Salisbury in early September, before returning by way of Wolsey's unfinished palace at Hampton Court.[22] It was during these years also that the Gentlemen of the King's Privy Chamber made their first appearance, beginning as somewhat amorphous 'minions' in the jousting celebrations of 1515. These young men were the King's chosen companions. They shared his tastes and his recreations, but had as yet no recognised place in the hierarchy of the court. It so happened, however, that Francis I was going through a similar phase, and his *mignons* were soon accommodated by the creation of the new rank of *gentilhomme de la chambre*. This was of no significance for Henry as long as relations between the two countries continued to be strained, but with the outbreak of peace in 1518, the situation changed. Francis' formal mission in September included a number of these *gentilhommes*, and they were naturally paired with Henry's chosen companions in the court celebrations which accompanied the mission.[23] No decision about the status of the latter is recorded, but they were thereafter known as the Gentlemen of the Privy Chamber, and that soon became recognised as a position with unique opportunities in the crucial matter of access to the

King. The Privy Chamber so constituted was independent of the Lord Chamberlain, and answerable only to the King. It was not long before abuses began to be alleged, and the Council became deeply suspicious of these free-spirited young men.

More seriously, 1517 saw an outbreak of xenophobic rioting in London, just when Henry was struggling to maintain good relations with the Emperor and the King of Spain. This appears to have begun with the agitations of one John Lincoln against the 'strangers' who, he alleged:

> grow into such a multitude that it is to be looked upon, for I sawe on a Sunday this Lent sixe hundred straungers shooting at the Popingay with crossbows, and they kepe such assemblies and fraternities, and make such a gathering to their common boxe that every Bocher will hold plee with the Citie of London ...[24]

They stole Englishmen's work, and their prosperity mocked the impoverishment of the natives. He succeeded in convincing one Dr Bele, who on the Tuesday in Easter week preached a sermon, during which he read part of Lincoln's 'bill', and expanded on the text *pugna pro patria*, to persuade his hearers that it was lawful to fight for their country by 'going upon' the strangers in their midst. Reports of this sermon reached the City authorities, but they did not apparently take it very seriously, with the result that:

> upon the xxviiith day of April diverse young men of the Citie assauted the Aliens as they passed by the strets, and some were striken, and some buffeted and some thrown in the canal ...[25]

This served to alert the Lord Mayor, but the precautions which he took were inadequate and over the next two days rioting spread through the city. The houses of Flemings and Frenchmen were sacked, and diplomatic representatives threatened and hassled. Death threats were issued to all in authority, including Wolsey, whose London residence was promptly fortified. The Italians, also forewarned, took similar precautions and beat off their assailants. By the evening of 1 May the Lords of the Council had flooded London with troops and the situation was brought under control. Upwards of 400 rioters were arrested, but remarkably, no one seems to have been killed.[26] The issue was internationally sensitive, and Lincoln, Bele and several others appear to have been executed out of hand within a matter of days. According to the Venetian ambassador thirteen were condemned to die, but some appear to have been respited, and only seventy were formally proceeded against.[27] Anxious to make some political capital out of what was in truth a fairly nasty little incident, Wolsey then seems to have decided that a grand gesture of reconciliation was called for, and persuaded the King and Queen to take part. The 400 delinquents remaining in custody, some of whom were women and some little more than children, were paraded in chains at Westminster Hall, crying out for mercy. Wolsey opened the proceedings with a suitable oration, and Catherine flung herself on her knees, with loosened hair in the classic mode of the female suppliant, before her husband begging him to show compassion. Wolsey then joined Catherine in supplication, and Henry ordered the prisoners to be released, to ostentatious rejoicings on all sides. The King had shown himself to be a worthy prince, not indifferent to the need for justice, but merciful towards those who could be represented as having been misled. It is safe to conclude that, thanks to the Chancellor's shrewdness, both Henry's and Catherine's images were suitably enhanced in the public mind.[28]

This was not the only service which the Queen had performed for her adopted country. On 18 February 1516, after enduring almost annual pregnancies which had resulted in miscarriages, stillbirths, and in one case in a short-lived son, Catherine was delivered of a healthy child. The rejoicings were muted because the child was a girl, but hope had been rekindled in the royal couple.

'The Queen and I are both young,' he told the Venetian ambassador, 'and if it is a girl this time, by God's grace boys will follow.'[29] However Catherine was no longer so young. She was thirty-one and on the threshold of middle age by the standards of the time, so her disappointment was probably the keener of the two, but she concealed it well. Nor was that the only thing which she had to conceal. In spite of her regular pregnancies, her beauty was fading, she was beginning to get plump, and Henry's eye was straying. It is difficult to know how seriously to take the constant rumours of the King's 'amours'. Dalliance was expected of him, and he played the game of courtly love with enthusiasm. It is probable that the story of his early involvement with Anne Hastings was no more than a malicious invention, and his falling-out with Ferdinand did not necessarily put a strain on his marriage, in spite of speculation to the contrary.[30] Catherine knew her duty too well to give him any cause for complaint. Jane Poppincourt, however, may well have been different. The evidence is purely circumstantial, but Jane was a Frenchwoman of a 'certain age' who had originally come to England as a companion for Henry's sisters in 1502. By 1512 she was receiving £5 a year as a member of the Queen's household, and playing a regular part in the revels of the court. In 1514 she was chosen by the King to partner him in the Twelfth Night masque at Eltham. That in itself need have no significance, but when she left England in 1516, Henry gave her the enormous leaving present of £100, which strongly suggests a payment for services rendered. Louis XII, who was not given to prudishness, had already censured her for promiscuous behaviour, although whether he had this relationship in mind we do not know. After returning to France she became the mistress of the Duc de Longueville, so she was not averse to that kind of adventure.[31] During much of 1514 Catherine would have been unavailable to her husband because of her fourth pregnancy, and that may also be a factor to be borne in mind. However, the case remains non-proven. Better substantiated is Henry's liaison with Elizabeth Blount, although the date when that commenced is similarly shrouded in uncertainty. Bessie Blount had been born with the century, and was a kinswoman of Walter Blount, Lord Mountjoy, a circumstance which had helped to gain her a treasured place among Catherine's attendants as early as 1512. By 1515 Bessie was playing an increasingly conspicuous part in the revels, and was undoubtedly a talented and attractive girl, but there is nothing particular to link her to the King. It is possible that their relationship may have begun as early as 1516, but more likely that it was Catherine's last pregnancy in 1518 which drove Henry to seek consolation with another, in which case they did not begin to sleep together until the summer of that year, when Catherine's condition was known.[32] At some point in 1519 she gave him the pledge of her affection, and proof of their relationship, in the shape of a bastard son, who was immediately acknowledged and named Henry Fitzroy.

When Elizabeth's condition became known, probably towards the end of 1518, Wolsey spirited her off to Blackmore Priory, near Chelmsford in Essex, where she spent her confinement in the prior's lodgings. Once the birth had taken place, probably in June, the Cardinal took over management of the child's affairs, also standing as Godfather at his baptism. A household was created for him, and Elizabeth disappears from the scene. It is probable that she played some part in his early upbringing, but that cannot be proved, and she did not return to court.[33] Her brief relationship with the King finished when the fact of her pregnancy became known, and at some point after the birth, perhaps before the end of 1519, she was married to Gilbert Tailboys of Kyme, a suitable match and one probably arranged by Wolsey. When an Act of Parliament was passed in Elizabeth's favour in 1524, it declared that by virtue of the said marriage Gilbert had received 'not only great sums of money, but also many other benefits', which strongly suggests the nature of the arrangement.[34] They first appear as man and wife in a grant of 1522, but the marriage had certainly taken place well before that. Henry was proud of his paternal achievement, and not at all reluctant to acknowledge the fact, a situation which must have been doubly galling for Catherine, whose pregnancy of 1518 had ended in yet another stillbirth in October. She was by that time thirty-three, and physically worn down by so many failures. There is no reason to suppose that Henry had given up on her, but she did not fall pregnant again, and may have passed an early menopause. At some point, perhaps in 1520, the King took another mistress in the person of Mary Boleyn, the elder daughter of his servant and courtier Sir Thomas Boleyn, and he and his wife began to drift apart.[35] Optimistic talk of a son persisted for some time, but as the years passed it became increasingly implausible. For the time being Henry Fitzroy would be the only son that the King possessed.

Meanwhile, Wolsey's carefully crafted treaty of London was beginning to fall apart. It had become clear as early as the summer of 1518, while the negotiations were still in train, that the Emperor was ailing, and that an Imperial election in the near future was likely. Maximilian's natural heir was his grandson Charles, the King of Spain, but it could not be assumed that he would be elected, and there were many who looked askance at the prospect of Spain and the Empire under the same ruler. Consequently when Maximilian died on 12 January 1519, the King of France also announced his candidature. At first Henry professed complete neutrality, as the treaty of London required, but as early as February Pope Leo X, alarmed at the prospect of either candidate succeeding, began looking for a third.[36] The chances are that Leo had in mind one of the German princes, probably the Elector of Saxony, who might be acceptable to the other electors and who would not suffer the disadvantage of being too powerful. However, Henry misinterpreted his references to a third candidate as an invitation to enter the lists himself, and by the end of May he had done so, pressing his candidature with some enthusiasm. Richard Pace was despatched to Germany to further his master's cause, but in spite of Pace's optimism, it is clear that he never stood a chance. The election became an exercise in competitive bribery, and the King of England simply did not have the resources. Critically, Charles was backed by the great Augsburg banking house of Fugger, who were prepared to make almost unlimited cash available, and the King of Spain was duly elected on 28 June.[37] A new Empire had come into being, which stretched from Bohemia to the Americas and from Friesland to Sicily. France was surrounded, and England reduced to the level of an also ran. It remained to be seen how long the treaty of London would survive in this new political climate. Francis was hugely chagrined at his failure, but not at first in any mood to challenge the new emperor, who, he probably reckoned, would have difficulties enough in rationalising the government of two such disparate regions. Henry appears to have shrugged off his humiliation, and by the middle of August was writing enthusiastically to the Pope about his willingness to support a crusade. This (as he probably knew) was a safe ploy to earn a little credit in Rome, because Leo had gone off the whole idea by then, and there was no realistic chance of his offer being accepted.[38] The Pope was more interested by this time in trying to defuse the potentially explosive situation created by the Imperial election and seeking to arrange a meeting between Francis and Charles. This was not to be, but the King of England could at least appear as an honest broker.

The treaty of London had provided for a meeting between Henry and Francis not later than July 1519. The Imperial election had frustrated that timetable. But the intention still remained, and in March 1520 Wolsey was given the go-ahead to make the necessary arrangements.[39] It was decided that the meeting would take place between Guines and Ardres, just outside the Calais Pale, in early June. Meanwhile, it became known that Charles was proposing to travel from Spain to Germany before that, and an invitation was extended to him to visit England on the way. Henry arranged an extraordinary election to the Order of the Garter for the new emperor, the insignia of which he sent to Spain with the envoy who bore the invitation for the visit. So it came about that Charles landed in England on 26 May, and spent four profitable days in discussion with Henry before the latter was constrained to depart for his rendezvous with Francis. They decided to meet again between Calais and Gravelines immediately after the Anglo-French discussions, which thus became sandwiched between two Anglo-Imperial meetings, a circumstance which aroused the liveliest suspicions in France.[40]

Consequently when the meeting took place at the Field of Cloth of Gold (so called from the venue rather than the accoutrements) on 7 June, the omens for success were not good. Protocol was strictly observed and the two monarchs expressed the warmest affection for each other, but the reality was rather different.[41] The meeting was, in effect, an exercise in competitive display, and Wolsey spared no expense in making a show. The entire court was involved, and over

5,000 people made up the trains of Henry and Catherine. A forest of exotic pavilions sprang up to house them, and a wooden and canvas palace was erected to provide a formal context for the King's Chamber. Henry himself, not perhaps trusting his hosts as far as he professed, was lodged in the nearby (English) fortress of Guisnes. Hundreds of pounds were spent on clothing the court in velvet, satin and cloth of gold, and tons of plate, cutlery and glass were shipped over; food also, for men and beasts, and rich furnishings for the temporary state apartments. Great timbers for the temporary palace, which were too long for any transport vessel, had to be floated down the coast from Holland, and laboriously dragged across country. From the beginning of March over 6,000 men were employed in creating the English quarters, and at least 2,000 of these were brought in from England or Flanders, who consequently had to be accommodated as well as paid.[42] In a sense the French preparations were equally lavish. Their numbers matched those of the English, and their arrangements for hospitality were just as great. However, being in their own country, they did not need the tents which formed so large a part of the English preparations, and Francis' temporary palace was so flimsily constructed that it actually blew down during a gale. The venue for the meeting had to be sculpted to ensure that neither side had an advantage, lists and galleries created for the jousts which were an inevitable part of such a celebration, and a sports field for the archery and wrestling competitions, surrounded by a high rampart. Wolsey oversaw every detail of this, worrying about the price of flour and the supply of game, as well as the stabling of the horses and the check lists for the jousts – it would not do for the opponents to be ill-matched.[43] In addition to this he had the difficult task of assuaging French fears about Henry's meeting with the Emperor, and arranging the logistics for Charles' visit. Never was his application and attention to detail to be put to a greater test. The outcome was a diplomatic fiasco, but that was none of the Cardinal's fault. He had set up the most elaborate 'summit meeting' of the century, and spent a fortune in ensuring that every event passed off smoothly.

The meeting lasted over a fortnight. Queen Catherine entertained the French King to dinner in Guisnes, and Queen Claude returned the compliment for Henry at Ardres. Jousts took place, at which the kings had to be assiduously kept apart, and the honours between French and English were studiously divided. The English (not surprisingly) excelled at archery, and the French at casting the bar and at wrestling. There was much banqueting and dancing, but little or no attempt at serious political dialogue. This was probably just as well, because in spite of the ostentatious back-thumping and embracing, it was fairly obvious that the kings did not like each other. When Francis threw Henry in an impromptu wrestling match, there was almost a diplomatic incident, and on the whole the less intimate their encounters the better. At last, on 23 June the sports came to an end, leaving each side with an impression of its own superiority, and Wolsey sang a solemn high mass at an altar set up at the place of the original encounter between the monarchs.[44] The sermon was on peace, and the following day Francis and Henry agreed to build a chapel to Our Lady of Peace on the site of the altar. Having thus done his duty, and enjoyed himself a good deal in the process, Henry returned to Calais, and to the second of his scheduled meetings with Charles V. On 9 July he rode to Gravelines to meet the Emperor and the Archduchess Margaret, where he stayed for a couple of days before accompanying them back to Calais, where they similarly stayed for two days. These meetings seem to have been more genuinely amicable than that between Henry and Francis, possibly because Charles offered no competition to the Englishman in the way of personal prowess, but they were not much more productive politically.[45] Since his election the Emperor had been trying to tempt Henry away from his French alliance, and particularly to abandon his undertaking to marry his daughter to the Dauphin, but the King was not to be drawn. He was prepared to reaffirm his commitments under the treaty of London, and not to enter into any new league or matrimonial undertaking, but beyond that he would not go. In thus affirming his neutrality, it is probable that he was acting under the influence of Wolsey, who was trying to maintain that treaty against the political logic of the Imperial election. What he was not going to do at this stage was betray his undertakings to Francis by entering into an alliance with Charles.[46] By the end of 1520 the two main continental powers were squaring up to each other, uttering threats and indulging in minor provocations, but Henry was genuinely trying to maintain the peace which had been his great achievement two years earlier.

One idea which did germinate at these Anglo-Imperial meetings, however, was that Cardinal Wolsey would make an excellent pope. This notion seems to have originated with the Emperor, but was taken up enthusiastically by the King. It was high time that a non-Italian was elected, and who better than his own minister? It would also be very useful to have an Englishman in St Peter's chair, and would place him in a good position to realise his aim of peace. Wolsey himself was less enthusiastic. He did not want to leave England, or the service of King Henry, and although he appreciated the honour, he at first declined to be considered. He was persuaded eventually that it would be very much to the advantage of his king if he were elected, and on the condition that the Emperor would support him, he was willing to be considered – when the time should come.[47] Leo X died in December 1521, and Wolsey put his name forward at the conclave, as he had agreed to do. Henry sent the indefatigable Pace to Rome to promote his cause, and did everything he could to secure his election, but his influence in the Curia was slight, and Charles appears to have changed his mind. A non-Italian was indeed elected, but it was Adrian of Utrecht, the Emperor's former tutor, who must have been in the frame for some time. At what point Charles switched his support to Adrian, and whether he had ever seriously considered Wolsey as a good prospect, we do not know. The Cardinal was not seriously put out over this rebuff, but Henry felt that he had been trifled with, and had some cause to feel aggrieved. When Adrian died in September 1523, Henry and Wolsey tried again, this time with a strange mixture of equivocation and bravado. The King undertook to come to Rome and to lead a crusade if Wolsey were elected, but at the same time his agents were instructed to support Cardinal de Medici if he were to emerge as the strongest candidate, and only to back Wolsey if the contest appeared to be more open.[48] Wolsey himself made conventional protestations of unworthiness, but this time his ambition may have been kindled, and the outcome more of a disappointment. Charles had again undertaken to support the Englishman, but his protestations were taken for what they were worth, more moves in the diplomatic game. Cardinal de Medici was indeed elected, and took the title of Clement VII. What might have happened to Henry's Great Matter a few years later if Wolsey had succeeded in this conclave is a fascinating but pointless speculation.

For understandable reasons, the King wished to appear very committed to the papal authority at this stage, and seized the opportunity presented by the activities of Martin Luther to make his point. He seems to have been swiftly and accurately appraised of the nature of Luther's protest in 1517, and had taken up his pen to refute such errors by June of the following year. His concentration span being limited, it is likely that Henry gave up on his self-appointed task soon after starting, but not before his manuscript had earned the critical approval of Cardinal Wolsey. It has been conjectured that this work was recycled as the first two chapters of the *Assertio Septem Sacramentorum*, which, being on the subject of Indulgences and the papal authority, are more relevant to his preoccupation in the summer of 1518 than to the *Assertio* itself.[49] On the strength of what he had seen, it is quite possible that Wolsey encouraged his master's literary ambitions, because three years later, in 1521, he produced his work on the seven sacraments, which he then presented to Pope Leo. By that time Luther had published *De Captivitate Babylonica*, and had been both excommunicated and outlawed, so he was fair game for any orthodox polemicist, but no one else approaching Henry's standing in the world took up the challenge. *The Defence of the Seven Sacraments* is not an impressive work of theology, and that is probably the best argument suggesting that the King himself composed it. It makes good use of the Bible (which we know Henry had mastered), but its grasp of Lutheran teaching is defective, and its exposition of Catholic doctrine on the sacraments is shot through with that semi-pelagianism which later Protestants were to find so offensive.[50] This was not quite the kind of response which Pope Leo had been looking for when he had urged all the monarchs of Western Europe to take action against the menace which Luther represented, but it was none the less welcome. It was printed in July, and presentation copies were sent to Rome in August, by which time there had also been a ceremonial burning of Luther's works at Paul's Cross. On that occasion John Fisher had preached, and Wolsey had presided. There was to be no doubt about the orthodox enthusiasm of the English government. Because the King's name was attached to it, the *Assertio* went through some twenty editions and translations in a few years, being twice translated into German within twelve months, and earned Henry the cherished title of *Defensor Fidei*. For so pedestrian a work, it was a remarkable success, and established the King's reputation not only as an orthodox prince but also as a defender of the Roman primacy – a remarkable irony in view of what was to follow.[51]

In addition to this concern over the discipline of his Church, Henry was also concerned about the order of his court and kingdom. As we have seen, the Gentlemen of the Privy Chamber had been formally constituted in September 1518, but then in May 1519 four of them, Nicholas Carew, Edward Neville, Francis Bryan and Edward Coffin, were expelled, together with some Knights of the Body, including Sir John Peachey and Sir Henry Guildford. In reporting this incident on 18 May, Guistiani, the Venetian ambassador, speculated about the reason. Some said that it was because Cardinal Wolsey had become apprehensive about their influence over the King. Others that it was on account of the fact that they were too favourable to the King of France in the impending Imperial election. The latter was the opinion of the Lord Treasurer, the Duke of Norfolk, but Guistiani himself was inclined to blame Wolsey, particularly as their replacements in the Privy Chamber were all the Cardinal's 'creatures'.[52] Modern research, however, has not endorsed either of these judgements. The replacement appointments were not specifically connected with Wolsey, but were all long-serving Knights of the Body – notably Sir Richard Wingfield – and the expelled minions were not disgraced, but rather sent off to honourable appointments elsewhere, particularly in Calais. They were not forbidden the court and their emoluments were not curtailed. The true explanation appears to be rather more mundane. The young men had indeed become 'Frenchified', but this was a moral rather than a political judgement. They had misbehaved themselves on a recent visit to Paris, they had developed an admiration for French dress and conduct, and had started 'playing light touches' with the King – none of which was conducive to his honour.[53] The Council, including, but not only, Wolsey, had become concerned, and had persuaded Henry to this course of action. Only he could modify the composition of the Privy Chamber, and the King was very sensitive to any aspersions upon his honour. He acted strictly *ad homines*, and other members of the Privy Chamber, notably the Groom of the Stool, Sir William Compton, were not touched. If Wolsey's jealousy had been responsible, Compton would have been the first to go! Far from denigrating the Privy Chamber, the intention seems to have been to upgrade it as a political institution by curtailing its informality. As a part of this operation, all its members were put on regular wages, and its distinctiveness from the general Chamber was finally recognised.[54] It may not be a coincidence that about a year later Thomas Howard, Earl of Surrey, was sent to Ireland with the title of lieutenant, in a short-lived attempt to upgrade the government there also. Wolsey was consistently preoccupied with his master's honour, and there were many routes to that goal, but they all involved convincing the King.

Guistiani made something of an issue of the 'expulsion of the minions' because he was looking for pointers to English policy in respect of the Imperial election, so too much has been made of his letter. The same is true of one of Henry's rare epistles to Wolsey, in January 1519, in which he asked him to 'keep good watches' on the Duke of Buckingham and 'others which you thought suspect'.[55] In the first place this relates to their reaction to some specific news, which is not disclosed, and in the second place it also includes the Duke of Suffolk and the Earl of Northumberland, neither of whom were in any sort of disfavour. Nevertheless, Buckingham's fall and execution just over two years later was a seismic event besides which the expulsion of the minions pales into insignificance. He was a man of no particular talent, and of endless indiscretions, but of enormous wealth. In his report of July 1519 Guistiani estimated his income at 30,000 ducats a year, more than twice that of the Dukes of Norfolk and Suffolk, and he held extensive Lordships in the Welsh Marches, which gave him a potential power base.[56] This, combined with the fact that he had a remote claim to the throne, derived from Anne, the daughter of Thomas, Duke of Gloucester, the youngest son of Edward III, made him a natural suspect as far as the Tudors were concerned. He had been a peripheral member of Henry VII's council, and occupied a similar position under his son, but Guistiani's opinion that if the King were to die without heirs 'he might easily obtain the Crown' was widely shared, and was no help to him at all. He tended to appear when Henry needed to be 'honourably accompanied', but his voice carried no weight in council, and his open contempt for the upstart Wolsey did him no favours either.[57] His lack of common sense was well demonstrated by the pertinacity with which he pursued what he took to be a hereditary claim to the Constableship of England, based on his descent from the de Bohuns This office, which was purely honorific, had been held by a number of incumbents since 1421, and Henry VI had specifically disallowed a claim by the Duke's grandfather, but his father had acted in such a capacity at the coronation of Richard III, and Edward Stafford considered that to be a sufficient precedent. His claim was granted, but for one day only, at the coronation of Henry VIII, and attempts to get the King to change his mind and make the position permanent proved to be futile. How far this rankled with the Duke we do not know, but in the wake of the Field of Cloth of Gold he retreated to his seat at Thornbury, muttering angrily about a 'conference of trivialities'.[58] His anger was directed at Wolsey rather than the King, but his sulky absence from the court was not well taken, and when he petitioned for permission to take 400 men on a tour of his Welsh lordships, further suspicions were aroused. It might have been considered that if he had had any sinister intentions he would hardly have asked leave, but it had been from Wales that his father had launched rebellion in 1483, and the King was understandably apprehensive.

Buckingham had not been without signs of royal favour. In August 1519 Richard Pace reported that he had made 'excellent cheer' for the King at Watford, and in November of the same year he had been granted the wardship of Thomas Fitzgerald, the young son of the Earl of Kildare.[59] However a year later the storm clouds were gathering, and Wolsey decided that the opportunity was too good to miss. When a messenger arrived at Thornbury on 8 April 1521, bearing a summons for the Duke to attend upon the King, he suspected nothing amiss, but within a week he had been consigned to the Tower and charges of treason were being formulated against him. Wolsey had agents within the Duke's household, but more importantly, he had succeeded in inducing a number of Stafford's former employees to testify against him. Some of these were disgruntled at having been dismissed, and it seems that the Duke was as contemptuous of his servants as he was of Wolsey – or of the King, but the most crucial was his former Chancellor, Robert Gilbert. Gilbert had been in the Duke's service for twenty years, and there were few secrets to which he did not have access.[60] Nevertheless the case assembled was almost entirely circumstantial, and based upon the way in which Buckingham had toyed with the idea of being heir to the throne. As far back as 1510 he had allegedly 'compassed and imagined' Henry's death, no doubt in the course of some such pleasurable speculation. He had consulted a certain 'Father Nicholas' at Hendon Priory, who claimed the second sight, and assured him that he would be king. It was claimed that he had planned to fortify Thornbury, and he seems to have complained loud and long about Henry's policies and the inadequacies of his councillors.[61] This last charge was no doubt true enough, but was proof of his indiscretion rather than his malice. Robert Gilbert's 'confession' was almost all in a similar vein. Stafford had complained about Wolsey, and about William Compton, alleging that favours were being given to mere boys. He grudged that the Earl of Warwick had been put to death (in 1499). He had sought to gain the favour of the

King's guard with bribes, and claimed that he could 'make a power' with like-minded noblemen. None of this was tangible treason, but in the delicate dynastic circumstances of 1521, it was worrying enough, and sufficient to convince the King that Buckingham would have to be dealt with.[62] He was tried before the Lord Steward's court on 13 May, and inevitably found guilty. By the end of May he had gone to the block on Tower Hill, and no one had lifted a finger to help him. All his boasted contacts, real and imagined, had failed to produce any movement in his defence, and he seems to have died in a state of frustrated bewilderment.

Buckingham's death was a coup for Wolsey, but it also marked a turning point in Henry's relations with his nobility. Before 1521 he had been inclined to look favourably upon the claims of lineage, which were a part of that chivalric culture which he so much admired, but the Duke's vague claims had been a wake-up call. As long as he remained without a son, he could not afford to encourage these Lancastrian ambitions. The cardinal was right to draw attention to the merits of his father's policy of keeping the nobility at an arms length, and of making new creations strictly dependent upon service to himself. In 1511 William Courtenay had been created Earl of Devon in recognition of his family claim, and in 1513 Margaret Pole had been restored to her father's title of Salisbury. In February 1514 Thomas Howard, Earl of Surrey, had been raised to the dukedom of Norfolk, at least as much in recognition of his father's status as for his victory at Flodden, but these were the last such creations. When Thomas Boleyn, Robert Ratcliffe and George Hastings were raised to the earldoms of Wiltshire, Sussex and Huntingdon in 1529, it was strictly for services to Henry himself.[63] Significantly, both William Courtenay's son Henry and Margaret Pole lost their heads for alleged involvement in a 'white rose' conspiracy in 1538, and the Duke of Norfolk was in the Tower under sentence of death for similar pretensions when Henry died in January 1547. The only exception to this service mode for new creations came in the titles of Richmond and Lincoln, bestowed upon his own bastard son and the young son of the Duke of Suffolk (born 1516) in 1525. With the exception of Charles Brandon, Henry's boon companions were not so honoured, and neither Seymour, nor Dudley nor Paulet had any claims to noble ancestry. When the sixth Earl of Northumberland died without issue in 1537, he was constrained to make the King his heir, rather than his brother Thomas.[64]

Meanwhile in Europe the inevitable had happened, and in the summer of 1521 an undeclared war had broken out between France and the Empire. Francis had offered the original provocation, but Charles had not been unwilling to respond. The fighting was inconclusive and both sides angled hopefully for the backing of England. In spite of an instinctive inclination to favour the Imperial side, Henry at first seemed determined to honour his treaty with France, and in diplomacy of great complexity (not untinged with deceit) offered his services as a mediator.[65] Wolsey was still ostensibly pursuing this priority when he went to Calais in August to continue discussions with both sides. However, by that time the King had changed his mind, and the Cardinal's discussions with the French were little more than a blind. In the midst of the negotiations, he took himself off to Bruges on the pretext of consulting the other side, and there, on 25 August, he signed a new agreement with the Imperial Chancellor, Gattinara. This was primarily a marriage treaty whereby the twenty-one-year-old emperor agreed to wed the five-year-old Princess Mary. He was not to contract any other marriage, and to espouse Mary *per verba de praesenti* as soon as she should reach the canonical age of twelve. Her marriage portion was fixed at 400,000 gold crowns, and her dower at 50,000 a year.[66] How seriously these professions should be taken is a matter of some doubt, given the normal role of dynastic marriages in renaissance negotiations, but they went into considerable detail, and occupied the first twelve clauses of the treaty. However, the agreement then proceeded to more immediate concerns. All existing treaties between the two parties were confirmed, mutual defence against attack guaranteed, and all other parties excluded from the agreement. If the existing war between the Emperor and France had not concluded by then, Henry bound himself to offer limited military assistance to Charles in May 1522, and in

March 1523 in any case both were to declare a new war. Neither party would enter negotiations with France without the other's consent, and the whole treaty was (for understandable reasons) to be kept strictly secret.[67] Both the principals in due course swore to the agreement which their agents had reached, but the aspiration to secrecy was quickly disappointed. By January 1522 Francis had a good idea of what had transpired, and was full of righteous indignation. He had given his 'good brother' of England no cause for such perfidy. The Duke of Albany had gone to Scotland against his will, and would be recalled; the depredations of French pirates were similarly contrary to his intentions; and in any case the English were equally active in that respect.[68] These protestations sound disingenuous, but they may not have been. In any case, as desultory fighting continued along the Franco-German border, Henry abandoned his mediatory role and prepared to offer the promised assistance to his future son-in-law.

5

THE COURT OF KING HENRY

The court was the King's context. It was where he lived, and where he conducted his business. Traditionally it was divided into two parts, the *domus providencie*, which was the household proper, and which provided for all the ordinary needs of the community – food, clothing, heating, transport and so on; and the *domus regie magnificencie*, where the monarch himself was on display, and where public and ceremonial events took place.[1] The household was divided into numerous functional departments, such as the kitchen, the scullery, and the woodyard, and was controlled by a financial agency called variously the Counting House or the Board of Greencloth. There the heads of the various departments met, determined policy and allocated funds. The Counting House was presided over by a senior official called the Controller of the Household, and he was answerable in turn to the Lord Steward. The Steward was appointed personally by the King, and had *ex officio* jurisdiction over the whole staff, and over all offences committed within the Verge, which were the topographical limits laid down for the court, wherever it happened to be.[2] The household normally had about 200 on the payroll, although shift work and the presence of numerous unpaid (and sometimes unacknowledged) hangers-on make an accurate headcount difficult. The whole organisation was stable and strictly hierarchical, patronage within the various departments belonging by tradition to the Sergeants (or departmental heads), and above that level to the Lord Steward. The King himself seldom interfered in the running of the household, which was self-contained and self-regulating.[3]

The *domus regie magnificencie*, or Chamber, was quite different. Its staff was about 50 per cent aristocratic, ranging from the Knights and Esquires of the Body to musicians and yeomen ushers, and it was much more directly controlled by the King. There were many variations of status within the Chamber, but no hierarchy, and no set pattern of promotion. The Lord Chamberlain presided, and allocated duties, as well as being responsible for accommodation when the court was on progress, but unlike the Steward, he had no judicial authority. The Chamber took its name from the fact that medieval kings, when they were not dining in public in the Great Hall, needed a retreat. They needed somewhere for the council to meet, somewhere to receive ambassadors and suitors, and somewhere to eat in what passed for privacy. The Great Chamber was never a single room, but a set of rooms of increasing dignity as the King's person was approached.[4] By the latter part of his reign, Henry VII had retreated further, into a Privy Chamber to which access was strictly controlled by servants who had no pretensions to being the King's companions. Henry emerged into the Great Chamber to dine in public and to conduct certain kinds of business; and it was in the Great Chamber that his household officers kept their tables, at which were fed those resident members of staff who were entitled to 'bouge of court'.[5] Henry's companions, in so far as he had any, were his councillors and the Knights and Esquires of the Body. It was the latter who performed the humble but honorific work of handing the King his shirt when he dressed in the morning, and of bearing the towels etc. while his barber shaved him. The Great Chamber was all about display, and the King's orchestra, his jesters, his players, his Wardrobe of the Robes and his Guard, were all members of the Chamber staff, along with innumerable gentlemen waiters and ushers. At the beginning of Henry VIII's reign the Chamber staff numbered about ninety, but here, even more than in the household, part-time

1. & 2. Two views of the Tudor Palace at Greenwich, massively and expensively rebuilt by Henry VII. Henry VIII was born there, and it remained his favourite residence. Nothing of the Tudor building now survives above ground.

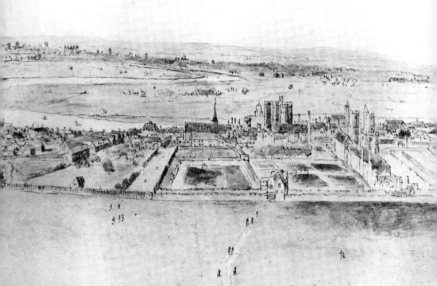

3. Richmond Palace, otherwise known as Sheen, rebuilt by Henry VII after a fire. It was home to Henry VIII for much of his childhood.

4. Henry VII as a young man. Attributed to Jacques Le Boucq, mid-sixteenth century. The original is in the Library of Arras.

5. Perkin Warbeck, the pretender whose claim to be Richard of York, the younger son of Edward IV, afflicted Henry VII from 1492 to 1497. This drawing, attributed to Jacques Le Boucq, shows the strong physical resemblance to Edward which first drew attention to him.

Above: 6. Henry VII's chantry in Westminster Abbey. Completed by Henry VIII after his father's death, with funeral effigies by Pietro Torrigiano.

Right: 7. Margaret Tudor, elder daughter of Henry VII, and Henry VIII's sister. She married in 1503 James IV of Scotland, and became by him the grandmother of Mary, Queen of Scots.

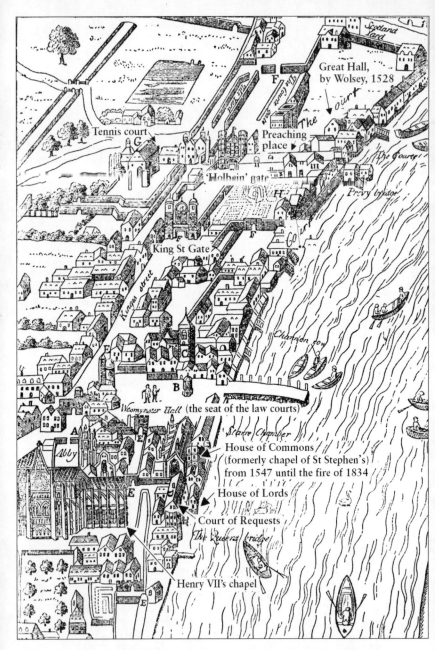

Tennis court

Great Hall,
by Wolsey, 1528

Preaching
place

'Holbein' gate

King St Gate

Weomynster Hall (the seat of the law courts)

Abby

House of Commons
(formerly chapel of St Stephen's)
from 1547 until the fire of 1834

House of Lords

Court of Requests

Henry VII's chapel

8. Plan of the palaces of Westminster and Whitehall, formerly known as York Place. From a later version of the 1578 map known as Ralph Agas's map, although not in fact by him. The Thames was the main highway connecting London, Westminster, Lambeth, Hampton Court, Southwark and Greenwich.

9. A view of Westminster, *c.* 1550, by Anthony van Wyngaerde. Westminster was the seat of the royal courts of justice, the meeting place of the parliament, and the nearest thing to a fixed capital that England possessed.

10. Whitehall palace, *c.* 1550, also by van Wyngaerde. As York Place this had been the traditional Westminster residence of the Archbishops of York, and had been extensively rebuilt by Cardinal Wolsey. It came into the King's hands on the fall of Wolsey in 1529, and was further rebuilt. It was used as a principal royal residence until largely destroyed by fire in the 1690s.

11. & 12. London from Westminster through the Strand (top) and St Paul's (bottom). *c*. 1550 by Anthony van Wyngaerde. These views show the closely packed nature of the City.

13. & 14. London bridge (top) and the Tower of London (bottom), *c.* 1550 by Anthony van Wyngaerde. The Tower was a fortress, prison, royal residence, and the home of the royal archives.

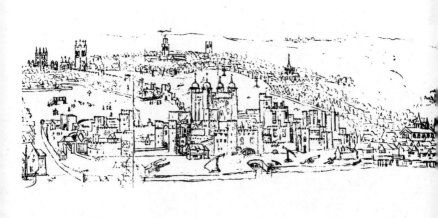

15. From a later copy of the parliament roll of 1512. The young king is shown going in procession to the opening of parliament, walking beneath a ceremonial canopy of blue and gold, blazoned with a Tudor rose. The canopy is borne by monks, and followed by peers of the realm bearing his train.

16. The coronation of Henry VIII, taken from an illuminated initial in the mortuary roll of John Islip, Abbot of Westminster (1500–1532). In this perspective the abbey is cut open to give a view of the coronation itself (24 June 1509), which was probably the highlight of Islip's incumbency.

17. An iron lock-plate, temp. Henry VIII.

18. 19. & 20. Henry VIII's Great Seals. The Great Seal, which was normally held by the Lord Chancellor, or Lord Keeper, was the ultimate authentication for acts of royal power. It was affixed (for example) to international treaties and to charters of grant. The Seal was changed periodically to express developing ideas of kingship – for example the Royal Supremacy over the Church.

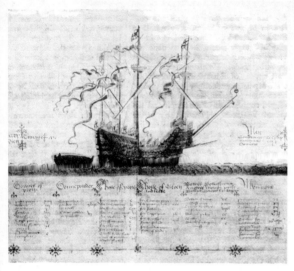

21. The *Henry Grace à Dieu*, taken from the Anthony Roll of 1545. When Henry's capital ship, the *Regent,* was lost in battle in 1512, Henry caused a replacement to be built '… such another as was never seen before in England, and called it the Henry Grace de Dieu …' It was launched on 15 October 1515, and displaced about 1,500 tons, making it by far the largest ship in the navy. Rebuilt in the late 1530s, it was reduced in size, and destroyed by fire in 1553. It was launched by Queen Catherine (then visibly pregnant), and the King, Queen and court enjoyed a splendid banquet on board.

22. Letter from Catherine of Aragon to Thomas Wolsey, as the King's Almoner. Dated from Richmond, 2 September 1513, and signed 'Katherine the Qwene', it recommends that Louis d'Orléans, Duke of Longueville, who had been taken prisoner at the battle of the Spurs (17 August), and sent to Catherine as a 'trophy', should be conveyed to the Tower 'as sone as he commethe' for 'it shuld be a grete combraunce to me to have this prisoner here'. Henry was still in France, and Catherine was ruling as Regent in his absence. The battle of Flodden was fought a week later.

23. Letter from Henry VIII to Cardinal Wolsey, March 1518. This letter, which is a holograph, shows the affable side of Henry's character. The King addresses Wolsey as 'Myne Awne good cardinall' and continues in the same vein to thank him for the 'grette payne and labour' that he has taken in the King's affairs. Henry sends the Queen's good wishes ('most harty recommendations'), and concludes 'Wrytten with the hand off your loving master, Henry R.'

24. 'Pastyme with good companye', Henry VIII's most famous composition. Henry had a good singing voice and was a (moderately) talented composer. Taken from 'Henry VIII's song book', in the British Library.

25. Illuminated capital from a plea roll of 1514. It was normal for these formal legal records to be decorated with initial letters depicting the king on his throne, sometimes (as here) in black and white, and sometimes in colour.

26. & 27. The meeting of the kings at the Field of Cloth of Gold, taken from plaster casts of the bas-reliefs in the Galerie d'Aumale at the Hotel de Bourgtheroulde, a noble townhouse in Rouen. Above, Henry VIII's party sets out from Guisnes. Below, the meeting of the Kings; Henry VIII is on the left, and Francis I on the right, a positioning reflecting French priorities.

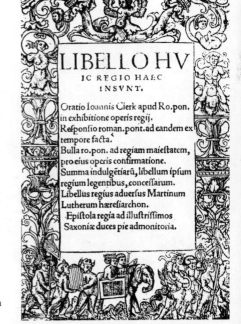

28. Henry VIII in the House of Lords, 1523 or 1529, taken from a later copy of a contemporary drawing 'ordered by the then Garter [King of Arms]'.

29. Title page of the 1523 edition of Henry VIII's *Assertio Septem Sacramentorum* against Martin Luther. This work was written and originally printed in 1521, but that edition was circulated only to a limited number of recipients (including the Pope). This title page describes the King as 'regiam maiestatem' (his royal majesty) a usage unusual before the break with Rome.

30. A drawing for the painting of Sir Thomas More and his family, by Hans Holbein,
c. 1527. The painting itself was copied by Rowland Lockey in 1593, and the original does
not survive.

31. Golden Bull of Pope
Leo X confirming the
grant of the title 'Fidei
Defensor' to King Henry
VIII in 1521. The papal
'bull' or seal was usually
cast in lead, but on
special occasions (as
here) might be cast in
gold. This one, designed
by Benvenuto Cellini,
shows as usual the twin
founders of the Church of
Rome, SS Peter and Paul.

32. Letter from Anne Boleyn to Cardinal Wolsey, *c.* 1528, when she was still hopeful that Wolsey would be able to clear a path for her marriage to the King. She thanks him for his services to her cause and promises that, after the attainment of her hopes, if there is anything that she can do for him 'you shall fynd me the gladdyst woman in the woreld to do yt'.

33. Letter from Anne Boleyn to 'Master Stephyns' (i.e. Stephen Gardiner, the King's secretary, in Rome, 4 April 1529). Dated at Greenwich and signed 'Anne Boleyn', the letter expresses the hope 'that the ende of this jorney shall be more pleasant' to her than its beginning. Gardiner was in Italy for a second time endeavouring to persuade Pope Clement VII to convert Wolsey and Campeggio's commission (then in England) into a decretal commission – from which there could be no appeal.

34. Holbein's design for a jewelled pendant, intended as a gift for Princess Mary, probably executed during his first visit to England (1526-28). At that time Mary was representing the King in the Marches of Wales, and was still in favour as the heir to the throne.

35. Anne Boleyn's clock. One of many artefacts given to her by the King as tokens of his affection. It has the initials H and A engraved on its weights.

36. A carving in wood from Canterbury cathedral, perhaps from a series caricaturing Henry's opponents. This shows Catherine of Aragon flanked by Cardinals Wolsey and Campeggio, in a clear reference to the failure of the Blackfriars court in the summer of 1529, when Catherine had aroused the King's anger by appealing directly to Rome, and Pope Clement had revoked the case. Wolsey's failure to prevent this led directly to his fall.

37. The Anglo-French treaty of Amiens, 18 August 1527, whereby Henry joined the
League of Cognac against the Emperor.

38. A grovelling letter from Cardinal Wolsey to the King, dated 8 October 1529, begging for forgiveness. It is signed 'Your Graces moste prostrat poore chapleyn, creature and bedisman'. In terms reminiscent of a prayer to God, the letter states that he, the King's 'poore hevy and wrechyd prest', daily calls upon his royal majesty 'for grace, mercy remyssyon, and pardon'. The King ignored him.

39. Letter from Wolsey to Stephen Gardiner, the King's Secretary in February or March 1530. The Cardinal never abandoned his hope for a recall to favour. Here he writes with reference to arrangements respecting appointments in the Province of York, to which he had been instructed to withdraw. He trusts ' yt wole now please hys maiste to shewe hys pety ... without sufferyng me any leynger to lye langwyshyng and consuming awey ...'

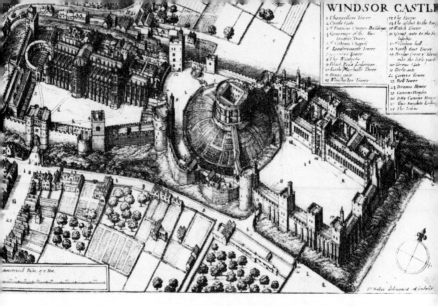

WINDSOR CASTL

1 Chancellors Tower
2 Castle Gate
3 S. Francis Commons Buildings in the Wiltshire Tower
4 Governour of the Knights Tower
5 Colemans Chapel
6 Lievtenaunts Tower
7 The Wardrobe
8 Black Rood Lodgings
9 Earle Marshalls Tower
10 Towne gate
11 Winchester Tower

13 The Keepe
14 The ascent to the towne
15 Watch Tower
16 Great gate to the the Islands
17 Timber hall
18 North East Tower
19 Broken frame v terrace into the little park
20 Norman Gate
21 Derbie-gate
22 Gardens Tower
23 Bell Tower
24 Dennis House
25 Canons House
26 Petty Canons House
27 Viar Singholde Lodgings
28 The Towne

40. Windsor Castle – a royal palace and fortress, and home of the Knights of the Garter. It was at Windsor on 11 July 1531 that Henry saw Catherine of Aragon for the last time.

41. Calais and its harbour from a sixteenth-century drawing. It was to Calais that Henry and Anne crossed in October 1532, for their meeting with Francis I, which occurred there and at Boulogne. Henry believed that he had secured Francis' diplomatic backing for his 'divorce' from Catherine, and while at Calais slept with Anne Boleyn for the first time.

Anglici Matrimonij

Sententia diffinitiva

Lata per sanctiss.imum. Dñm Nostrum. D. Clementem. Papã. vij. in sacro Consistorio de Reuerendiss.morum Dominorum. S. R. E. Cardinalium consilio super validitate Matrinonij inter Serenissimos Henricum. VIII. ¿ Catherinam Anglie Reges contracti.

PRO.

Eadem Serenissima Catherina Anglie Regina,

CONTRA.

Serenissimum Henricum. VIII. Anglie Regem.

Clemens Papa. vij.

Hristi nomine inuocato in Trono iustitie pro trib.nali sedentes, & solum Deum pre oculis habentes, Per hanc nostram diffinitiuam sententiam quam de Venerabilium Fratrum nostrorum Sanctæ Ro. Ec. Car. Consistorialiter coram nobis congregatorum Consilio, & assensu scimus in his scriptis, pronunciamus, decernimus, & declaramus, in causa, & causis ad nos, & Sedem Apostolicam per appellationem, per charissimam in christo filiam Catherinam Anglie Reginam Illustrem a nostris, & Sedis Apostolice Legatis in Regno Anglie deputatis interposi tam legitime deuolutis, & aduocatis, inter predictam Catherinam Reginam, & Charissimum in christo filium Henricum. VIII. Anglie Regem Illustrem, super Validitate, & inualiditate matrimonij inter eosdem Reges contracti, & consumati rebusq̃ in aliis in ectis, cause & causarum huiusmodi latius deductis, & dilecto filio Paulo Capissucho causarum sacri palaty tunc decano & pro pter ipsius Pauli absentiam Venerabili Fratri nostro Iacobo Simonee Episcopo Pisaurien. vnius ex dictis palaty causarum Auditori bus locumtenenti, audiendis instruendis, & in Consistorio nostro Secreto referendis commissis, & per eos nobis, & eisdem Car dinalibus Relatis, & mature discussis, coram nobis pendentibus, Matrimonium Inter predictos Catherinam, & Henricum An glie Reges contractum, & inde secuta quecunq̃ fuisse, & esse validum, & canonicum validaq̃, & Canonica, suosq̃ debitos de buisse, & debere sortiri effectus, prolemq̃ exinde susceptam, & suscipiendam fuisse, & fore legitimam, & prefatum Henri cum Anglie Regem teneri, & obligatum fuisse, et fore ad cohabitandum cum dicta Catherina Regina eius legitima coniuge, illamq̃ maritali affectione, & Regio honore tractandum, & eundem Henricum Anglie Regem ad premissa omnia, & singula cum effectu adimplendum condemnandum ommibusq̃ iuris Remedijs cogendum, & compellendum fore, prout condemnamus, cogimus, & compellimus, Molestationesq̃, & denegationes Per eundem Henricum Regem eidem Catherine Regine super inualiditate, ac see dere dicti Matrimony quomodolibet factas, & prestitas fuisse, & esse illicitas, & iniustas, & eidem Henrico Regi super il lis ac inualiditate matrimony huiusmodi perpetuum Silentium imponendum fore, & imponimus, eundemq̃ Henricum Anglie Re gem in expensis in huiusmodi causa pro parte dicte Catherine Regine coram nobis, & dictis omnibus legitime factis condem nandum fore, & condemnamus, quarum expensarum taxationem nobis imposterum reseruamus.

Ita pronunciauimus .I.

Lata fuit Rome in Palatio Apostolico publice in Consistorio die. XXIII. Martij. M. D. XXXIIII.

Blosius.

42. A copy of Pope Clement VII's 'definitive sentence' in favour of Catherine of Aragon and against Henry VIII. Issued on the 23 March 1534, after vain calls to Henry to give up Anne and return to his first wife. It was ignored in England.

43. The Act in Restraint of Appeals (25 Henry VIII, *c*.20) of 1533. The preamble opens with the portentous claim 'that this Realme of Englond is an Impire', and goes on to state that it is governed by one supreme head and king, whose jurisdiction is competent to adjudge all spiritual cases which may arise within the realm. All appeals to the Pope, and to any 'foreign princes and potentates' are absolutely forbidden. In passing this act, the parliament claimed jurisdiction over spiritual causes in a manner which had never hitherto been thought possible. Before it was passed, Archbishop Cranmer had received from Rome the pallium which confirmed his metropolitan authority, and this Act enabled his decision to be definitive.

Right: 44. Letter from Cranmer to the King, dated from Dunstable 17 May 1533. The Archbishop informs Henry, with apologies, that his great matter cannot be resolved until Friday, because of the liturgical calendar.

Below: 45. Extract from the Treasons Act of 1534 (26 Henry VIII, *c*. 13). This provides that 'everie offendour … hereafter laufully convicte of any maner of high treasons shall lose & forfayte to the kynges highnes his heirs and successours all suche landes tenements and heriditaments whiche any suche offendour … shall have of any estate of inheritaunce yn use or possession by any right title or menes within this realme of Englonde'. Its innovation lay in the fact that it extended the definition of treason to include the Royal Supremacy over the Church, which many contemporaries saw as making treason out of mere words.

Bottom: 46. The Act of Supremacy, 1534 (26 Henry VIII, *c*.1). This act declared that 'the kynges maiestie iustley and rightfully is & oweth to be the supreme heed of the churche of England …' It was carefully phrased to make it clear that Parliament was recognising a title which the King already possessed, not conferring it upon him. By Letters Patent of 15 June 1535, Henry formally added the phrase 'in terra supremum caput Anglicane Ecclesie' to his royal style and title.

47. An imaginative nineteenth-century portrayal of Queen Catherine before the Blackfriars court in 1529. This shows the proceedings of the second session on 21 June, when the King was also present.

48. A nineteenth-century representation of the death of Catherine of Aragon at Kimbolton in January 1536. Although allegedly very much afraid of poison, it is almost certain that she died of coronary thrombosis.

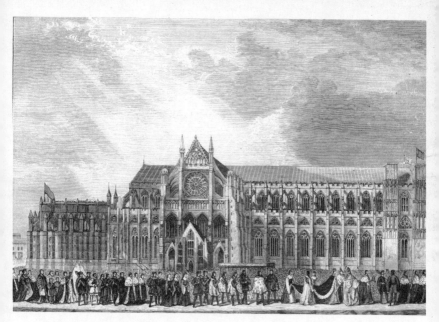

49. The coronation procession of Anne Boleyn approaches Westminster Abbey, 1 June 1533. A published account shortly after did its best to portray spontaneous rejoicings, but in fact a number of prominent individuals boycotted the proceedings, including the King's sister, Mary, his daughter and the Imperial ambassador.

50. A nineteenth-century representation of the execution of Anne Boleyn. The Calais executioner, with his sword, stands waiting on the right.

King Henry the eyght.

52. Page from the original manuscript of 'The Institution of a Christian Man' (The King's Book), showing the extensive corrections made in the King's own hand. Henry lost no opportunity to emphasise, clearly and in detail, his repudiation of the Roman jurisdiction.

53. The barn at Wolf Hall, near Marlborough, the seat of Sir John Seymour. Jane Seymour was allegedly born in the house, which was long ago demolished. The barn, however, survived until it was burned down in the early twentieth century. Local legend has it that Henry and Jane were married in the barn, but in fact that happened at Whitehall (originally York Place) on 30 May 1536.

Opposite: 51. Henry VIII in council. This appears to be a formal session, with the King seated under his 'cloth of estate'. In practice the council normally met without the King, and attendance was usually about a dozen.

Left: 54. Monumental brass of Thomas Boleyn, Earl of Wiltshire. Following the executions of his daughter Anne and son George in 1536, Thomas lost the Privy Seal, but was allowed to withdraw to his estates, and not otherwise penalised. He died at Hever Castle on 13 March 1539.

Below: 55. Declaration by the bishops, probably of 1536, explaining that two disputed scriptural texts (John 20:21 and Acts 20:28) confer spiritual but not political power upon the episcopate.

Opposite: 56. Title page from the Great Bible, printed by Richard Grafton and Edward Whitchurch, 1539. Enthroned as God's vicar, Henry symbolically hands out the Word of God to the spiritual and temporal hierarchies of his realm, headed by Thomas Cranmer on his right, and Thomas Cromwell on his left.

¶ The Byble in Englyhe, that is to saye the content of all the holy scrypture, bothe of ý olde and newe testament, truly translated after the veryte of the Hebrue and Greke textes, by ý dylygent studye of dyuerse excellent learned men, expert in the forsayde tonges.

¶ Prynted by Rychard Grafton & Edward Whitchurch.

Cum priuilegio ad imprimendum solum.
1539.

...vnyte to be had in the same.

Whereupon after a great and longe debate and argued disputacion and consultacion had and much conteyning the saide articles as well by the consent of the kynges highnes as by thassent of the lordes spuall and temporall and other lerned men of this clergie in they convocacion and by the consent of the comons in this present assembled it was and is fynally resolued, accorded and agreed in maner and forme following, that is to say fyrst that in the most blessed sacrament of the aulter by the strengthe and efficacy of Chrystes myghtie worde it beinge spoken by the prest is present really vnder the forme of bread and wyne the naturall body and bloode of our saviour Jesu Christe conceyued of the virgyn marie and that after the consecracion there remayneth noo substance of bread or wyne nor any other substance, but the substance of Christe god and man, Secondly that communyon in bothe kindes is not necessary ad salutem by the lawe of god to all persons And that it is to be beleued and not doubted of but that in the fleshe vnder forme of bread is the very bloode and with the bloode vnder forme of wyne is the very fleshe as well apayrte as thoughe they were bothe together, Thyrdly that

priestes after the order of priesthode receyued as afore may not marry by the lawe of god, fourthlie that vowes of chastitye or wydowhode by man or woman made to god advisedly ought to be observed by the lawe of god And that it exemptes them from other libertyes of christen people which without that they myght enioye, fyftly that it is mete and necessary that pryvate masses be contynued and admytted in this the kynges Englishe churche and Congregacion wherby good christen people ordeynge them selfe receyue bothe godly and goostly consolacions and benefight And it is agreeable also to goddes lawe, Syxtly that Auricular confession is expedient and necessary to be retayned and contynued vsed and frequented in the churche of god, ffor the which most godlie stodie payne and travaile of his maiestie and exquysicion and resolucion of the premisses his most humble and obedient subiectes the lordes spuall and temporall

Top: 57. The Act of Six Articles (31 Henry VIII, *c*.14). This conservative measure enforced all the traditional doctrines of the mass, including transubstantiation – the conversion of the bread and wine in the Eucharist into the physical body and blood of Christ.

Left: 58. Henry VIII as King David. One of several beautiful illuminations decorating a manuscript book of the psalms produced for the King's personal use in 1540.

BEATVS vir qui non abiit
in consilio impiorum, & in via
peccatorum non stetit, & in cathedra pe=
stilentiæ non sedit

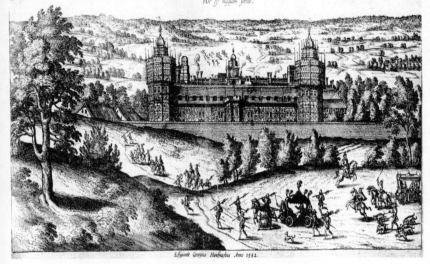

Effingit Georgius Houfnaglius Anno 1582.

59. Henry VIII's new palace of Nonsuch, built (roughly) in imitation of Francis I's chateau of Chambord. It was never finished in Henry's lifetime and was demolished in the late seventeenth century. It was allegedly constructed partly using materials looted from the dissolved monasteries.

60. Oatlands in Surrey, another of Henry's palaces, which was upgraded from a hunting lodge. It was here that the King married his fifth Queen, Catherine Howard, on 28 July 1540. The palace was subsequently demolished and archaeological investigations were carried out in the 1950s.

61. Third Succession Act (35 Henry VIII, *c*. 1), 1544. This was the act which designated Mary and Elizabeth to follow Edward if he should die without heirs, and broke new ground in that it authorised the succession of illegitimate children.

62. Design for a timepiece by Hans Holbein. This was made by Nicholas Kratzer for Sir Anthony Denny, and presented by him to the King for a New Year's gift in 1545.

63. Henry VIII's will, dated 30 December 1546. It was signed with a dry stamp, not with the King's own hand, which was a cause of later disputes.

64. St George's Chapel, Windsor, which was the home of the Garter Knights, and which Henry chose for his last resting place in preference to his father's chapel at Westminster. This was probably because he wanted to be beside Jane Seymour, who had been interred there in 1537.

and unpaid officers, who attended as required, make numbers hard to calculate.

The new king also had somewhat different requirements from his father. He had no use for privacy in the earlier sense; what he wanted was to be surrounded by congenial young aristocrats who would share his numerous pastimes – hunting, jousting and making music in particular. These boon companions were there from the beginning of the reign, but at first they lacked any organisation or any recognised status. However, during the friendly contacts with France which at first followed the accession of Francis I in 1515, a Privy Chamber took shape on the French model.[6] Henry VIII kept his father's retreat with its menial servants, but added to them a new kind of animal called a Gentleman of the Privy Chamber, as previously mentioned. These were people like Charles Brandon and William Compton, and their appointment belonged to the King alone. They were presided over by the most intimate and highly favoured of their number – the Groom of the Stool.[7] It became a matter of some contention whether they were in theory subject to the Lord Chamberlain, but in practice their loyalty was exclusively to the King, and successive Lords Chamberlain treated them with kid gloves. The Privy Chamber in its new form was created between 1515 and 1518, and it was not long before its members were causing concern to the King's political advisers. They were perceived as being too intimate – 'playing light touches' – with the King, and as misbehaving themselves in public, thus bringing dishonour upon their master. In May 1519 Henry was persuaded to dismiss four of them and to draft in four Knights of the Body (perceived as older and more responsible men) to take their places. It used to be thought that Thomas Wolsey was responsible for this purge, but it now appears that the whole council was involved, and it may well have been that unanimity which persuaded Henry that he must act.[8]

Both the size and the nature of the Privy Chamber changed as the King got older. It showed an inexorable tendency to inflate in numbers, and every so often the brakes had to be applied, but the average number through the reign was about twenty. By the 1530s the jousters and 'wild boys' had disappeared, and the appointments look more political in nature. Because they had unsupervised access to the King, his Gentlemen were much sought after as patrons and promoters of causes, and Thomas Cromwell, in particular, was careful to secure places for some of his own friends and supporters. They could be positions of danger as well as honour. Ease of access might embrace the Queen as well as the King, and both Henry's queens who were accused of adultery – Anne Boleyn and Catherine Howard – brought down members of the Privy Chamber with them. The King used his Gentlemen as private messengers, and was in the habit of entrusting delicate missions to them, both at home and abroad. Wolsey is alleged to have surrendered the Great Seal to the Duke of Norfolk only when he noticed that he was accompanied by a Gentleman of the Privy Chamber, thereby demonstrating that his mission was really from the King.[9] As we have seen, Henry was also suspected of wooing Anne Hastings by proxy, in that case using Sir William Compton. Because of its intimate nature, and because the King was the centre of all politics, the Privy Chamber inevitably became a centre of pressure. Between 1529 and 1533 it was purged of supporters of Catherine of Aragon; and in 1536 of the Boleyns and their clients.[10] However, no such purge followed the fall of Thomas Cromwell in 1540, so from then until the end of the reign, the Privy Chamber formed a sort of 'alternative council', often giving the King contradictory advice to that which was being handed down by the Council proper. The latter was under conservative control by then, while the former retained many of Cromwell's men. This could only have happened because Henry so willed it, and if he took Privy Chamber advice from the likes of Sir Anthony Denny, it was because his mind was moving in that direction. In the political and religious conflicts of the last decade of the reign, the Privy Chamber was an active player.

The rise of the Privy Chamber was probably the most important change to occur in Henry's court, but it was not the only one. From 1509 to 1537, from 1540 to 1541, and again from 1543–47 there were separate establishments for Henry's successive queens. In each case the consort chose her own intimate servants, and had at least some say in the appointment of her household officers. In Catherine of Aragon's case this meant the employment of a fair number of Spaniards and Italians, and thereafter usually of the consort's kindred, both male and female. Each consort was given a substantial endowment in land, from the proceeds of which she was expected to keep up her own residences and pay their staff, but those who attended her at court were paid by the King.[11] The royal children, Mary, Elizabeth and Edward, were also given their own establishments, which fluctuated in size with the status of the child, and hence with the politics of the reign. These were all paid for from the Chamber accounts, and while Mary was in Wales from 1525 to 1529, she was costing her father £4,000 a year. The other main change was structural, but it is arguable as to how much difference it made. Thomas Cromwell, like Wolsey, became worried about how much the household was costing, and rightly believed that this was largely due to the existence of large numbers of traditional perquisites. He therefore decided to abolish both the chief offices, the Lord Chamberlain and Lord Steward, replacing them with a single Lord Great Master. Like the Privy Chamber this was modelled on the French system, and was intended to improve efficiency by unifying control.[12] Ironically, the changes were implemented in the very year of his fall, 1540. The King must have consented to them, but he had no will to persist. As early as 1543 he had appointed a new Lord Chamberlain, and the Lord Great Master thereafter became little more than the Lord Steward under another name until the whole traditional structure was restored in 1553.

The court was constantly on the move. This was partly to enable the King to show himself to his people, but more because contemporary hygiene was primitive, and after several weeks of residence by 200–300 people even the most commodious palace became insalubrious. Henry went on progress every so often, most notably to York in 1541, but most of his migrations were simply from one to another of his own residences in the Home Counties. He had nearly sixty houses by the 1540s, some as far away as Ludlow and Newcastle upon Tyne, but seldom visited more than about six or eight of those within easy reach.[13] Greenwich, Westminster and Windsor were his early favourites, but once he had acquired Hampton Court from Wolsey in 1525 that became the most favoured of all. The great new palace which he built at Nonsuch was visited from time to time to oversee work in progress, but was never finished in his lifetime. When not in use, these palaces were on a care-and-maintenance basis, with a skeleton staff in each, because most of the furniture and fittings required when the court was in residence arrived in an enormous baggage train a few days before the King himself. Consequently last minute changes of plan were extremely unpopular with the marshals and harbingers who had to organise the transit. Particularly in his younger days, Henry was also in the habit of going off hunting. He had a number of hunting lodges within easy reach of London, of which Oatlands in Surrey was probably his favourite. Such visits were usually small scale (20–30 people) and of relatively short duration. If the King's intentions were known in advance, some servants would be sent down from the court to look after him and his party, but if they were not, a scratch staff would be recruited locally, and those living close to the more popular lodges became accustomed to such demands

How much all this cost is very difficult to ascertain, because a number of separate accounts were involved. In 1531–32, for example, the Cofferer accounted for £27,947, but that was just on the Household, and the Chamber accounts are confused by the fact that the Treasury of the Chamber was also a public spending department and was used for many other things apart from the Chamber wages.[14] At this time the Chamber proper was probably costing about £20,000 a year, which was to rise to £25,300 by the last year of the reign. If we assume that the average cost of the whole court between 1530 and 1547 was £45–50,000 a year, that would probably not be far out. At the same time the ordinary revenue of the Crown, exclusive of direct taxation and windfalls like monastic lands, was about £130,000.[15] The King always held a Privy Purse, which was administered by the Groom of the Stool, and for which he accounted to nobody. This was used for such matters as gambling debts, special rewards, unscheduled alms, and the occasional purchase. It amounted to about £3–4,000 a year, and was replenished from such windfalls as the French pension, paid by Francis (when there was no war, and when he felt like it) in accordance with the terms of the treaty of 1514; and also from the sale of lands or the produce of estates. During the last decade of the reign there was also another office, called the King's Coffers. At the end this was held by Sir Anthony Denny in his capacity as Keeper of the Palace of Westminster.[16] Denny eventually accounted for over £100,000, spread over several years, when it was noted that £11,359 in cash had been secreted in the Jewel House at the time of Henry's death. This money seems to have come mainly from Augmentations, but it also absorbed all the other casual sources, and the Privy Purse drew on it. It was also used rather as the Treasury of the Chamber had once been used, for state purposes, particularly diplomatic, but also occasionally military. In addition the King used it to fund his building projects. The Treasury of the Chamber had been returned to its earlier function when the financial administration was reorganised in the 1530s, and the King's Coffers seems to have taken its place – except that it was subjected to no regular accounting procedure. When Denny eventually accounted in 1548, it was before a special commission.[17] There were thus no clear distinctions drawn between the King's private expenditure, and the expenditure of the state. In a sense the court was the government, or at least the political end of it. The administration and judiciary had long ago gone 'out of court', as it was significantly expressed, so the Chancery and the Court of King's Bench no longer functioned within the verge, but in every other sense the court was central, and the tendency to financial confusion reflects that.

Security, as that is understood in the modern world, was almost non-existent. Henry VII had established, soon after his accession, a bodyguard of 200 (or so) archers, known as the Yeomen of the Guard. At the time this was a sensible protection against the most obvious kind of threat, a physical attack upon the court, which was a real possibility, particularly on progress. However, by the time that his son was settled on the throne, the Yeomen served mainly ceremonial purposes. There were always some of them on duty, but they are not known to have been called upon in earnest until the time of the Wyatt rebellion in

1554.[18] Henry VIII, as we have seen, loved military display, and in 1511 attempted to set up a new ceremonial guard, of higher social status, known as 'the Spears'. For some reason or other this was a short-lived experiment, and it was not until 1539 that such a group became established. It was then known as the Gentlemen Pensioners, the idea being to provide honourable employment for old soldiers, as well as to safeguard the King. The Gentlemen numbered fifty, had their own officers, and were paid at the dignified rate of £50 a year.[19] Members of the band served in shifts, and usually had other occupations, sometimes also around the court. These Gentlemen guarded the Privy Chamber, and would no doubt have been reasonably effective if they had ever been called upon. The Privy Chamber (again a suite of rooms, not a single one) was the one part of the court to which access was tightly controlled. Elsewhere the public came and went, almost at will. It was said that all you needed to get past the porters on the gate was a presentable appearance and a little money to pay an inducement. The merest pretext of legitimate business (plus further inducements) would have enabled the interloper to pass various Chamber doors, theoretically guarded by yeomen or gentlemen ushers. When a tournament or some other display was in hand, the gates were in any case open to all, who were invited to come and be overawed by the royal splendour. In spite of his controversial policies and opinions, no one (as far as we know) ever made an attempt upon Henry's life – or on those of any of his courtiers. The courtiers themselves probably constituted a greater danger at a time when it was common for a gentleman to wear a sword, honour was sensitive and tempers were short.[20] Nevertheless, an absolute ban on weapons in the Privy Chamber, and the most draconian penalties for bloodshed in the royal presence seems to have kept the problem under control. Henry liked receiving petitions; it added to his sense of being respected, and deliberately made himself available to receive them from time to time, usually when he was on his way to the Chapel Royal, or off hunting. Petitions could be presented at other times, but only through the mediation of a well-placed courtier, who was likely to charge heavily for his assistance. Successive queens were also energetic petitioners, and their ladies developed a clientele of their own for a similar purpose.[21]

The more general security of the household at large was even less strict. One of the main problems was that the King's lavish lifestyle (necessary for his honour) meant that a great deal more food was cooked than was consumed. Some of this was distributed to the normal servants by way of perquisites, and some was regularly distributed in alms, but much was up for grabs by anyone who could infiltrate the kitchen or the scullery. Consequently, there were always a lot of unauthorised extra hands in those departments. If they did not fight, or make nuisances of themselves, the Sergeants tended to turn a blind eye, and sometimes, if there was a push on, it was useful to have their labour. Every so often the senior officers conducted a purge of these undesirables, but they always came back.[22] The other problem was caused by the fact that there was a chronic shortage of women. Even in the Chamber the Queen's ladies and their female servants constituted only a small minority; in the Household it was much worse. Apart from the laundresses (an indeterminate number and not a department), there were none in legitimate service. As a result, whichever palace the court was in was besieged by the local prostitutes, who did a roaring trade. Again the departmental officers tended to turn a blind eye; undesirable as they might be, these women performed a necessary function, and in any case their activities were preferable to encouraging the 'detestable sin of buggery', which was the realistic alternative.[23] Only a small minority of the more established servants were married and lived in, or nearby, with their wives and children. As with the 'vagabonds and boys', these whores were periodically driven away by the senior officers, but nothing could deter them for long. Rather surprisingly, given this ease of access, there were no recorded riots in the lower reaches of the court, and no one tried to poison the King's soup. Venereal disease was probably a different matter, but no statistics were kept.

As the court surrounded the King, and the Council always met within the verge, in a sense all the politics of the reign was also the politics of the court. However, it would be unrealistic to treat most of the problems of government in that way. The most obvious point of contact was the King's sex life. Insofar as this constituted successive marriages and the question of getting an heir, this will be dealt with separately, but there was always rather more to it than that. It would not have been surprising if a young man who prided himself upon his virility as much as Henry did, had run a series of mistresses alongside his legitimate wives. However, Henry did this only to a very limited extent, and the fact probably is that he was never actually as good in bed as he liked to think he was.

The politics of the court always depended, ultimately, upon the will (or whim) of the King. Factions, in the sense of groups of like-minded individuals sharing a common goal, certainly existed, and his successive consorts, although not necessarily leaders, were often the symbols of these factions. This was most obviously the case with the Boleyns, who with their supporters constituted an anti-papal and pro-French pressure group for about ten years, from 1526 to 1536. In that case Anne was the real leader as well as the figurehead, but both their success and ultimate failure depended upon Henry and the nature of her influence over him. Catherine and Mary were not leaders in the same sense, but were equally the centre of a contrary faction, which fought tooth and nail to resist Boleyn influence. Catherine was no match for Anne as a king-pleaser, but after her death, when the boundaries shifted somewhat, they also enjoyed their moment of success – because the King changed his mind. Mary's surrender destroyed them after 1536 because they no longer had a focus and the Princess refused to be used as a pressure point against her father. Jane Seymour played no such part, and the rise of her kindred cannot be associated with any cause, but the Howards were another family-based faction, who during Catherine's brief ascendancy undoubtedly influenced the King's mind. However, the total eclipse which they suffered as a result of her indiscretions should warn us against supposing that they had any control over Henry. It would also be a mistake to think of the religious conservatives after 1540 as having any kind of coherence, even after the rehabilitation of the Howards. They were, perhaps, a group of factions. Their rivals, the evangelicals, certainly shared the common aim of securing influence and resisting their rivals, and they certainly used Queen Catherine Parr as a rallying point, but they also were a miscellaneous bunch, and whether Catherine was a real leader is still an open question. At an earlier date, the Duke of Buckingham had been brought down by the King's suspicions, and by his own stupidity, not by factional rivals, and although Wolsey had many enemies, they had no consistent purpose beyond discrediting him. It is slightly more realistic to see Anne Boleyn and Thomas Cromwell as victims of faction; certainly their enemies were organised, but in both cases those enemies efforts would have come to nothing if they had failed to convince the King.[24] The point is emphasised, not only by the survival of Catherine Parr, but even more by the survival of Thomas Cranmer, who was the target of factional hostility on at least two occasions. Henry was always the master in his own house, although he did not always appear to be. For a variety of reasons, commentators, both contemporary and historical, have often sought to explain his apparently abrupt changes of favour and direction in terms of who had the King's ear – 'evil counsellors' in fact, who included unsympathetic consorts. Henry was not immune to influence, even pressure, but his erratic behaviour sprang from deep roots within himself. His concentration span was limited, particularly in his younger days, and on some occasions he may simply not have been paying attention to what he was told. In later life he acquired a range of prejudices and dislikes, which his courtiers and advisers simply had to take account of, and steer around – unless, like Catherine Howard, they were too stupid. His successive marriages, and the rise and fall of his consorts' kindred, tell us a great deal about the sensitivities of the court environment. His first, second and fourth marriages all had international implications which will be dealt with elsewhere, but the Seymour, Howard and Parr unions raised only domestic issues. Each in turn refocused the court, readjusted its personnel, and to some extent altered its climate. But the man who had to be satisfied, pleased and humoured, was always the King.

6

WAR & POVERTY, 1522–1525

By the treaty of Bruges, Henry was bound to make war on France in May 1522, provided that no peace had been declared between Charles and Francis in the meantime. He was not, however, bound to launch any Army Royal until the following year. This rather curious provision reflects the ambiguous nature of English foreign policy at the time. The King was broadly supportive of the Emperor and hostile to France, but was hoping to use Imperial pressure, plus the threat of his own involvement, to extract a favourable settlement from the latter. On this occasion the strategy did not work, and Henry found himself committed to a war at sea, for which mobilisation had begun as early as the previous December.[1] It was, however, at best a half-hearted effort. The Great Ships were prepared, and were at sea by the end of May, but no effort had been made to augment the fleet, either by building or by purchase. The intention seems to have been to attack Le Havre, and the ships were duly brought round from the Thames to Southampton, where soldiers were embarked on 21 June. However the Earl of Surrey, who was in charge of the expedition, was not a happy man. In letters both to the King and to Wolsey, he expressed his unwillingness to set out until his fleet had been properly victualled. Supplies promised from Kent and Essex had not arrived, and there was no money to pay the brewers, who would not provide beer except for ready cash.[2] Some provisions must have reached him, because he set off a few days later – not for Le Havre, which was too strongly defended, but for Morlaix in Brittany, which he seized and partly destroyed on 1 July. By the 3rd he was writing again urgently requesting additional supplies, without which any intention to go further and attack Brest would prove abortive.[3] They clearly did not arrive, because a few days later he was back at Portsmouth, where his forces were disbanded. Somewhat paradoxically the King was pleased with the gesture which had been made, and it must be wondered whether the shortage of victuals was not deliberately contrived by Wolsey to restrict Surrey's activities without appearing to do so.

While this expedition was actually at sea, the Emperor was in London, ostensibly on a goodwill visit, but probably to keep his ally up to the mark. 'Now', as Grafton commented, 'was the warre open of all parties betweene England, France and Spayne'.[4] On 6 June, Charles entered London to a lavish reception, including 'rich sumptuous and costly pageants' and the emblazoned slogan:

Carolus, Henricus. Vivant defensor uterque
Henricus fidei, Carolus Ecclesie

They dined with the Duke of Suffolk, and hunted at Windsor and Winchester; and all the time Charles pressed his host for a more earnest commitment to the war; pressure which Henry just as assiduously avoided.[5] When they parted on 7 July, the Emperor can hardly have been satisfied with the results of his visit. He had been forced to concede the postponement of the major joint offensive upon which he had set his heart until 1524, and to listen without enthusiasm to talk of a possible truce. Nor was the King best pleased either, because at the same time he had to press the City of London hard to loan him £20,000. Opposition to the war was building among the taxpayers who would ultimately have to pay for it.[6] One of the reasons for discontent was that war with France nearly always spelled trouble from Scotland, a kingdom whose hostility could be a costly nuisance. In November 1521 that bird of ill-omen, the Duke of Albany had returned, ostensibly without the consent of King Francis, but in reality to do his work for him. With considerable difficulty, the Duke managed to persuade a number of Scottish peers to back him in an attack across the border, but their hearts were not in it, and when the English Warden, Lord Dacre, offered them a truce, they took his offer and disbanded their army. Albany was left with little option but to return to France and plead for some more reliable forces. Paradoxically, Henry was displeased with Dacre's action, perhaps because it had been taken without his permission, or perhaps because he was anticipating another Flodden, but Wolsey was relieved. The exposure of Albany's weakness had opened the way for a longer-term settlement with Scotland – perhaps even extending as far as a marriage between Princess Mary and the young James V.[7] The fact that the treaty of Bruges had committed her to Charles, and forbidden all other negotiations, was a mere inconvenience. If a deal could be struck with France, then the Imperial alliance became dispensable. Secret negotiations had begun. They had so far made little progress, but the Emperor was right in suspecting that his ally was less than wholehearted about the war which was then ongoing.

Nevertheless skirmishing continued around the Calais Pale, with both sides sharing the aggression, and at the end of August Henry launched a more substantial attack from the same base, when the Earl of Surrey at the head of 15,000 men began a burning and plundering campaign into neighbouring Picardy. He encountered only local resistance, and spent the month of September destroying villages and small towns.[8] The French seem to have been taken by surprise by the scale of this operation, and did not attempt to mount a counter-attack. Surrey's orders in any case were to avoid battle, because when he judged that he had done enough, and 'seeing that it was no time to keepe the field, [he] turned backwards in good order of battayle, and came to Calice the sixtene day of October ...'.[9] Surrey's foray did not amount to a serious act of warfare. It was probably aimed partly at Charles, and partly at the English taxpayers, but most of all intended to encourage those secret negotiations which seemed to be stalled in the autumn of

1522. It would have been a good idea if Francis had settled with him before he did a deal with the Duke of Bourbon, who was by this time on the brink of open rebellion. A coalition of Henry, the Emperor and the Duke would present the King of France with problems which he would be well advised to avoid. This type of thinking was more typical of the Cardinal than of the King, but there is no reason to suppose that they were in serious disagreement. At this level of diplomacy, Henry's wishes always prevailed – but he was open to persuasion. The trouble was that the Duke of Bourbon was not, in English eyes, a very convincing player, and the King was not persuaded that the enthusiastic Emperor would actually deliver in the joint campaign that he was urging.[10] In June 1523, however, there came a change. Bourbon had reached a point of no return in his relations with Francis, and this apparently convinced Henry (or at least Wolsey) that he now had no choice but to rebel openly. At the end of June an envoy was sent secretly to the Duke, offering him terms, and a month later an agreement was signed between Henry, Charles and the Duke, committing all three to a joint attack on France. Instead of waiting until 1524, the Emperor would get his eagerly sought campaign almost immediately.[11] In spite of Wolsey's appeals of poverty, English money was poured into Bourbon's pocket, and a deal was finally confirmed on 6 September. By the time that this happened, the Duke of Suffolk, leading an English expeditionary force, was already on his way. Commissioned to raise troops on 24 July, he reached Calais a month later at the head of 10,000 men.[12]

Meanwhile, Wolsey had taken the King's financial needs to Parliament. War, even in the somewhat limited form then being waged, was immensely expensive. The last effort, between 1511 and 1514, had cost £892,000, and had emptied the treasury. There was no reason to suppose that the current effort would be any less of a drain. Preparations for this had not been neglected, and in March 1522 the Cardinal had sent out commissioners to assess the military and financial potential of each county.[13] This covered landholding, individual wealth and the possession of harness, armour and weapons. Wolsey was not only anticipating a new taxation demand, but was also intending to use the county levies as an alternative method of raising troops – a tactic quite consistent with his distrust of the military pretensions of the aristocracy. For some unknown reason, this first survey was found to be unsatisfactory, and the commissions were reissued in July. It was upon these returns that the forced loan which was demanded in the autumn of 1522 was assessed. This, and a similar loan early in 1523, raised some £350,000, which was over £40,000 short of what was required to pay for the Earl of Surrey's foray and the precautions which needed to be taken on the Scottish border.[14] By the time that Parliament met in April 1523, the King's need was urgent, and Wolsey demanded a subsidy of four shillings in the pound, which would have realised about £800,000. He was bitterly resisted in the Commons, partly on the grounds of the loan which had been recently raised, and the repayment of which was uncertain, and partly because the members were unconvinced of the need for war. After a great deal of haggling, the Cardinal was finally forced to accept a subsidy of two shillings in the pound, which would not be due for payment until the spring of 1524.[15] Parliament dissolved on 13 August, and during October Wolsey tried to anticipate the tax by sending out a commission to demand early payment from all those assessed at over £40. The result was negligible, except in generating resentment, and the sums then being promised (and paid) to the Duke of Bourbon had to be funded by borrowing. This was probably the main reason why England refrained from any major military operations during 1524, to Charles' mounting frustration and disgust.

Suffolk's expedition thus took place against a background where the rhetoric hardly matched the reality. The Emperor saw Bourbon's defection as a golden opportunity to put fetters on Francis' ambitions in Italy, and possibly to create a new state based on the Duke's extensive lands. Henry saw a similar opportunity to revive his claim to the crown of France, and persuaded Bourbon to swear allegiance to him in that capacity.[16] Neither of these dreams paid much attention to the military and financial situation which actually existed. The Archduchess Margaret was supposed to provide cavalry and artillery for Suffolk, and did so, although not on the scale agreed, but Charles, who was expected to find 100,000 crowns toward the expenses, delivered only 48,000, and that was late. Nor was a strategy agreed until the very last minute. When Suffolk landed at Calais, he was still expecting to proceed to the siege of Boulogne. It was only during September that the Emperor persuaded Wolsey, and Wolsey persuaded the King, that Boulogne should be abandoned in favour of a dash towards Paris, to link up with Bourbon, who was supposed to be coming from the east.[17] Moreover, the campaign had got off to a shaky start. There was plague in Calais, and on 10 September Suffolk was constrained to move his men out of the town into a camp nearby to avoid the infection, which he did not entirely succeed in doing. In spite of all efforts, disease continued to be a steady drain on the army. Because of this, and because he was waiting for his Flemish reinforcements, it was early October before Suffolk moved out of the Pale. The strategy then was to move fast, bypassing strongly fortified places rather than wasting time in sieges.[18] At first this seemed to work well. Small towns and villages were overrun, and because they were well supplied, his forces had no need to live off the country, a fact which no doubt helped to persuade many of the people to accept an oath to Henry VIII as King of France. He crossed the Somme at Ancre and Bray, and marched on towards Paris. Although heavily dependent upon the experienced Flemish commander, Floris van Buren, Suffolk proved himself to be a competent and decisive commander, paying due attention to his Council of War, but making critical decisions himself.[19] Unfortunately, the Duke of Bourbon turned out to be useless. When Suffolk reached the Somme, his friends were nowhere to be seen, and the Emperor had proved unable without his backing to prevent Francis from reinforcing Paris in depth. Faced with this prospect, and increasingly bogged down by exceptionally wet weather, after taking the town of Montidier Suffolk and van Buren decided to retreat. At first this was conducted in good order, but an exceptionally severe frost in early November turned this orderly retreat into something resembling a rout. 'Many a soldier died for cold, some lost fingers and some toes, but many lost the nails of their hands, which was to them a great grief …'[20]

The horses suffered similarly, and morale, already adversely affected by disease, slumped to a disastrous level. When they got close to the Pale, van Buren disbanded his force, and left the Duke to extricate himself as best he could. Thus it came about that Henry's decision to maintain Suffolk's army in winter quarters for a new campaign in the spring, was met by the news that the army no longer existed. Of the 10,000 men who had landed so hopefully at the end of August, by the end of November less than half remained, and their resolve and their discipline had alike disintegrated. When it became obvious that Margaret's support was no longer to be counted upon, Suffolk refused to deploy his remaining forces into garrisons for her defence, and instead disbanded them.[21] They returned to England in dribs and drabs, as shipping became available.

Henry swallowed this disappointment with a surprisingly good grace, choosing (not unreasonably) to blame the Duke of Bourbon and the circumstances rather than the Duke of Suffolk for the failure. Politically, however, the impact was considerable. Gone was the expansive rhetoric of the autumn, and a cautious ambivalence returned in its place. Charles and Margaret continued unabashed to press for a further English effort, but Wolsey and Henry were determined only to respond when they became convinced that the Duke of Bourbon was a player with anything other than words. A new campaign was not ruled out, and in April the council even decided to advocate a further expedition on the lines of the previous year. Troops were raised; 9,000 English infantry and 1,500 horse were projected, to join with 3,000 German horse and a further contingent to be led by van Buren. The latter offered sensible advice, and Suffolk was named as the overall commander in August.[22] But nothing happened. Wolsey was unconvinced by the Duke of Bourbon, and it was decided that no more money was to be expended on German mercenaries. Suffolk remained enthusiastic, and even sent Sir Richard Jerningham to the Low Countries to begin the necessary organisation, but the critical commitment was never made. The only thing which the events of 1524 prove conclusively is that Suffolk's reputation, both political and military, had suffered not at all from the humiliation of 1523. He was still the King's first choice for any serious enterprise.

While Suffolk was occupied in France in October and November 1523, the Duke of Albany resumed his efforts to create a second front. Evading the English navy, he had returned to Scotland by the western route in September 1523, bringing with him some 5,000 French troops, and 'the traytor Richard De La Pole'.[23] The presence of the latter made his purpose clear, and within a few weeks the summons had been sent out to the Scottish Lords, who duly assembled 'with vitaille, gunnes and all other artillery ...' on 17 October to 'go upon' the English. They advanced to the border at Coldstream, and the Duke sent a formal challenge in due form to his opposite number the Earl of Surrey, who was by then encamped at Alnwick. Surrey replied in a similar vein, but nothing happened until 30 October, when the Scots crossed the border and laid siege to Wark Castle. Rather to their surprise, the castle was vigorously defended, and when Surrey advanced to its relief, on 2 November they backed off.[24] They may have been outnumbered, but that seems unlikely, and the true explanation for this retreat probably again lies in divided councils. Albany may have been keen to try conclusions with the Earl of Surrey, but the Scots were only too conscious of what had happened when James IV had done a similar thing ten years earlier. They were quite happy to carry out the traditional border raids, but anything more sustained, let alone any furthering of the ambitions of the White Rose, was not part of their agenda. Seizing her opportunity, Queen Margaret proposed a truce between the kingdoms, and this, with which Albany had no choice but to concur, settled the affairs for the time being.[25] The Earl of Surrey returned to the south, and Richard de la Pole went back to France. French influence remained predominant in the northern kingdom, but its limitations had been exposed. Border raiding continued in spite of the truce, but the main consequence for Henry was that the bill for keeping Surrey and his forces on standby in the north added significantly to his financial difficulties. At the beginning of 1524, English strategic thinking seems to have been going on at a number of different levels. The King, naturally belligerent, was still talking of 'winning his ancient rights' in France, and of the importance of recruiting the support of the new Pope, Clement VII, but his council, and particularly Wolsey, were doing their sums and realising that they did not add up.[26] Although the subsidy was due to be paid soon, that was already spoken for, and in any case would be insufficient to support the kind of war which Henry was threatening. By the spring, official spokesmen were declaring that although (of course) the King was willing to launch a new offensive, he would only do so once Charles and Bourbon were already in the field, and until then, no more money would be forthcoming.[27] The ambiguities of English policy in the first half of 1524 therefore reflect Henry's own uncertainties. It was not so much a question of being restrained by his councillors as being aware of the force of their arguments. Consequently, when Clement VII sent agents to all the belligerent powers urging a settlement, his initiative was well received, as was a representative of the Queen Mother of France who came secretly to discuss possible terms. On the other hand, the King was still publicly urging Clement to join the alliance against France, and sent Richard Pace to the Duke of Bourbon to discuss new terms for an alliance.[28]

Pace was enthusiastic, and by the early summer was writing to Wolsey, urging him to commit men and money to the Duke's cause. By the end of July, Bourbon was in Provence, and preparing to besiege Marsellies. Never, wrote Pace, would such a golden opportunity recur. The Cardinal was unimpressed. Bourbon would be more convincing if he turned his guns against Lyons, and at least pretended that he was conquering part of France in the King's interest instead of confining himself to his own lands. Moreover, his demands for money were exorbitant.[29] What he did not say was that the secret talks with France in London and Calais were making good progress. Henry appeared briefly to be more persuaded by Bourbon, but even he made intervention conditional upon an attack on Lyons. Moreover, neither he nor the Emperor were in any position to move quickly to the Duke's assistance, whatever they might pretend. This was just as well because Bourbon's campaign against Marseilles collapsed as quickly as it had been mounted, and his defeated army retreated precipitately into Italy. Although he talked of a new campaign in 1525, it was fairly obvious that his role as an Imperial ally had come to an end. Wolsey was relieved that his caution had been thus justified, and tried to shift Henry off his preoccupation with securing the Crown of France. The abandonment of such a claim would be essential for any settlement between the kingdoms, but for the time being Henry was not to be budged.[30]

Meanwhile, Francis had moved back into Italy to secure his position in Milan, and there near Pavia on 14 February 1525, he suffered a shattering defeat. His army was destroyed and the King himself captured. Henry received the news on 9 March, and fell into a rapture of joy and thanksgiving. Not only had his arch-rival endured a crashing fall, but the Earl of Suffolk – the White Rose – had died on the field of battle.[31] The King's ambitions, dormant since the previous summer, were now thoroughly reawakened. Now was the time for the Great Enterprise to go ahead. The Emperor and the King of England should jointly invade the stricken kingdom, and help themselves to its territories; even the useless Duke of Bourbon could be accommodated. On 11 March:

> ... in the Citie of London for these tydinges were made great fiers and triumph, and the Mayor and Aldermen road about the citie with trumpettes, and much wine was layed in divers places of the citie, that every man might drinke.[32]

More thoughtful heads were less sure, anticipating the financial demands which such a rekindling of ambition would provoke, but for the time being the bonfires blazed and Wolsey sang a solemn high mass at St Paul's. Orders went out for the mobilisation of troops, and envoys were despatched to the Low Countries to organise hoys, horses and wagons to transport the anticipated host and its guns. The council saw the implications of these actions at once. The King was determined to grasp this opportunity in person, and 'remembryng that it was determined that the kyng in proper persone should passe the sea, they considered that above all thynges great threasure and plenty of money must nedes be had in a readiness'. Consequently as early as 21 March commissioners were appointed to raise another levy, optimistically called an Amicable Grant.[33] This was never intended to be a loan, and was not so described, but was to be a contribution based on the assessments made in 1522. Through April and May the commissioners laboured, using a sliding scale. Those assessed at £50 and over were to pay 3s 4d in the pound, and so on down to those valued at between £1 and £20 who were to pay 1s. Their work was bitterly resented, and 'the burden was so grievous that it was denied, and the commons in every place were so moved that it was like to have grown into a rebellion ...'[34]

London, Kent and East Anglia proved particularly recalcitrant, and Wolsey was persuaded that he would have to modify his demands. By the end of April the King had cancelled the 3s 4d levy, replacing it with a request for a benevolence, that is a grant the size of which is up to each particular donor. This change took the form of a letter from Henry to Wolsey, acknowledging the difficulty which men were finding in paying on the assessment, and authorising changes which appear to have varied from county to county.[35] The result was confusion, as some communities felt that they were being dealt with more severely that others. On 12 May Archbishop Warham was instructed to defer the clergy assessments until the laity's was completed, and the commissioners were advised to 'practice' with six or seven leading men from each community in the hope of making progress. Eventually, about the middle of May, the assessment was abandoned, because it was judged that the ill will being generated more than outweighed any money which might be raised.[36] The taxpayers strike had been successful, and as far as we know not a penny of the Amicable Grant was ever paid. Wolsey had been the main moving force behind the demand, and quite rightly took the blame for its failure, but the pretence that the King knew nothing about it was disingenuous. Henry not only knew, he was actively involved right up to the moment when it was decided to abandon the demand – a decision which only he could have taken. The ramifications of this failure were extensive. Not only was the King unable to wage war without money, but it is fairly clear that his trust in his Chancellor's judgement was shaken. This was not immediately apparent, but less than two years later he decided to negotiate with Rome behind the Cardinal's back, a strategy which would have been unthinkable before the Amicable Grant fiasco. Given his powers of self-persuasion, it is quite possible that Henry really believed that he had been misled over that demand, and the old relationship of trust was never fully restored.

Meanwhile an embassy had been sent to Charles in Spain to discuss the best way to exploit the opportunity which Pavia had created. The instructions are full of high-flown rhetoric. God had punished the insatiable ambition of the King of France, and the time had now come to 'remove and utterly extinct' his whole line and succession in the interest of the legitimate heir – Henry of England. Let them jointly march on Paris, where Henry can be crowned. Charles will receive Provence, Languedoc and Burgundy; Bourbon can recover his patrimony, and the King of England will take the rest! The Emperor is also to be reminded that if he honours his undertaking to marry Mary, he may also add England and Ireland to his many titles.[37] Henry did not expect Charles to take all this at face value; it represented a bargaining position, which could be scaled down in response to the Emperor's reaction. Ultimately Henry would settle for Normandy or Picardy, plus Boulogne and a few other towns. The King realised well enough that his bargaining position was not strong. Since Suffolk's incursion in the autumn of 1523 he had contributed only words, and some money, to the joint cause. Now he was expecting to ride in triumph on a victory which belonged to another, and the advantages of which were more equivocal than they looked. The Emperor's response was disappointing, if predictable. He had no time for Henry's high-flying ambitions; if the King of England wanted to conquer France, then let him do it for himself. He was penniless, and his intention did not extend beyond extracting a favourable treaty from his prisoner. Mary's inheritance might be tempting, but it was not assured, and the child was still only nine years old. Although he had not admitted it as yet, he was already negotiating for the hand of a Portuguese princess of a more suitable age, with whom he might reasonably expect to get an heir. In fact his attitude to his ostensible ally was chilly if not actually hostile.[38] For this Wolsey was partly at least to blame. Although he had dutifully followed his master's lead, he had always been sceptical about the grand alliance, and, since day-by-day diplomatic exchanges were always left to him, he had been gratuitously offensive to the Imperial ambassador.[39] This may have been intended to cool the King's ardour, and it certainly cooled the relationship. Charles would have nothing to do with Henry's inflated ambitions, even in their scaled-down version. He intended to make his own settlement with Francis, in which it was highly unlikely that England would feature at all.

By the time that news of this rebuff reached London, the Amicable Grant had collapsed, and it was clear that there would be no great enterprise. The alliance was effectively dead, and Henry was mortified. However, this left the hitherto-secret negotiations with France as the only viable option. French envoys had actually been on the point of seeing the King when the news of Pavia sent them scuttling home. Three months later, the whole political landscape had changed. Not only peace, but an Anglo-French entente was now on the agenda, and John Joachim, hitherto the Queen Mother's confidential agent, returned to London on 22 June on a mission of public reconciliation.[40] France, without its king (still imprisoned in Madrid), and in need of all the diplomatic backing it could get, proved amenable, although she would concede no territory, and on 30 August a treaty was signed at the More, Wolsey's residence in Hertfordshire, which brought an end to three years of intermittent and often confused warfare.[41] Charles had been anticipated, and he was not pleased, but at least he felt that Henry's action had absolved him from his 1521 commitment to Mary. He married the Infanta Isabella of Portugal in the following year, and Henry was free to express his outrage at having been so rejected and humiliated. In the autumn of 1525 there was a party on the Council which was in favour of disengagement on the grounds that England could no longer afford a proactive foreign policy. However, this did not represent either Wolsey's position or the King's, both of whom were committed, although for different reasons, to playing the role of arbiter in the high politics of Europe. At this stage Henry was still toying with the idea of persisting in his overtures to the Emperor in the forlorn hope of resurrecting the great enterprise.[42] Had he received a flicker of a response, he would have been prepared to ditch the treaty of the More and return to the policies of the alliance. However, no such flicker came, and that gave Wolsey his opportunity. He had built up a considerable portfolio of grievances against the Emperor, who also owed the King an enormous sum of money. These he worked on to convert Henry from his hankering after an Imperial alliance. It made no sense, he argued, and was not conducive to the peace of Europe, to be in alliance with so overwhelming a partner as the Emperor had now become. Much better to ally with France, and with that cluster of Italian states surrounding the Pope to impose some kind of curbs upon Imperial ambition. By the time that Francis was freed from his Spanish prison in January 1526, his scheme was bearing fruit.[43]

By that time, too, Henry's matrimonial link with Charles was in serious difficulties. The trouble was that Catherine had borne him no son. She was in most respects an exemplary consort, faithful, loving and pious, but her repeated pregnancies had resulted in only one daughter, a pretty precocious child now aged nine, but no substitute for a boy. Mary had played her part in her father's international diplomacy, as the affianced bride of the Emperor, but that role was now over. Catherine might have been an intercessor in easing the pain of that breakdown, and indeed Charles seems to have assumed that she would, but the letter announcing his intention in the summer of 1525 was mishandled by the ambassador in London, and the Queen was not consulted.[44] The King was merely informed of the fait accompli, which he interpreted as an unfriendly gesture, and vented some of his resentment on his wife. Bessie Blount's son, Henry Fitzroy, was now aged six, and had been reared in comfortable but decent obscurity by agents of the Cardinal. On 18 June he was knighted, and created in turn Earl of Nottingham and Duke of Richmond and Somerset. Shortly after he was named as Lord Admiral and Lieutenant in the North Parts. It looked as though he was being groomed for the succession, and Catherine was loud in her protests at what seemed to be an infringement of her daughter's rights.[45] In fact it does not seem that Henry had any such intention, and his purpose (apart from annoying his wife) was rather to give substance to one of Wolsey's schemes for the improvement of central government. By bestowing these high offices upon a royal child (albeit a bastard) he could ensure that the actual work was done by deputies, who would be loyal servants of his own. At the same time the child would symbolise the King's personal involvement, and give dignity and status to the deputies. The Duke's Council in the North would be in effect a royal council, directly controlled from the centre.[46] Similar thinking inspired the almost simultaneous despatch of Mary to Ludlow, to act as a 'front' for the re-established Council in the Marches. Significantly, Mary was not created Princess of Wales, but was treated as though she were, and was given a suitably dignified household. Catherine again was grieved at losing the daily contact with her daughter which had been such a feature of the child's upbringing, but consoled by the fact that her old friend Margeret Pole, the Countess of Salisbury, who had been out of favour because of her alleged association with the Duke of Buckingham, was now restored and given the responsible position of Lady Governess.[47]

However, none of this addressed the issue of the succession. Catherine was now forty-one, in indifferent health, and would clearly bear no more children. The royal couple still appeared in public together from time to time, and even shared some of the intimacies of their earlier days, but these moments had become rare. For the most part the Queen lived alone, and consoled herself with piety and with works of charity. Henry kept his court elsewhere, and reserved his embraces for his new mistress, Mary Boleyn. Mary's tenure of the royal bed is something of a mystery, and might have gone unnoticed if the King himself had not confessed it some years later. The most plausible scenario is that she succeeded Bessie Blount late in 1519 or early in 1520, and that her marriage to William Carey, which probably took place in the latter year, was designed to cover or conceal that relationship.[48] William began to receive royal grants in 1522, and their first child was born in March 1526. Some thought at the time that Henry Carey was the King's son, but that is almost certainly wrong. Having made such a fuss of his first acknowledged bastard, there would have been no reason for the King not to have recognised a second. The child was almost certainly conceived as soon as Mary began to sleep with her husband, which his date of birth confirms to have taken place not later than the summer of 1525.[49] Mary's failure to bear the King a child may be ascribed to some contraceptive knowledge (which she would have concealed from her partner), but more plausibly to Henry's erratic fertility. She was no help when it came to resolving the succession issue. Just when the King gave up sleeping with his wife we do not know, but it was probably some time between 1522 and 1524. By 1525 their sexual relationship was over, and Henry had to decide what to do.

He could seek to have Henry Fitzroy legitimated, but the obvious way to achieve that, by the subsequent marriage of the parties concerned, was no longer an option, and probably would not have been contemplated anyway. Any other route would involve a special dispensation, which was always open to challenge, and would certainly have been challenged in a case such as this. In spite of conferring the royal title of Richmond on the child, and in spite of rumours emanating from the circle around the Queen, there is no evidence that the King ever contemplated taking such a course. The second alternative was simply to accept the situation as it was, and to prepare Mary to become queen. This was obviously the solution favoured by Catherine, but it had a number of drawbacks. England had never had a ruling queen, and the nature of her authority was open to question. She would marry, and her husband would become king, but his rights over the realm were indeterminate.[50] If he were an English nobleman, that would be a disparagement, and would open the door to all manner of factional strife. If he were a foreign prince, it might result in England being drawn into some continental empire, and thus losing its independence. The main consolation when Charles repudiated his agreement to marry her was that the possibility of a Habsburg takeover disappeared. The best way out of this dilemma would be to marry her early, and to trust to God that she would bear a son who would grow to adulthood in his grandfather's lifetime – in other words to bypass her – but the drawback with that was that Mary was physically a slow developer. Even if she had been married immediately, their was no prospect of her bearing children for at least another six or seven years, and, given her mother's problems, even that was by no means certain.[51] There was, however, a third alternative, and that was repudiate Catherine and start again. By 1525 this was beginning to look appealing, as her physical attractiveness faded and her health and spirits declined. She was also bitterly hostile to Wolsey, and blamed his pro-French policies for the breakdown in relations with her nephew the Emperor. In other words she was becoming a personal and political liability. Divorce was out of the question, because the Queen had given no grounds, and Henry's infidelities were irrelevant, so it became a question of annulment. The King was genuinely troubled as to why Catherine had failed to bear him any son who had survived infancy. It was conventional wisdom that women were always responsible for such misfortunes, but this was clearly a judgement upon him, and he had (obviously) done nothing wrong. So he began to rethink the circumstances of his marriage, and immediately hit on a possible explanation. He knew perfectly well that there had been doubts from the first on the grounds of consanguinity, because Catherine had been married to his brother, Arthur, and a papal dispensation had been required for the marriage to go ahead.[52] Suppose, however, that the prohibition rested on something stronger than the law of the Church? There was, in the Book of Leviticus, a verse which prohibited a man from taking his brother's wife. This surely constituted a law of God, which no pope had the power to dispense. The idea worked its way into Henry's mind, and became a conviction. The fact that the Levitical text did not exactly match his circumstances and that there was a similar passage in Deuteronomy which appeared to contradict it were set aside. The penalty decreed by Leviticus for the offending couple was that they should be childless, but Catherine had borne Mary, whose only offence was to be of the wrong gender.[53] By 1525 Henry, who had remarkable gifts of self-persuasion, was convinced that his marriage had offended against a law of God and that the papal dispensation which had authorised it was invalid. In spite of sixteen years of cohabitation, and all the extravagances of devotion which he had once displayed, Catherine had never been truly his wife.

The chronology of this advancing conviction is uncertain. We can be reasonably sure that it was in place by the summer of 1526, but it is not in the nature of such a development to be sudden, and it was probably germinating as early as 1524. Wolsey knew of it by the end of 1525, and realised the difficulties which it might involve. He may well have been thinking of a French replacement before Francis was released in January 1526, because that would have been the best way to attract the French support in Rome which would clearly be necessary to secure an annulment. We cannot be sure, but what is reasonably certain is that Anne Boleyn had nothing to do with it at this stage. Even the most optimistic assessment of her relationship with the King does not register anything before the summer of 1525, and that is circumstantial, based on the evidence for the ending of Henry's involvement with her sister. The King's active pursuit of Anne cannot be dated before Shrovetide 1526, by which time she had been a courtier for about four years.[54] Anne was the younger of the two siblings, and much the more talented. She was the daughter of Sir Thomas and of Elizabeth, daughter of the Duke of Norfolk, so she was in a sense a member of the Howard clientage. Nevertheless, her first big break was organised by her father, who used his diplomatic contacts with the Low Countries to place her in 1513 in the court of Margaret of Austria at Mechlin. This was something of a coup, because such places were eagerly sought after and competed for, but Margaret was given no cause to regret her indulgence.[55] Anne was an intelligent girl of about twelve, and a gifted linguist who made an immediate impression in that cosmopolitan environment. So much so, that the Archduchess was sorry to lose her when, after about a year, she was transferred to the service of Mary, the new Queen of France, whom she joined in October 1514. There she also joined her sister, but the fortunes of the two girls were soon to diverge. When the Queen was widowed after a few weeks, Mary Boleyn returned with the new Duchess of Suffolk in May 1515, but Anne stayed on in France, joining the household of Francis I's consort, Queen Claude, who was a girl not much older than herself.[56] She was already proficient in French, and probably skilled on various musical instruments; however, Mechlin would not have given her much opportunity to learn the subtle arts of flirtation, which were essential for survival at the court of Francis I. If a girl wished to protect her honour, she had to know how to go about it graciously, and this was an art in which Anne became highly proficient. In 1522, with war looming between the realms, Sir Thomas retrieved his daughter, and so arranged it that she was able to rejoin her sister in the service of Queen Catherine. For the time being it was Mary who caught the King's attention, but it was Anne who was the star, her French education immediately making itself apparent. A few years later one commentator reminisced that it was difficult to believe at this stage that she was not French – and that was intended as a compliment![57]

It was the objective of every courtier to see his daughters well married, and Sir Thomas Boleyn had two girls to make arrangements for. Mary's liaison with the King was a help rather than a hindrance in that connection, and it was quite probably Wolsey rather than Sir Thomas who arranged her match with William Carey, a young and promising member of the Privy Chamber for whom Henry had a warm regard. Anne was more problematic, because she had a feisty independent streak in her which was quite lacking in her elder sister, and which may well have turned off some otherwise eligible suitors.[58] It may well have been to curb that streak that Sir Thomas planned to use her in a dynastic manoeuvre to secure control of the lands of the Irish Earldom of Ormonde. He was the heir general, through his mother, to that inheritance, which was actually in the possession of Piers Butler, who styled himself Earl of Ormonde but was not so recognised at the English Court. Piers was indeed the heir male, but was a fairly remote cousin of the last undisputed earl, who had died in 1515.[59] The plan was to unite the two lines by marrying Piers' son, Thomas, to Anne. This, it was calculated, would reconcile Piers to the King, and guarantee an undisputed succession to their children. Wolsey was an enthusiastic promoter of this scheme, and may even have been its originator, given that his grasp of the Irish situation was much superior to Sir Thomas'. Anne, however, was not keen on marrying a man she did not know, and the negotiations straggled on for several years until Piers Butler finally lost patience. While this was going on, she made a conquest, probably in 1523 or 1524. Henry Percy, the twenty-one-year-old son of the Earl of Northumberland, was living in Wolsey's household at the time, and became 'much enamoured' of her. Unfortunately, the younger Percy was already contracted to Mary Talbot, the daughter of the Earl of Shrewsbury, an arrangement which Wolsey was particularly keen to promote.[60] Anne seems to have been equally attracted and the young people came to some sort of an understanding which fell short of a consummated relationship, but was more binding that mutual interest. At that point the Cardinal got wind of what was going on, and moved decisively to separate them, calling in the Earl to admonish his son in no uncertain terms. Sir Thomas' attitude to these developments in not known, but given that he was still pursing the Ormonde negotiation at that stage, he was probably relieved by Wolsey's action. Anne was understandably frustrated, and it was later alleged that her subsequent antipathy to the Cardinal dated from this episode. The Talbot/Percy marriage duly took place, and was an absolute personal disaster, but that was no consolation to Anne.

Perhaps because of the Ormonde complication, ordinary suitors do not seem to have been queuing at Anne's door. She is alleged to have had a romantic attachment to the poet Sir Thomas Wyatt during these years, but the evidence for that is late, and hostile.[61] The two had known each other from childhood, since they came from neighbouring gentry families in Kent, and it is only too likely that their friendship was resumed when she returned from France in 1522. He was estranged from his wife, and may well have sought consolation in her companionship. It would have been difficult for them not to have been thrown together in the intimate atmosphere of the court, but there is no contemporary suggestion of anything more in their relationship. The story that the King and Wyatt clashed over her, and that the latter tried to warn Henry that the lady of his choice had had many lovers, comes from

Nicholas Sander and dates from the later sixteenth century, when her controversial role in the events of the next decade was already history. What is clear from contemporary descriptions is that Anne was no conventional beauty, inferior in that respect to Bessie Blount, but that she knew how to make the best of herself, particularly of her attractive eyes and magnificent mane of dark hair.[62] She was also, thanks to her French experience, an accomplished flirt, and it may well have been that aspect of her personality which first caught the King's eye. Henry was thoroughly accustomed to playing Courtly Love with the ladies of his wife's Privy Chamber, but as soon as he made a pass at Anne, he realised that she was something different. It may well have been that these initial passes went back to 1525 – or even before – and it is entirely likely that just as Henry was coming to the conclusion that he would have to end his marriage, he found himself caught by this mysterious damsel. About the end of 1525 Anne was coming to the conclusion that she had hooked the big fish, and would have to think very carefully about how to exploit the advantage which that gave her. The trouble with assessing Anne at this juncture is that so much depends on hindsight. For example, the story that she had six fingers on one hand comes from Sander, and depends for its plausibility on the fact that at the time of her fall in 1536, she was accused of witchcraft. The extra finger was the hallmark of the witch. There is no suggestion that anyone at the time noticed any abnormality.[63] Contemporaries were clear that she was an elegant, striking-looking young woman, gifted in music and in dancing, and that she knew how to manage men. This last quality caused doubts to be cast on her claims to virginity, but they also came later, when she was enmeshed in controversy. She was also naturally pro-French in her politics, and the beginning of 1526 was a good time to have such an orientation. Henry did not live his life in separate compartments, and it may well have been that at this stage Wolsey was also inclined to look indulgently on the King's new favourite. The time had not yet come when she was to be a serious rival to him.

The court reflected the ambiguities of Henry's foreign policy during these years, as various missions were ceremoniously received, or unceremoniously brushed under the carpet. For those in favour banquets and jousting were the order of the day, and never more so than during the Emperor's visit in 1522, when 'the king ran at the Duke of Suffolk six or seven courses, and at every course brake a spear'.[64] Charles' reaction is not recorded. Henry still regularly jousted at those 'feats of arms' which marked the seasons of the year, an occupation which was a constant source of anxiety to his councillors, and Suffolk was his regular opponent until an event occurred in 1524 which effectively put an end to this partnership. On 10 March the King 'having a new harnese made of his own devise and fashion, such as no Armourer before that time had seen ...' decided to try it out, and devised a joust for that purpose. By some mischance, and perhaps because of the novel design, he did not close his headpiece properly, and the Duke's spear actually struck the inside of his helmet, filling it with splinters, none of which mercifully caused any injury.[65] There were immediate recriminations. Some blamed the armourers, and some the Marquis of Dorset for allowing the King to go into the lists with his face uncovered, but Henry (rightly) insisted that the blame was his alone, because he had hoped that the new headpiece would have given him better vision than turned out to be the case. The Duke of Suffolk was horrified at the thought of the damage which he might have inflicted, and then and there vowed that he would never run against the King again, an oath which he appears to have kept.[66] He was in any case forty years of age, and his athletic career was coming to an end. He did joust again, but Henry never found a partner of comparable excellence among the younger members of the court, and Suffolk's oath may well have hastened his own decision to quit the sport, which appears to have come about three years later. In March 1524 he made light of the whole incident, and taking his spear ran six additional courses in order to demonstrate that he had taken no hurt 'to the great joy and comfort of all his subjects there present'. Time, however, was beginning to catch up with him. Not only was he no longer the youthful athlete of ten years earlier, he was no longer rich, and no longer the hopeful family man that he had been then either. Between his own military expenditure and subsidies to Maximilian, his first war had cost almost a million pounds, and far outrun the treasure which his father had left him. Tournai cost £40,000 a year to run, until Wolsey persuaded him to relinquish it in 1518. Even during peacetime the expenditure of the Chamber was running at some £70,000 a year, and further subsidies to Maximilian and to Charles absorbed another £80,000 in 1515 and 1516, when war was being discussed but not waged.[67] Repeated grants of fifteenths and tenths, and subsidies which should have yielded £270,000 were passed by Parliament in 1514 and 1515, but these were imperfectly collected and came nowhere near bridging the gap. Consequently, as we have seen, the war of 1522 was launched against the stark background of empty coffers. Somehow, by a mixture of forced loans and subsidies the bills were paid, but two subsidies to the Duke of Bourbon of 100,000 crowns each in 1523 and 1524 had to be funded by commercial borrowing. By 1525 the reality had to be faced. Henry could not afford to make war unless or until a more satisfactory system of raising and collecting taxes could be devised. Even the ordinary revenue account was running at a deficit by then, and the future was bleak. Wolsey's philosophy was that the money was there, and means had to be devised of getting at it, but as his experience with the 1523 Parliament showed, that was easier said than done. As he faced the new year of 1526, Henry was effectively bankrupt.

The marriage also, which had seemed so full of hope and delight in 1509, had run its course. Catherine was past the menopause, and the King had no legitimate son. Doubt had turned to recriminations and then to hostility. But Henry was, in many respects, the man he had always been, full of self-conceit and determined to get his own way. His ego had been bruised in different ways by Ferdinand and by Maximilian, who had cheated him, by Francis I, who had beaten him at his own game, and by Charles, who had outmanoeuvred him, but still in 1525 he could see himself as the arbiter of Europe. He needed a new wife, and that required work in Rome, but he had a Cardinal Legate as his Chancellor, and that would surely guarantee success. Wolsey was a good servant, who did not mince his words, but who ultimately knew who was the master. He had done sterling work in raising the King's power and honour, both within the realm and in Europe. Now he was to face a new challenge. Henry could not have envisaged the traumas that the next six or seven years would bring him and his realm, but one thing was clear in his mind. God was on his side, and whatever he might decide to do would carry the stamp of Divine approval.

7

THE ORIGIN OF THE 'GREAT MATTER',
1525–1529

The chronology of Henry's relationship with Anne Boleyn is notoriously hard to reconstruct, because it seems to have been a passion which grew out of a courtly love dalliance of a fairly conventional kind. The Shrovetide jousts in February 1526, when he appeared displaying the device of a heart in flames, and the motto 'Declare I dare not' could be an example of either. His brush with Sir Thomas Wyatt, who had also been dallying with Anne, if it ever occurred at all, belongs to the courtly love context, and may well have come at the same time, or even earlier.[1] Henry's first surviving letter, which has been dated to the autumn of 1526, accompanied the present of a buck, and chides her gently for not having answered a previous epistle. It ends 'Thanking you heartily for that it pleaseth you still to hold me in some remembrance', which is surely the language of the gallant rather than of the passionate lover. At some point late in 1526 or early in 1527, Henry appears to have proposed that she become his mistress, but she treated this as another move in the courtly game, and sent him teasingly equivocal signals. Her response, as he pointed out in a subsequent letter, left him confused. He had been, he declared, 'kept ... for some little time from calling you my mistress, since if you do not love me in a way which is beyond common affection, that name in no wise belongs to you ...'[2] It may have been reluctance on her part, or it may have been the consideration that

191

another bastard would not be of much use to him, which caused the King to up the stakes at some time before May 1527. He began to talk of marriage, and that was an altogether different proposition. After about a year, his 'scruple of conscience' and his desire for Anne Boleyn came together. When he had secured the annulment of his existing marriage, they would wed, and he was not thinking in the long term. Within a few months at most, he would be free. How long it took Anne to accept this proposal is not known; it may have been a few days, it may have been several months. What we do know is that by August 1527, she was regarding herself as the queen in waiting, and she was also not prepared for a long delay.[3]

Meanwhile, the King had started legal proceedings. In May 1527 Wolsey, acting in his capacity as papal legate, set up a secret tribunal in his residence at Westminster, and cited the King to appear to answer the charge of having for eighteen years unlawfully cohabited with the widow of his brother. Archbishop Warham was the assessor, and the King appeared briefly, just to confirm the facts of the situation. Sessions were held on the 17th, 20th and 23rd of the month, and in those sessions Richard Wolman, the King's counsel, built up his case against the bull of Julius II, by authority of which the marriage had taken place.[4] Catherine was not informed, and the proceedings have rightly been described as 'a conspiracy'. Whether Wolsey was gambling on being able to resolve the issue using his own authority, or whether he was assuming that a fait accompli would be accepted in Rome, we do not know.[5] Whatever assumption he may have been making, it was destroyed by events in Italy, because on 1 June the news arrived that the City of Rome had been sacked by an Imperial army, and that the Pope was a prisoner in the castle of San Angelo. These horrifying events had occurred about three weeks previously, and lost nothing in the telling by eyewitnesses. An unpaid and unfed army under the notional but ineffective command of the Duke of Bourbon, had burst into the Imperial City, overcoming some determined but sporadic resistance, and had then gone on a rampage. They had desecrated churches, and looted private homes, torturing and murdering the citizens. Clement, whose main force had been disbanded some weeks earlier, had been quite unable to check this onslaught, and was now under siege.[6]

In one sense this news was a disaster for Henry, because it meant that the Pope was no longer a free agent, and (even if he had been disposed to do so) would be unable to confirm any judgement of nullity which Wolsey's court might reach. The Legatine tribunal was abandoned. On the other hand, as Wolsey was quick to perceive, it presented a golden opportunity. With the Pope out of action, steps would have to be taken for the government of the Church in the immediate future. What better solution than that the Cardinal of England, who had twice almost been elected to St Peter's chair, should be authorised to exercise authority on his behalf, backed by the 'free' cardinals assembled at Avignon?[7] Not only would this appeal to his vanity, it would also enable him to pronounce in the King's favour on the delicate issue of his marriage. On 12 July Wolsey set off for France as the King's plenipotentiary, with a draft authorisation in his pocket and an agenda which included a marriage negotiation for Henry with a French princess. He was well aware of Anne Boleyn's existence, but not aware that the King had proposed marriage to her, nor of any response which she might have made. As far as he was concerned, Henry was a free agent.[8] It was, however, essential that the Emperor be kept in ignorance of his intention. Charles was not particularly close to his aunt, but her repudiation would be a slur upon his family honour, and one which he would probably do his best to prevent. Given the situation in Italy, he was in an excellent position to do that, and might well succeed in derailing Wolsey's entire programme. So it was important that Catherine should not find out what was going on. Henry, however, was in a state of high emotional tension, and not disposed to make calculations. He may also have had a guilty conscience about the collusive suit in which he had been engaged, because on 22 June he confronted Catherine with the news that they had never been truly married, and that they had been living in fornication.[9] She exploded in tears and in furious denial – everyone knew that God had approved their marriage in answer to her prayers – how dare he question it after all these years! Henry retreated in confusion, but the damage had been done. It now became essential for Catherine to inform her nephew of what was afoot, and equally important, as the King now realised, to prevent that information from getting through. Not realising that Henry understood the reason for her action, she prompted one of her servants, Fernando Felipez, to ask the King for leave to return to Spain. Knowing the nature of his mission, the King dissimulated, granting him a safe conduct but arranging that he should be arrested as he passed through France. As was explained to an anxious Wolsey, Felipez was to be 'let impeached and detained in some quarter of France' without Henry knowing anything about it.[10] Catherine's messenger, however, appears to have travelled by sea, and about the end of July, within a few days of Wolsey's departure on his hopeful mission, reached Valladolid safely and told Charles the whole story.

The Emperor reacted very much as expected. He wrote to Catherine pledging his full support, and to Henry, begging him to desist. More importantly, he also wrote to the Pope, urging him to cancel Wolsey's legateship and, if Henry should persist, revoke the case to Rome. Clement was in no position to resist such pressure, and as soon as he got wind of Wolsey's proposed alternative government, took steps to scotch that plan as well.[11] It later transpired that if Henry had been able to offer prompt diplomatic support immediately after the sack, and more important speedy financial relief, he might have won his case, but the opportunity slipped by, and by the time that Charles' letter reached him, Clement had decided that his best course lay in humouring the dominant power. He absolutely forbade any of the cardinals remaining in Rome (the majority) from travelling to Wolsey's alternative conclave in Avignon, with the result that only four turned up to back his plan and it had to be abandoned. The Cardinal's great schemes, which had included a new effort for a European peace, were in tatters by the end of August, and worse still, he had evidence that Henry was listening to other advisers behind his back. The King, he was told, 'passeth the time in hunting ... he suppeth in his Privy Chamber ... there suppeth with him the Dukes of Norfolk and Suffolk, the Marquis of Exeter and the

Lord of Rochford'. Rochford was Anne Boleyn's father, and these were just the councillors which Wolsey had most cause to fear.[12] Proof of this alternative programme was not long in coming. Probably before the end of August the King had decided to send his secretary William Knights, direct to Rome bearing a draft brief permitting him, in effect, to commit bigamy. Wolsey found out about this ill-advised venture and intercepted Knight at Compiègne, meanwhile persuading Henry to abandon it. Before he could catch his breath, however, Knight received fresh instructions from London that he was to proceed to Rome anyway. This, as the Cardinal had not discovered, was because the secretary was also carrying a second brief, presumably to be proffered if the first was ill-received. This authorised the King to marry any woman he chose, even if she were related to him in the fourth degree of affinity, provided that his first marriage had been annulled.[13] As such it was a revealing document, because Anne was related to Henry in just that degree through the illicit coitus between him and her sister, but it was also useless because of its proviso. Knight's mission duly proceeded, but met with not the slightest success, as might have been anticipated. The real significance of these events lay not in Rome, but closer to home. Wolsey was no longer in the King's full confidence, and Anne had succeeded in intruding herself between Henry and his chancellor. At the end of September, when he returned to England, the Cardinal found the King closeted with his mistress, and was forced to wait upon the latter's convenience.[14]

Meanwhile the fighting in northern Italy continued, bloody and confused, but with the Imperialists generally retaining the upper hand. The Duke of Bourbon was killed, but some measure of discipline was restored to the forces which he had led, and an Anglo-French peace mission to Spain in the middle of 1527 was repulsed.[15] The League of Cognac was making no progress at all, and the French princes remained in custody in Madrid. By December Charles felt that it was safe to release the Pope from San Angelo and he retreated, battered and diminished, to Orvieto. This could also have been a moment of opportunity for Henry, because Clement was undoubtedly resentful at the way in which he had been treated, but the moment passed and in a more rational mood he realised that he should do nothing to upset the Emperor.[16] The latter's wrath was still formidable, and the French could offer no effective protection. English diplomatic initiatives consequently continued to fall on deaf ears in Madrid, and having failed to make peace, Henry and Wolsey took the next logical step. On 21 January 1528 they declared war on the Emperor. It soon became apparent that this was a mere gesture, because it was quickly followed by a commercial truce with the Low Countries, and no preparations were made for any campaign either by land or sea. Indeed the King's Great Ships do not appear to have emerged from their dockyards at any time during the year.[17] The only Imperial territory within reach of an English army was the Netherlands, and neither Wolsey nor Henry had any intention of disturbing relations with Margaret. England would supply encouragement, and even some money, to the combatants in Italy, but had no intention of allowing the fighting to spill out of that region, and continued to press for peace. No doubt it was felt that being a recognised belligerent gave her an additional right to do that. By March 1528, Wolsey felt that success was in sight. 'Hitherto,' he told the French ambassador, 'I have had little hope of peace ... Now I regard it as certain.' He was too optimistic, and the emissary whom the allies sent to Spain at the end of May was kept kicking his heels in Madrid for six weeks after his arrival. Charles was not in a conciliatory mood, and by the end of September the mission had effectively failed.[18] In November Sylvester Darius, who had been chosen to undertake it because he was a papal servant and therefore neutral, was back in France, empty-handed.

Meanwhile, papal-Imperial relations had taken another twist, because by October 1528 Clement was back in Rome, from which the German soldiers had long since been expelled. Although the city was a shell of its former self, the Pope had recovered his self possession. Still alarmed at the thought of Imperial power, he had nevertheless decided that his best course lay in being on the winning side, and sought an active rapprochement with Charles – 'to live and die an Imperialist' – and that was the worst possible news from Henry's point of view.

Knight's mission having failed, the initiative had returned to Wolsey. Henry must have known of this, and given his approval, although it gave the impression in Rome that the right hand did not know what the left hand was doing.[19] Just before Christmas 1527, and just after the move to Orvieto, Gregory Casale had gained access to Clement with instructions to persuade him of the invalidity of Julius II's bull of dispensation. Casale also bore with him the draft of a decretal commission empowering the commissioners to investigate that bull, and to apply the law to any deficiencies. This would have had the effect of invalidating the dispensation, and thus declaring the marriage void, and because it was a decretal commission, no appeal would have stood against it. Unfortunately, in spite of Wolsey's optimism, Clement was not persuaded, and his legal advisers cut the draft commission to shreds.[20] What Casale emerged with was precisely what Wolsey did not want – a general commission to investigate the case without the power to give sentence, and with no immunity from appeal. In other words, like Knight, he had failed to budge the Pope an inch in Henry's favour. Clement, who had many other troubles to worry him, was puzzled and a little irritated by English persistence in this matter, especially at receiving two different embassies within days of each other, which seemed to bear different instructions. Let Wolsey deal with the matter in England. Henry could then take a new wife, and only if that marriage was challenged need the matter come to Rome. In taking this line, however, Clement was not concentrating, because the Emperor had already expressed an interest in the King's matrimonial affairs. It was inevitable that any sentence of nullity pronounced in England would be appealed, and therefore his suggested course of action was a mere waste of time.[21] By February 1528 Wolsey had realised that Casale's commission was useless. So he scrapped it and tried again. This time the ambassadors were his secretary Stephen Gardiner and the King's almoner Edward Foxe. They were to try again for a decretal commission, emphasising the gravity of the situation, and professing Henry's undying devotion to the Holy See. They reached Orvieto on 21 March and spent the next fortnight closeted with Clement and his chief advisers, sometimes for several hours each day. Although backed by the nuncio in France, whom Francis had sent to Rome specifically for that purpose, they got nowhere.[22] The most that they could obtain was another general commission, although cast in rather more generous terms and backed by an undertaking to confirm its findings, embodied in a draft bull. With this they had to be satisfied. It was sealed on 13 April, and although he was warned that it would not satisfy the King, Clement protested that in his circumstances, it was the most that he could possibly offer.[23]

This new commission was to be issued to Wolsey, and to another cardinal, who was swiftly identified as Lorenzo Campeggio, and Fox left Orvieto immediately, bearing this dubious trophy homeward as fast as he could. At first Henry was somewhat inexplicably elated by this news, and his faith in the Cardinal's negotiating powers appeared to have been restored. However, closer examination of the terms of the commission brought swift disillusionment. It would not do, and in mid-May Gardiner was sent back to Orvieto to try again. What had been conceded would suffice for public consumption, but what was still required was a decretal commission, no matter how secretly it was issued. However, by the end of June there was no sign of the decretal, and no sign either of Campeggio. Henry's temper began to fray and a letter from Gardiner was lost in transit. It probably contained only news of further delays, but its loss was infuriating, at least to the King.[24] Then in July his mind was distracted by an outbreak of the sweating sickness in London. It was brief, but extremely virulent, and directly affected the court. Sir Francis Pointz, Sir William Compton and William Carey all died, and Anne Boleyn herself fell sick. The King fled, first to Tittenhanger and then to Ampthill, 'accompanied by few', and redoubled his spiritual exercises. He is alleged to have confessed daily, and his surviving correspondence is full of nostrums and remedies.[25] Wolsey similarly retreated, but only from Westminster to Hampton Court, where he remained fully in touch with business. He may, or may not, have fallen ill himself, but he never stopped work. Henry, whose gallantry was always more apparent in words than in deeds, wrote to Anne lamenting their separation, but warning her not to seek to return too soon. Meanwhile, although there was still no positive news from Gardiner, Campeggio had at least set out. Travelling with extreme slowness because he was afflicted with gout, he reached Lyons in September, and proceeded thence via Paris to Calais. He landed in England on 29 September, and reached London on 9 October.[26] By then the sweat had long since abated, Anne Boleyn was back at court, and the great and good turned out in strength to do the Cardinal honour. He was a sick man, and evaded the celebrations as far as possible, so that it was to be another fortnight before he felt up to meeting the King at Bridewell. Anne was discreetly sidelined for that meeting, and it appeared that Campeggio had actually brought with him the secret decretal commission which Gardiner had been commissioned to obtain. This was to be shown only to the King and Wolsey, and it turned out not to be quite what was pretended. Gardiner may have thought that he had won, but this commission required confirmation by a second letter of authorisation which had not yet arrived, and was full of ambiguities which could be exploited by a resolute opponent who was well versed in the canon law. It turned out also to be a fraudulent document, because although Clement did confirm it in writing, he had no intention that it should be used, and had given Campeggio secret instructions that he was to contrive every possible delay, and in no circumstances to find in the King's favour.[27] Henry (and Anne) were consumed with impatience, and apparently deceived as to the completeness of the Legate's powers. His first step, however, was logical enough; he went to see Catherine to determine whether there might not be some other way out of this dilemma short of a decree of nullity. Suppose she was to take the veil? That would, in the view of most canonists, free her husband to marry again without impugning the validity of her marriage or the legitimacy of their child. In spite of her formidable piety, Catherine absolutely refused to contemplate such a way out. She was the Queen, and had every intention of retaining that status. Wolsey backed his colleague's pleas, and a delegation of English prelates came on the same errand, but the Queen would not budge.[28] She had, with Henry's permission, appointed counsel to represent her, and she would abide the decision of the Holy See. Whether she would accept the verdict of the Legates appointed to hear her case remained to be seen.

Meanwhile, news of the King's intentions was being gossiped on the streets of London. The people, and especially women that favoured the Queen, 'talked largely, and said that the king for his pleasure would take another wife, and had sent for this Legate to be divorced from his Queen, with other foolish words .' or not so foolish as it transpired.[29] Realising that his 'Great Matter' was now in the public domain, in November Henry sent for a gathering of nobles, members of Parliament and other élite gentry to come to Bridewell to hear his side of the story. There he talked largely of Catherine's virtues, and of the love that was between them, of his own scruple of conscience and of how hard he had tried to resolve his doubts. The Legates had now come to settle the issue, and he hoped that everyone would accept their decision as final – as he himself was determined to do. His effort was not well received. As Edward Hall observed:

> To see what contention was made amongst the hearers of this oration, it was a strange sight, for some sighed and said nothing, other were sorry to see the king so troubled in his conscience. Other that favoured the Queen much sorrowed that the matter was now opened, and so every man spake as his heart moved him ...[30]

The King was deeply disappointed by this reaction. If he had failed to convince his own subjects, would he stand any better chance with Campeggio? Wolsey was a prey to conflicting doubts and hopes. He may not have been aware that the Legate had destroyed his 'decretal commission' as soon as he had shown it to Henry and himself, but he strongly suspected that Campeggio was prevaricating. It was absolutely essential, not only for the King but also for his own credibility, that the Legates find in Henry's favour, but he was beginning to doubt that that would ever happen. Even before the King's oration at Bridewell he had written to Casale in Rome, expressing his fears as to what might transpire.[31] So convinced was Henry of the righteousness of his own cause, that any failure to reflect that might well result in his decision to repudiate papal authority altogether. 'I close my eyes before such horror ...' the Cardinal wrote with an excess of hyperbole which it would be hard to equal. It was absolutely essential for the future of the English Church that Clement not only confirm the commission which he had issued, but instruct Campeggio to get on with the job. 'After Christmas (1528) and all Lent until Easter was none other thing communed of but only of the king's marriage ...' The King's Great Matter had moved centre stage.[32]

So why, apart from the politics of the Emperor's family, was the issue so difficult? The problem was partly one of biblical exegesis. The Levitical text was quite unambiguous, but it referred to a brother's wife, not his widow. Although it could be stretched to cover a relict, the obvious interpretation was polyandry – a woman could not marry two brothers at the same time. There was also in the book of Deuteronomy a text which urged the so-called 'levirate', that if a man died his brother (if he had one) was bound to take his widow and 'raise up children unto his brother'.[33] It was thus quite possible to argue that the Levitical text did not cover Henry's situation at all, and that the penalty 'they shall be childless' did not apply to him either. Consequently, even if it were admitted that Leviticus created a Divine Law which the Pope could not dispense, that was irrelevant in this case. In fact the issue was not quite so straightforward, and there were theologians prepared to argue on both sides, but the theology of Henry's case needed both good luck and very skilful management. It got neither.[34] There was also the question of the dispensation, which operated at two levels. First there was the doubt as to whether any pope was entitled to dispense from a biblical prohibition. The Pope, it was argued, could dispense any penalties inflicted by the canon law for breeches of its decrees, and even from the sins incurred in similar breeches, but not from penalties incurred under the Divine Law for breeches of scriptural precepts.[35] The second level was technical. Did the dispensation in fact address the issues to which it was ostensibly directed? That was relevant in this case because Julius had assumed that Catherine's marriage to Arthur had been consummated, and he therefore dispensed from the relevant degree of consanguinity. Catherine had always denied that such consummation had ever taken place, and that the only bar between Henry and herself was that constituted by the 'public honesty' of their betrothal. This may seem a slender argument, but it would have been sufficient to have invalidated the dispensation upon a technicality.[36] Although Wolsey had urged the King to accept Catherine's statement of her virginity at the time of their marriage, Henry had consistently refused to do so. Perhaps he did not want it to be thought that he had not recognised a virgin when he saw one!

There was also a political issue attached to this dispensation, because the papacy was edging towards an official statement on its own infallibility. Clement was therefore extremely reluctant to declare that his predecessor had made a mistake. One of Martin Luther's more notorious heresies had been to declare that the Church could err – not only popes but also General Councils – so there was an understandable sensitivity on the subject in Rome. If Henry's case had been absolutely unequivocal, he would have had no option, but it was not, and Clement, who was not given to bold or decisive action, would make no move against Julius.[37] Nor was it entirely clear which dispensation was in question. Henry was working from the text which his father had received, but it transpired in the autumn of 1528 that another version existed, which had been sent to Isabella to satisfy certain doubts which she had expressed about the original. This had never been sent into England, and the only known text was in Spain. It addressed the question of 'public honesty', and remedied one or two other minor defects which Isabella, or her advisers, had clearly noticed. Someone in Spain saw the relevance of this document for Catherine's case, and sent her a copy, which she produced, thus undermining such progress as had been made in discrediting the English text.[38] Wolsey's first thought was to denounce the Spanish version as a forgery, but his agents were unable to get a sight of the original, so such a response had only rhetorical value. By January 1529 his arguments against the validity of the dispensation were therefore looking extremely fragile, and as Campeggio continued to equivocate and delay, he was forced back upon the theological arguments based on scripture. Catherine might protest that she was a poor neglected woman, helpless and alone, but in fact her counsel were well briefed and she had a battery of arguments at her disposal which could have torn Henry's case to shreds.

All this while, Henry was theoretically at war with the Emperor; a war which gave the latter the pretext to seize English merchants and their goods when they took advantage of the absence of hostilities to venture into his waters, but did not prevent him from maintaining accredited agents in England.[39] Wolsey meanwhile kept up a steady round of negotiations with France, and signed an agreement committing Princess Mary to marriage with the Duke of Orléans, Francis' second son, who was at this stage a boy of nine. These moves were not popular in London where 'the people sore lamented the chance for all merchandise was restrained to pass into any of the emperor's dominions, and merchants were desired by the Cardinal to keep their marts at Calais, to which in no wise they would consent …'[40] Instead they continued to trade illicitly into the Low Countries, and the Regent Margaret turned a blind eye to their activities. Although the prohibition allegedly made Wolsey very unpopular, it is unlikely that he was much disconcerted by their defiance, because the whole purpose of his tortuous manoeuvres was to bring about peace, to get the belligerents to the negotiating table. He realised perfectly well that this meant pressurising Charles into modifying the terms of the treaty of Madrid, so he caused Henry to make threatening noises, and even to send money to support the French cause in Italy. The only trouble was that the more effective his pressure was, and the more alienated the Emperor became in consequence, the more distant did any solution to the King's Great Matter become. The only things to be said for England's foreign policy between 1526 and 1529 are that it was a reasonably effective way of cultivating the French support which could be necessary to get a favourable response from Rome, and that it was gratifying to the pro-French Anne Boleyn and to the family-based faction which was beginning to gather around her at court. Now that he understood the nature of her position, Wolsey was careful not to antagonise Anne, and she responded positively because throughout 1527 and 1528 he seemed to offer the best hope for a solution to the King's matrimonial problem. It might be an exaggeration to describe them as allies, but at least their aims were congruent.[41]

It would also be true to say that Wolsey's reticent foreign policy was also due to a keen awareness of the King's poverty. Even if he had been anxious to launch the Army Royal which was occasionally threatened, and for which sporadic preparations were made, he knew that he could not afford to do so. With the harvests of 1527 and 1528 much diminished by storms and unseasonable rains, and trade disrupted by the war, economic hardship was very real for many people, which meant that money generally was in short supply, and the civil order under constant pressure. He might pretend, in April 1527, that he had succeeded in raising the French pension to a level which would make Henry one of the 'richest princes in the world', but he must have known that that was not true, because the true value of the pension was a mere 10,000 crowns a year.[42] As we have already seen, by the summer of 1525 Henry was aware that he was under extreme financial pressure, and that was no doubt one reason why Wolsey was permitted to overhaul the Household in January 1526. According to Edward Hall, he came to Eltham on 8 January 1526, and stayed until the 22nd, 'In which season the cardinal and other of the King's council set for a direction to be made in the King's house ...' Many servants were put out, and officers 'sent to their countries', which meant for the most part reduction from full-time to part-time rates. On the same basis sixty-four of the Guard who had been paid 12*d* a day were reduced to 6*d* a day, and instructed to come only when sent for. At the same time the regulations governing the conduct of the Household were reissued in a more stringent form, and the duties were more clearly specified.[43] Hall concludes:

At this season, the cardinal made many ordinances concerning the King's House, which he at this day called the Statutes of Eltham, the which some said were more profitable than honourable ...

In the perpetual battle between magnificence and economy, economy had won a round, but it was a temporary victory which checked the rise in household bills only for a while. The Cofferer was supposed to dispense £19,400 a year, that having been the sum assigned to him at the beginning of the reign, but by 1526 he was regularly exceeding that sum, and by 1532 expenditure 'in ordinary' had risen to £25,812. So the Eltham Ordinances marked only a brief respite in the steady rise of the King's housekeeping bills.[44] Nor was economy aided by the special 'entertainment' provided for Mistress Anne. Catherine, whose bills were paid out of the traditional consort's endowment with which she had long since been provided, was moved out of Greenwich in December 1528 to Hampton Court, and Anne was moved into the Queen's apartments next to Henry's. This not only signified an enhancement of her status, so that she was able to preside at the King's side over the Christmas festivities which followed, but also a major increase in her expenditure, because she was now keeping a virtually royal state, with all the enhanced service which that implied.

As far as the King's Great Matter was concerned, the end of 1528 was dominated by the papal brief which Catherine had turned up in Spain. Under extreme pressure, the Queen wrote to her nephew, begging him to send the original to England, because only in that way could it stand in her interest in a court of law.[45] For some extraordinary reason the messenger entrusted with this letter was her own loyal servant Thomas Abel, who promptly sabotaged Wolsey's plan by telling Charles to ignore the letter, hang on to the brief and continue his efforts to persuade Clement to halt the annulment proceedings forthwith.[46] Charles did not follow his suggestion, but then neither did the brief leave Spain. The English ambassadors were welcome to read it for themselves, but under no circumstances would he part with it. Either Henry must trust to Campeggio's increasingly suspect mission, and effectively ignore the brief, or he must try to tackle the threat in Rome by sending another mission. Before the end of December such a mission was despatched. Led by William Knight and Francis Bryan, it was armed with threats as well as arguments, but its main purpose was to persuade Clement that the Spanish document was a forgery. For that reason they were given secret instructions to examine the original in the Vatican archive, and detect, if they were able, any error in its draftsmanship. They were to urge the Pope to instruct Charles to send his copy to England, because it was only there that the truth of the matter could be determined. They were also to reopen the question of Catherine's possible withdrawal into a religious order. Suppose that she agreed to co-operate with such a plan on the condition that Henry did likewise. Would the Pope then be willing to absolve him from the vows which he had taken under constraint?[47] This and other equally bizarre plans were apparently to be canvassed in all seriousness. Would the Pope permit bigamy? Would he grant a new decretal commission with full powers to resolve the problem once and for all? At this time, Clement was very much the centre of Henry's diplomatic world. In addition to the question of his marriage, he was expected to establish a general truce which would lead to European peace, and to crown Charles as Emperor (he was technically only King of the Romans until he was crowned). Rumours of Clement's death in early February therefore spread panic in London, where it was thought that the negotiations would have to begin all over again. These reports were soon refuted, but the Pope was undoubtedly ill, and that meant further delays.[48] Not until the end of March was he in a fit condition to receive the ambassadors. Meanwhile, Knight and Bryan had found no trace of the Spanish brief in the archives, which confirmed their suspicions that it was a forgery. When this circumstance was drawn to Clement's attention, he was unconvinced, and merely referred the investigation to a third party, supposedly indifferent, but in fact hostile. Then in early March, Catherine had written secretly, asking the Pope to recall her case to Rome, and towards the end of April Charles' agents in Rome protested against the concessions so far made to England, and formally petitioned that the case be revoked.[49] The English mission was stalemated, and the representatives conferred anxiously about how they were to break this news to the King.

Meanwhile, the case had not yet been revoked, and unless or until that happened, the legates in England had a clear duty to proceed on the basis of the powers which they had received several months before. More in desperation than in real hope, Henry instructed his agents in Rome to make one final plea for the Pope's promised confirmation of the Legate's decision, and then to come home, whether they had achieved it or not. There was no point in their remaining in such a hostile climate. By the end of May, Henry was desperate for the action to commence, and berated Campeggio's unfortunate secretary, blaming the Italian for the delays – in which he was fully justified, as we have seen. On 29 May he issued a licence under the Great Seal for them to proceed, and unable to prevaricate any longer, they named Blackfriars as the venue and 18 June as the date for the commencement of the trial.[50] The King and the Queen were both summoned, and whereas Henry appeared by proxy, Catherine came in person, no doubt to the huge embarrassment of the court. Such was her intention, because having denounced the incompetence of the judges, she announced her appeal to Rome and immediately withdrew. Realising that he was in danger of being outmanoeuvred, the King came in person a few days later, and made an impassioned plea:

> My Lordes, Legates of the sea Apostolique which be deputed judges in this great and waightie matter, I moste heartily beseech you to ponder my mind and intent, which is onely to have a final end for the discharge of my conscience; for every good Christian man knoweth what paine and what unquietness he suffreth which hath his conscience grieved …[51]

Whereupon Catherine, who was also present, came and knelt at his feet, begging him not to dishonour himself or her, or their child. Only in Rome, she urged, could a decision be reached. Each having made their ritual gesture, the court then announced that Catherine's appeal was disallowed, and she withdrew, not saying anything more, but adamantly refusing to return when summoned, for which she was pronounced contumacious. It was the King's only success, because as the sessions progressed, the Queen's case was compellingly made by her proctors, including a thunderous speech by Bishop John Fisher of Rochester, delivered on 28 June, which left him a marked man in Henry's eyes.[52] The Court scrutinised Julius' bull, examined the brief, and heard evidence about Catherine's first marriage and its possible consummation. It was working swiftly and apparently purposefully in early July. Meanwhile, news of Catherine's appeal had reached Rome, and on 13 July Clement, under intense pressure, agreed to halt the English proceedings, and recall the case to his own jurisdiction. This decision was promulgated in the Curia on 23 July and copies immediately despatched to all the relevant parties.[53] The proceedings in England were not merely terminated, but also quashed, so that everything which had been achieved there became a mere waste of time. By the time that news of this debacle reached London, the court at Blackfriars already stood adjourned. Campeggio employed swift and confidential messengers, so just as Clement was being kept regularly informed of progress in London, the legate was only days behind in his information from Rome. By the middle of July he knew that Catherine's appeal had been received, and what the outcome was likely to be.[54] So he began to discover technicalities to slow proceedings down, and by 27 July Wolsey was reporting with some bewilderment that the whole case seemed to have become a quagmire of legal difficulties. The reason for this soon became apparent when Campeggio announced that since this was a Roman court, it would follow the Italian calendar and adjourn at the end of the month until October.[55] Henry protested furiously, but the legate was unmoved. On 31 July he duly announced the adjournment, leaving the King speechless with indignation. Long before there could be any question of its reconvening, the letters of recall had arrived from Rome, and Henry was cited to plead his case in person in the Holy See. More than two years of intense diplomatic effort had been totally defeated, but the situation could not return to where it had stood then. Henry and Catherine had both had their day in court, and their estrangement was public knowledge. It was also generally understood that Mistress Anne Boleyn was the lady in waiting, so the French had no interest in providing diplomatic support. Above all, Thomas Wolsey had lost his aura of invincibility, and stood exposed as never before to the machinations of his enemies – including by this time Mistress Anne.

Not only had Wolsey failed to secure the annulment of the King's marriage, his foreign policy was also going nowhere. Since 1526 England had been supportive of the League of Cognac, a French-led group of states attempting to curb Charles V's power and to modify the treaty of Madrid. This had involved a series of understandings between Henry and Francis, occasional threats of intervention, and constant pressure for a peace negotiation. Charles had responded, or not responded, to these initiatives, depending upon the military situation in Italy. On 21 June 1529 the French had been decisively defeated at Landriano and a few days later he signed the treaty of Barcelona with the Pope, who had decided that further support for the League was a waste of time.[56] This was not without its relevance for the events then taking place at Blackfriars, but it also demonstrated the extent to which English diplomacy had been sidelined. In fact peace talks between the two sides had been going on for several months, which had owed nothing to English initiative. Wolsey had known about these negotiations but had not, apparently, taken them very seriously, until, in July 1529 he suddenly realised that they were close to success.[57] The final round of talks began at Cambrai on the 5th of that month, and after some very hard bargaining, agreement was reached on 3 August. This was the so-called 'Ladies Peace' because it was brokered by Margaret of Austria and Louise of Savoy, and it was essentially a modification of the treaty of Madrid, whereby (most crucially) Charles gave up his claim to Burgundy in return for a payment of two million gold ecus.[58] The Dauphin and the Duc d'Orléans were to be returned to their father, and Francis in turn would immediately marry the Emperor's sister Eleanor. Only some very rapid diplomatic footwork ensured that England was comprehended in this treaty. Her interests were accommodated to a very limited extent, and the whole negotiation was effectively a humiliation for her. More than three years of intensive effort had been crowned with success – but it was a success towards which Wolsey had been able to make no contribution at all! By the end of August, Eustace Chapuys, the Imperial ambassador in England, was reporting that the Cardinal was finished.[59] Affairs of state were in the hands of Norfolk, Suffolk and Rochford, foreign ambassadors were being denied access to him, and even a request for a personal interview with the King had been turned down.

This last was true, and it was an adverse sign, but it was not necessarily the end of a relationship. Henry had never relied exclusively upon Wolsey, useful though he was, and adverse signals had been reported before. The King had not confided to Wolsey that he had proposed to Anne, so that he went off to France in 1527 with only half a story, but during the following year Henry's increasingly intricate negotiations in Rome had depended more than ever upon the Cardinal's expertise. Edward Hall, who repeatedly emphasised his unpopularity, was not only hostile to the Cardinal personally, he was also hostile to the French connection which was the hallmark of his diplomacy from 1525 onward, so he is not necessarily a reliable witness. In spite of the unpleasantness over the Abbess of Wilton,[60] as late as the summer of 1529 Anne Boleyn was going out of her way to be courteous to him, and Henry was intermittently entertaining him in the old familiar manner. However the failure of the Blackfriars court, and the narrow escape at Cambrai which followed within days, do seem to have wrought a change. When Campeggio was due to take his leave on 19 September, he cannot have expected more that the frosty courtesy which was extended to him, but Wolsey got a much more mixed reception. Having been told that there was no accommodation for him in the palace, he was nevertheless received by the King in an extended private audience.[61] The following day, whether by accident or design, the King was out riding all day, and by the time that he returned the cardinals had gone, Campeggio on his return journey to Rome and Wolsey to nurse his anxieties at the More. His worries by this time were fully justified, and two days later he received the King's command to hand over the Great Seal. Somewhat ill-advisedly, the Cardinal insisted on receiving this instruction in writing, but then there arrived a messenger from the

King, bearing a 'privy token' and word that Henry had cast him down only for a show to satisfy certain 'hostile spirits', and would raise him up again.[62] Understandably elated, he went on to Esher, whither he had been commanded to retire, and awaited his rehabilitation. It never came. Either the King spontaneously changed his mind, or the Cardinal's enemies lobbied effectively against him. Instead the next thing that happened was that a charge of praemunire was lodged against him, and he was found guilty. He submitted and the King pardoned him, but stripped him of all his temporal possessions, provoking him to remind the council 'to put no more into his [the King's] head than will stand with a good conscience'. In spite of this implied rebuke, Henry took York Place, although it belonged to the archdiocese rather than to the Cardinal.[63] The one thing that Wolsey did not do in this crisis was to stand on his dignity as a prince of the Church. Throughout his ordeal, he would admit only to being the King's 'good subject' – to be plundered at will, apparently. Then Henry relented again, sending another 'privy token', his physician at Christmas when Wolsey was ill, and several cartloads of furnishings to Esher at Candlemas. A few days later, he gave the Archbishop of York leave to withdraw to his diocese (which he had never visited).[64] This may, or may not, have been the work of his enemies. Certainly it would have the effect of removing him from the King's presence, but on the other hand it gave him a recognised status. Wolsey's relationship with the King remains baffling to the very end, but as far as public policy was concerned, he was now off the scene and the King would have to make shift without him. On 26 October Sir Thomas More received the Great Seal on the understanding (it was alleged) that he would not be involved in the King's Great Matter, and on 4 November Parliament convened at Westminster.

8

CRISIS & CHANGE, 1529–1536

In the autumn of 1529 Henry's kingship faced a number of challenges. He wanted to marry Anne Boleyn, but the Pope had refused to clear a way for that to happen. Was Clement entitled to be so obstructive when the future security of England might well hang on the outcome? There was also the problem of what to do about Thomas Wolsey, that faithful if sometimes overbearing servant who had been his alter ego for the last fifteen years. Wolsey had failed, and the King's anger had expressed itself in a number of ways. Henry had to demonstrate that he was the master in his own house, but how far should he allow that anger to carry him?[1] He was also short of money, and keenly aware of the anti-clericalism which had grown up, particularly in London, in the aftermath of the Hunne affair. Wolsey had smoothed that over, and it had simmered down, but it had not gone away. So Henry had to decide what it meant to be a king. He could take counsel where it pleased him, promote whom he chose to high office, and elevate peers at his own discretion. Even before Wolsey's fall, he had begun to take the advice of his Lord Treasurer, the Duke of Norfolk, of the Duke of Suffolk and of Viscount Rochford. In December 1529 the latter became Earl of Wiltshire, and his allies George Hastings and Robert Radcliffe, Earls of Huntingdon and Sussex respectively;[2] Thomas More became Lord Chancellor and the Earl of Wiltshire Lord Privy Seal. However, he could not get rid of his wife.

The Church, he decided, was the main problem; not just the papacy but the whole ecclesiastical establishment. Bishops were too keen on wealth and jurisdiction, and not keen enough on preaching the gospel. Abbots were too interested in protecting their legal rights, and not sufficiently interested in serving God in prayer.[3] He had no quarrel with the parish priest who heard confessions and administered the sacraments, but whose subject was he, the King's or the Pope's? The last time that Parliament had tried to restrict the benefit of clergy in 1512 it had provoked a furious reaction from Abbot Richard Kidderminster, who had preached that Parliament had no authority to overturn a papal decree, and that secular courts had no jurisdiction over the clergy.[4] It had been in that context that Henry had observed that he recognised no superior authority on earth. It is not likely that he had thought out the implications of his statement at that time, and the controversy had been smothered, but it surfaced again now. The King believed that he enjoyed a special relationship with God – why else had he been anointed? But he was unsure how far that relationship extended. Where did the boundary between secular and spiritual authority actually lie? Most important of all, on which side of the boundary did matrimonial jurisdiction lie? On 28 October, Henry had a most interesting conversation with the new Imperial ambassador, Eustace Chapuys, which revealed both the direction and the uncertainties of his thinking.[5] It was a great pity, he said, that Luther was a heretic, because much of what he had said about the vices and corruptions of the clergy was true. The Pope and his cardinals, who should have been setting an example of apostolic living, instead were preoccupied with vain pomp and ceremony. The Church was indeed in need of reform, and if Luther had stopped at that, instead of going on to attack the sacraments, Henry would have written in his support. It was the duty of all Christian princes, and most of all of the Emperor, to promote such reform, and he, as the King of England, would do no less within his own dominions. These observations were not unprecedented. The Gospel and the Fathers had often been called upon by reformers in the past, and Henry himself had tolerated some pretty strong anti-clerical propaganda when it had been aimed at Campeggio during his recent visit.[6] The King's mind had moved a long way since the somewhat unreflective papalism of the *Assertio Septem Sacramentorum*; moved partly by force of circumstances, and partly (perhaps) by the writings of William Tyndale and Simon Fish. Thomas Wolsey may have been a good servant, but he had also been an exemplar of all that was wrong in the upper reaches of the Church. His pride and his magnificence may have been conducive to the King's honour, but they were not compatible with his status as a churchman. It would be better in future to keep the secular and spiritual dignities apart, and to induce in the latter a little of the humility which was supposed to be the mark of a true faith.

It was probably with some such agenda in mind that Henry convened Parliament in August 1529. A parliament was not necessary to deal with Wolsey, and in any case the King had taken most of the relevant steps before it ever assembled. However, something of importance was in the wind, because considerable effort was expended to make sure that the House of Commons was biddable.[7] This may have been because of the difficulties which the Council had had with the last parliament in 1523, when the King had demanded money, but such was not his intention on this occasion, and as Edward Hall noticed, 'the most parte of the Commons were the Kynges servauntes'. It seems likely that Henry was bracing himself for some kind of attack upon the Church, although how far he intended to take it is unclear. Hostile observers certainly interpreted it in that light, and John Fisher's first biographer was later to write that '… the Common Howse was so parcially chosen that the king had his will almost in all things that himself listed'. It consisted, he alleged, of 'roystnge courteours, servingmen, parasites and flatters of all sorts …'[8] This, as the returns show, was scarcely fair to a normal assembly of gentlemen and lawyers, but an anti-clerical inspiration was soon apparent. Within days the Commons had presented a petition to the King, asking him to confront the spiritual peers on the issues of temporal possessions, secular office, pluralism and non-residence, an agenda which closely resembled that of the *Supplication for the Beggars*, which had recently appeared in London.[9] Henry received this petition favourably, but he did not do what he was asked. Instead the questions of fees and pluralism were recycled as Bills, which together with others on probate and mortuary fees emerged eventually as Acts, with a distinct anti-clerical tone. There were four of these Acts, which became law when they received the royal assent on 17 December: an Act restricting sanctuary; an act 'concerning fines and sums of money to be taken for probate'; an act concerning the taking of mortuaries; and an act 'for the farming of benefices, for pluralities and for residence'.[10] The King was steering a delicate course, because he did not want to be thought a heretic, and heresy was the usual cry of the clergy when under attack. In spite of Henry having issued an elaborate proclamation against heretical books in March 1529, Bishop Nix of Norwich reported to the Duke of Norfolk in May 1530 that he was having great difficulty in enforcing it because 'many say openly that the king favours such books' and that it was 'the king's pleasure that the New Testament in English shall go forth'.[11] Nix was an arch-conservative, who was trying to deter Henry from his reforming course, so it is probable that he misrepresented the situation in Norfolk, but the King was clearly sending out contradictory signals. He was ambitious to control the Church within his dominions, but not yet willing to repudiate the Pope's overall authority. Indeed his attitude towards Rome was ambiguous, because while he was determined to settle his dispute within his own realm, he was also anxious to gain the Pope's authority to do so.

In the late summer of 1530 this muddled thinking clarified somewhat, perhaps influenced by a document known as the '*collectanea satis copiosa*', which seems to have been put together by a group of his most trusted advisers (including by this time Thomas Cranmer) at some point during the winter of 1529–30.[12] This proposed, using a mixture of scriptural and historical arguments, that Henry could legitimately claim sovereign powers over England, including its Church, and could similarly claim an Imperial status for himself, whereby he was not subject to any superior authority on earth. This went beyond the limited immunity which Henry had claimed before the Blackfriars court, and was well on the way to describing the papal authority as 'usurped', which was to be a feature of the regime's later rhetoric.

Paradoxically, this went hand in hand with continued efforts in Rome to secure recognition for the more limited immunity which had been claimed before. On 7 October 1530 Henry wrote to William Benet and Edward Carne, his representatives there; why, he asked, should he be compelled to have a case tried in Rome which not only concerned his own conscience, but the succession to his Kingdom?[13] Because of his supreme authority, he could prevent any of his subjects from appealing to the Holy See, so why should he be summoned himself? If these reasonable arguments were not accepted, then they were to seek for a delay while the respective privileges of England and Rome were investigated. Having been so impatient for a decision while the case was being heard in England, it now appears that the King himself was seeking respite, perhaps while he put his still disordered thoughts into some presentable form. His next move was potentially more radical. In the Michaelmas term 1530 fifteen clergy were summoned to appear in King's Bench to answer charges of praemunire. They included a number of Catherine's more prominent friends, such as Bishop John Fisher, and the charges involved connivance in the offences for which Wolsey had already been convicted, and to which he had confessed.[14] The main motive for this attack (apart from punishing the Queen's allies) seems to have been to convince Clement that Henry's caesaropapist claims were seriously meant. However, it was not pressed home. Someone noticed that there was little logic about this selective approach. Wolsey's guilt embraced the whole Church, so the logical thing to do would be to indict the whole clerical body of praemunire. This was duly done, and the whole system of Courts Christian was implicated in the allegedly illegal submission of the clerical estate to Wolsey's authority as papal legate. It was a bizarre charge, but one full of menace for the traditional Church, whose courts, to be lawful, would in future have to be part of the royal jurisdictional system.[15] The charges were formally presented in January 1531, when Parliament was also recalled, presumably to give some anti-clerical stiffening because it was not involved in the prosecution. The convocations had reconvened with the Parliament, and it did not take long for them to decide that there was little point in trying to fight the accusations, unjust though they were. On 24 January 1531 the southern convocation submitted to the King, and received a royal pardon; a few days later the northern equivalent followed suit. The price of this acquiescence was high: £100,000 for the southern province and £18,000 for the northern.[16] The King was mollified, but not satisfied, and when, in the wake of their pardon, the convocations petitioned for some definition of praemunire to give positive protection to the ecclesiastical courts, he refused. It was the very vagueness of that offence which made it such a valuable weapon. Nor were the terms for the payment of the clerical fine satisfactory. Henry wanted his money more quickly, because although he had persuaded the last session of parliament to cancel his debts, he had not asked for any new grant.[17] Henry seems to have been thinking on his feet at this point, because having accepted their submission, he decided that he wanted some additional clauses inserted. The Archbishop of Canterbury was summoned to the Council, and informed that the text was not satisfactory. The King should be styled 'Supreme Head' of the English Church; it should be made clear that the cure of souls was committed to him; and that the privileges of the Church, which he was called upon to defend, were to be defined as those not detracting from the other laws of the land.[18]

This was virtually the whole agenda of the Royal Supremacy, but at this stage it was a bargaining position, and the clergy did not roll over. They were prepared to concede the title of 'Supreme Head', but only 'as far as the law of Christ allows', which could mean anything, but in their own eyes meant 'not at all'. At the same time, by fiddling with the word order they contrived to reduce his claim for the cure of souls to a general care for the souls of those entrusted to the clergy. For the time being, Henry allowed these amendments to pass, but when he received strongly worded protests, probably from the Lower Houses of the two convocations, he reacted with further charges of praemunire. Only Cuthbert Tunstall's moderate and carefully worded remonstration was treated to a similar moderate response.[19] Henry had, Tunstall argued, shifted the boundary stones between the spiritual and the temporal jurisdictions, leaving the former with nothing but the ministry of the word and of the sacraments – the *potestas ordinis* as it was traditionally known. In reply, the King admitted the charge, but argued that that was how 'spirituality' should be understood. He was claiming the *potestas jurisdictionis*, which consisted of the right to licence bishops, and grant their temporalities; control over the clergy's temporal goods; and control over the Courts Christian which operate 'by our sufferance'. 'There is no doubt,' he went on, 'but as well might we punish adultery and insolence in priests, as emperors have done, and as other princes do at this day …'[20] Which other princes he had in mind is not clear, but it was in this last claim that the novelty of his pretensions lay. There would be little room for the papacy in a world where all ecclesiastical courts were controlled by the lay rulers of their respective realms. However, all this was thinking in progress, and when the pardon of the clergy was confirmed by Parliament in March 1531, none of it was mentioned.[21] Henry was still capable of making eirenic observations about the papacy, and the chances are that if Clement had suddenly given way and granted the annulment which he sought, all this threatening rhetoric would have been forgotten. He was trying to alarm the Pope, and also probably endeavouring to convince himself of the validity of the arguments which he was putting forward. He was far more successful in the latter quest than he was in the former.

Meanwhile, Benet and Carne were pursuing their hopeless quest to get Henry's case handed back from the Rota to a court in England. To do that, they had to frustrate the proceedings in Rome, and in the early part of 1531, they were achieving that fairly successfully. Edward Carne did not disclose that he had been granted proctorial powers, because they were for use only in an emergency, and in the absence of such powers he was not admitted to plead before the court. Perhaps by that means he hoped to bring the case to a halt, on the assumption that it could not proceed in the absence of one of the litigants. However this was a false assumption, and instead Henry faced the prospect of being declared contumacious, which could only have hastened the decision against him.[22] So Carne lodged an appeal against his exclusion, and spent many weeks arguing his case before the Consistory, which had jurisdiction in such matters. The Imperialists needless to say opposed him, and that dragged matters out still further, so it was November before a final decision against Carne was given. However, this was made by the Rota and not by the Consistory, which provoked a vigorous counter-attack from Henry, denouncing the decision as invalid, and demanding that the whole issue be referred back to the Consistory. His reliance on the Consistory was based upon the fact that many of the cardinals who comprised it were 'men of the world', that is were accessible to lobbying or bribery, and he employed both these methods successfully.[23] As a result the Consistory agreed to look again at the matter, and gave the English two months to present their case. Imperial agents tried to obstruct them in the gathering of evidence, and the Pope was appealed to personally to put a stop to this. Altogether these procedural wrangles took so long that it was February 1532 before the substantive debate could begin, and June before the relevant decisions were made, by which time the Consistory was exhausted. It was concluded that the Rota was the right place to hold the proceedings, and that Carne could not be admitted without proper credentials. However, the Roman vacation was then upon them, and nothing would be done until October.[24] Clement was of the opinion that October would finally see the end of this protracted case, but he did not, of course, know that Carne still had his secret instructions to fall back on, and if admitted to the Rota would be able to begin the process of obstruction all over again.

While the case was thus wending its unsatisfactory way through the Roman courts, other attempts were still being made to reach a settlement. Clement suggested moving the hearing to Cambrai, which both Catherine and Charles rejected. Henry would have preferred Calais, but that was rejected by Clement, as was the King's hopeful suggestion for a court of four judges, to be nominated by the various parties.[25] In the summer of 1531 a further attempt was made to pressure Catherine into abandoning her appeal and asking the Pope to return the hearing to England, but that was a mere waste of time. Henry tried being conciliatory; he tried threats; he even offered on one occasion to come to

Rome in person – on certain conditions which he knew would not be fulfilled. Finally, in the summer of 1532, he resorted to the 'public honesty' argument. Julius' bull was invalid because it dispensed from the wrong impediment.[26] However, this did not take account of the Spanish brief, and was not presented with any conviction. As a concession in the debate, it was both too little and too late. Although there was the prospect of another round in October, the most that could be hoped for from that was further delay, and both Henry and Anne were desperate for a solution. The King had at last made up his mind to take the law into his own hands, and to fulfil some at least of the threats which he had been making. Then in August 1532 a window of opportunity opened when the aged William Warham, Archbishop of Canterbury, died. Warham had been too good a royal servant to be openly obstructive of the King's proceedings, but his reluctance to co-operate had become more and more apparent.[27] Now he had an opportunity to appoint his own man to the primatial see.

Meanwhile, Henry and Anne Boleyn were in love. 'The King's affection for La Bolaing increases daily,' Chapuys reported in September 1529. 'It is so great just now that it can hardly be greater; such is the intimacy and familiarity in which they live at present.'[28] She presided at court ceremonies, and in many respects occupied the position of queen. But Catherine was still at court, and Henry still visited her from time to time. They dined together on 30 November, and quarrelled inevitably over the state of their relationship. The King took refuge with Anne, who immediately denounced his efforts to placate his wife:

> Did I not tell you that whenever you disputed with the Queen, she was sure to have the upper hand? I see that some fine morning you will succumb to her reasoning, and that you will cast me off ...[29]

She apparently declined to take part in the Christmas festivities which followed, but by February he was spending all his time with her at York Place, leaving Catherine alone at Richmond. For the time being the *ménage à trois* continued. It was not so much that lust was driving him, as that Henry was still trying to work out what sort of a king he was supposed to be if he could not get rid of a useless wife and replace her with someone more agreeable. For this purpose his new council were no help at all. The Duke of Norfolk, for example, had been Wolsey's enemy, and did not have much thought beyond his fall.[30] He successfully kept the King and the Cardinal apart during that crisis, but could not prevent the latter's pardon on 12 February, nor the 1,000 marks pension which he was granted out of the see of Winchester, in the King's hands by virtue of his surrender. The archbishopric of York appears never to have been sequestered, and by May 1530 the Council was apparently discussing the Cardinal's possible return to office.[31] Henry was not best pleased with the efficiency of those who had replaced him. However, the one person who did not pretend to be placated by the King's change of mood was Anne Boleyn. She had conceived a mortal hatred of Wolsey in the aftermath of the Blackfriars fiasco, and did not relent. By the spring she was making it clear to the French that she was a better friend to Francis I than the Cardinal had ever been. It was probably his obvious failure to convert Anne which drove Wolsey to make the fatal mistake of trying to engineer a rapprochement with the Imperialists. By October he had succeeded in persuading Clement to issue an order to Henry to stop cohabiting with Anne. News of this possibility reached the English Court, and drove Anne into a frenzy of activity. Badgered by her, the King made it clear that no such edict would be accepted, and, probably alerted by the French ambassador, identified Wolsey as the cause of the problem.[32] It was this which led to his arrest for treason, and death at Leicester on his way south to face interrogation.

Wolsey's demise, however, did nothing to solve the main problem. Neither Norfolk, nor Suffolk nor Wiltshire had any new ideas, and More and Gardiner, who might have done, did not come up with any. The only new contribution came from Dr Thomas Cranmer of Jesus College, Cambridge, who, when he was lodged near to the Court at Waltham Abbey in the autumn of 1529, had suggested to his old friend Stephen Gardiner that the King should seek the advice of theologians rather than canon lawyers.[33] When interviewed by the King in October, Cranmer had suggested consulting the theology faculties of various European universities, and was promptly whisked off to write a treatise to that effect. This task must have been swiftly completed because, when in January 1530 the Earl of Wiltshire was sent off on yet another mission to Charles V and Clement, Cranmer was added to his staff for the purpose of beginning the consultations. He had shown the King a possible way to bypass the Curia altogether, and obtain direct confirmation from the Fathers of his private conviction that his marriage offended against the laws of God. In spite of the weakness of the Council, ideas were beginning to build up: the *Collectanea*, in which, as we have seen, Cranmer had a hand; the notion derived from *The Obedience of a Christian Man*, that 'the king is in the person of God, and his law in God's law'; and now Cranmer's new initiative.[34] Anne had no direct hand in Cranmer's efforts, but she was responsible for introducing Henry to the *Obedience*, probably without disclosing that it was the work of a known heretic – William Tyndale. She also kept up the anti-clerical pressure by showing the King the *Supplication of Beggars*, that virulent attack on clerical avarice and immorality. According to the author, Simon Fish, the clergy did not scruple to use heresy charges to protect themselves against proceedings in the King's courts:

> ... if any man in your sessions dare be so hardy to indict a priest of any such crime, he hath, ere the year go out, such a yoke of heresy laid in his neck that it maketh him wish he had not done it.[35]

Fish was another heretic, but the King immediately put his pardon in hand, and recalled him to England, from which he had fled in 1526.

All this did not amount to much in terms of political action, but in the summer of 1530 it was proposed to send a petition to the Pope, signed by all the worthies of England, begging for the annulment in the national interest, and vaguely threatening to find 'some other way' of resolving the issue. This was considered by the Council in June, and subsequently sent around the country for signature. Most of those approached subscribed, and although it had no impact at all in Rome, it did serve to identify Catherine's more determined supporters.[36] At the same meeting Henry canvassed the idea that if the theologians of the Western Church supported him, he might go ahead and remarry without obtaining papal approval. The result was a stunned silence, followed by pleas not to do anything so radical. There was apparently still a large gap between the thinking which was beginning to appeal to Henry, and the practical politics of the situation. However, the ideas of the *Collectanea* were having an increasing appeal, and in October 1530, the King broached for the first time the idea that Parliament could be used to authorise the Archbishop to proceed, irrespective of papal refusal. He did so, however, to an assembly of clerics and lawyers who immediately responded that Parliament had no such power.[37] Angrily, Henry prorogued the session until January 1531, and began to busy himself with the production of propaganda in his own interest. Before the end of the year *The Glasse of Truth* had appeared, a Latin disputation between a cleric and a knight, and Christopher German's *New Additions*. In the first of these, at least, the King is known to have had a hand.[38] The manner in which the clergy purchased their pardon in the new session of Parliament should probably be seen as another triumph for Boleyn thinking, but as yet the increasingly radical rhetoric had remained just that. The Pope would not budge, and nor would his own clergy, and there were signs of resistance not only from the Queen's known supporters but from the conservative political élite in general. Getting rid of Wolsey had increased the political power of the Boleyns and their status at court, but it had so far come nowhere near solving the burning issue of the day – how was Henry to get rid of Catherine?

The court was divided. Those who supported Anne unequivocally were mostly her family, the Earl of Wiltshire, and her brother George, Lord Rochford, who had of course their clients and dependants. Thomas Cranmer was scarcely a courtier of any significance at this point. The Queen's open supporters were no longer welcome at court, but there were many senior members whose attitude was equivocal,

66. Henry VII by an unknown artist *c.* 1500.

ELIZABETHA VXOR HENRICI.S VII

67. Henry VII's Queen, and Henry VIII's mother, Elizabeth of York. She holds a Tudor rose, as a symbol of her dynastic significance.

Above left: 68. Westminster Abbey. The site of Anne Boleyn's greatest triumph when she was crowned queen of England.

Above right: 69. Lady Margaret Beaufort. The matriarch of the Tudor dynasty, through whom Henry VII derived his tenuous claim to the throne, Lady Margaret narrowly outlived her son, to die early in her grandson's reign. Like her son, she is buried in what is in effect the Tudor mausoleum, the Lady Chapel he built at the back of Westminster Abbey.

Right: 70. Henry VIII portrayed in all his magnificence at King's College, Cambridge.

73. Henry VIII tilting before Queen Catherine, celebrating the birth of his short-lived son, February 1511. From the Great Tournament Roll of Westminster.

KATHERINA VXOR HENRICI . . VIII.

Left: 71. Cartoon of Henry VIII with his father by Hans Holbein, 1536-37. Drawn in black ink with watercolour washes. Paper, mounted on canvas. *Above*: 72. Catherine of Aragon as a slightly younger woman (c.1520?).

Above: 74. The tomb
of Henry Fitzroy,
Duke of Richmond,
Henry VIII's bastard
son. At St Michael's
church, Framlingham,
Suffolk.
Above right: 75.
Elizabeth (Bessie)
Blount, Henry's
mistress and the
mother of Henry
Fitzroy. From her
funeral effigy.
Right: 76. Cardinal
Thomas Wolsey
(1471 or 1475-1530).
From a drawing by
Jacques le Boucq.

78. The Field of Cloth of Gold, 1520, depicting the temporary palace built at Henry's orders especially for the occasion. The King takes centre stage.

Above left: 77. Thomas Cranmer (1489-1556). He was appointed Archbishop of Canterbury following the death of William Warham. From a painting by Gerhard Fliche.
Above right: 79. Design for a pageant tableau, probably intended for use by the merchants of the Steelyard at the coronation of Anne Boleyn in 1533. Anne was apparently upset by the fact that it was surmounted by an Imperial eagle rather than by her own badge of a white falcon.

ANNA BOLLINA   VXOR HEN VI

81. Anne Boleyn. Her relationship with Henry VIII from 1525 to 1532 was fraught with consequences, because of her insistence of marriage as a condition of sharing his bed. She failed to adapt to the role of Queen after 1533, and was executed in 1536.

82. Stained glass from Wolfhall. The glass showing Jane Seymour's phoenix badge and other royal images was moved to Great Bedwyn Church following the destruction of Wolfhall. The feathers under Jane's Phoenix badge show her to have been the mother of the Prince of Wales.

Above left: 80. Thomas Wyatt the elder, by Hans Holbein. Wyatt was a royal servant and diplomat who had, allegedly, been one of Anne Boleyn's 'lovers' in the 1520s.
Above right: 83. Jane Seymour, who was generally reckoned to be a comfortable creature rather than a great beauty. Drawing by Hans Holbein.

Above: 86. Henry VIII and his family, artist unknown, but about 1545. The Queen depicted is Jane Seymour. On the King's right is Prince Edward. Mary is further out on his right, and the twelve-year-old Elizabeth on his left. The figure on the extreme right is alleged to represent Will Somers, the King's jester.

Right: 84. A depiction of Henry VIII in a stained-glass window at Canterbury cathedral. The dependence of the design on Holbein's original is obvious.

85. Henry VIII, from a window in the chapel at Sudeley Castle.

Above left: 87. Drawing of
Sir Thomas More by Hans
Holbein, *c.* 1527. This drawing
is pricked for transfer to
canvas, and is the original of
the painting by Holbein now
in the Frick gallery in New
York.

Above right: 88. Drawing of
Archbishop William Warham
by Hans Holbein, *c.* 1527–28,
which is the original of the
painting now in the Louvre,
Paris.

Left: 89. Thomas Howard,
3rd Duke of Norfolk, Henry's
Lord Treasurer until his fall
in December 1546, and uncle
to both Anne Boleyn and
Catherine Howard. By Hans
Holbein.

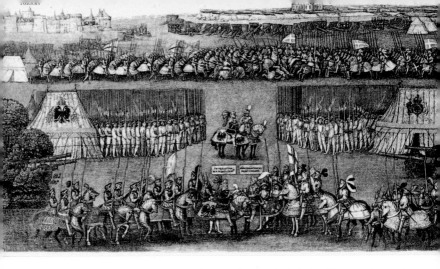

92. The meeting of the Emperor Maximilian I and Henry VIII during his campaign against Boulogne in 1544. Artist unknown.

Below: 90. Anne of Cleves, Henry's fourth wife. This is the portrait by Hans Holbein that misled the King into thinking that he was marrying a beauty. The marriage was dissolved after three months on the grounds of non-consummation.
Right: 91. Catherine Howard, Henry's fifth wife, as the Queen of Sheba. From a window at King's College Chapel, Cambridge.

95. The great Gate at Hampton Court. One of Henry's major additions to the palace.

Above left: 93. Henry's last Queen, Catherine Parr, from a window at Sudeley Castle. After Henry's death, Catherine married Thomas, Lord Seymour of Sudeley, and died there in childbirth in 1548.
Above right: 94. Desiderius Erasmus, the great Dutch humanist scholar, who spent some years at Cambridge in the early sixteenth century. From a contemporary engraving.

96. Edward VI as Prince of Wales
c. 1542. From a drawing by Hans
Holbein.

Right: 97. Edward VI, from a window
in the chapel at Sudeley Castle.
Above: 98. Mary Tudor, by an
unknown artist. Mary had little sense
of image, and failed to parade herself
convincingly for her subjects.

Above left: 99. Elizabeth I at prayer is the frontispiece to *Christian Prayers* (1569).

Above right: 100. Mary Stuart, Queen of Scots. Mary came to the throne of Scotland at just over a week old, in December 1542. Her claim to the English succession was ignored in Henry VIII's final Succession Act of 1544.

Left: 101. Thought to be Margaret Zouch, a lady-in-waiting to the Queen. A drawing by Hans Holbein.

The Dutchess of Suffolk.

The Lady Henegham

Above right: 102. Catherine Willoughby, a ward of the Duke of Suffolk, who became the second duchess after Mary's (the King's sister) death in 1536. She was a close friend of Queen Catherine Parr, and shared her reforming tastes in religion. She was a fugitive on the continent during Mary's reign. A drawing by Hans Holbein.

Right: 103. Margaret Shelton, later Lady Heveningham, in whom Henry was rumoured at one time to be interested. A drawing by Hans Holbein.

Above: 104. Jane Grey, from a stained-glass window at Sudeley Castle. Jane was the granddaughter of Henry's sister, Mary, by Charles Brandon, Duke of Suffolk. By the terms of his will, she was next heir to the Crown after his own three children, Edward, Mary and Elizabeth. In 1553 Edward attempted to promote her above Mary and Elizabeth, and she was Queen for about a fortnight following his death. In the contest between the two women, Mary prevailed, and Jane was executed in February 1554.

105. Henry VIII in later life, *c.* 1542, a drawing by Hans Holbein.

and who wished profoundly that the King would change his mind. The Duke of Suffolk was much influenced by his wife, and Mary (who absented herself as much as she could) was strongly sympathetic to Catherine.[39] Even among Henry's chosen companions, like the Marquis of Exeter and Nicholas Carew, there were those who had grievous doubts about the course which the King seemed increasingly likely to take. Most ambiguous of all was Thomas Howard, Duke of Norfolk. He was Anne's uncle, and had supported her vigorously against Wolsey, but he was deeply conservative by instinct, and shied away from any radical courses. His position was also complicated by the fact that he was estranged from his wife, Elizabeth, by virtue of his affair with Bess Holland. The Duchess was a strong supporter of Catherine, and this fact tended to keep the Duke somewhat tentatively on the Boleyn side, particularly in his dealings with Eustace Chapuys.[40] These alignments were also complicated by the need for French aid in Rome. Various agreements, going back to 1526, bound the two monarchs together, and in writing to Sir Francis Bryan, his ambassador in France, early in 1530, Henry was effusive in his references to his 'dearest brother' the King of France. Fortunately France had just acquired two new cardinals, and in one of these, Gabriel de Grammont, Bishop of Tarbes, the King placed especial trust. It was of no avail, and in March of the same year, Henry understood that 'the pope little regardeth the request made by our good brother the French King …'[41] Nevertheless, French pressure offered just about the only hope of countervailing Charles' influence in the Curia, and by the summer of 1531 there was talk on both sides of arranging another personal meeting between the monarchs to discuss the issue – and other things. The Boleyns were inevitably strongly supportive of this French connection, but others, including but not exclusively Catherine's friends, believed that the best way ahead was to do a deal with the Emperor, and these were the people to whom Chapuys principally talked, giving his reports that lop-sided air which makes them so suspect as a source.

In spite of the continuing deadlock, by 1532 events were moving on both sides. Elizabeth Barton, the so-called 'Nun of Kent', was escalating the political significance of her prophecies. Elizabeth seems to have been a woman of genuine holiness, but somewhat simple minded. She had begun in about 1527, apparently spontaneously, issuing dire threats as to what would happen to the King if he abandoned his wife, and to the Pope if he allowed it. She was taken seriously enough to impress both Wolsey and Warham, but was not at that stage considered to be much of a threat.[42] However, by 1532 Elizabeth had been taken up by a conservative clerical group led by her spiritual director, Dr Edward Bocking, who began to use her in a more coherent fashion. As the threat of such an outcome grew closer, she began to prophesy that Henry would cease to be king if he married Anne Boleyn, and that he would die a villain's death. Her utterances were 'authenticated' by a letter written from heaven by Mary Magdalene, and it began to be suspected that Bocking and his allies were planning to use her to provoke a rebellion in Kent, if Henry went ahead with his plans.[43] In various ways the stakes were increased, and the word treason began to be used, but it was not until after his second marriage had taken place (and her prophecies in a sense discredited) that the King struck. In July 1533 the Nun and her accomplices were arrested and taken to the Tower. On the other hand, Henry had acquired a new servant, and one who was to make a considerable difference to his plans. This was Thomas Cromwell, an erstwhile servant of Thomas Wolsey, who had done his best to protect his master's interests in the interval between his fall and his death just over a year later. Neither Cromwell's loyalty nor his efficiency passed unnoticed, and at some point early in 1530 he also entered the royal service – such 'dual citizenship' was not unusual – and by the end of that year had been sworn of the council.[44] It was probably Cromwell, who by 1532 was an important councillor, who orchestrated the 'Supplication against the Ordinaries' which went through the House of Commons in its session between January and March. This was principally an attack upon the legislative autonomy of the Convocations, which:

> have made and daily make divers fashions of laws and ordinances concerning temporal things; and some of them be repugnant to the laws and statutes of your realm, not having ne requiring your most royal assent to the same ...[45]

This was just the sort of attack to be devised by a lawyer to appeal to other lawyers. It was not submitted to the peers, and never made it to the statute book, but it was sent to the King, and was just the kind of backing which he was looking for at this stage of his campaign. Taking it to be an unofficial expression of opinion, Stephen Gardiner, the new Bishop of Winchester, undertook to reply to it on behalf of the clergy, an indiscretion which he was compelled to redeem the following year with the tract *De Vera Obedientia Oratio*.[46] Thanks to Cromwell, the supplication was as near to being a statement of the King's own opinion as makes no difference. Thomas Cromwell was made Master of the King's Jewel House in April 1532 – no doubt as a reward for his efforts.

By the autumn of 1532 Henry seems to have made up his mind to grasp his personal nettle. An act of Parliament, passed in the summer session, encroached upon spiritual jurisdiction to the extent of declaring that 'the unlawful payments of annates and first fruits ... shall from henceforth utterly cease', and that if Rome responded by withholding episcopal appointments, then the Archbishop was to go ahead and consecrate the elect person anyway – a direct infringement of the Roman prerogative.[47] In a fit of exasperation he had already dismissed Catherine from the court in July 1531, thus bringing the *ménage à trois* to an end. Now, as he prepared for his long-discussed meeting with Francis I he decided to give Anne the status necessary for her to accompany him. On 1 September he created her Marquis of Pembroke in her own right, a unique sign of royal favour. Margaret Pole had been recognised as Countess of Salisbury in 1513, but that had been in acknowledgement of an ancestral claim. Anne had no similar claim to her title, and it was to be the only one of its kind created by the Tudors.[48] No expense was spared to equip her for the event, and Catherine was humiliatingly stripped of her jewellery in order to adorn 'the scandal of christendom'. A retinue of some 2,000 nobles and others accompanied the couple when they sailed to Calais on 11 October, but it was noted that the thirty or so ladies who formed Anne's retinue all belonged to families associated with the Boleyns. Many prominent Englishwomen were missing, including the King's sister Mary, and it must be assumed that they had boycotted the event.[49] For about ten days Henry and Anne lived together at the Calais Exchequer, and then the King set off (on his own) to meet Francis at Boulogne. There he enjoyed 'great cheer', and presumably did some business, before accompanying Francis back to Calais on the 25th for the return visit. The French King had come equipped with a magnificent diamond as a present for the Marquis, but she did not at first appear, and Francis' lodgings were at some distance from the Exchequer. It was not until the banquet held on the 27th that Anne made her entrance, leading a masque of six ladies in magnificent costumes. All the ladies were disguised, and each chose a Frenchman to dance with, Anne of course choosing Francis.[50] Then the disguises were removed, amid scenes of great mirth, and the dancing continued. Anne and Francis, however, were observed to spend much of the time in earnest conversation. The following day was spent in sports of various kinds, which were better managed than those at the Field of Cloth of Gold and did not include jousting. Nor did Henry risk another fall at wrestling, so the amity of the occasion was conspicuously better than it had been twelve years earlier, and on the 29th Francis took his leave, the English King ceremoniously escorting him to the border.

News could travel fast in the sixteenth century, and within a week of the event Wynkyn de Worde had *The Manner of the Triumph at Calais and Boulogne* on sale in London, a neat piece of propaganda which contrived to make it appear that Mary Carey (who had been present) was actually the Princess Mary (who had not).[51] There was no way in which Catherine's daughter, then aged sixteen, would have countenanced such a triumph by her mother's supplanter. The royal couple travelled back more slowly. Detained by bad weather until 12 November, they continued together at the Exchequer, and after a painfully slow crossing finally landed at Dover on the 14th. Henry only reached Eltham on the 24th, and part of the explanation lies in dalliance by the way. At some point, and probably at several points, in early November, Henry and Anne actually slept together for the first time. Both were sufficiently confident by then that Henry had found a solution to the Great Matter which had been plaguing them both since 1527. On or before 1 October, Thomas Cranmer had been recalled from his mission to Germany and notified, much to his alarm, that he was to be the next Archbishop of Canterbury.[52]

The Archdeacon of Taunton was by no means an obvious man for this job. He was not a bishop, and had no administrative experience outside of Cambridge University. He was, however, a theologian and biblical scholar of some merit, and above all he was absolutely committed to the King's cause in the one issue which mattered above all others at that time – the question of Henry's marriage to Catherine. In early January 1533 Anne began to realise that she was pregnant, and this forced the issue. The child that she was carrying – hopefully a boy – must at all costs be born legitimate, and that gave them seven months to come up with a solution. About 25 January the couple were secretly married. It is not known who performed the ceremony, or what witnesses there may have been. Not even Cranmer was told, and it was not until March that the French ambassador found out.[53] Carlo Capello, the Venetian envoy, was the first to record such knowledge in writing, and that did not come until 12 April. Meanwhile, on 21 February Cranmer had been provided to the see of Canterbury. His views on the marriage question were well known – he had after all been on various missions to promote Henry's cause – so it was anticipated that the Pope might make some difficulties about awarding the *pallium*. However, Clement seems to have been willing to do anything within his power to avoid provoking the King of England further, and although he must have had a shrewd idea of what would happen, duly confirmed the appointment. Cranmer was consecrated on 30 March.[54] Meanwhile Parliament, which had convened on 4 February, had prepared draft legislation empowering convocation to resolve the issue of the King's first marriage, and a royal household had been created for Anne. On 9 April Catherine was informed that she would have to reduce her status and establishment to that of Dowager Princess of Wales, and on Easter Day, 13 April, Anne went to mass for the first time as queen. Although the enabling act for convocation had not been proceeded with, the Act in Restraint of Appeals, which received the royal assent on the day that Parliament was prorogued, 7 April, had the same practical effect.[55] Even before that Act became law, and after a protracted debate, on 5 April the southern convocation had declared that Henry's first marriage broke the law of God which no pope had power to dispense. There was some significant dissent from this verdict, and it was reached in open defiance of the papal ban on all discussion of the case, but neither of these things now mattered.[56] All this made the outcome of Cranmer's special court, convened at Dunstable on 10 May, a foregone conclusion. Catherine, who declined to recognise the Archbishop's jurisdiction, refused to appear, and was declared contumacious. This made the court's task easier still, and after only four sessions it declared the King's first marriage void. Catherine was now the Dowager Princess, Mary was illegitimate, and a few days later, on 31 May, Anne Boleyn rode to Westminster for her coronation.[57]

After such a protracted struggle, the conclusion was brief and painful. Opinion in London was generally hostile to the new queen. When preachers called for prayers for her, the congregations walked out, and the spontaneous enthusiasm generated for her coronation was carefully orchestrated, when it was not made up by the author of *The Noble Triumphant Coronation of Queen Anne*, a propaganda tract issued immediately after the event.[58] Several prominent figures boycotted the ceremony, including the Duchesses of Suffolk and Norfolk and the ex-Chancellor Thomas More, who had resigned the Great Seal when convocation had submitted to the King in the previous May, but whose approbation for the new order had been surreptitiously sought. The Imperial ambassador was also conspicuous by his absence, and confined his involvement to the writing of snide descriptions for the benefit of Charles V.[59] In spite of the efforts which were made to make it appear to be a glamorous triumph, Anne's coronation was in fact a thoroughly ambiguous event. The lavish river procession which preceded it, the salvos of gunfire which greeted her arrival at the Tower, and the exhausting banquet which followed being matched by the ominous silence of the crowds, most of whom kept their hats firmly on their heads and exhibited more curiosity than enthusiasm. Nor had the thinking which made it possible advanced as much as might appear. The historical arguments which underpinned the Act in Restraint of Appeals had been in the royal armoury for months, if not years, and the jurisdictional autonomy of the English Church was a claim which went back at least to 1529. What had changed was the emergence of a political will to make these various claims real. Henry had been advised that Parliament did not have the authority to challenge the spiritual estate, but the King thought differently, and it is probable that the man who convinced him was Thomas Cromwell.[60] By the end of 1532 Cromwell had emerged as the King's chief adviser. He was more intelligent than Norfolk or Suffolk, and more resolute that Wiltshire. He picked up the ideas already canvassed in the *Collectanea*, by William Tyndale and by Christopher St Germain, and formed them into a legislative programme. The 'Supplication against the Ordinaries' had been the first step, and the Act in Restraint of Appeals was the second. Cromwell was uninhibited by tradition, unlike Henry himself, but he had to be careful not to run faster than the King was willing to go. He may, or may not, have been a man of constitutional vision, but he was quite astute enough to see that Parliament offered by far the most promising way out of the jurisdictional impasse which had held up the King's second marriage for so long. Although its representational quality was somewhat notional, Parliament spoke for the whole realm, the clergy as well as the laity because of the presence of the bishops in the House of Lords. Moreover the King was a part of the Parliament, which could therefore act in his name as well as that of the other two estates.[61] It alone could make new law, and it had a determining voice in the interpretation of existing law. There were also good precedents for its operating on the fringes of ecclesiastical jurisdiction, not only in the celebrated Acts of provisors and praemunire, but also in restricting the benefit of clergy and the rights of sanctuary. When therefore the Act in Restraint spoke of cases:

within this realm, or within any of the king's dominions or marches of the same, wherein they concern the King our Sovereign Lord, his heirs or successors, or any other subjects or resiants within the same of what degree soever they be ... [they] shall be from henceforth heard, examined, discussed, clearly finally and definitely adjudged and determined within the king's jurisdiction and authority, and not elsewhere, in such courts spiritual and temporal ... as the nature of the causes ... shall require.[62]

It was not in a sense claiming anything very revolutionary. The revolution was implicit rather than explicit, because it was claimed that Henry was reverting to an earlier tradition, supported by 'divers sundry old authentic histories and chronicles'. A tradition which had been subverted by papal pretensions connived at by the King's progenitors.[63] The Act was clear enough in most respects. Henceforth all ecclesiastical cases were to be heard and finalised within the realm, using the Courts Christian established for that purpose. What was not clear was whether it was retrospective, and whether it covered the appeal which Catherine had already made before such a restriction was even thought of. Nor did it renounce papal authority altogether, and certainly did not seek to cut England off from the Western Church. One thing at a time, Cromwell may well have thought. What he had done was to provide a legal basis for Cranmer to proceed against Henry's first marriage, and to declare the second marriage valid. Anne's child would be legitimate, at least by English law, and what happened next would depend upon the Pope's reaction. In Consistory on 11 July, Clement solemnly condemned the King's separation from Catherine and his second marriage, giving him until September to return to his wife, under pain of excommunication.[64]

After the coronation, the party continued in the Queen's chamber. 'Pastime,' as one observer wrote, 'was never more.' Years of pent up frustration could now be released, and it is not clear what (if any) role the Queen played in the mourning which Henry was obliged to enter into for his sister, Mary, who died on 24 June. It would have been hypocritical of Anne to have mourned a woman who had for years been one of her most outspoken opponents. Her principal reaction was no doubt one of relief. Catherine and the younger Mary, however, continued to be recalcitrant. Neither would accept their new status, and initial attempts to reduce their households were met by the dumb loyalty of their servants.[65] Requested to give up the splendid christening robe which she had brought originally from Spain, Catherine absolutely refused, realising that it was intended for use by Anne when she had given birth. 'God forbid,' she is reported to have said, 'that I should ever be so badly advised as to give help, assistance or favour, directly or indirectly, in a case so horrible as this', and that was surely her sentiment, if not her actual words.[66] Seldom can a royal confinement have been awaited with the eager anticipation which preceded this one, and preparations for Anne's lying in began at Greenwich in early August. Henry cancelled his planned summer progress in order to be on hand, although what he thought he could do if anything went wrong is not clear. However, all was well, and Anne 'took to her Chamber' on 26 August. Elizabeth was born on the afternoon of 7 September, after an easy labour, a perfect and flourishing child, who took after her father. Her sex was a disappointment to both her parents, and Chapuys could scarcely conceal his mirth – all that effort for another girl![67] The planned jousts were abandoned, but apart from that the rejoicings were genuine enough, and next time, it would surely be a boy. She was christened in the church of the Observant Friars at Greenwich on 10 September, and named for her paternal grandmother. It was a time for reconciliation, and several of Catherine's friends played prominent roles in the ceremony, including Gertrude, Marchioness of Exeter, who stood Godmother. Thomas Cranmer was Godfather, and inevitably the Queen's Howard and Boleyn kindred were also prominent, although to see this as a 'Boleyn triumph' seems to mistake the intention.[68]

Mary – or the Lady Mary, as she should now be called – had no part in any of this. Her opposition was just as determined as that of her mother, and considerably less discreet. She told her father's commissioners that the title of princess was hers by right, and that she had no intention of surrendering it. By 10 October Catherine felt it necessary to warn her not to countenance any movement of open opposition to the King's proceedings, because there is some evidence to suggest that political enemies of the King, encouraged by Chapuys, were looking to her for a lead. She was only seventeen and her inexperience might easily lead her into danger. By early November, Henry had decided that Mary was a threat, because Anne, in spite of her celebrations, was vulnerable.[69] She had not produced the son which would have finally consolidated her position, and the King now had two daughters, both of doubtful legitimacy. It must be unequivocally asserted that Elizabeth was his rightful heir, so he dissolved Mary's household (for which he was paying) and sent her with a handful of servants to live in the new household which had been created for the real princess. It was a martyrdom which was to last for nearly three years, and which Mary herself consistently blamed on the malice of Queen Anne.[70] The evidence for this interpretation is mixed – it depends on which sources you credit – but Anne would certainly have had grounds for being harsh to a young woman who went out of her way to be offensive to her whenever an opportunity presented itself. During these years Mary seems to have been an affliction to herself and to everyone who had dealings with her, and the stress induced by these circumstances affected her health for the rest of her life.[71]

Meanwhile, September had come and gone, and the papal sentence of excommunication was due to take effect. News to this effect disrupted the Duke of Norfolk's mission to the French court and caused Henry to try and dissuade Francis from going ahead with his planned meeting with the Pope. Francis, however, had other business with the pontiff apart from the affairs of the King of England, and duly met Clement at Marseilles on 13 October. The meeting was amicable, and resulted in a marriage agreement between the Pope's niece, Catherine, and Francis' second son, Henry. The only sour note was provided, unsurprisingly, by the English, when on 7 November a special mission arrived, consisting of Stephen Gardiner and Edmund Bonner. Bonner had been briefed to remonstrate with the Pope, to demand the recall of the King's case to England, and to appeal from Clement's sentence of excommunication to a General Council of the Church.[72] The Pope was unmoved. The most that he would concede, on the intercession of Francis, was a further stay of two months on the sentence of excommunication. Henry was not the slightest bit grateful for this effort, and when he heard of the friendly nature of the Franco/Papal discussions, denounced his 'good brother' as a fickle villain. Francis was outraged. He and his cardinals had done the best they could for Henry, and might even have succeeded further if it had not been for Bonner's inept intervention. In spite of years of practice, the King of England had not the faintest idea how to negotiate with Rome.[73] In the event the delayed sentence of excommunication was never promulgated, but relations between England and France suffered long-term damage.

The late summer and autumn of 1533 were tense as the King awaited both Anne's confinement and the papal sentence against him. In July Elizabeth Barton was arrested and all the copies of *The Nuns Book* were seized and destroyed. Strenuous efforts were made to implicate Catherine and some of her more prominent supporters such as Fisher and More in her treason, but they had, for the most part, been far too discreet to get caught. Only Fisher was indicted for misprision, and that charge was not proceeded with.[74] On 20 November a large gathering of councillors and others debated the case, and on the 23rd the accused were exposed to public humiliation at Paul's Cross. A few days later Barton herself, Edward Bocking and four others were attainted of high treason, although it was not until the following April that they were executed. The King, who took a strong personal interest in the case, may have been hoping to extract further damaging confessions, but if so, he does not appear to have succeeded.[75] It had also been intended to recall Parliament in the autumn, and a draconian programme of legislation was drawn up for it, possibly to meet the threat of papal excommunication. Anyone recognising that sentence or otherwise supporting the Pope would have been guilty of high treason, and half the lands of the Church were to be seized to provide for the King's defence. In the event the delay of the sentence probably caused Parliament to be deferred until January 1534 and the draft legislative programme disappeared. When it did reconvene, its programme was both less punitive and more constructive, although equally anti-papal. Cromwell's fingerprints are all over it, although it is clear that Henry approved of what was being done. First an Act in Restraint of Annates confirmed and made effective the statute of the previous year, which had been posted mainly as a threat. Second, an Act for the Submission of the Clergy gave statutory form to the surrender of convocation in May 1532; and thirdly a Dispensations Act cancelled all other dues normally paid to Rome, thus completing the English Church's isolation from the Holy See.[76] All these were effectively tidying-up acts, completing processes already begun. More original, and again reflective of Cromwell's thinking, was the succession Act. This firstly confirmed that the King's marriage to Catherine had been unlawful, and that his second marriage was good and sound. Mary was thus disinherited, and the succession settled on any son who might be born to Queen Anne. In default of such a son, Elizabeth was to inherit. This was the first time that Parliament had been used to pronounce on such an issue, and was a reflection of the enhanced status which that institution was coming to enjoy. When a similar problem had been brought to the Lords and Commons in 1460, they had disclaimed any right to adjudicate in so high a mystery.[77] It was only logical therefore, that when Parliament assembled for a further session in November 1534, that it should have been invited to pass the Act of Supremacy, roundly declaring that the Bishop of Rome had no more jurisdiction in England than any other foreign bishop, and that:

> the king our sovereign lord ... shall be taken, accepted and reputed the only supreme head in earth of the Church of England, called the Ecclesia Anglicana, and shall have and enjoy annexed and united to the imperial crown of this realm as well the style and title thereof, as all honours dignities ... [etc.] ... to the said dignity of supreme head of the same church belonging and appertaining ...[78]

The denial of this was to be high treason.

Henry's relations with the Pope and the Emperor could hardly have been any worse by this time anyway, so the formalisation of the English schism scarcely made any difference. He had also fallen out with Francis, and was in serious danger of being isolated in Europe, a circumstance which turned his diplomatic attentions towards the Schmalkaldic League of Germany. These princes might be Lutherans, but at least they were determined opponents of Charles V, and that commended them to Cromwell, and through him to the King. Fortunately, perhaps, the Emperor was preoccupied with plans for a counter-attack against the Moors, and the King of France was temporarily quiescent, so foreign policy was not at the top of Henry's agenda. Then in September 1534 Clement's troubled pontificate came to an end, and the King's interest in Rome reawakened. The conclave selected Alessandro Farnese, who took the title of Paul III, which should have been good news because he had earlier expressed an interest in bringing the English schism to an end. Shortly after his election he sent for Gregory Casale, who was still in Rome although without any status, to ask how to recover English allegiance.[79] Casale reassured him that he would only have to be reasonable. Unfortunately Paul's idea of reasonableness did not relate to Henry's, who demanded nothing short of a total papal climbdown, including the recognition of the Royal Supremacy. This being so, immediate negotiations were out of the question, although subterranean lines of communication remained open in case one party or the other should change his mind. It was not until the summer of 1535 that hopeful signals began to pass to and fro, and then the execution of John Fisher for treason effectively put an end to such exchanges, for the time being at least.

Meanwhile, Henry's relationship with his second wife was becoming a subject for fascinated speculation. Anne became pregnant again within about three months of Elizabeth's birth, but this time miscarried in July 1534, a circumstance which seems to have given the King an attack of *déjà vu*.[80] Court gossips, and particularly the Imperial ambassador, were full of salacious stories about the King's supposed amours, and of the Queen's alleged reaction to them. Some of these stories were pure invention, others may have had some substance, particularly as Anne was unavailable to him during the early months of 1534, and she was not accustomed to being upstaged in such a fashion. For years she had enjoyed a monopoly of Henry's sexual attentions, and it would have come as a shock to discover that such was no longer the case. Nor was she accustomed to mincing her words when affronted. That Henry became angry at these outbursts is likely enough, although reports of their quarrels are interspersed with others declaring that 'the Lady's' influence was as great as ever. The real problem probably was that Anne never learned to behave like a conventional sixteenth-century wife – and Henry was nothing if not conventional. As a mistress she could be fretful, jealous and demanding, but as a wife she was supposed to be submissive and tractable. During their prolonged courtship, the King had found her tantrums exciting and even stimulating, but when she continued to behave in the same way after their marriage, he began to find it tedious.[81] There was also the problem of Mary, that wilful obstinate child for whom Henry nevertheless retained a strong affection. Anne's language about Mary was frequently violent – in self-defence as much as anything else – and the King did his best to repress her. But he was not prepared to do anything more, and that annoyed Anne when she was in one of her more vengeful moods. Her hostility to the girl was well known, and that had the advantage of enabling Charles V to blame her for Mary's harsh treatment, a treatment allegedly unknown to the King. He was therefore able to remain on more or less civil terms with Henry, in spite of the schism, and that was an advantage when it came to keeping him away from any fuller commitment to France.[82] Anne also reacted badly when discussions with Francis turned in the direction of a marriage alliance during 1534. She was provoked by the fact that the French still seemed more interested in Mary than in Elizabeth, in spite of her illegitimate status. In fact this suggestion had emanated from the Emperor, and was part of a package proposal advanced in November 1534 to settle disputes between himself and Francis. In that respect Elizabeth was largely irrelevant, but Anne still pressed her case, and became exceedingly put out when the French King rejected it.[83] At that point, early in 1535, Henry needed all the friends he could get, and his queen's reaction was no help at all. Anne's dual function as councillor and consort brought its own problems, but in spite of all the rumours, there is no sign of a serious rift between the royal couple until the autumn of that year. Anne was unpopular, and a liability to the King in terms of his public relations, and that also helped to fuel the rumours. There was a constituency which wanted rid of her, and Henry was aware of that. However, their relationship continued along its erratic and passionate course until it eventually cracked under the strain of so many pressures.

Catherine may well have been amused at this situation, which Henry had so obviously brought on himself, but her opinion no longer counted for much, as even Chapuys admitted. Sequestered from the King's presence, she had retired with her household to Ampthill, retaining for the time being the status and establishment of a queen. When her title was reduced to that of Princess Dowager, she had perforce to remove from Ampthill, which was a royal residence, and settled instead at the Bishop of Lincoln's palace at Buckden in July 1533.[84] Her household was reduced, but not by very much, and the royal commissioners studiously ignored the fact that her servants went on addressing her by the royal title. In theory this was a treasonable offence, and under the terms of the Act of Supremacy they should all have sworn an oath not to do so. However, Henry instructed that the oath was not to be administered to Catherine, and the practice continued.[85] In spite of being so obviously out of favour, and harassed from time to time by royal commissioners, Catherine was on the whole treated quite generously, and well served by her local supporters. Her main affliction was the ban on communication with her daughter. In terms of written messages this could be circumvented using loyal servants, but being deprived of her company, even in times of illness, was hard. In May 1534, perhaps as a precaution, or perhaps because of Anne Boleyn's paranoia, she was moved again from Buckden to the rather less salubrious mansion of Kimbolton. Her household had been reduced again at the end of 1533, but was still costing the King £3,000 a year, so the scale of her housekeeping was generous.[86] Chapuys' story of Catherine and her ladies cooking their own food over a fire in the Privy Chamber may have been true, but that had nothing to do with constraints on her lifestyle.

She was undoubtedly afraid of being poisoned and may have chosen that as a remedy. A full kitchen establishment was available, if she chose to use it. The ambassador, who was not allowed to visit Kimbolton, was dependent upon informants, and they, knowing what he wanted to hear, gave their imaginations full rein. Chapuys' despatches present a consistent story of dishonour, hardship and abuse, but the reality was rather different. Henry was extremely scrupulous in treating his former wife according to the dignity which she then enjoyed, that of Princess Dowager. Realising that she would never countenance open resistance to his will in her own name or that of her daughter, Henry decided to tolerate her dissent.

This toleration, however, could not be extended to her more high-profile supporters. Both Sir Thomas More and Bishop John Fisher refused the oath required by the Act of Supremacy, and brushing aside a suggestion from Cranmer that they be allowed to swear to the succession only, Henry consigned them both to the Tower in 1534. Brought to trial in 1535 both were inevitably convicted and executed in July of that year.[87] They were not alone. Several Carthusian priors, leaders of that most respected of the mendicant orders, had also refused submission and suffered the same fate. These executions signalled a new phase in the King's thinking. He was absolutely determined to have his own way, not only in his political relations with the Pope and the Emperor, but in enforcing the obedience of his subjects. The legislation of 1534 spelled out a programme which was to be imposed in detail, and nobody, clergy or laity, were exempt from it, unless the King so chose. Realising that he faced a struggle to impose his vision of kingship, Henry was sufficiently convinced of his own righteousness to create and enforce extreme laws, and in terms of what he was attempting to achieve he was right. The Royal Supremacy was launched in blood, and that persuaded most of those who were unhappy with it to conceal their opposition on the assumption that once the succession was settled Henry would forget his rhetoric and negotiate a deal with the papacy. There was no point in running such an extreme risk for the sake of a temporary aberration.

So Henry acquired a European reputation for tyranny. The execution of Fisher, recently created a cardinal, caused particular offence and Paul III drew up a fresh edict of excommunication, deposing Henry and releasing his subjects from their allegiance. This was done on 30 August 1535, but again it was not promulgated because Paul wisely decided that there was no prospect of securing its enforcement.[88] The Emperor was preoccupied with his campaign against Tunis, the King of France was too friendly to Henry, and the King's own subjects were either too intimidated or inclined to support his policies. So at the end of the year the threat still remained suspended, merely a symbol of the total breakdown in relations between England and Rome. Meanwhile Anne Boleyn was pregnant again, giving renewed hope of the birth of a prince, and at Kimbolton Catherine's health was collapsing. Mary was not allowed to visit her mother, to the great anguish of both of them, and then on 7 January 1536 the former queen died. Henry is alleged to have 'worn yellow for mourning', but whether or not he did so, he must have felt a profound sense of relief. At last the papal order to return to her had become meaningless.

9

THE LORDSHIP &
KINGDOM OF IRELAND

Tudor policy in Ireland was not a success. Although when the nine years' war eventually came to an end in 1603, the Irish were subdued, that in itself was a failure in terms of the aspirations which had prevailed earlier in the previous century. The English, or rather Anglo-Norman, presence in Ireland went back a long way, to the days when Hugh de Lacy had been appointed Justice and Custos in 1172.[1] By the late fifteenth century the island was divided roughly into three zones. The first was the Dublin Pale, which was under effective English rule, where the common law was applied, and where the King's writ ran without question. The second was the so-called 'obedient land', of Leinster and Munster, which was ruled by Anglo-Irish peers such as the Earls of Kildare and Desmond. These peers acknowledged the overlordship of the Kings of England, and used common law and Gaelic custom as appropriate. The third zone was 'wild Irishry', which was ruled by Gaelic chieftains, without reference to the King, where his overlordship was not acknowledged, and where Gaelic custom was the only law. Gaelic Ireland was in no sense united, and in the perpetual small wars which prevailed there, alliance with the Anglo-Irish peers, or with the English Governor himself was not out of the question.[2] In theory the whole of Ireland was a lordship under the English Crown, but in practice the King's effective rule extended to less than a third of the island, and tended to fluctuate with the strength of the English Crown at home. Both Lambert Simnel and Perkin Warbeck found support in Ireland for their pretensions to the English throne, and Henry VII was, by and large, happy to settle for the submission of

243

the Anglo-Irish peers, while allowing them to continue governing the country in the King's name.[3]

At first Henry VIII was equally happy to continue with this situation, and reappointed Gerald, the 8th Earl of Kildare, as Chief Governor immediately after his accession. Any understanding of what followed is dependent upon an appreciation of the nature of Kildare's position. On the one hand he was *Gearoid Mor* (The Great FitzGerald), a chieftain of power and resources, respected and feared by the Irish clans.[4] On the other hand he was the King's representative, whose authority to govern the Pale depended entirely upon a royal commission. At the same time, on his own great estates he had a *manred* which was both English and Irish, and whose first loyalty was to him as their overlord. His position could thus be compared to that of the great English magnates of the fifteenth century, such as the Earls of Warwick or Northumberland, whose capacity to make trouble for the King was so great that he was virtually forced to govern through them. Kildare was Old English, proud of his connections with the English Crown and court, and contemptuous of Irish manners. But he was also an amphibian who could operate in both media. Gaelic political consciousness was highly particularist and dynastic, and the Fitzgerald family could be fitted into that context with little adaptation. The 8th Earl's children were married into both communities.[5] The Celtic praise singers might laud his position as the royal governor rather than the High King of Tara, but the substance of what they were saying was much the same. It is hardly surprising that the Earl therefore saw any strengthening of his position among the tribes as an enhancement of the authority of the Crown. Nor is it surprising that his activities when viewed from London, took on a rather different perspective. A man who was as at home in the Gaelic language and culture as he was in English exposed himself to misunderstanding, yet such expertise was essential to his position.

The distinction between the Irish and English communities, in terms of language, law and lifestyle was clear enough, and there was plenty of mutual antagonism, but there were also big areas of overlap. Land titles in the marcher areas were fearsomely complicated, a complexity increased by the fact that the area of English settlement had shrunk during the troubles of the mid-fifteenth century. This had left some places in Gaelic occupation, and presently subject to Celtic law, but to which English title remained. This could be exploited as settler fortunes revived, but only at the cost of confused legal process, and often violence. Some English settlers also preferred brehon law for certain purposes. It was less draconian than the common law, and allowed (for example) composition for homicide.[6] In the marcher lordships that option was available. Similarly some Irish tenants in the same lordships preferred English law for property disputes, because of the greater clarity and firmness of the remedies which it offered. To the Irish tribes the King of England was not so much an ethnic or ideological enemy as an alien presence which had to be accommodated, and which could be a useful ally when the circumstances were right. If the English of the Pale had a complaint against government from London in the first decade of the sixteenth century, it was that they saw too little of it. The Fitzgerald ascendancy was not unacceptable, but it could be oppressive, particularly when the Earl was juggling his priorities with the 'Wild' Irish. There was a parliament in Ireland, modelled on that in England, but until 1494 it was not entirely clear who had the right to summon it. In that year the Lord Deputy, Sir Edward Poynings, secured the passage of an Act which rested the initiative firmly with the English Crown, and prescribed that only matters initiated by the council in London should be considered for legislation. This so-called 'Poyning's Law' governed the operations of the Irish Parliament thereafter.[7] Partly for that reason it was never as independent or as important as its English counterpart, and of course it only represented the Pale, the obedient land, and the English towns of the South, such as Galway and Limerick. The native Irish were unrepresented, and did not recognise its jurisdiction.

The 8th Earl of Kildare died in 1513, having made no noticeable adjustments to his style of government, and not having been called upon to do so. He was succeeded in office by his son, the 9th Earl, and everything seemed set to continue as before. However, Henry VIII was more inquisitive about what happened in the 'other island' than his father had been, and more inclined to bestow Irish offices upon his English courtiers. He appointed Sir William Compton, the Chief Gentleman of his Privy Chamber, as chancellor. Compton never went to Ireland, and discharged his office through a competent deputy.[8] He similarly appointed John Kite to the archbishopric of Armagh in 1513, before translating him to Carlisle in 1521. Unlike Compton, Kite did reside on his cure – which he regarded as a kind of exile – and his recall to the remotest, and one of the poorest, English sees, says a lot about the priority with which Ireland was regarded. Kildare lacked his father's sureness of touch, and the feeling began to grow among the gentry of the Pale that the FitzGerald ascendancy might not be the unmitigated blessing which they had supposed. In 1514 the Earl made the mistake of dismissing two of his baronial council, William Darcy and Robert Crowley, who promptly made their way to London and began to bend the ears of the King's council about the Chief Governor's mismanagement.[9] He had, it was alleged, made war and peace without the consent of his council, and introduced both Irish men and Irish customs into his government to an unacceptable degree. Apart from a small area around Dublin, the 'Englishry' was losing its identity, and if nothing was done the whole colony stood in danger of disappearing. Kildare was summoned to London in 1515, and confronted his accusers. Their charges, it soon transpired, were personally motivated and wildly exaggerated. The Earl was exonerated and confirmed in office. However, the whole episode had served as a timely reminder of the Chief Governor's ultimate dependence upon the King. This time he had not only been endorsed, but significantly rewarded; next time he might not be so successful, and almost immediately after his return, a caltrop was thrown into his path by the death of Thomas Butler, Earl of Ormond.

Thomas died without a direct male heir, and the inheritance was disputed between his cousin, Sir Piers Butler, and his two daughters. Piers looked to his friend Kildare for support, but Henry had unequivocally instructed his Chief Governor to recognise the claims of Anne St Leger and Margaret Boleyn, both well connected at the English Court.[10] Margaret indeed was the mother of Sir Thomas Boleyn and grandmother to Mary and Anne, the former of whom was just beginning to attract the King's favourable notice. In December 1515 Henry gave livery of all the Ormond lands in England, Wales and Ireland to the two women, but Kildare and the Irish council accepted the claims of Sir Piers, and the Irish lands went in practice to him. He began to style himself Earl of Ormond, but Henry did not for some time recognise him as such, and feeling that the Chief Governor had let him down, Butler quarrelled bitterly with FitzGerald in 1520. Henry, on the other hand, considered that his instructions had not been obeyed, and when further complaints arose against the Chief Governor's regime, he was less inclined to look on him with favour. By 1520 the Kildare ascendancy was beginning to unravel, and Henry, prompted no doubt by Wolsey, was thinking that the devolved government of Ireland, which had worked for nearly thirty years, was no longer performing satisfactorily. In March 1520 he sent across a reliable English nobleman, Thomas Howard, Earl of Surrey, as Lord Lieutenant in Kildare's place.[11]

Howard's instructions were sweeping: 'to inform [his] highness by what means and way [his] grace might reduce this land to obedience and good order'. He was to recall the marcher lords to their direct allegiance, and to levy the King's revenues throughout the obedient land.[12] Kildare was summoned to London, and kept there for the time being. Unfortunately, the resources which the Earl was given (and over which there was a good deal of haggling) were not sufficient for so ambitious a programme. In spite of ostensibly proposing a sweeping programme of change, the English gentry of the Pale offered little in the way of practical support, and the backing of the noble affinities was patchy and unpredictable. By 1521 Surrey's lieutenancy was costing the King £10,000 a year above the revenues of Ireland, and had achieved virtually nothing. The Earl was insistent that only a military conquest could subdue even the Anglo-Irish feudatories, let alone the 'Wild Irish', but Henry was unconvinced, looking instead for a process of more or less peaceful pressure.[13] This soon became a fundamental disagreement, because the traditional English attitude towards the Irish was that they were a subject people, who could be expropriated at will. This was, by and large, the position which Surrey adopted, but the King and Wolsey favoured instead an attempt to win over the Irish chieftains, which, ironically, was much closer to the practice of the Anglo-Irish peers. Not for the last time, the English government became bogged down in the contradictions and illogicalities of Irish politics. Meanwhile, the FitzGeralds were seething with discontent, and Kildare himself was returning to favour at court. In September 1521 Surrey was recalled. In tangible terms he had accomplished nothing, but what his mission had done was to set out in stark terms the alternatives which confronted the King in his other realm. Either he must commit the large resources of men and money which would be required for a military conquest, and to go on doing so for a long time in support of a regime controlled directly from England, or he must fudge and compromise with the various factions and groups which constituted the Englishry, and try by gradual persuasion to improve relations with the native Irish. Meanwhile, Kildare still not being fully rehabilitated, Henry appointed no less a person than Piers Butler as Lord Deputy, presumably on the grounds that he controlled the second-largest affinity in the obedient land, and was a reliable opponent of the Geraldines.[14] He offered him favour, and a good marriage, but did not recognise him as Earl of Ormond until 1528.

Piers' estates, it soon transpired, were in the wrong place, his resources inadequate and the Geraldines uncontrollable. At the same time a third Anglo-Irish peer, the Earl of Desmond, complicated the issue further by entering into direct negotiations with Francis I during the second Anglo-French war, and by recognising Richard de la Pole as King of England![15] This was little more than a nuisance as far as Henry was concerned, but the deteriorating situation prompted him to receive Kildare back into favour in 1523, and to despatch the Earl back to Ireland to pacify his kindred. Butler and Kildare immediately quarrelled, and in the summer of 1524 Wolsey attempted another cheap direct involvement by sending a special commission over to resolve the dispute. Ostensibly this was successful, and both peers entered into bonds to keep the peace towards each other, but the equilibrium was again upset when Kildare was restored as Chief Governor later in 1524, whereupon his feud with Butler promptly flared up again. Complaints and counter-complaints were soon flying backwards and forwards across the Irish sea, and it was alleged that Kildare was inciting the Irish tribes to attack his rival's estates. Although the Earl's reappointment restored order to the Pale, this continuing quarrel, plus Kildare's failure to apprehend the rogue Earl of Desmond, prompted another rethink in 1528. Both protagonists were summoned to London and detained, while the governorship was placed in the hands of Thomas FitzGerald of Leixlip, as Lord Justice.[16] This reduced the main faction fight to skirmishing, but weakened the government in the face of Irish incursions, and pleas for more money and military resources were soon resumed. Only in one respect was the situation eased; the Earl of Desmond died in June 1529, and the desire of his successor for royal recognition led to his submission and the settlement of that particular issue.

Uncertainty seems to have prevailed during the last days of Wolsey's ascendancy. First Piers Butler was restored in August 1528, now recognised as Earl of Ormond, and then in June 1529 the King's illegitimate son, Henry Fitzroy, Duke of Richmond, was appointed Lord Lieutenant.[17] This appears to represent a complete change of direction, because Fitzroy never visited Ireland, and for about a year the office was discharged by a 'secret council' headed by John Allin, the Archbishop of Dublin. After Wolsey's fall, in the summer of 1530, William Skeffington was appointed deputy. Skeffington, who was backed by a modest but effective military force, succeeded in bringing an end to the feud between Desmond and Ormond, and persuaded Henry to send Kildare back to Ireland, with the specific brief of managing the borders with the Irish tribes. The improvement, however, was purely temporary. By the summer of 1531 Skeffington and Kildare had fallen out, the Parliament of October 1531 threw out the subsidy bill, thus reducing the government to impotence, and in the summer of 1532 Skeffington was recalled and charged with all sorts of malpractices.[18] Apparently despairing of any better solution, the King restored Kildare to office, only this time as deputy. However, by the summer of 1533 Thomas

Cromwell was turning his omni-competent gaze towards Ireland, and not liking what he saw. He began a policy of 'subliminal intervention', securing control of Irish patronage, and promoting Ormond or Desmond supporters to lesser but significant offices. Kildare was summoned to London, but sent his excuses, and there was talk of sending William Skeffington back to Ireland. By late 1533 English politics were having their impact in Ireland, and resentment over the King's Proceedings were adding further fuel to the many fires of controversy. Early in 1534 Kildare rethought his position, and decided to obey the summons on being given permission to appoint his son Thomas, Lord Offaly, to act in his absence.

This was the signal for a crisis. By May Kildare was facing charges of treason, and on 11 June Lord Offaly stormed into the Irish Council, resigned his office, and denounced the King's policies from every possible angle.[19] Exactly what persuaded Offaly to ignore the subtleties and ambiguities of Irish politics in this forthright way, we do not know, but within a month he was in open rebellion, murdered the Archbishop of Dublin, and laid siege to Dublin Castle. 'Silken Thomas', as he was known, claimed to be leading a Catholic crusade against the schismatical King of England, and sought support, both among dissident peers in England and also from the Emperor. For a variety of reasons, none was forthcoming. Charles V was interested for a while, but eventually was not drawn, and men like Lord Darcy, who sympathised with his ostensible intentions, were not prepared to act.[20] Had the Irish revolt coincided with the Pilgrimage of Grace it might have been a different story, but it did not. In Irish terms, however, it was a considerable conflagration, being partly religious in its motivation, and partly provoked by the increasing signs of central interference in the affairs of the lordship. Although Kildare was off the scene, his affinity rallied to his heir, as did many of those whom Kildare had appointed to office before his departure. Both the Pale gentry and their natural enemies, the Irish tribes, were involved. This combination had its drawbacks, because those most opposed to the Kildare affinity, or most hostile to the native Irish, had every incentive to remain loyal. Viewed from outside, the rebellion looked more like a civil war. Neither the King nor Cromwell showed the slightest inclination to compromise, and although it took some time to mobilises a response, Henry happened to be free from other military commitments at that point.[21]

At first the rebels had the better of a very confused conflict, but the return of Skeffington in October 1534 with over 2,000 troops transformed the situation. This was a very large army by Irish standards, where battles were normally fought by scores or hundreds, and it quickly restored the Pale and most of the obedient land to its allegiance. As his English followers dropped away, or were defeated, Offaly found himself increasingly dependent upon his Irish allies, and this gave a new, and ultimately sinister twist to the conflict. After his own main fortress of Maynooth had fallen to the royal forces in March 1535, 'Silken Thomas' took refuge with the tribes, and during the summer of 1535, the war acquired an ethnic dimension of Gael against Gall, which had not been present before. It may be that Offaly (by this time the 10th Earl of Kildare)[22] was himself perturbed by the implications of this, because in August of that year he surrendered and the rebellion came to an end. It may well be that Kildare expected that this conflict would end, as was normal in Ireland, with submission, composition, and eventually a return to favour. He probably expected no worse than a period in the wilderness, such as had often been inflicted on his family in the past. If so, he was to be disillusioned. He had insulted the King, and sought foreign allies. Meanwhile the Pilgrimage of Grace reminded the King that he could no more afford to be tolerant of opposition in Ireland than in England. After the end of the Pilgrimage, in February 1537 the 10th Earl and his five uncles were all executed in London. The Kildare ascendancy had been brought to a bloody end.

This marked an important turning point, because Ireland was now a welter of competing affinities and interests, no one of which had the edge. After the death of the Duke of Richmond in the summer of 1536, it was decided that the country would have to be governed more directly, by an English deputy supported with a sizeable garrison. Lord Leonard

Grey was actually appointed before Richmond's death, and it was under his auspices that the Irish Reformation Parliament met in 1537, which dutifully extended the Royal Supremacy to the Church in Ireland.[23] In spite of the fury which the implementation of such a policy had seemed to threaten only three years before, these measures were accepted without serious resistance. However, there was still no agreement as to general policy in Ireland. Grey, backed by the Irish administration, favoured a full conquest of the island, arguing that the collapse of Silken Thomas' insurgency presented a unique opportunity.[24] Henry, on the other hand, was acutely conscious of the cost of such a 'forward' policy, and of the risks of getting literally bogged down in the tribal lands. Between September 1537 and April 1538 a specially appointed commission for Irish affairs examined the options, and recommended that in future the Council in Dublin should confine itself to governing and defending the Englishry, and that administrative reforms should be introduced to increase control over the obedient land. Relations with the Irish chieftains should be confined to the giving and taking of pledges for the peace, and otherwise there should be no attempt to expand into tribal land.[25] Lord Grey, who was not happy with these recommendations, was replaced in 1540 by Sir Anthony St Leger, who was to remain as Lord Deputy for the rest of the reign – and beyond. By this time Cromwell had also gone, and the way was open for a new initiative.

St Leger's name is always associated with the last, and the most hopeful, phase of Henry's Irish policy, which was symbolised by his erection of the traditional lordship into a kingdom in 1541.[26] This was in part a natural consequence of the rejection of papal authority, because there was a general (and well-founded) belief that the King of England held the lordship of Ireland as a fief from the Pope. Henry would have nothing to do with such a view, and chose this way in which to demonstrate his sovereignty. However, it was also intended to indicate an 'equal but separate' system of government. Instead of embarking upon a vastly expensive and confrontational policy of conquest, he would attempt to incorporate the tribal lands into the new kingdom by a policy of inclusion and reconciliation. This was the policy of 'surrender and regrant', which was attempted by St Leger between 1541 and 1547. The basic idea was simple. Each tribal chieftain would surrender his lands to the King of Ireland, and receive them back as a fief to be held of the King in chief. Along with each grant would go a barony, which carried with it a place in the Irish House of Lords.[27] It was assumed that a process of anglicisation and 'civilisation' would then follow. The early results were promising. After the ritual gestures of coercion which were part of the traditional liturgy of Irish politics, McMurrough, O'More, O'Connor, Desmond, Burke of Clanrickard and O'Neill all sought reconciliation, and entered into indentures to recognise the King as their lord, and to apply for crown grants and the peerages which went with them. Unfortunately, nothing in Ireland was as simple as this would suggest. In the first place, by Gaelic law the land belonged to the tribe, and not to the chief, in other words it was not his to surrender; although if he managed to get away with it, the new grant would confer a valid title by English law which would be vested in himself alone. This meant that the chiefs were very much keener than their followers and kinsmen, and when it came to the actual details, the negotiations frequently broke down.[28] So tortuous did these negotiations often become that the whole policy was effectively suspended in 1543, when only a small number of transactions had been completed. It was not abandoned, and no fresh initiative took its place in Henry's lifetime, but it was a big discouragement to St Leger, who found himself effectively marking time in his relations with the Irishry.

The Irish Church, like the community itself, was divided into zones. Within the Pale, which roughly corresponded with the archdiocese of Dublin, the standards of discipline and education were much the same as they were in England, and similar systems of patronage applied. The provinces of Armagh and Cashel each covered part of the obedient land, and dioceses such as Cashel itself and Meath were rather similar to Kildare or Ferns; but they also included Irish lands where different practices were followed, and even the succession of the bishops is often uncertain.[29] The whole of the province of Tuam was Gaelic country, and there even the archbishops are shadowy. By the standards which applied in most parts of the western Church, the clergy of the tribal lands were in serious need of reform. Parishes were very large and ill-defined, the priests often being kinsmen of the clan chiefs. The ancient Celtic habit of relying on the regular clergy for parish ministry was still followed in many places. Sometimes this was respectable enough, and the friars were busy and very well regarded in this mode, but in other places in meant that the parish priest doubled as the abbot of the local monastery, and might well be a married man with a large family.[30] There was, consequently, a considerable racial division within the Church, and provinces, or even dioceses, might have two sets of administrators – one dealing with the clergy *inter Anglicos* and the other with the clergy *inter Hibernicos*. About a dozen sees were normally in English hands, and there the bishops were provided by the Crown and confirmed by the Pope, as in England. In the first twenty years of the sixteenth century Anglo-Papal relations were good, and there were no problems. Thirteen sees were regularly in Gaelic hands, and there the Pope tended to provide without reference to English wishes, because the English had no temporal control. The other nine dioceses varied, and it was there that the main problems arose. Sometimes these sees were held by absentee Englishmen, sometimes by residents, and sometimes by resident Celts. There were double provisions, quarrels and uncertainties in such places, and it was there that the sharpness of racial antagonism was most marked.[31] Royal and local interests were constantly in conflict, and this required regular process of negotiation and compromise. By the 1520s double provisions, at least, had been largely eliminated.

Rather surprisingly in view of the stand which Lord Offaly had been claiming to make, the Royal Supremacy was accepted in Ireland with remarkably little fuss. The Parliament enacted the necessary legislation in 1537, with the only dissent coming from the 'third chamber', the proctors of the lower clergy who (in contrast to England) formed a house of the parliament. One result of this, of course, was to sharpen the distinction between the Englishry and the Irishry, because the latter paid no attention whatsoever to the new laws, and continued to deal directly with Rome as they had done before.[32] To what extent the Curia actually understood the condition of the Irish Church may be doubted, because one of the consequences of this was the preservation (and indeed promotion) of the clerical dynasties which were one of the features of the tribal lands. The fact was that the Gaelic Church was very far from being a jewel in the papacy's crown. Although the liturgy was in Latin, education in the normal sense was very sparse. As in Wales, the bards had a learning of their own, which they imparted to selected laymen, but this served mainly to perpetuate the distinctiveness of their culture, and did not build any bridges either to England or to mainland Europe.[33] Although some parts of the scripture had been translated into the Gaelic tongue, humanism as that was normally understood had made no impression in Ireland. Piety, even by English standards, was primitive and superstitious. 'Holy warriors' gave their services to chiefs in battle, water poured into saints' bells cured sick animals, and visions and minor local miracles were a constant ingredient of popular faith. Moreover, the *mores* of tribal conflict were regularly reflected in the behaviour of senior clergy. In 1444 Cormac MacCoughlan, Bishop of Clanmacnois, his son the Archdeacon and the Prior of Clontuskert were all killed in battle with a rival sept. In 1466 O'Brien of Thomond was allegedly slain by the evil eye, and as late as 1525 Abbot Kavanagh, the Archdeacon of Leighlin, murdered his own bishop, Mauricius O'Deoradhain in the King's highway, allegedly to secure his see.[34] Although the latter crime, being committed within the obedient lands, attracted a savage justice at the hands of Lord Deputy Kildare.

Altogether, there was much in the Celtic Church which stood in need of reform. Discipline as that was normally understood was virtually non-existent. The great exception to this generally depressing picture was, however, the growth and strength of the mendicant orders.[35] Although for the most part of Irish birth, these friars had normally been educated abroad, and brought with them different standards of both conduct and ministry. Above all, they stood apart from tribal loyalties and affinities, in marked contrast to the secular clergy. During the fifteenth century nearly fifty houses of Dominicans, Franciscans and Augustinians had been established, mostly in the tribal lands. Between 1460 and 1530 many of these houses also converted to strict observance, and this was greatly respected among a laity whose lives were far from strict. There was a down side to this, in that chiefs, and even bishops, jostled to be buried in a friar's habit in the belief that some of this sanctity would rub off on them; but there is no doubt that the mendicants in general provided a quality of spiritual guidance and example which was not otherwise available. They were also able and willing to preach in Gaelic, which was an invaluable asset, because otherwise most of those who had the language did not have the ability, and those with the ability did not have the language. Some houses were also established in English-speaking towns, but a sensible policy of deployment did not usually waste Gaelic speakers in places where they could do no good. In the Englishry, as in England itself, the friars were generally reckoned to be at the sharp end of theological debate, and in so far as there were reformers in Ireland, they tended to be located in the mendicant houses. By contrast, monasticism was in full decline, and in 1538 there were no more than half a dozen communities with more than six monks.[36] The rot in that quarter went back a long way, again because monastic property tended to be regarded as a part of the tribal endowment. Abbots frequently and individual monks not uncommonly were married, often non-resident, and made almost no pretence of observing their rule. In 1466, for example, the abbey of Lough Key was burned to the ground by the inadvertence of a canon's wife bearing a lighted candle.[37] Pluralism was also frequent, and monastic sites were sometimes turned into strongholds for the purposes of tribal warfare.

The Cistercians, who had been in the forefront of earlier reforms, were in a desperate condition by the end of the fifteenth century, and in 1496 the General Chapter established a National Congregation, which appointed special *reformatores* in the hope of re-establishing discipline. A surviving report from Abbot Troy of Mellifont, one of these special agents, makes the scale of the problem clear. Only two communities, his own at Mellifont and one in Dublin, still observed the rule and wore the habit; the others scarcely made a pretence of maintaining any corporate life or liturgy. They were caught up in local wars, dominated by tribal chieftains, and in the obedient land riven by racial animosities. He begged to be excused from visiting any more Gaelic houses, because of the violence to which he had been subjected, and because of what had been threatened.[38] The abbot's brief was to be impartial, and he may not have been, but there is no evidence to suggest that he was mistaken. The other orders appear to have been little better. Within the Pale, the standard was more acceptable, but even there the monastic orders were in decline, lay benefactions going mainly to confraternities and Third Order groups – and, of course, the mendicants. Ormond, in the obedient land, was visited by a royal commission in 1537, and the picture painted was almost as black as that of the tribal lands; the abbot and monks of Inishloughnaght each had a concubine and a household; the Priory of Cahir did not celebrate the liturgy; at St Katherine's Waterford the community had split up and divided the revenues – and so on.[39] This is all rather reminiscent of the reports of similar commissions in England, and may have been deliberately designed to justify dissolution. By the time that this visitation took place, thirteen of the more decrepit houses had already been dissolved by statute, and the Irish properties of English houses had been seized.[40] Pressure for more sweeping measures came mainly from official circles, and was closely linked with the desire to find more resources for military deployment. As in England there were also pressures from private interests which hoped to benefit. In September 1538 Henry decided on total suppression, and this process was carried out by another royal commission, which was issued in April 1539. This was a direct exercise of the Royal Supremacy, without any specific legislation by the Irish Parliament. By November 1540 another forty-seven houses had been added to the thirteen suppressed earlier.[41]

The monks were pensioned in accordance with the resources of their houses, and (where possible) redeployed as secular clergy. There was remarkably little resistance, or even complaint, because monasticism was little respected – for all the reasons suggested – and the friars, who were regretted, were immediately redeployed into the parishes where they greatly enhanced the quality of the ministry. The effectiveness of the King's action varied in accordance with the general effectiveness of his government. In the Pale, Wexford, Ormond and the English towns of the south, suppression was total; in the obedient land partial, according to circumstances, while the tribal lands were virtually untouched. Altogether about 80 of the 140 monasteries which had existed in Ireland in 1530 were dissolved, and a similar number of the 200 mendicant houses. The mendicants survived better, not because of their higher standards, but because they were more numerous in Gaelic Ireland. The pickings were nothing like as rich as they were in England, but a similar policy was followed. The largest number of recipients were Old English, from the Pale, followed by a group of English outsiders, some of whom took up residence in Ireland, but most of whom remained absentees.[42] A proportion also went to the Anglo-Irish peers, and to Gaelic chiefs who wanted to establish town houses within the Englishry, a distribution which can be linked to the policy of surrender and regrant. Most of this property was not granted away or sold, but leased, usually for twenty-one years, which was different from the policy followed in England, and possibly the result of the need to be much more careful in the newly established kingdom. Where the monasteries were dissolved they were little missed, and where they remained performed no useful function in the preservation of the faith.

Reform in the sense that Cranmer or Cromwell would have understood it had hardly touched Ireland by 1547. No part of the kingdom was under Canterbury jurisdiction, and although the calendar was altered and the English Bible used in some places, that was very much at the discretion of the local diocesan. Had it applied to Ireland, the Act of Six Articles would have been warmly endorsed. There was no tradition of heretical discourse in Ireland, and no institution of higher education to attract dissident intellectuals. Quasi-Protestant evangelicals like Hugh Latimer were unknown, and when they began to arrive in Ireland after 1547, the shock was profound. In the course of the 1530s Henry had largely destroyed the traditional system of devolved government, replacing it with a system much more directly answerable to London. Although this was resented in some quarters, the weakening of the grip of the Anglo-Irish nobles, and the reduction of their endless feuding, was generally welcomed. It was the failure of the surrender and regrant policy, accompanied by the introduction of Protestantism, which turned the Irish polity inside out, and led first to colonisation and then to an ethnic polarity of religious ideology which bedevilled Ireland in the Elizabethan period and after. At the end of Henry's reign his second kingdom was probably more governable than it had been at the beginning, but in bringing about this improvement, he had sown the seeds of future trouble in a big way.

A KING IN HIS SPLENDOUR, 1536–1542

Henry had been writing essays and letters in defence of his position over the marriage since about 1527. Most of these efforts survive only in manuscript and in a fragmentary form, so there is much debate over their dating and provenance.[1] He encouraged scholars and others sympathetic to his cause to do likewise, so that it is often hard to tell who was responsible for the surviving documents. One written in the first person singular and known from its opening words as '*Henricus octavus*' appears to have been his contribution to the debate at Blackfriars. However, later evidence suggests that he did not write the whole of it. A letter from John Stokesley to Cromwell in 1535 identifies himself, Edward Foxe and Nicholas de Burgo as being the principal authors of the Latin original, which was then translated into English with 'additions and chaungynges' made by Cranmer.[2] In other words the same team which had produced the *Collectanea satis copiosa* a little earlier, except that in this case the King undoubtedly had a hand in it, and wanted it to be thought his own work. To this collection of tracts was added, between 1529 and 1530, the opinions of certain European universities, and the whole was published as the *Censurae Academiarum* in April 1531. Henry was particularly concerned to emphasise the Levitical argument, and that formed the basis of the questions posed to the universities, whose responses Cranmer and others had begun to collect during 1529. There was clearly felt to be an urgent need to publish, and to assert the European scope of the consultation, because the *Censurae* of Oxford and Cambridge, which had been available for about twelve months, were not included. In order to make it more available to the domestic market at large, the *Censurae* was translated and published as *The Determinations of the moste famous and mooste excellent universities of Italy and France* in November 1531.[3] These works were the tip of an iceberg of effort, which at one time or another involved Reginald Pole, John Stokesley, Richard Croke, John Longland, Geronimo Ghinucci and Gregory Casale as well as Cranmer, and endless politically fraught encounters with nervous academics from Salamanca to Marburg. Nor was it only university faculties which were canvassed. The librarians of notable libraries, and individual scholars were also approached, and a varied, but surprisingly numerous collection of favourable opinions was assembled.[4] So worrying did the Imperialists find this evidence of success that they induced Clement, on 21 March 1530 to issue a bull forbidding anyone to write in Henry's favour. It appears to have had no effect, and although the King's campaign suffered some spectacular reverses, on the whole his agents did what was required of them.[5]

However, persuading Henry's English subjects of the validity of his cause, although necessary, was not the main point of all this effort. The main purpose was to convince the Pope and the Consistory, and in that he enjoyed no success at all. No matter how many authoritative opinions he received, Clement remained unconvinced, because just as many could be found to argue the other way. A battle of the books developed, starting with John Fisher's *De Causa Matrimonii Serenissimi Regis Angliae*, published at Alcala in 1530, and to which the *Censurae* may have been intended as a reply. Petropandus Caporella, Ludovico Nozarola and Johann Cochlaeus all contributed to the assault on the English position between 1530 and 1535.[6] Against this barrage, the English response was at first limited. Apart from the *Censurae* and the *Glasse of the Truth*, most of their arguments were concentrated on the Rota. It was only after Thomas Cromwell took over the management of the King's campaign in about 1535 that the defence of Henry's position really began, and the leading writer became Richard Morison. Morison wrote one book in Latin, the *Apomaxis* in 1537 which was specifically intended to refute Cochlaeus, but for the most part he wrote in English, and concentrated his efforts on the defence of the King's authority against attacks of all kinds. Altogether he wrote six books, starting with *A Lamentation* in 1536, and ending with *An Exhortation to stirre all Englyshe men to the defence of theyr countrye* in 1539, each of which was directed against a specific threat, but underlying them all was an evangelical conviction of the rightness of the King's position in respect of the Church.[7] It was, after all, the Royal Supremacy which was causing most of Henry's problems, and the defence of that became Morison's (and Cromwell's) chief priority. The theological controversy, conducted in Latin, did not go away, indeed it was still raging in Elizabeth's reign, but by 1540 the main political issues had moved on.

The early part of 1536 saw a number of changes in the King's circumstances. Catherine's death led to an easing of relations with the Emperor. Charles had begun to find his aunt an embarrassment, and he had been warned by his council that his feud with Henry over her treatment was a private matter, not justifying any public action against England. The King had shown no violence to his ex-wife, and in material ways had treated her decently, so there was no occasion for a political response.[8] Indeed the Emperor was always concerned to prevent Henry from becoming too close to Francis, and in that he found a valuable ally after January 1536 in Thomas Cromwell. Cromwell did not trust the French, but he had gone along with the alliance as long as it seemed necessary to provide against any attempt by Charles to reinstate Catherine by force. After her death that was no longer a possibility, and the Secretary's foreign policy advice began to move in response. Anne also became vulnerable. As long as Catherine was alive, the King was compelled to defend his second marriage against all detractors, but in fact he was finding her less than satisfactory. Not only was she given to tantrums, she was far more politicised than a good wife should have been.[9] Above all, she had not borne him a son, which had in a sense been the whole point of marrying her. Like many couples whose relationship is intensely physical, they went through periods of emotional reaction, and Chapuys could write of the King's alienation from Anne, and of her reaction to it. In January 1536 all appeared to be well, and Anne was pregnant for the third time. However, on the 27th of the month Henry had a heavy fall in the tilt yard at Greenwich, which left him unconscious for several hours, and allegedly in reaction to the stress which this induced, two days later, the Queen miscarried.

Edward Hall does not mention the gender of the foetus. Unsubstantiated reports, both at the time and subsequently, declared that it was male, but since it was also reported that the Queen's period was only fifteen weeks, that must have been hard to determine, given the primitive nature of medical knowledge at the time, and the absence of any experienced midwife to confirm such a diagnosis.[10] It was also alleged, many years later, that the foetus was deformed, and that the King took this as evidence that he was not the father. This is plausible only insofar as it was a widespread belief at the time that a deformed child was evidence of misconduct on the part of one or both parents. Obviously Henry had not been guilty of any such misconduct, so it followed that the Queen had been playing away.[11] There is, however, no contemporary evidence to support any such thesis. What we do know is that the King, when he was sufficiently recovered to be told, was bitterly disappointed, and remonstrated with his wife as though the misfortune was all her fault. His talk of having lost 'his prince', however, must have sprung from general disappointment rather than from any specific knowledge. What does seem to have happened is that Henry began to doubt the validity of his second marriage. He had for years accepted that Catherine's failure to bear him a son had reflected a divine judgement on his marriage. Was he now faced with a second marriage which had offended the Almighty? We do not need to accept Chapuys' stories of estrangement between the couple in the spring of 1536 to believe that the seeds of doubt had been sown in the King's mind.[12] The ambassador picked up all sorts of stories from those unsympathetic to Anne, one of which was that the King was muttering about having been ensnared into this marriage by witchcraft, which would, of course, have exonerated him from all responsibility. Henry seems to have been genuinely undecided, and this was reflected in erratic displays of affection, alternating with bouts of hostility and grumbling.

The person who picked up this display of uncertainty most significantly was Thomas Cromwell, who saw in it an opportunity to remove from the scene the one politician who was not amenable to more orthodox pressures, and who stood firmly in the way of any rapprochement with the Emperor.

The story of events in the fraught days at the end of April and beginning of May is confused by hindsight and special pleading, but only makes sense if we assume that Cromwell was improvising his tactics as he went along, meanwhile keeping a sharp eye on the King's reactions to the disclosures as they were made. For example, a commission of Oyer and Terminer was issued on 24 April for the trial of treasons, and it has been argued that the King was already planning to act against his wife and her accomplices.[13] However such a commission was a routine matter, and it is not clear that Henry was in any way involved. Similarly a parliament was called on 27 April, and this was unusual because it was only a fortnight since the last one had been dissolved. An emergency of some kind seems to have been envisaged, and in this case the necessary action would certainly have had to be taken by the King, but it does not follow that a matrimonial crisis was anticipated. Again the relevant agent would have been Thomas Cromwell. As late as 25 April Henry was referring to Anne in public as his 'entirely beloved wife', and there is no reason to suppose that he was dissimulating.[14] Yet on 2 May she was arrested and sent to the Tower. What seems to have happened is that Cromwell was aware of tensions between the royal couple, and was doing his best to exploit them. He may well have had informants among Anne's ladies, and was certainly keeping a wary eye on Sir Henry Norris, about whom he had been warned for reasons which had nothing to do with Anne. Had events fallen out differently, the commission would have remained dormant and Parliament would no doubt have been prorogued. As it was, an event on Saturday 29 April played right into his hands. Irritated by his failure to 'come on' to the young lady whom she had looked out for him, Anne accused Norris of preferring herself, and said that if 'ought but good' should come to the King, he would look to have her.[15] This incredibly rash statement was soon all over the court, and of course Henry heard about it, which may well explain the scene which Alexander Ales recorded for Elizabeth's benefit twenty-three years later. Anne, bearing Elizabeth in her arms, allegedly sought out the King to plead with him. Ales admitted:

> I did not perfectly understand what had been going on, but the faces and gestures of the speakers plainly showed that the king was angry ... [and] it was obvious to everyone that some deep and difficult question was being discussed [16]

However, if this scene actually took place, angry as the King was, he did not take immediate action. He even allowed the May Day jousts, in which Norris was a participant, to go ahead. It was not until the jousts were over that he suddenly rode off, accompanied by only half a dozen servants, without taking leave of anyone, 'whereat,' as Edward Hall commented, 'many men mused'. As well they might, because he had left Anne behind at Greenwich without a word of explanation.[17] The following day she was arrested and charged with treasonable adultery.

What had apparently triggered this reaction was the arrest on the 30th of Mark Smeaton. Mark was a young musician, probably of Flemish birth, who was attached to the King's Privy Chamber. He had been mooning after Anne for some considerable time in an adolescent crush which he revealed (with incredibly bad timing) in the Queen's apartments on the 29th. Informed immediately of this indiscretion, Cromwell pounced, and after about twenty-four hours of interrogation, accompanied by numerous threats and promises, he confessed to adultery with the Queen. This was almost certainly wish fulfilment, but it served the Secretary's purposes admirably. He promptly informed the King, who reacted by quitting the jousts in a fury. Cromwell had successfully bounced Henry into the conviction that his once-adored wife had been playing him false.[18] Seizing the opportunity created by this success, over the next twenty-four hours he also implicated others in the same offence, notably Sir Henry Norris, William Brereton of the Privy Chamber, Francis Weston, and Anne's own brother George, Lord Rochford, whose ready and frequent access to his sister suddenly became ground for suspicion. With that capacity for maudlin self-pity which was one of his most unlovable characteristics, Henry was suddenly prepared to believe almost any charge which was fired against his wife. She was a witch who had seduced him; she had had a hundred lovers; she had plotted to poison the Duke of Richmond and Princess Mary. Nothing was too bad to be believed.[19] In this extremity, Anne did not help her own cause. Although she consistently denied the charges against her, nervous gossip with her remaining attendants in the Tower revealed the extent of the flirtations which had fuelled the original suspicions, and which seem to have been second nature to her. However, one problem stood in the way of prosecution. Whatever Henry might believe '... no man will confess anything against her but all-only Mark of any actual thing. Where of ... it should much touch the king's honour if it should no further appear ...'

William Fitzwilliam, who had interviewed Anne the day after her arrest, was clearly unconvinced of her guilt, probably regarding Smeaton's confession with justifiable suspicion.[20] Cromwell, therefore, had to assemble his case with care, which he did, making it appear that both the doubts over the Queen's conduct and the investigations into them went back far further than was actually the case. This has created a fog of misinformation which has afflicted interpretation of the case from that day to this. Norris and Rochford were included as suspects from the beginning, and the events of that fraught weekend were carefully downplayed.

It was decided to proceed against the commoners first, and a grand jury was empanelled on 9 May to process the indictments. This was duly done, and on 12 May Norris, Brereton, Weston and Smeaton were arraigned at Westminster Hall. There was no pretence that this would be a fair trial, and Cromwell had ensured that as hostile a jury as possible had been assembled. Some were dependants of his own, others were devoted to the Lady Mary. All were hostile to the Boleyns.[21] Eventually only Mark Smeaton pleaded guilty, but all the defendants were convicted, and sentenced to suffer the penalty of treason. It was as tidy a piece of judicial assassination as could well be imagined. It also left the outcome of the Queen's own trial as a formality. Nevertheless the due form was carefully observed. It was conducted in the King's Hall in the Tower, and presided over by the Duke of Norfolk as Lord Steward. Anne showed admirable composure, and defended herself eloquently, 'she made so wise and discreet answers to all things laid against her, excusing herself with her words so clearly as though she had never been faulty to the same …'. For the first and last time in her life, Anne attracted a good deal of public sympathy in her ordeal. Even her arch-enemy Eustace Chapuys found the proceedings against her 'very strange'.[22] It was all to no avail; she was found guilty and sentenced to be burned or beheaded at the King's pleasure. When the sentence had been passed, the Queen addressed the court as was customary, admitting that she had not always borne herself with fitting humility to her lord, and that sometimes she had been jealous of him, and concluding (according to one well informed source), 'But God be my witness if I have done him any other wrong'. She did not challenge the justice of the verdict, but the implication was clear enough.[23] There then followed the trial of her brother George, Lord Rochford, against whom the charges were even flimsier. George made mincemeat of the crown case, ill-advisedly treating it with some of the contempt which it deserved. The audience was convinced that he would be acquitted, but the Lords, of course, knew their duty and he was convicted like his sister. He again accepted the verdict without admitting any kind of guilt, and seemed more concerned with the debts that he owed than with his own fate. They were both executed at the Tower on 19 May.[24]

By the time that she died, Anne was no longer queen, nor Marquis of Pembroke, both of those titles having been stripped from her by her attainder. Nor was she Henry's wife. On 17 May in a special tribunal convened at Lambeth, Archbishop Cranmer declared their marriage null and void, in a judgement supposedly based on Henry's previous relationship with her sister. However, since the cause papers have disappeared, we cannot be certain of the real grounds. It must have been a very painful decision for him to have made, but the King was insistent that he had been duped, and that left the Archbishop no option.[25] He had been close to Anne, and had tried unsuccessfully to intercede for her when she was first arrested, but had been one of those kept away from the King by Cromwell's vigilance. His decision of course created work for the Parliament which assembled on 8 June, because those statutes which had insisted on recognition of the King's second marriage, and of Elizabeth as heir, had to be repealed. Henry now had two bastard daughters – but no legitimate son. Steps were quickly taken to provide a remedy. In the first week of June, Henry married Jane Seymour, 'daughter to the right worshipful Sir John Seymour, knight, which at Whitsuntide (4 June) was openly showed as Queen ...'.[26] Jane was about twenty-seven, and had been around the court for a number of years, so it is by no means certain when she first caught the King's eye. She was probably not at Wulf Hall when Henry and Anne had called there during the progress of 1535, but was certainly an item on the agenda by the time that Anne was arrested. Indeed the poisoning stories told against the Queen are alleged to have originated from the Seymour circle, and some contemporaries believed that the King's infatuation with her was one of the main reasons why he wanted rid of his second wife. The politics of the situation were actually not that straightforward, because as we have seen Thomas Cromwell regarded the Boleyns as dangerous enemies, which was why Anne and Rochford had to die, instead of being simply discarded. The Seymours did not have an agenda in the same sense, and Cromwell probably encouraged Henry's attraction mainly to give him more leverage against the Boleyns. Jane was no great beauty, but the fact that she was unmarried at twenty-seven probably had more to do with Sir John's lack of means – and the fact that he had several other daughters to provide for – than with any lack of appeal on the part of the lady. Henry seems to have found in her just the restful submissiveness that he was looking for. 'The king hath come out of hell into heaven for the gentleness in this and the cursedness and unhappiness in the other ...' wrote Sir John Russell at the time, and apparently with some justification.[27]

Jane was a helpmate, and no challenge either politically or intellectually, but her emergence was not without political significance nevertheless. It was members of Jane's circle, rather than the new

Queen herself, who encouraged Mary to think that Anne Boleyn's fall spelled the end of her troubles. Somewhat puzzled by her father's silence, she wrote to Thomas Cromwell on 26 May, asking for his intercession, now that the woman who had caused their estrangement was no more. Cromwell's reply does not survive, but seems to have been along the lines that obedience would be a necessary precondition for reinstatement.[28] If that was the case, then his meaning seems to have been misunderstood, because a few days later she wrote again, asking to see her father, and offering to be 'as obedient to the King's Grace as you can reasonably require of me'. That, however, was not sufficient because she had always withheld obedience on the grounds of conscience from those two points upon which the King insisted – the Royal Supremacy and his second marriage. The latter issue was now resolved without any effort on her part, but the former remained, and with it the question of her own legitimacy.[29] Unknown to her, Henry had already made his position clear in conversation with Chapuys a few days earlier:

> As to the legitimation of our daughter Mary ... if she would submit to our Grace, without wrestling against the determination of our laws, we would acknowledge her and use her as our daughter ... But, [he added with one eye on the Emperor] we would not be directed or pressed therein.[30]

An explicit submission was called for before any reconciliation could be considered, and that would not necessarily go as far as recognising her as his heir. An exchange of letters followed in early June, in which Mary still attempted to reserve her conscience, and Henry made it clear that that would not do. Indeed she was now in danger from the 1534 Act which had declared it to be treason to withhold from the King any of his titles, of which Supreme Head was one, and the Council was earnestly debating whether to proceed against her. On 15 June she was visited by a royal commission headed by the Duke of Norfolk, and flatly refused the submission required of her.[31] At this point, Cromwell intervened again to avert a crisis. He had no desire to see Mary facing the executioner's axe, and no intention of forcing the King into such a cruel decision. So he sent her a carefully worded set of articles to sign, with a covering letter offering a full and unconditional submission. Emotionally and physically exhausted by her ordeal, Mary yielded to this gesture of apparent kindliness, and signed both without reading either.[32] When news of this reached the court on 22 June, there was an audible sigh of relief. Her friends consoled themselves with the thought that now she would live to fight another day, while her enemies reckoned that her political teeth were drawn without the need for drastic action.

Nothing now stood in the way of a perfect reconciliation with her father. On 6 July the King and Queen visited Hunsdon, and stayed for several days. There were rumours that her household would be reinstated, and hopeful servants began to canvass for positions.[33] In Rome it was believed that she would be recognised as heir to the throne, and even that the King would return to his obedience. With Catherine and Anne both dead, the issue of the King's marriage was water under the bridge, and Paul III waited hopefully for an initiative from London. In the event none came, because Henry was by this time quite convinced that the Royal Supremacy represented the will of God, and there was no place for the papacy in his reconstructed Church. Mary's household, or rather her chamber, was reconstituted by 16 August. For the time being the joint household with Elizabeth was retained, but it was now 'served on two sides', and Mary, as an adult, clearly had the superior status.[34] Probably the implementation of this arrangement was delayed by the final illness, and death on 23 July, of the eighteen-year-old Duke of Richmond. Whatever plans his father may have had for him were laid to rest with his body, and this inevitably affected perceptions of his elder sister, who, whatever her official status was now generally recognised as Henry's heir. Since she was twenty years of age, Mary was not deemed to need the services of a lady governess any longer, but she was given fourteen gentlewomen and six gentlemen to serve her Privy Chamber. Most of these she chose herself, and a number of them had been in her service before 1533, so it must have been a happy reunion.[35] Jane had a gift for friendship, and seems genuinely to have liked Mary, so the latter returned to court with every sign of favour in the autumn, and was soon noted as being the 'second lady', after the Queen.

One of the reasons why Henry remained indifferent to the signals emerging from Rome in the summer of 1536 was that he was embarking upon his own programme of reform. He had already in 1535 constituted Thomas Cromwell his Viceregent in Spirituals, and in 1536, probably in August, authorised him to conduct a royal visitation, the injunctions for which show the King in his reforming mode. The convocations had just recently, in July, passed the Ten Articles, and Henry had authorised an English translation of the Bible, both of which feature in the Injunctions.[36] More importantly Parliament, which had dispersed on 18 July, had passed an Act for the dissolution of the small monasteries. Henry had been taking stock of the assets of the Church since commissioning the *Valor Ecclesiasticus* in 1535. This great survey had immediately provoked rumours of intended confiscations, but such was not its purpose. It was a sensible piece of housekeeping, intended not least to keep track of the Crown's complex rights of patronage, without reliance on the goodwill of diocesan authorities. It also revealed the wealth of the shrines, derived from the offerings of pilgrims, a practice which the King was already severely discouraging and was shortly to ban altogether. The wealth of the Church was shown to be very unevenly distributed, and that was also valuable information for a Supreme Head with a reforming agenda.[37] Henry had been brought up as a humanist, and that involved a contempt for 'superstitious ceremonies', among which pilgrimages featured. He also had no time for monks, following Erasmus in regarding them as idle drones. Withdrawal from the world was no way in which to tackle its manifold needs and weaknesses. The vital life of the Church was to be found it its parishes, in the sacraments, and in the Bible. The piety of earlier generations had also endowed these religious houses with wealth far beyond their needs – even supposing that those needs could be justified. So the King had not objected when Wolsey dissolved a number of minor and troublesome houses to fund his colleges in Oxford and Ipswich, indeed he encouraged the process. Now, in 1535–36 the issue was raised again, and the King had in his service the agent who had been responsible for Wolsey's dissolutions, namely Thomas Cromwell. Henry and Cromwell were agreed that the monasteries could and should be pruned. Many of the smaller houses were struggling, with fewer than half a dozen inmates, not sufficient even to maintain that *opus dei* which was their main responsibility, and there were strong suspicions that their way of life left a lot to be desired.[38] Commissioners were sent out to investigate towards the end of 1535, and not surprisingly, soon came back with horror stories in plenty. They knew that part of their brief was to find fault, so unsubstantiated accusations came back as proven facts, and feuds among the brethren were exploited to provide such tales. The nunneries came off particularly badly, not because they were necessarily more scandalous, but because the female religious seem to have been more adept at sniping at one another. Given the circumstances, it is surprising that so many houses were given a clean bill of health.[39]

Armed with these findings, the government had a number of options as to how to proceed. The first intention seems to have been to operate piecemeal, using a method analogous to that employed by Wolsey. However, different counsels soon prevailed and it was decided to proceed against the smaller houses by statute, as being the safer option, given the authority of Parliament. An arbitrary cut-off point was fixed at £200 in annual revenue, and any house with an income below that level was to be dissolved, and its property given to the King. The inmates were given a choice: either they could be transferred to a larger house of the same order, or they could take pensions and return to the world – as secular priests if they were ordained, otherwise as laymen or women.[40] The implication clearly was that the larger houses would continue, and indeed the statute spoke of 'divers and great solemn monasteries, wherein, thanks be to God, religion is right well kept and observed'. Yet within five years, and without any further legislation, the whole lot had gone, and the King was a very rich man.[41] The reason for this change of heart seems to have lain in two things. The first was the defeat of the Pilgrimage of Grace, which had made an issue of the minor monasteries, and the second was the overwhelming interest shown in acquiring the property of the dissolved houses. Gentlemen came metaphorically knocking on Cromwell's door with shopping lists of desirable properties, sometimes on their own behalf, sometimes that of clients. Because of their special status, the lands of these abbeys had been exempt from the market for many generations; now they were freed and the opportunity was too good to be missed. Cromwell had originally intended, it appears, to retain these lands in the hands of the Crown as an additional source of income, and to have leased them out through the newly created Court of Augmentations. However, the creation of a vested interest in the Royal Supremacy by encouraging investment in its proceeds was an unexpected bonus, and the lands began to be sold almost at once.[42] Sometimes these were granted at preferential rates, but most went at the standard rate of twenty years' purchase. The land-holding community proved to have unexpected reserves of cash, and this offered a means of tapping that which was far less controversial than taxation. Somewhat cynically Edward Hall had observed that 'there was given to the king by the consent of all the great and fat abbots all religious houses that was of the value of CCC marks and under, in the hope that their great monasteries should have continued still …'[43] but this rush of eager purchasers changed the King's mind. Pressure began to be applied to the 'great and fat abbots' and one by one they surrendered. In many cases this was brought about by forcing the resignation of obstructive incumbents, and replacing them with more amenable monks from within the relevant houses. In other cases the pressure was more direct. Many abbots and priors were sympathetic to the old ways, including the papal primacy, and if they made this apparent in any way, then prosecution could be threatened. Between 1536 and March 1541 122 greater houses surrendered, bringing to the Crown a net annual income of some £135,000.[44] A further statute in 1539 confirmed that all this property now belonged to the King, and not to the heirs (if any) of the original founders. The last to go was Waltham in Essex, and with it went over 1,000 years of Church history. Buildings were either converted into manor houses, or stripped of their lead and left to fall down; their valuables were removed to the royal treasury; and their libraries usually dispersed. The reformers were averse to traditional rites, and some liturgical manuscripts ended up as butter wrappings. The inmates were pensioned, and most eventually found employment as incumbents, curates or cantarists within the parish system. The servants usually stayed put to serve the new owners of the estates, which were granted or sold away in the same way as for the lesser monasteries. By the end of the reign some £2 million had been realised in this manner.[45]

There was surprisingly little opposition to this process. The distress caused to those with genuine vocations, or to the elderly who now saw their security removed, was real enough. The modest pensions might be enough to live on, with care, but that was hardly the point. However, monasteries had been peripheral to most men's religious lives, a part of the landscape rather than vital functioning units for many years, and support for the King's action was not lacking. This was especially true among taxpayers, who saw in this accretion of wealth to the King good reason why the pressure upon their own purses should be relaxed. There were, however, important exceptions to these generalisations. On 2 October 1536 the men of Louth, in Lincolnshire, rose in rebellion. At first this was a small-scale riot, caused by suspicion that the royal commissioners visiting the town were about to confiscate the goods of the parish church. There was no such intention, but they had come to dissolve the nearby nunnery at Legbourne, and they were roughly handled by an indignant mob, stirred up by conservative clergy.[46] That part of Lincolnshire was clearly ripe for trouble. Commissioners for the assessment of the subsidy were operating at Caistor, and made jumpy by the events at Louth, attempted to run away. They were captured and brought back in what was effectively another act of rebellion.[47] Suspicion of the government's intentions was rife all over the county, and rumours about the closure of parish churches and the confiscation of property were widely believed. Lincolnshire was a conservative area and the King's reforming initiatives, such as the introduction of the English Bible, were much resented. Here the religious houses still served a local need, both of hospitality and of education, and the dissolution even of the minor houses, caused heightened anxiety. There were also 'gentlemen's grievances' caused partly by the Statute of Uses, and partly by the intrusive influence of that royal favourite the Duke of Suffolk in the county. Suffolk was endeavouring to build up a power base, and had received a number of grants of property which had escheated from local families. Inevitably he installed clients of his own as stewards and other officials on these manors. His son, Henry, had indeed been Earl of Lincoln from 1525, but Henry had died in 1534, and his father's attempt to perpetuate that situation caused more resentment.[48] The Statute of Uses was an attempt to protect the King's feudal interests by restricting a gentleman's freedom to dispose of his property by will. Triggered by events in Louth and Caistor, rebellion spread all over north and east Lincolnshire during the first week of October. The standard tactic was for groups of commoners to 'abduct' prominent gentlemen, and to make them swear the rebels' oath. Given the ease with which this often happened, it would appear that Henry was justified in his slightly later comment that the gentlemen in the affected area 'were not as whole as they pretend'. About 10 October some 10,000 rebels marched on Lincoln, ostensibly led by the sworn gentlemen, who then persuaded them to send a set of articles to the King, and to await his response before proceeding further.[49] Meanwhile, the King was mustering forces to send against them at Ampthill, and it was rumoured that he would lead his army in person. On 11 October, Lancaster Herald reached Lincoln, with the intention of parlaying and delaying the rebels' advance. He found them less resolute than he expected, and by working on the gentry leaders succeeded in persuading them to disband without waiting for an answer to their articles. The gentlemen then sued for pardon, which was mostly granted, and the Lincolnshire rising was effectively over.[50] It would seem that the commons' respect for their leaders, however acquired, was greater than their sense of grievance, or perhaps, once the first flush of anger was passed, they realised that their chances of success were not great.

Meanwhile, the articles sent to London were five in number, and bear the marks of both gentry and clerical leadership. The first was a protest against the dissolution, 'whereby the service of God is not well maintained', and the fifth a complaint against 'divers bishops of England of your Grace's late promotion' who did not have the true faith in them; who were (although the word was not used) heretics. The fourth article was an objection to the King's use of 'base born' councillors, Thomas Cromwell being particularly mentioned. All these may well have represented popular points of view, but the remaining two, about the Statute of Uses and the assessment of the parliamentary fifteenth, would hardly have touched the commons at all. They were 'gentlemen's matters' and reflect the extent to which the county élite were striving to use the commons insurrection as a means of securing their own ends.[51] They need not have bothered. The King rejected their representations, with withering contempt for the inhabitants of 'one brutish shire', who would attempt to dictate to him how he should compose his Council, or who he should appoint to run his Church. By the time that this response arrived, the rebels had in any case gone home, and the King had disbanded his army. It was rather a tame ending, or would have been except that some 112 persons were prosecuted for participating, or whom 46 were executed, including some of the more prominent gentlemen.[52] The reason for this severity, however, lay less in the threat posed by Lincolnshire than in the fact that it became the preamble to a larger and more dangerous movement over the border in Yorkshire – the Pilgrimage of Grace proper.

Events in Yorkshire arose directly out of the earlier movement, because the first disturbance took place at Beverley on 8 October in sympathy with the men of Louth. The motivation was much the same; discontent over the King's reforming ecclesiastical policies, combined with rumours of church closures and confiscations. Some gentlemen were coerced into joining, others said that they were. The movement spread outwards from Beverley like a bush fire, and soon the town was only a minor element in the general conflagration. Different areas, like Holderness, reacted in different ways, but always the initiative came from the commons, inspired, more often than not, by sermons, letters and personal communications from traditional clergy, or from the monks and abbots of threatened houses.[53] Unlike Lincolnshire, however, the Yorkshire rising soon found a leader of authority and commitment in the person of Robert Aske. Aske was a lawyer, and had originally been a Percy dependant. More important in this context, he was a gentleman with an agenda, and it was that agenda which formed the basis of the articles which were presented to the Duke of Norfolk at Pontefract towards the end of November.[54] Once the seale of the movement had been appreciated at court, Norfolk was immediately commissioned to go north. He had the title of King's Lieutenant, but quite inadequate forces to confront the rebels, and his main task was to play for time, and to negotiate. By the end of November the Pilgrims had about 20,000 men at Doncaster, and Norfolk's main task was to prevent them from sweeping south. They were led by Lord Darcy, an elderly and extremely traditional peer, backed by a fair selection of the Yorkshire gentlemen, many of them at the head of the commons contingents from their home areas. Darcy professed his loyalty to the King throughout, but he was convinced that Henry had been misled and dishonoured by the men whom he had chosen to serve him, and his agenda was not dissimilar to that of the Lincolnshire gentry.[55] However the ideological leadership provided by Aske ensured that the articles presented to Norfolk at Pontefract were both more coherent and more far-reaching than those which had been transmitted at Lincoln. Starting with a round condemnation of Luther, Wycliffe and other heretics, they demanded that the heretical bishops presently in post should receive 'condign punishment by fire or such other ...'; that the friars and other religious should be restored to their houses and that the Royal Supremacy be abandoned. As a corollary to that, they demanded that the Lady Mary be recognised as legitimate and the heir to the throne; that baseborn councillors should be dismissed and punished, and that those responsible for the recent survey of the monasteries should also be called to account for their evil deeds. The remainder of the twenty-four articles were filled out with specific grievances, like the Statute of Uses, the treason laws recently enacted, the demands of taxation, and (for some mysterious reason) the Statute against handguns and crossbows.[56]

Altogether it was a thoroughly conservative manifesto, demanding the reversal of most of the King's policies of the previous decade. It was also very conventional, in that it carefully blamed 'evil councillors' for the policies objected to rather than the King himself. It was this ambiguity which eventually proved the downfall of the whole movement, because when the King, through Norfolk, offered concessions and further negotiations, they had to decide whether to trust him. Although the balance of force favoured them at that moment, the leaders were only too aware that time was not on their side. Keeping 20,000 men under arms within easy reach of their own homes was simply not practicable for any length of time, especially if they could be given nothing to do. Moreover, the great northern peers whose support they had been looking for, particularly the Earls of Derby and Shrewsbury, held themselves aloof, declaring for the King, and in Derby's case preventing the Pilgrimage from spreading onto his patch in Lancashire.[57] Darcy and his council, including Aske, therefore decided to trust the King and sent their supporters home. Only Aske may have been aware that their demands had been far too radical for Henry to stomach, and that the opportunity for a decisive military victory was now passed. If they had attempted to assemble again, the King would have had forces to send against them.

The main problem with the Pilgrimage was that it was deeply divided, and in spite of the coherence of its main demands, the miscellaneous nature of the supporting articles reflects that. The gentlemen were concerned about taxation, the parliament and border tenure, the commons about enclosures, and the clergy about their status and privileges. There was also division about how to respond to the King's offer. The more radical of the commons leaders were all in favour of pressing on while the advantage lay with them, but were persuaded by the more cautious gentlemen that such a reaction would ill accord with their professions of loyalty to the King.[58] Robert Aske and some of the other leaders actually spent Christmas at court negotiating with the Council, and seem to have been persuaded of the King's good faith. In that they were deceived, because the policies to which they were objecting were Henry's own, and the Royal Supremacy was non-negotiable. What might have happened if Yorkshire had remained quiet we do not know, but it did not. As things stood, the Doncaster agreement committed the King to visiting the north, convening a parliament in either Nottingham or York, and pardoning all those who had been involved in the protest.[59] A document drawn up, probably by Cromwell, before Christmas, clearly reflects the Council's unhappiness with those commitments, and uncertainty as to how to proceed. The Duke of Norfolk was to be sent back to the north, and provided with adequate military backing; there was a proposal to convene a Great Council; only the pardon seemed to be clearly established.[60] These doubts were reflected in the north, where in January 1537 rumours began to circulate that the Duke of Norfolk was coming with a great force to seize Hull and Scarborough, and Aske had considerable difficulty in persuading the people to be patient. Then, on the 16th, a fresh stir erupted in the East Riding. This was largely provoked by John Hallam, an arch-sceptic of the Doncaster agreement who had been trying to persuade his neighbours for several weeks that it was useless, but it was fronted by Sir Roger Bigod, who had not featured prominently in the original movement.[61] Why Sir Roger became involved at this point is not clear, because he seems to have been a man of reformed religious views, but his scepticism about the royal intentions was clearly profound. He attracted relatively little support, and his rising was soon suppressed, but it gave Henry the perfect excuse to renege on his word. The Yorkshiremen had broken their side of the agreement, so he was under no obligation to keep his. Norfolk was commissioned to investigate the circumstances of the original Pilgrimage, and in early April Aske, Darcy and Sir Robert Constable were arrested and sent to the Tower. Darcy was tried by his peers and beheaded on 30 June; Constable was hanged at Hull on 6 July and Aske at York on the 12th. Altogether 132 people were executed for their part in the Pilgrimage, and the royal policies which had been so strenuously objected to were not deflected in the slightest.[62] Mary, who had been the subject of such strong representations, remained in favour at court, having given no countenance whatever to her self-styled supporters, while Cromwell,

Cranmer and Audley, that triumvirate of evil councillors, continued to be high in confidence. Ostensibly, the Pilgrimage had achieved nothing, yet within a few years the Statute of Uses had been modified, the Act of Six Articles passed, Cromwell had fallen and Mary had been reinstated in the succession. Although he could not admit it at the time, Henry was perhaps rather more alert to what was being said than might at first appear.

Meanwhile, Pope Paul III had called a General Council to meet at Mantua in 1537. In 1533 Henry had appealed to such a Council against the papal sentence, but that had not been in any expectation of one meeting. Now he was alarmed, because any council convened by the Pope was likely to confirm the Pope's actions, so he directed his diplomatic efforts to frustrating it. In this he was joined by the Lutheran princes of Germany, for much the same reason.[63] What they wanted, they claimed, was 'free council', convened by the princes of Europe, which would be able to look at papal actions objectively. Richard Morison wrote a tract to this intent, entitled *A protestation made for the most mighty and moste redoubted kynge of Englande*, which was translated into Latin for the benefit of the Schmalkaldic League.[64] However, it was not the efforts of either Henry or the Lutherans which frustrated Paul's intention, but rather the continued warfare between France and Empire which made both unwilling to participate. So the Council of Mantua was postponed *sine die*, and Henry was free to continue his ambiguous role between Charles and Francis.

It was small thanks to English diplomacy that the Council was called off, but 1537 was nevertheless a momentous year in the reign. In the spring, Queen Jane was found to be pregnant, and as the summer advanced Henry became increasingly solicitous of her well being. He had been this way many times before, and always hitherto the outcome had been a disappointment. At the end of September she 'took her chamber' and Hampton Court. The King withdrew to a safe distance, because there was plague in the area, and the court waited with bated breath. Then:

... on saint Edwards even (12 October) was born at Hampton Court the noble imp Prince Edward, whose Godfathers at the Christening were the Archbishop of Canterbury and the Duke of Norfolk, and his Godmother the Lady Mary the

King's daughter, and at the bishop was Godfather the Duke of Suffolk ...[65]

The country exploded with rejoicing, 'and great joy [was] made with thanksgiving to Almighty God which hath sent so noble a prince to succeed to the crown of his father ...' At last the succession had been secured! Although infant mortality was high, the child appeared to be healthy, and no more could be done for the time being. Occasion had even been found to demonstrate the reconciliation of the Lady Mary. Queen Jane had lived up to her credentials of coming from a good breeding stock, and no doubt there would be more where this one had come from. Henry returned for the christening, and to see his wife, who had suffered severely from a protracted labour. She had seemed well enough as she sat in the ante-chapel to receive congratulations from the assembled courtiers. However, she contracted puerperal fever from the inadequate hygiene of her surroundings, and died on the 24th.

Of none in the realm was it more heavily taken than of the King's Majestie himself, whose death caused the king immediately to remove unto Westminster, where he mourned and kept himself close and secret a great while ...[66]

Henry had been genuinely fond of Jane, and may well have mourned her as lost love. However, he also mourned the chance of begetting more sons through this, his most successful of marriages. Fortunately, Edward continued to flourish, and it is unlikely that he lost very much by being deprived of his mother at such a tender age. His basic needs would in any case have been satisfied by the services of a wet nurse.

Towards the end of 1536 Reginald Pole, recently created cardinal and the only Englishman in the College of Cardinals, had been sent north in the hope of being able to stimulate either Francis or Charles into taking advantage of the Pilgrimage of Grace. He was to issue an ultimatum to the King of England, and if that failed, to implement his excommunication by force of arms.[67] However, by the time that he actually set out, in February 1537, the rising had been suppressed, and he soon discovered that both the Emperor and the King of France were more interested in securing Henry's alliance in their perpetual warfare than in taking any action against him. He did not have the resources to act independently, even on a modest scale, and so his mission was a complete waste of time. What it did do was to convince Henry that Reginald was a double-dyed traitor. He had been persuaded that he was an ungrateful miscreant by the arrival of Pole's 'letter', *De Unitate Ecclesiae*, in June 1536, which criticised in scathing terms every aspect of the King's policy since 1527.[68] This would have been bad enough as a private communication, but it was also published in Rome, without the author's knowledge, as he averred, which stoked the fires of anti-English feeling in the Curia and effectively killed off any talk of reconciliation. Henry was not interested in reconciliation, but he was very indignant indeed against Reginald Pole, and that indignation was now confirmed by Pole's part in the abortive crusade against him. Any communication with him was therefore regarded as treasonable, and his family remaining in England were brought into acute danger.[69] On 29 August 1538 his brother Geoffrey was arrested and taken to the Tower. Under intense interrogation, and possibly threatened with torture, he began to make damaging revelations. Of course he had been in touch with his brother, and so had several other members of his family circle, including their elder sibling, Henry Pole, Lord Montague, and Henry Courtenay, Marquis of Exeter. Montague and Exeter were arrested on 4 November, and another member of their circle, Sir Edward Neville, the following day. On 15 November the sixty-five-year-old Countess of Salisbury was placed under house arrest, and the interrogations continued.[70] What was revealed was a communications network, centred on Reginald, and implicating all the other suspects. No overt act of treason was disclosed, but rather a group of important people fundamentally out of sympathy with the King's proceedings. Moreover both Montague and Exeter had remote claims to the throne, and given the fragile state of the King's nursery, that was also a factor to be borne in mind.[71] Cromwell's agents had been active, collecting data from miscellaneous servants and other dependants which confirmed the general drift of what was going on. The trials were conducted between 2 and 5 December, the peers by the Lord

Steward and the commoners by commission of Oyer and Terminer. To the modern mind their treason was no more than implied, but Cromwell had assembled a damning case in contemporary terms, and all were found guilty. On 9 December Montague, Exeter and Neville were beheaded on Tower Hill, while four of the others suffered a more lingering fate at Tyburn. Margaret remained in prison, not tried but included in the Act of Attainder, until a pretext was found to execute her in 1541.[72] Geoffrey was pardoned, and left to the tender mercies of his conscience, a fact which seems eventually to have unhinged him. Cromwell was the agent, but Henry was the cause of these executions, because he did not believe that he could afford to tolerate dissent at such a high social level. Henry Courtenay had been a boon companion in the 1520s, but he had fallen out of favour over the King's annulment, and had distanced himself from the court thereafter. The King believed, probably rightly, that he had sufficient influence in Devon to make an unresisted landing there a real possibility, and that was a risk which he could not afford to take, especially as there were signs that the Franco-Habsburg wars might be coming to an end.

Mutual exhaustion rather than goodwill had led to negotiations being opened towards the end of 1538, and on 12 January 1539 a treaty was signed at Toledo. Francis and Charles agreed not to enter into any further agreements with Henry, and there was talk of their ambassadors being withdrawn.[73] That did not eventually happen, but the warning was obvious, and something like panic gripped England. Thanks to the dissolution of the monasteries, Henry was not short of money at this juncture, and immediately began a massive building programme, throwing up fortifications all along the south coast from St Mawes to Rye. The fleet was mobilised, and musters were held right across the South of England.[74] Paradoxically this invasion scare served to strengthen the King's position. If there was one thing calculated to rally the English people behind their King, it was the prospect of foreign intervention against him, and in 1539 that was a real possibility. Reginald Pole, even more alienated by the fate of his family, again appeared in the north to rally support for a new crusade against the schismatic regime, and this time his prospects looked decidedly brighter. However, it was not to be. The Emperor already had quite enough problems with the Turks and the Lutherans, and he had no desire to take on fresh burdens. Pole was so dispirited by this encounter that he decided to send emissaries to Francis instead of risking another personal rebuff. The King of France expressed sympathy with the aims of the Cardinal's mission, but was only prepared to act if the Emperor would do so first. He advised Pole not to visit France, and in March he renewed his ambassador in England.[75] The following month he wrote a friendly letter to Henry, saying that the military preparations in which he was engaged were not aimed against him, but against Charles. By July all danger was past, as the great rivals began to square up to each other again, and Pole was recalled to Rome, a move which did at least have the advantage of frustrating the kidnappers and assassins which Henry had set on his tail.

While these threats were reducing, but before they had actually gone away, Henry had other issues on his mind. 1539 was a year of stocktaking, because not only was the succession still in a fragile state, but he was aware that his religious policy was sending out contradictory signals. His council were urging him to remarry, and he was considering various attractive options. The trouble was that the whole of Europe seemed to be lined up either on the French or the Imperial side, and to marry into either of those camps would constitute a level of commitment which he was anxious to avoid. His suggestion to Francis for a beauty parade of eligible candidates was probably not seriously intended, and in any case provoked from the French King the response that his kinswomen were not cattle.[76] It was for this reason that Henry began to get interested in a negotiation with the Duchy of Cleves. This had been going on in a low-key fashion since 1538, because Duke John was a determined opponent of the Habsburgs, although not a Lutheran, and was keen to recruit Henry as an ally in a long-running dispute with Charles over the Duchy of Gelderland. John died in February 1539, but his son and heir was equally enthusiastic for the same reason. There was no way in which Henry was going to become embroiled in the Gelderland controversy, but William had an unmarried sister who might be worth a second look.[77] Having received a very flattering image of the lady, and an equally flattering description, Henry became serious. Negotiations began in August and a treaty was concluded on 4 October committing the King to marry Anne of Cleves. Meanwhile, Henry was becoming uneasily aware that his Church might be drifting away from him. He had always been clear in his own mind that his dispute with the papacy was purely jurisdictional. It had started as a personal quarrel with Clement VII, but by 1535 he had accepted that it was more than that – it was a constitutional issue between Rome and England. What it was not was a theological dispute. Henry remained devoted to the sacraments and to many of the traditions of the old faith, and had no time at all for such heretical notions as justification by faith alone.[78] The Church needed reform, but that affected its practices, not its doctrine. Images and pilgrimages were abused, the Bible was neglected, and money was poured into the pockets of useless monks and friars. All these issues he had addressed, and in consequence many believed him to be an evangelical, even a sort of Protestant. Thomas Cromwell had not helped in this because many of the preachers he was patronising and protecting were indeed evangelicals, and all this was being done in the King's name. Even his cherished Archbishop of Canterbury was guilty to some extent of this kind of indiscretion, and the time had come for Henry to spell out exactly where he stood. His more conservative advisers, such as Stephen Gardiner and the Duke of Norfolk had been urging him for some time to take a stand against this creeping evangelicalisation, and he did so now in the act 'abolishing diversity in opinions', otherwise known as the Act of Six Articles.[79]

This measure, which became law on the proroguing of Parliament on 18 July, was mainly a thumping affirmation of the traditional doctrine of the mass. The bread and wine did really and corporeally become the body and blood of Christ when the words of consecration were spoken; it was not necessary for the laity to receive the cup in communion; and it was a laudable practice for the priest to say mass in private 'no man communicating with him'. Clerical celibacy was reaffirmed, and vows taken in religion were to continue to be binding, although the individual concerned had returned to the world. Denial of transubstantiation became heresy, to be punished by death, and denial of the other clauses of the Act became felony without benefit of clergy.[80] Although it was introduced in the House of Lords by the Duke of Norfolk, this statute undoubtedly reflected the King's own views, and should have come as no surprise to those who knew him well. For the time being at least, Cromwell and Cranmer had been defeated in their battle to control the public face of the Church, and the limits of their influence over the King painfully exposed. Conservatives rejoiced, but it was a limited victory. There was no sign of second thoughts about religious houses, and it was as pure an action of the Royal Supremacy as any that had preceded it. Henry meant to be master in his own house, and this was the traditional aspect of that idiosyncratic Church which he was building. The path of safety in ecclesiastical matters came to mean following the King, and not adhering to the agendas which either papalists or evangelicals wished to implement.[81] Cranmer had been excused attendance at Parliament while the measure was under discussion, because Henry knew that it would offend his conscience, but that did not mean that he had forfeited the King's confidence. Cromwell drew in his horns and kept quiet, because he realised (as did his opponents) that the proof of the King's intentions would come in the enforcement of the Act rather than in the Act itself. Henry had had his say, and it remained to be seen how seriously he had meant it.

For nearly two years the King had resisted pressures to remarry. This was partly because, in spite of the manner in which he had rebuffed her attempts at political intervention, he had really loved Jane; and partly because at forty-seven he was beginning to feel old. Although he professed himself satisfied with the arrangements made for the Cleves marriage, there was none of the eager anticipation which had characterised each of his first three matches. Nor was there much urgency on the other side. Anne set off on her journey to England at the end of October, and by 11 December had got no further than Calais. There she was lavishly received, and made a very good impression. In spite of speaking no language but low German, she was sweet tempered, and it was judged that she would be an easy mistress to serve.[82] There was pleasurable speculation about how long it would be before a Duke of York appeared. Then things began to go wrong. Bad weather delayed her at Calais until 27 December, forcing the King to spend a lonely Christmas at Greenwich, and Henry decided to indulge in a little knight errantry. Driven largely by curiosity, he intercepted her incognito at Rochester, invading her chamber with a gang of disguised companions. Not surprisingly, the poor girl was bewildered and terrified, thinking that she was about to be abducted.[83] What kind of reaction he was expecting is not apparent, but having reassured her by revealing his identity, he withdrew deeply disappointed. 'I like her not,' he is alleged to have said. Perhaps he was looking for the witty play-acting with which Catherine would have greeted such a foray, or the sharp response to such nonsense that he would have received from Anne Boleyn. This Anne was quite incapable of such role play. The fact was that she was ill-prepared to be the consort of such an educated and sophisticated monarch as Henry. She had been trained in the domestic virtues appropriate to a minor German princess, knew no languages, and was completely innocent of theology. Even the dances which she knew were those of her homeland, which did not feature among the French and Spanish fashions prevailing at Greenwich or Hampton Court.[84] According to her portraits she was passably good looking, but that was not the point; she was completely lacking in the wit and polish which the King was looking for, and he began immediately to seek for a way out of his contract. There was none, and the formalities of greeting and wedding were gone through with due decorum. He was courteous and considerate, and she apparently completely unaware that there was anything wrong. The wedding night was a fiasco, because he was impotent, and she so ignorant of the facts of life that she did not even know what was supposed to happen. 'At this rate,' one of her ladies commented sourly, 'it will be a long time before we see a Duke of York.'[85] For the time being the uninformed spectator would have noticed nothing. The new Queen had been given a household of 127 persons, including a number of her own German servants, and her dower lands were duly settled on her in April. However, below the surface feet were paddling fast. It was decided to use non-consummation as the grounds for annulment, and on 25 June Anne was visited by the King's commissioners at Richmond and informed that her marriage to the King was over.[86] She could have made a fuss, and resisted the decision, but in fact it probably came as a relief to her. She submitted to the King's will, and accepted the settlement which he provided for her, showing no inclination to return to her homeland. Her brother the Duke similarly accepted the situation; after all, if she was not prepared to object, why should he? Anne spent the rest of her life in England, on the fringes of the court. She never married, and died in 1557.

The politics of early 1540 were fraught, not so much because of Anne as because the Lord Privy Seal was under mounting attack. He had made enemies in his climb to power, most notably Stephen Gardiner and the Dukes of Norfolk and Suffolk, and they were constantly on the lookout for ways of undermining him with the King. For several years this was unavailing, but then Cromwell began to make mistakes. His patronage of evangelical preachers went a little too far, and was rewarded with defeat over the Act of Six Articles. The treaty with Duke William of Cleves, for which he was mainly responsible, was also a failure, not only because Anne failed to please Henry, but also because William, who was supposed to marry Mary, went off after a French bride.[87] The negotiations with the Schmalkaldic League had broken down, and Charles' victory over the rebels in Ghent in February 1540 made it more necessary than ever to place some curbs upon him. The obvious solution would have been closer ties with France, but Cromwell did not trust the French and was averse to such a course. Then he misjudged the situation in Calais, and left himself open to charges of supporting not just heretics, but sacramentarians.[88] It was this last factor which gave his opponents their critical opportunity. Parliament reconvened on 12 April, and there his management skills appeared to be as indispensable as ever, so that when he was created Earl of Essex and Lord Great Chamberlain on the 18th, it appeared that the Lord Privy Seal had won again. This time, however, appearances were deceptive. Exactly when, or why, Henry decided to abandon Cromwell is not clear, but it was sometime in late May or early June, and the critical factor seems to have been that the King became convinced that not only did his Lord Privy Seal support sacramentarians, but he was one himself.[89] Henry's horror of this radical heresy was paranoid, and he came to believe that it was Cromwell the secret radical who was stirring up all the theological controversy which was erupting in the pulpits and on the streets of London, threatening the good order of the city. On 10 June, he was arrested at a council meeting, and sent to the Tower. To have charged him with treason on the evidence available would have been impossible, even for Henry VIII, so he was condemned by Act of Attainder (ironically a method which he himself had developed). This Act became law when the Parliament was dissolved on 24 July, and Cromwell was executed at the Tower on the 28th.[90]

From then on there were to be no more chief ministers, and the King would govern as well as rule. Nevertheless, the legacy of Cromwell's years in power was of profound importance. Whether he is regarded as an originator or a facilitator, he was heavily involved in a number of developments which helped to reshape the English polity. First and foremost his use of Parliament transformed that institution from the medieval estates into something much closer to a modern sovereign legislature. A whole range of Acts reduced the Church from the status of an independent franchise to an aspect of the state – a department of ecclesiastical affairs. Further statutes reduced the secular franchises and shired Wales.[91] The succession was determined by the same method, again breaking new ground. His offices, whether of Secretary or Lord Privy Seal, became the great clearing houses for royal business of all kinds, and largely controlled the Crown's patronage. This was not continued by his immediate successors, but was picked up and made permanent by Sir William Cecil under Elizabeth. Another long-term legacy, although one for which he was less certainly responsible, was the reorganisation of the Council. Cromwell never enjoyed a monopoly of Council, but he did manage its business – very largely in his own interest. When he fell from power, it was reconstituted into the Privy

Council, less a pool of advisers and more a management committee. Professor Elton attributed this to Cromwell's own initiative, but it has been pointed out that it was not in his interest to surrender his personal control in this fashion, and that the idea almost certainly came from the King.[92] This Privy Council, consisting of office holders, meeting to a regular agenda, and keeping formal minutes, remained the central institution of the executive until its role was taken over by the cabinet in the eighteenth century. Less significant in the long term, although important at the time, was Cromwell's reorganisation of the royal finances. He reduced the role of the King's Chamber Treasury (over which he could not exercise control), and instead diverted most of the revenue income to new financial courts, such as Augmentations, First Fruits and Tenths and Wards and Liveries, which he could control through the appointment of his agents to run them. The Exchequer remained largely an accounting department, until the reign of Mary when the new courts were abolished and income returned to a reformed Exchequer.[93] So in this respect his reforms lasted only about fifteen years, except that the Exchequer took over the modern system of double-entry bookkeeping which had been characteristic of the Court of Augmentations – a great improvement on its traditional (and arcane) practices. Only in Ireland was his legacy largely negative, because, dissatisfied with the quasi-autonomy enjoyed by the Earl of Kildare as deputy, and disillusioned with the feuding of the Earls of Ormond and Desmond, he decided to impose stricter English control over the obedient lands.[94] These lands constituted the Dublin Pale and the Anglo-Irish Earldoms of the south and south-east. Over the 'wild Irish' who occupied the rest of the island, there was no English control anyway. Kildare was summoned to London, but allowed to leave his son, Lord Offaly, to govern in his place. Angered by attempts to control him from England, in 1534 Offaly renounced his allegiance and rose in rebellion, supported by those Old English settlers who were opposed to Henry's religious policy. By 1535 the rebellion had been suppressed, and Offaly was captured and executed, but not before a legacy of bitterness had been created between the Old and New English. Towards the end,

Offaly had also sought the support of the Irish tribes, and that also had long-term consequences. Cromwell's policy in Ireland not only failed at the time, but left a situation which made constructive initiatives more difficult in the future.[95] The long-term consequence was the disastrous Elizabethan expedient of the Plantation, which created permanent divisions in Irish society.

Apart from Ireland, in terms of its efficiency and authority, Henry's government moved on quite a lot under Thomas Cromwell's guidance, but one thing did not change – the King's need for further children. In that respect the omens in the summer of 1540 were much better than might have been expected. The Duke of Norfolk had a niece, the eighteen-year-old Catherine Howard, whom her uncle began thoughtfully to dangle under the King's nose once it was clear that all was not well with his fourth marriage. Henry took the bait, and from about April began to lavish gifts upon her. She responded coyly, and once convocation had cleared the way by declaring his existing entanglement null and void on 9 July, Henry married her at Oatlands on the 28th – the same day, ironically, which saw the end of Thomas Cromwell.[96] The Howard ascendancy at court was now complete, and the King excited speculation among the spectators by his assiduous attentions to his new bride. It was observed that he could barely keep his hands off her, even in public. Her lavish household, which cost Henry some £4,600 a year, was quickly filled with numerous Howard family members and clients of all kinds. Resentment smouldered, and the Cromwell years suddenly seemed a lot more endurable.[97] Had Catherine become pregnant as a result of all these attentions, she might have been given the benefit of the doubt, but she did not, and unlike Anne Boleyn, was not astute enough to fend off the criticisms when they came. Meanwhile, she was given a far larger jointure than Jane Seymour had enjoyed, including much of the estate of the late Earl of Essex. Jewels, rich clothes and public adulation were lavished on her, and her numerous enemies were silenced by the King's favour. This was just as well, because Catherine was a young lady with a past. She had been brought up in the rambling and ill-disciplined household of the Dowager Duchess of Norfolk at

Horsham, who may or may not have known what was going on, but in any case regarded it as all part of a girl's education. Catherine had taken at least two lovers, and one of them, Thomas Culpepper, was now a member of the King's Privy Chamber.[98] This, of course, was concealed from the King, who seems to have assumed that she came to him as an innocent virgin, and even celebrated her in that mode. Others knew differently, and at least one of her former 'bedfellows' had to be bought off with a place in her household, lest she make inconvenient disclosures.[99] The new queen was also temperamentally vulnerable. Her attitude towards her aging husband was one of mingled awe and gratitude. She took the unexceptionable motto 'no other will but his', but she also found him a very unsatisfactory lover. It is by no means certain that their union was ever consummated, and Henry's early euphoric confidence soon evaporated, leaving him restless and fretful. In March 1541 the chronic leg ulcer which permanently afflicted him closed up, and he was seriously ill for about a week. During that time, he could not bear his wife to be near him, and that added to her discontent.

During the summer of 1541, Henry made his long-delayed progress to the north, having, as he thought, persuaded James V of Scotland to meet him at York, to discuss relations between the two kingdoms. He also wished to persuade his nephew to follow his lead in relations with Rome, a break which James had no incentive to make.[100] The King reached York on 18 September with a train the size of an army of occupation, but James did not come. His council did not trust the English, and he could hardly come at the head of an army. Henry waited until the 29th, and then headed rapidly south, in a foul temper at having been 'mocked' by the Scots. Had he known what was going on in his own chamber, his mood would have been even more thunderous, because the Queen, out of patience with his sexual withdrawal, began again to entertain lovers. In this she was fatally abetted by Jane Rochford, her Chief Gentlewoman. Jane should have been aware of the perils of such behaviour, as she was the widow of Lord Rochford who had lost his head for alleged indiscretions with his sister, Anne Boleyn. However, she admitted Thomas Culpepper and another old flame, Francis Dereham, and seems to have encouraged their advances. Just how serious these encounters were is not apparent, but it was an incredibly foolish way to carry on, given that servants were everywhere in a Tudor court. Ironically,[101] however, the first revelations to throw Catherine out of her stride came not from these adventures but from her earlier life. The Howards had enemies, not least among the evangelicals who blamed them for the downfall of Thomas Cromwell, and one of these, John Lascelles, had a sister who knew all about the goings on at Horsham. She told her brother what she knew, and he sought out the Archbishop of Canterbury, and passed the stories on to him. This happened on 1 November 1541, the very day upon which the King had held a special thanksgiving service for the virtues of his wife.[102] What he heard was so circumstantial and convincing that Cranmer realised at once that it would be his unpleasant duty to break the news to Henry. The next day he passed a discreet note to the King during mass, with the request that he read it in private.

Henry's first reaction was one of incredulity. Someone was trying to blacken his wife's name, which was only to be expected in the fraught atmosphere of the court. He ordered a secret investigation, but only for the purpose of clearing her of suspicion. The Earl of Southampton was sent to examine Lascelles, and then down to Sussex to see his sister, Mary Hall. They both repeated their story with persuasive detail. Henry was still not convinced, but Catherine was ordered to keep to her chamber and await his pleasure. Meanwhile, news of her activities during the progress must have leaked out, because Sir Thomas Wriothesley arrested Francis Dereham, allegedly for piracy, but immediately began to question him about his relations with the Queen.[103] He also picked up another of her familiars, one Henry Mannox, and both under pressure confessed to adultery. On 6 November the King returned to London without speaking to Catherine, and immediately called the Privy Council into emergency session. Dereham under interrogation had implicated Thomas Culpepper, and the whole sorry story began to emerge. Under the weight of this evidence, Henry's delusions finally collapsed into an orgy of self-pity. He threatened to torture the ungrateful girl to death, but the fact was that he was an old and tired man, who had failed to satisfy the sexual appetite of a nubile teenager.[104] The King was genuinely hurt by these disclosures; more hurt, probably, than by anything else in his life. He left the unravelling of Catherine's infidelities to Thomas Cranmer, and took himself off hunting 'for the purpose of diverting his ill humour'. He may not be able to joust any longer, to play tennis or to make love, but he could still hunt, and make war. His thoughts began to turn in the latter direction. On 7 November Cranmer went to Hampton Court for the embarrassing task of interrogating the Queen, and at first she denied all the charges, with copious tears, but the following day he got the whole story out of her, interspersed with fits of hysterics. She admitted prenuptial intercourse, but claimed:

> I was so desirous to be taken unto your grace's favour, and so blinded by the desire of worldly glory, that I could not, nor had grace, to consider how great a fault it was to conceal my former faults …[105]

Dereham claimed a contract of marriage, which would have made her union with the King illegal because bigamous, but this Catherine strenuously denied. Then Culpepper was arrested and admitted to an adulterous relationship with the Queen since her marriage. This Catherine also denied, but Jane Rochford, deeply mired herself, claimed that she believed intercourse to have taken place. On 13 November the Queen's household at Hampton Court was closed down, and her jewels and other possessions were inventoried.[106] The whole situation is confused by special pleading, but it is probable that intercourse did take place between Catherine and Culpepper in the course of the summer progress, and that was sufficient not merely to bring them within the scope of the 1534 Treasons Act, but also to constitute 'ancient treason' – the violation of a queen. On 22 November Catherine was deprived of her title, and on 1 December Dereham and Culpepper were arraigned for high treason. On the 10th they were executed at Tyburn. The Howard ascendancy at court had been destroyed and on the 22nd the whole clan, with the exception of the Duke, were found guilty of misprision for concealing Catherine's offences.[107] They were eventually pardoned, but their political influence was over, and that was to be of great significance for the last period of the reign. Parliament was convened on 16 January 1542, and a bill of attainder against Catherine and Jane Rochford was introduced into the House of Lords on the 21st. It received the royal assent on 11 February, and the two women were executed on the morning of the 13th. Catherine was almost too unnerved to walk to the block, and merely confessed her faults in a few words, inviting the assembled crowd to pray for her. She was just twenty years old.[108]

The conservative ascendancy had unravelled. Just after Cromwell's execution, on 30 July 1540, Robert Barnes, William Jerome and Thomas Garrett had gone to the fire for heresies which remain obscure to this day, but by 1542 enforcement of the Act of Six Articles was slack and Thomas Cromwell's friends who remained in the Privy Chamber, were recovering influence, William Buttes and Sir Anthony Denny in particular. Henry was also hankering after a new Imperial alliance. For much of 1541 he had been locked in negotiations with Francis for the marriage of his daughter Mary, who was now twenty-five, but these had broken down because the King obstinately refused to allow her to be described as legitimate. In spite of the fact that he was then onto his fifth wife, he would not admit that he had been wrong in nullifying his first marriage. He was also beginning to find those regular French allies the Scots troublesome. James V seems to have had no aggressive intentions, but he was much influenced by clerical advisers, and he had snubbed Henry's efforts to persuade him into an anti-papal stance. Moreover, there were always border raids in plenty to provide pretexts for a hostile posture, should the King wish to adopt one for other reasons. By the summer of 1542 such reasons were beginning to build up.[109] After tentative negotiations in the early part of the year, in June he sent Thomas Thirlby to the Emperor to settle terms for an alliance which would lead to a joint invasion of France in the summer of 1543. This was successfully done, and immediately followed up by an agreement with Mary of Hungary, the Regent of the Low Countries. On 10 July,

Francis and Charles resumed their warfare, which had been broken by the peace of Toldeo in 1539, and Henry began to assemble ships, guns and money for the projected campaign. But first he decided to take out the Scots.

The reasons for the King's bellicosity at this juncture were probably psychological rather than political. Although he would not admit it publicly, his dream of conquering France, or at least a large part of it in the manner of Henry V, was now dead. If he was to secure any further territory on the far side of the Channel, he needed the Emperor as an ally. Moreover, joining in an attack on France was a good way of protecting himself from any papally inspired coalition. His confidence was also not what it had been thirty years earlier. Then, as a young man eager for glory, he had been prepared to take on the world; now, after years of buffeting in the diplomatic field, his aims were more limited. But above all, he needed reassurance. Having been mocked and humiliated by a slip of a girl, he needed to convince himself that he was still a great king. One symptom of that was the tenacity with which he clung to the Royal Supremacy. Thomas Cromwell had been right about that, and perhaps he had been over hasty in getting rid of him; certainly none of his present servants could match Cromwell for efficiency or devotion. Another symptom was his desire for war; and war, moreover, which he would wage in person. Although he might have difficulty in squeezing his body even into the generous suits of armour with which he was now provided, he was determined to lead the campaign in France himself. Henry needed to rediscover his manhood.

11

THE RETURN TO WAR, 1542–1547

In the summer of 1542 Henry committed himself to war with France. However, no campaign was to take place until the following year, and in the meantime he had to decide what to do about the situation in the north. James V had no aggressive intentions, but on the other hand he had no intention of submitting to his uncle's leadership, let alone his claims to suzerainty. He was not prepared to abandon his clerical councillors, nor to surrender his special relationship with France, and it was this latter factor which Henry found particularly worrying.[1] In the middle of September English commissioners met their Scottish counterparts in York, and confronted them with a number of provocative demands. These included reparations for border incursions, and a visit by King James to England to make up for his missed appointment of the previous year. The Scots may have been intimidated, but they gave Henry the impression that they had agreed to these demands. This, however, was not what the King wanted, and shortly after he upped the stakes by demanding hostages for their King's appearance.[2] This the Scots commissioners were not empowered to concede, and while they dithered and prevaricated, Henry ordered his army to march. Just over a fortnight later, the Duke of Norfolk led his army across the border at Coldstream, and marched on Kelso. For about a week he burned and destroyed everything in sight, meeting virtually no resistance from the totally unprepared borderers.

Once back in Berwick, he received instructions from the King to keep his army in being to deal with any retaliatory strike, and ordering him to collect victuals from across the north to feed them.[3] It soon transpired that his belligerence had had the opposite of its intended effect, as he apparently suspected that it might. Instead of being intimidated, James responded in kind. Issuing ritual appeals to the Pope and all Christian princes for aid, in the middle of November he launched about 20,000 men into the Debateable Land, north of Carlisle.

This was a larger riposte than Henry was looking for, and in the wrong place. However, Sir Thomas Wharton, the warden of the West March, had about 3,000 experienced troops at his disposal, plus a force of some 700 cavalry, and on 24 November, while the invading army skirted the bogs of the Esk valley, he struck. Inexperienced, and caught at a major tactical disadvantage, the Scottish infantry broke and ran.[4] As a battle it was a minor affair, not to be compared to Flodden, but it left a number of Scottish lords and gentlemen as prisoners in English hands, and they were to contribute significantly to Henry's cause in the exchanges which followed. About a fortnight after the battle, the Queen of Scots, Mary of Guise, was delivered of a daughter, and a week later, James V unexpectedly died, leaving his realm in confusion and his field army in tatters. Had Henry wished to do so, he could probably have conquered Scotland at this point, but he had no such intention. His main aim had been to keep Scotland out of his war with France, and that now seemed to have been accomplished. It was also a golden opportunity to assert his overlordship, and that he attempted to do by proposing a marriage between the newborn Queen of Scots and his own son, Edward, aged five.[5] It was to this programme that the captured Scots were sworn, the intention being to make them the nucleus of an 'English party' in Scotland, committed to the King and his interests. They were brought to court for the Christmas celebrations, duly sworn, and allowed to return home. Most of them were back in Edinburgh by the end of January. However, these plans were largely derailed by the actions of the Scottish Council, which, without consulting Henry, made its own arrangements for the minority government. On 3 January it appointed James Hamilton, Earl of Arran, to be Governor of Scotland until Mary came of age. Henry was offended, and made a half-hearted attempt to have Hamilton arrested and Mary brought to England, but that was beyond the power of the English party, even if they had been so inclined.[6] Moreover, Arran soon began to make conciliatory noises. He wrote to Henry about the need to reform the Kirk, and to negotiate a peace and marriage treaty with England. The King responded positively, and issued safeconducts to the envoys to come and negotiate. On 20 February a three-month truce was offered and accepted. It looked as though Henry was going to get his own way in spite of the Council's gesture of independence. However, nothing happened and the King, who did not understand the intricacies of Scottish politics, sent Ralph Sadler to Edinburgh in mid-March to find out what was going on. Sadler found, as he had feared, that the pro-French party was rallying round the Cardinal Archbishop of St Andrews, David Beaton, and that French ships and munitions were surreptitiously arriving in the north.[7] Nevertheless, the King continued to be optimistic. He sent Arran instructions as to how best to reform the Kirk, and continued to make arrangements for Mary to be sent to England. However the Duke was playing his own hand, trying to navigate around the conflicting interests of France and England in order to retain his power. Eventually, in June, he sent the promised ambassadors to England, and on 1 July 1543 they signed the treaty of Greenwich, which appeared to give Henry the majority of what he wanted. Most importantly, they accepted the proposed marriage, and agreed to send hostages to England for Mary's safe delivery. The Queen herself, however, was not to come until she was ten years old, and that pushed the implementation of the treaty comfortably into the future. For some reason, Henry chose to regard this equivocal agreement as a triumph for himself, and as representing the submission of Scotland to his will. It was soon apparent that it was nothing of the kind.[8]

The reason for this delusion lay in the dynamics of his relationship with the Emperor. In February 1543 he had signed a new Anglo-Imperial agreement, which was kept secret until the end of May, and it was the last week in June, when he was convinced of his success in Scotland, that Henry finally delivered to the French ambassador the ultimatum which meant war. At the beginning of July, 5,000 English troops crossed to the Low Countries to aid in their defence. And the first skirmish occurred between English and French ships in the Narrow Seas about 6 July.[9] It was now, however, too late to mount the great joint offensive which had originally been intended, and the Emperor reluctantly agreed to postpone that until the following year. Each was then to mount an army of 42,000 men, not later than 20 June 1544; Charles to enter France via Champagne, and Henry via the Somme, on the direct route to Paris. For this programme to work, Henry had to believe that the situation in the north was under control. However, by the middle of August civil war threatened in Scotland, as Beaton and his allies rallied against Arran, and on the 31st Suffolk was ordered to gather a large army to go to the Governor's assistance. On 5 September the Duke suddenly changed sides, and joined the Cardinal at Stirling, thereby derailing Suffolk's preparations, and leaving Sadler and Henry fuming.[10] The leadership of the English party now devolved upon the Earl of Angus, and the King began to hurl instructions in his direction which were totally unrealistic in their scope. He was to capture the Cardinal, the Earl of Arran and the Queen, and he could have whatever men and money he might require out of England for the purpose. Even with this proposed support, such a programme was completely beyond Angus' capabilities, and nothing happened.[11] At the end of September Henry announced that he was at open war with the Scots because of their failure to renounce the auld alliance and to honour the treaties between the kingdoms – but again nothing happened. On 11 December the Scottish Parliament solemnly repudiated the treaty of Greenwich, and on the 15th renewed all Scotland's existing agreements with France, in a deliberate insult to the English which Henry's failure to act on his earlier threats had probably encouraged. A year after the battle of Solway Moss, the King had gained precisely nothing, and his northern frontier was more insecure than it had been in 1542, thanks to the aggravation which he had caused.[12]

This time, however, he was determined upon revenge. When it had appeared that the 1543 campaign against France would go ahead, in the autumn of 1542, he had recalled the Dukes of Norfolk and Suffolk to London for consultations. In October the Warden General of the Marches, the Earl of Rutland, had stood down on the grounds of poor health, and had been replaced by John Dudley, Viscount Lisle, who took over his duties on 1 December. It therefore fell to Dudley to deal with the day-by-day consequences of the instability in Scotland following the death of James V, including the murder of an English envoy by renegades in Edinburgh, an event which Henry decided not to turn into a crisis. He mobilised local forces, exchanged formalities with the Earl of Arran, and provided for border defence, but his tenure of office was short, because in January 1543 he was also appointed Lord Admiral in succession to the Earl of Hertford.[13] For about three months he doubled the functions of admiral with those of Lord Warden, which made some sense as most of his naval preoccupations related to ships mobilised in the north-east for possible use against the Scots. On 19 April Lord Parr of Kendal was briefed to succeed him in the marches, and by the 21st he was back in London. The appointment of Lord Parr signalled a downgrading of the military potential of the office, and when the King was contemplating a punitive strike in the autumn of 1543, he entrusted it to the Duke of Suffolk, not to the Lord Warden. Although officially at war, because of the tense situation in Scotland, Henry's efforts against the French at this time did not amount to much. Individual letters of Marque began to be issued on 4 August, and these were upgraded to a general permission by a proclamation of 20 December.[14] At the beginning of November the King appears to have intended a strike against the French fishing fleet as it returned from Iceland, but he did not give sufficient warning to his admiral and the necessary warships could not be prepared in time. Henry could not very well evade the obligation which he had undertaken to attack France a second time, and early in 1544 began the major mobilisation which such a large campaign would require. However, in the immediate future, he had to decide what to do about Scotland. The leaders of the English party, the Earls of Angus and

Lennox, were not powerful enough to achieve anything very much, so by the end of January the King had decided to launch a large-scale raid, targeting this time not the borders, but the capital city of Edinburgh itself. He would give those treacherous Scots a bloody nose that they would not forget![15]

At the end of January 1544 the Duke of Suffolk was nominated to carry out this operation, an appointment which he accepted on 2 February, asking that Hertford and Lisle should be designated to accompany him. The 'enterprise' was to deploy some 17,000 men and was to take place before the end of March. However, the King then had second thoughts. He was still determined to go ahead with the invasion of France which he planned for the summer, and he would need Suffolk with him since he had decided to campaign in person. He therefore relieved Suffolk of his northern command, and entrusted it to Hertford instead, instructing Lisle to provide the necessary shipping for the whole operation to be carried out from the sea.[16] This inevitably led to delays, and it was 21 March before Lisle went down to Harwich to muster the necessary ships. Meanwhile Stephen Gardiner and William Paulet, Lord St John, had been commissioned to provide the support services, and on 24 March wrote bitterly complaining of the difficulties which they were having.[17] At the end of the winter, victuals were in short supply. By the end of the month, Hertford had almost a full muster of troops at Newcastle, but nowhere near enough ships, and if they did not arrive quickly, his soldiers would have consumed the rations which had so far been provided for the campaign. In the event, thanks to adverse winds, it was 20 April before Lisle reached the Tyne with his fleet. He brought with him eleven warships and fifty-seven transports, which were enough for the purpose, but victualling continued to be a headache. On 28 April Hertford issued his fleet with battle orders, which were specifically designed for an amphibious operation, and embarked 12,000 men.[18] The other 5,000 were to go overland via Haddington, possibly to deceive the Scots as to the strength of the expedition. On 1 May the ships were still trying to get out of the Tyne, but on the evening of that day the wind changed, and early on the 2nd they arrived opposite Inchkieth, about two miles from Leith, where they landed on 3 May. The town was virtually undefended, and was comprehensively plundered, the English finding 'such riches as they thought not to have found in any town of Scotland', which probably reflects the soldiers' contempt for Scotsmen rather than the exceptional opulence of the place. The next day the Scots made a gesture of resistance, but it was little more than that and Hertford wrote an amused report mocking the somewhat comic opera style of Cardinal Beaton, who had led them – and been the first to run away![19] Thoroughly alarmed, and realising that they were next for attack, the citizens of Edinburgh sent emissaries to Hertford, offering to ransom the town, but he rejected their offer on the grounds that his instructions were to destroy. Meanwhile, his warships carried out a similarly destructive mission on such forts and strong places as they could find in the vicinity, encountering little in the way of resistance. On 8 May, Lisle blew in the main gate of Edinburgh with a culverin, and, making light of some fierce resistance, led his men on a rampage through the town, at the end of which they torched the entire place. Hertford had neither the time nor the resources to besiege the castle, which held out, its guns inflicting some severe casualties upon the invaders, which were glossed over in the official reports.[20] Meanwhile the English cavalry raided as far as Stirling, destroying everything in their path. On the 15th, having burned Leith for good measure, the English retreated, the army going overland, and the ships, now laden with plunder and looted guns, returned as they had come, doing such damage as they could on the way. In spite of the difficulties and delays which it had encountered, it had been a brutally successful operation.

In political terms, however, its effect was not great. Both Arran and Beaton were discredited and a special convention held at Stirling in June transferred the Governorship to the Queen Mother, Mary of Guise. Mary was able to talk to Angus and Lennox in a way which Arran could not, and that was a gain from an English point of view, but otherwise there was little advantage. Mary was equally, if not more, committed to the French cause than her predecessor, and there was no question of reviving the treaty of Greenwich.[21] The Scots did not invade when Henry went to France, but it is by no means certain that they would have done so in any case. At the same time the English party was reduced to total impotence; with friends like Henry VIII, who needed enemies? On his return to Newcastle, Lisle paid off the foreign ships which he had hired for the expedition, and the remainder headed south to join the musters being prepared for the invasion of Picardy. Most of the army was similarly redeployed, except for those who were retained in the north to reinforce the border garrisons. Some 4,000 were sent immediately to Calais, and Hertford and Lisle rejoined the King, who was already engaged in bickering with the Emperor about the strategy of the campaign.[22] Charles was less than impressed by Henry's decision to take part in person, pointing out (although without using such words) that the King was past it. Henry had still not made up his mind what his strategy was to be when his army crossed to Calais at the end of May, led, for the time being, by those veteran war lords the Dukes of Norfolk and Suffolk. The army numbered about 32,000 foot and 4,000 horse, and the logistical preparations had been enormous, complex and expensive. It was also, in a sense a revolutionary body because, apart from the royal household, which numbered about 2,000, it was largely recruited from the counties by way of the musters. Previous hosts had been composed of noble and gentle retinues, but, because Henry mistrusted the military pretensions of the nobility, that was no longer the case; and the army of 1544 was recruited and officered by the county gentry.[23] It has been described as 'the last hurrah of the royal affinity', but it would be more realistic to call it the first citizen army, and its officers' loyalty was due only to the King, without any question of intermediary allegiances. By the middle of June it had moved eastwards into French territory, so far unresisted but with its purpose still indeterminate. It was not until 14 July that Henry finally disembarked at Calais, and the period of waiting came to an end. After surveying the situation and talking to his leading advisers, the King decided that his objective was to be Boulogne.[24]

The English immediately moved to besiege Boulogne and Montreuil, and Charles protested that this was not his idea of a joint campaign.

Henry was supposed to march on Paris, not to become bogged down in sieges, to which the King responded that to advance into France leaving such strong places unsubdued behind him would be asking for trouble. What he did not confess was that his ambition extended no further. His title as King of France was a useful pretext for such an invasion, but he no longer expected it to be realised. The opportunity for that had passed nearly twenty years before, but Henry did not remind Charles that he had been responsible for thwarting his ambition then, and would no doubt have done the same again if the circumstances had repeated themselves. He settled down to enjoy the siege. Bad weather and shortage of powder held up the operation, and it was not until early August that the full power of his artillery was deployed. Thereafter the King supervised every detail, and was, it was reported, in better health and spirits than he had been for years.[25] On 11 September all this firepower was rewarded when the castle was blown up, and the garrison sued for terms of surrender. These were swiftly negotiated, there being no sign of a French relieving army, and Henry entered in triumph on the 18th. He stayed there for twelve days, supervising arrangements for the fortification and defence of his new acquisition, and returned quietly to England on the 30th. Norfolk was instructed to disengage at Montreuil, which he did with some difficulty thanks to the belated attentions of the Dauphin at the head of substantial force, and to retreat to Boulogne.[26] The bad news was that the Emperor, despairing of his ally and desperately short of money, had come to terms with Francis on the very day that Henry had entered Boulogne, and signed the peace of Crespy. The King would have to defend his new conquest unaided, and Francis now had 50,000 men in the field. In the face of this threat Norfolk and Suffolk abandoned Boulogne and retreated to Calais in early October, to Henry's extreme anger. They felt that they had no option because their German cavalry had followed the Emperor's lead and gone home. From Calais they quickly began to ship their men to England, but remarkably Boulogne did not fall. Its makeshift garrison under Lord Lisle held out, and redeemed something from a campaign which had seemed destined to sink into dishonour and disaster as the supply services finally collapsed under the strain.[27] The Council was left to vent its impotent rage on the unfortunate commanders. It had been estimated that the campaign would cost £250,000, but when the bills were presented they added up to £650,000, leaving the King in desperate straits for money. In spite of the sale of monastic land and a variety of loans and benevolences, he was reduced to debasing the coinage to make ends meet, and that was to create an economic timebomb in terms of inflation, the worst consequences of which he did not live to see. By the autumn of 1544, the treasurer of the armies in France, Richard Rich, was reporting that the soldiers at Calais were dying daily 'for weakness and lack of victual', and the Flemish debt was costing £40,000 a year in interest.[28]

After his return from France, Henry kept his options open. Peace was a possibility, and negotiations were opened at Calais as early as 16 October. However, the King's insistence on retaining Boulogne, and his demand that the French abandon the auld alliance with Scotland meant that no progress was made, and Francis withdrew his delegation early in November. Henry had gained a little breathing space, because the winter precluded further military operations for the time being, and he was able to fortify and reinforce Boulogne. Then on 25 February 1545 the Scots defeated Sir Ralph Eure at Ancrum Moor. This was not a major reverse, but it was a warning that the Scottish front was still active, and an incentive to launch another destructive raid under the Earl of Hertford later in the year. Unusually as 1545 advanced, Henry's thinking was defensive rather than offensive. This was partly occasioned by shortage of money, and partly by political isolation. In April he sent Christopher Mont to Germany to see what potential allies he could drum up, but his embassy met with little response. The most that he could obtain was a defensive alliance with the Schmalkaldic League, which was likely to be of more use to them than to him.[29] Having (in Henry's eyes) abandoned him at a critical time, the Emperor now recycled himself as a mediator between the belligerents, a service for which he got small thanks as Anglo-Imperial relations continued to deteriorate. Charles made little progress with the French either, as Francis was now determined upon a major stroke to recover Boulogne. Rightly perceiving that command of the sea was the secret to English success in maintaining themselves there, he determined to take out the English fleet by destroying its base at Portsmouth. Henry had by this time about fifty warships of varying sizes, including several Great Ships, like the *Henry Grace à Dieu* and the *Mary Rose* which had recently been rebuilt and re-equipped with the latest guns.[30] He also had an admiral of efficiency and enterprise, and Lisle was determined to disrupt the French preparations. On 24 May he led out a warfleet of some thirty ships to attack the navy which was assembling at Le Havre. His tactic apparently was to use fireships on the assumption that his enemies would be immobilised, and unable to move for some time. He had also learned that galleys from the Mediterranean station were expected as reinforcement, and he was anxious to strike before they arrived. However, bad weather disrupted his preparations and when he did attack on 6 July, he was repulsed, and retreated to Portsmouth to re-provision. In fact d'Annebault, the French Admiral, was nearer to being ready than Lisle realised, and led out his armada on 12 July, hard on the heels of the retreating English.[31] It was a massive operation involving between 30,000 and 50,000 men, and somewhere between 150 and 200 ships and galleys – the largest invasion fleet ever to have been mounted against England – and he entered the Solent on 19 July, landing 5,000 men on the Isle of Wight. As a naval confrontation, however, it was not as uneven as these figures might suggest, because most of d'Annebault's fleet consisted of troop transports. He deployed about 30 large fighting ships and 25 galleys, while against him Lisle mustered 80 vessels, all warships, although only about 20 of them could be classed as large (over 400 tons).[32] It appeared that a great naval battle was impending, but it did not happen. The English were within the harbour, and d'Annebault marshalled his fighting ships into three squadrons, keeping his transports well out of the way, but a total absence of wind frustrated their attempts to encounter. Only the French galleys remained mobile, and they advanced, firing their basilisks or forward guns, only to little effect because of the range. Then in the late afternoon a fitful wind sprang up, and the English fleet moved out to attack. The galleys retreated in some haste, and it was at that juncture that the *Mary Rose*, executing a turning manoeuvre, was caught by a squally gust and sank. There has been a great deal of speculation as to why this happened, but it appears that the gunports had been left open, and the water entered as she turned. Only a handful of men escaped, the Captain, Sir George Carew, being among the dead.[33] Thereupon the wind failed again, but Lisle was able to make skilful use of the tides and currents to get his ships into position. Frustrated by the lack of wind, and without the benefit of a similar local knowledge, d'Annebault tried for two days to engage, and then, because he was running short of victuals and disease was spreading among his men, he retrieved his landing party from the Isle of Wight, and quitted the Solent on the 24th.

Although this was a negative success, it was a great victory for the English. Henry had mustered three armies, totalling about 90,000 men, to meet the invasion scare, and was actually at Portsmouth when the French arrived. So he witnessed the whole sequence of events, including the sinking of the *Mary Rose*, and although distressed by that disaster, was generally well satisfied with what he had seen.[34] D'Annebault, whose whole operation had been intended to support an attack on Boulogne, landed part of his army to reinforce the siege there, and then demobilised in some haste because the plague was becoming rampant on his crowded ships. The siege of Boulogne also failed, the army being attacked by the same disease, so that Francis was left with nothing to show for a summer of immense effort and expense, and Henry was able to congratulate himself on having survived a major crisis. Survival, however, was the most that could be said for his situation, because as Stephen Gardiner wrote:

We are at war with France and Scotland, we have enmity with the Bishop of Rome; we have no assured friendship with the Emperor ... our war is noisome to our realm, and to all our merchants that traffic through the narrow seas ...[35]

In early November Sir Thomas Wriothesley, the Principal Secretary, was desperately scraping the barrel for money, and wrote to Gardiner: 'I assure you … I am at my wits end how we shall possibly shift for the three months following …' By the end of the year Henry was effectively bankrupt, and at Trent the long-delayed General Council of the Church was at last assembling. It would be hard to say which constituted the greater threat.[36]

The King spent the last eighteen months of his life in a round of diplomacy which could be described as frenetic or desperate, according to your point of view. He had two general purposes in mind: to secure a peace with France which would enable him to keep Boulogne, and to bring the Emperor back into alliance. In both these objectives the odds were stacked against him, but in the words of Professor Scarisbrick, Henry 'thrust and parried like a master', showing no weariness or lack of grasp even in the last weeks of his life.[37] Not the least of his opponents was his own Council, which as early as late September 1545 was anxious to trade the captured town in return for a deal with Francis. In spite of his financial plight, the King would have nothing to do with such defeatism, and was only narrowly dissuaded from sending an additional 4,500 troops. In this intransigence he was supported by the Earl of Surrey, who fell out quite seriously with his father the Duke of Norfolk in consequence.[38] By the end of 1545 Norfolk was by far the most senior of the King's advisers, the Duke of Suffolk having died in August, and he was adamantly opposed to continuing the war. In October 1545 Henry was pursuing two diplomatic courses, apparently quite independently; on the one hand he was seeking 'clarification' of the existing Anglo-Imperial treaties, which meant prising Charles out of his neutrality; and on the other he was entertaining envoys from the Schmalkaldic League, which suddenly had need of his support against the Emperor. The latter negotiation made the better progress, because the League was also wooing the French for the same reason, and on 21 November persuaded Henry to accept their mediation in the conflict between the two countries. However, by the middle of January, after six weeks of wrangling over Scotland and Boulogne, these talks broke down, and neither of the October initiatives produced any result.[39] On 17 January 1546 the King decided to send the Earl of Hertford to France to prepare for a major 'enterprise' in the spring. This would require 16,000 English troops, 10,000 Italian and Spanish mercenaries and 4,000 cavalry. Where the money for the mercenaries was to come from is not apparent, but agents were sent to Antwerp to raise further loans, and arms and equipment were gathered. Hertford went to France on 23 March, accompanied by a large number of English levies, and it looked as though full-scale hostilities were about to be renewed.[40] However, that did not happen. Whether he was daunted by the cost, or inhibited by the Emperor's obvious intention to strike at the Schmalkaldic League, within a few weeks Henry had decided to settle for what he could get. By early April a Venetian intermediary was passing backwards and forwards between London and Paris, carrying proposals for renewed peace talks, and on 17 April Lisle, Hertford and Sir William Paget were commissioned to begin negotiations at Calais. These talks began on 24 April, and proved just as difficult as the earlier ones. Eventually Scotland was abandoned, and a face-saving formula was adopted over Boulogne, whereby the English were to keep it for a period of years, at the end of which time it would be ransomed for 2 million crowns.[41] Meanwhile Francis was to pay Henry the arrears of pensions owed under earlier treaties. It was a fudge, and Henry entertained doubts about it until the last minute. However, persuaded apparently that the French would never be able to afford the redemption payment on his prize, he signed on 6 June. Francis ratified this treaty of Camp, as it was called, on 1 August, and when the French attended Henry's ratification they were splendidly entertained, but it was a loveless peace, full of tensions and rancour.

Partly for that reason, diplomacy continued to be actively pursued. The King stalked Francis suspiciously, evading pressures to become involved in the increasing tensions of Germany, and did his best to keep the Emperor and the King of France apart. Scotland remained unfinished business, and in November 1546 Henry charged the Scottish envoys who had come to talk peace with having broken the last treaty.

They were so convinced that he was about to attack again, that they immediately appealed to France for aid, which provoked the King in the last month of his life to prepare another force to strike north, and prompted him on his death bed to instruct the Earl of Hertford to carry out this last coercive intention.[42] When Henry died at the end of January 1547, he did not have a friend anywhere in Europe, and when Guron Bertano arrived in England to discuss possible terms for a reconciliation with the papacy – and participation in the Council of Trent – he was dismissed empty-handed. Although he would probably not have wanted to admit it, the diplomacy of the last months of Henry's reign had left England in not-so-splendid isolation, and that broke all the rules of renaissance politics.

Meanwhile, the King had married again. This time there was no rush, no passionate affair, and no international complications. Unlike Ferdinand of Aragon, he did not remarry late in life in order to secure a diplomatic advantage, nor even to strengthen the succession, but simply to gain that 'heart's ease' which had eluded him since the early days of his reign. The lady of his choice was a sober good-natured widow of thirty-one, Catherine, Lady Latimer, better known by her maiden name of Catherine Parr.[43] She was the daughter of Sir Thomas Parr of Kendal, a courtier who had been knighted at Henry VIII's coronation, and she had consequently been brought up on the fringes of the court. She had been married twice before, and when Henry first encountered her early in 1543, her second husband, John Neville, Lord Latimer, was still alive. Neville, who was based in Yorkshire, had come south in 1537 for the sake of his health, and Catherine had quickly renewed her court connections, becoming particularly friendly with Mary, the King's daughter, and with various members of the Seymour family.[44] Indeed, when Lord Latimer died in March 1543, his widow was quickly pursued by Sir Thomas Seymour, the Earl of Hertford's brother, who would probably have married her if the King had not intervened. No intermediary seems to have been involved, and indeed the act of attainder against Catherine Howard had placed the pitfalls of treason around any attempt to introduce young women to Henry, so it would have been a bold man (or woman) who would have taken that risk.[45] Exactly how Catherine came to the King's attention we do not know, but it seems that Henry dealt with her directly; perhaps it was as a friend of Mary's that he first met her. By the middle of June it was noticed that Lady Latimer and her sister Anne Herbert were being rather conspicuous, and on 12 July the King married her in a small ceremony conducted in the Queen's Closet at Hampton Court.[46]

Catherine was not particularly beautiful, nor was she highly educated. Indeed she seems only to have begun to learn Latin after her return to court; but she was possessed of a serene dignity and a robust common sense. It was probably this quality, rather than any theological knowledge, which inclined her towards the evangelical party; that, and an intense interest in the Bible, which she read perforce in English, her Latin being elementary. Such an interest would have drawn her and the King together, and helps to explain the religious discussions which they apparently held from time to time with members of their respective Privy Chambers. As he got older, Henry's interest in theology intensified. *The Bishops' Book* was issued on the authority of convocation in 1537, and when he got around to studying it, the King found many things in it which did not please him. It was too evangelical, particularly on the sacraments, and he covered his copy in manuscript notes and amendments.[47] It was partly to correct the impression which this book had given that the Act of Six Articles had been passed two years later. An amended version was clearly called for, and that was published at the end of May 1543 as the *King's Book*. This was a substantially rewritten version of *The Bishops' Book*, and although significantly more conservative, began with a thumping preface in the King's name, supporting the English Bible:

> Like as in the time of darkness and ignorance, finding our people seduced and drawn from the truth by hypocrisy and superstition, we by the help of God and his word have travailed to purge and cleanse our realm from the apparent enormities of the same; wherein by opening of God's truth, with setting forth and publishing of the scriptures, our labours (thanks be to God) have not been void and frustrate ...[48]

The King's Book was thus a realistic expression of that idiosyncratic doctrinal position which Henry had reached by the end of his reign, and was intended to be a manual of orthodoxy. It was enforced by the power of the Royal Supremacy, backed up by the heresy clauses of the Act of Six Articles. Its distinctive balance also helps to explain a curious story told about the Queen by John Foxe. According to this tale, for which there is no contemporary evidence, Stephen Gardiner and his conservative clerical allies, were plotting against the evangelical Catherine.[49] Taking advantage of her forthrightness in theological discussions with the King, they persuaded Henry that his wife was trying to 'school' him, and that she was a heretic. They even drew up articles against her, which they induced him to sign. This is likely enough, but the story then takes an implausible turn, because a copy of these articles was allegedly dropped accidentally by a councillor, and brought to the Queen. Realising the peril which she was in, Catherine then sought out Henry and made a total submission, convincing him that all that she desired was to learn from his great wisdom. Flattered by this evidence of devotion, the King then affected a total reconciliation, and when the Lord Chancellor arrived with an armed escort to take her (as he thought) to the Tower, he was sent away with a stinging reprimand. This may, or may not, have happened, but it is clear that Catherine was a leading member of the evangelical party at court, and that her advent, following the eclipse of the Howards, signalled the revival of that influence. However, it had to be influence over the King; no independent action was possible.

Foxe is full of conspiracy theories, of which this is only one. In April 1543 charges were brought against Archbishop Cranmer by a group of conservative prebendaries and gentlemen of Kent. Sending for the Archbishop, Henry quickly revealed that he knew a great deal about the latter's unorthodoxy (including the fact that he was married), but that he did not propose to do anything about it.[50] Frustrated of their intention to use agents, the conservative councillors, led by Norfolk and Gardiner, then tried denouncing Cranmer directly, and thought that they had gained the King's support. However, when they came to arrest him they discovered that Henry had secretly given Cranmer his own signet ring, with the instruction that he was to appeal directly to the Supreme Head. Summoning all parties into his presence, he then denounced them for factional strife, and made it apparent that the Archbishop retained his full confidence.[51] Henry appears to have enjoyed playing such games with his Council, but the source for the stories is Ralph Morice, who at the time was Cranmer's secretary, so they are not free from the same suspicion that attends the tale of Catherine and her submission. What does seem to be authentic is the fact that when Anne Askew was in trouble for sacramentarianism in 1545, a serious attempt was made to involve some of the ladies of the Queen's Privy Chamber. Askew was undoubtedly a heretic, who was subsequently burned, but the charges could not be made to stick, largely because Anne, even under torture, refused to implicate anyone.[52] It was still a dangerous business to be convicted of heresy, and three minor members of the court were burned for that offence at Windsor as late as 1546. However, it was the King alone who determined the fate of such offenders. He decided what was acceptable and what unacceptable, and his egotism was the salient feature of the Church of England as he approached the end of his life.

It was he, therefore, and not the Queen, who was responsible for the education which was decreed for his son. Catherine quietly brought the royal children back together, largely through her friendship with Mary. Mary, of course, was not a child; she was twenty-seven in 1543, and was the Queen's ally in this respect rather than her agent. However, she did not have an independent establishment (or income) of her own, and resided much of her time at court, on the 'Queen's side'.[53] The same was true of Elizabeth, who was ten and who had tutors of her own, when she was not sharing lessons with her six-year-old brother. Edward did have his own establishment, and was a frequent visitor to the court rather than being resident there, but his affection for his stepmother appears to have been equally great. His tutors, Richard Foxe and John Cheke in particular, were committed evangelicals, and may well have been suggested by Catherine, but they were appointed by the King, who was ultimately responsible for the curriculum which they drew up. This consisted primarily of Latin, classical texts and ancient history, but it also included the study of the Bible, and such theology as Henry deemed to be appropriate. A separate tutor, Jacques Belmaine, was appointed to teach him French. It was all rather intense for so young a child, but Edward seems to have taken to it well, and his precocity was much commented upon, especially for the King's benefit.[54] All these tutors later emerged as Protestants, but there is no evidence to suggest that they had crossed that shadowy boundary before Henry's death; nor is there any proof that they taught their charge any characteristically reformed doctrine before that date. They would scarcely have dared to do so, given the care with which the King monitored their proceedings. By 1545 Henry was keenly aware that his son was likely to succeed as a minor, and much preoccupied with the fate of the Royal Supremacy in that event. In spite of his self-induced conviction that this was an ancient authority, he was keenly aware that there were no precedents for its exercise by a child, and he was deeply suspicious that his more conservative advisers, given the chance, might be prepared to abandon it for a deal with Rome. This, he was determined, must not happen, and his favour to the evangelical party at court has to be seen in that light. If they were inclined to Protestantism, he did not want to know. They were the most committed anti-papalists, and that was what mattered, so when he came to draw up his will, they dominated the body of executors, and opportunists like the Earl of Hertford and Viscount Lisle, the roots of whose favour lay in other causes, were swift to perceive the advantages of being evangelical in the atmosphere of 1546.

As his health, and his temper, became more uncertain after 1543, the succession loomed increasingly large in his thoughts. He knew, better than anyone, that the chances of begetting a second son were now remote, and he took the obvious step of initiating a further Succession Act in the Parliament of that year.[55] This started conventionally enough by confirming Edward's position as heir apparent, and making correct noises about any son begotten between the King and his present Queen. It then, however, became innovative, because in the event of Edward dying without heirs, and there being no son by his final marriage, the succession was to pass to his elder daughter, Mary. After her, there being no heir 'of her body lawfully begotten', the Crown was to pass to Elizabeth, and after her to anyone whom the King might appoint by his last will. Neither of his daughters was legitimated by this act, or by any other, and the arrangement can only be described as eccentric. It was also idiosyncratic in another respect. When he came to make his will, the undoubtedly legitimate descendant of his older sister Margaret, namely Mary, Queen of Scots, was totally ignored. Had he been following the principal of indefeasible hereditary succession, which in other respects the will indicates, the Queen of Scots should undoubtedly have taken precedence over Frances Brandon, currently the Marchioness of Dorset and the mother of three young girls. The proviso that it could be confirmed or altered by the King's last will and testament was an unusual reservation. So the King was given the final say, although with parliamentary approval. This had the undesirable consequence of making Henry's last will, which should have been concerned with the mundane disposal of property, into a political document of the highest sensitivity.[56] Not only would it have to decide the succession to the Crown, it would also (in all probability) have to determine the arrangements for the minority government. When Henry left for his campaign in France in 1544, he constituted the Queen as the Governor of the realm in his absence, as he had done with her predecessor thirty years before. Would Catherine occupy a similar position when the King died? The Queen herself seems to have thought that she should, but in the event was to be elbowed aside by ambitious politicians. Unlike 1513, Henry's absence of two months in 1544 embraced no crisis, and Catherine was given no opportunity to prove her mettle, which was perhaps just as well as she seems to have had little capacity for affairs of state. The King had good reason to be grateful to his Parliament for what it had enabled him to achieve over the years, and he bade farewell to it in fitting style when the 1545 session was prorogued on 24 December. Having listened to (and no doubt enjoyed) a flattering oration from the Speaker of the Commons, he then asked the Lord Chancellor's leave to usurp his function and reply in person.[57] He was, he declared, thanking them for their goodwill and willing service; he never stood higher in his estate royal than in the time of Parliament. Yet, he added, he had one matter to reprove them with – a lack of charity. They abused each other mercilessly, with terms like 'heretic' and 'papist', and he would that all such quarrels might cease in the name of God. The fact that he was largely responsible for these quarrels was blandly glossed over, and he became the loving father issuing a clarion call for unity and peace. It was all very correct, and what the members really thought of it we do not know. Their recorded comments were suitably complimentary.

War, as we have seen, was the forcing house of innovation. It had been war which had caused the formation of the Royal Navy in 1514, and the establishment of gun foundries in the Weald and at Hounsditch. It had been war which had prompted the refashioning of the army in 1544, and the downgrading of the noble retinue. There would be far less incentive to licence such retinues if they were no longer required for fighting purposes, and without such backing a nobleman would be much less likely to try to take the law into his own hands. It was war, or the prospect of war, which caused the technological revolution of iron gun casting, which began in 1542 and led eventually to England becoming self-sufficient in the production of artillery.[58] It was also war which caused the naval administration to be recast, creating in the Council for Marine Causes a new department of state. Before 1545 naval administration, as distinct from the operational command of the fleet, had been somewhat hand to mouth. In Henry VII's time there had been a Clerk of the Ships, who was responsible for maintaining the handful of ships which the King then possessed. The increase in the size of the navy which accompanied the first French war, led to the establishment of a second office, that of Clerk Controller, with responsibility also for the dockyards at Deptford and Greenwich. John Hopton, who occupied that office, died in 1524, and then a third position, that of Keeper of the Storehouses was created. However, each of these officers accounted separately, and the only overall control was exercised by the Council in the person of Cardinal Wolsey.[59] Wolsey's fall appears to have led to development rather than change, in that the Keeper of the

Storehouses, William Gonson, began to be entrusted with rather wider financial duties. He began to receive warrants for money to be passed to his fellow officers, accounting for no less that £15,589 between 1532 and 1537. He also began to receive general warrants for money to be expended on 'the affairs of the sea', rather than specific requisitions. In short, he began to look like a Treasurer of the Navy, although he was not so called, and money continued to be paid direct to the other officers.[60] This worked, more or less, as long as Thomas Cromwell's vigilant eye was on it, but with the withdrawal of that oversight in 1540, and more particularly with Gonson's death in 1544, it became apparent that some new system was needed. There were models available. Both the office of the King's Works and the Ordnance Office had been reconstituted after 1540, each under a master, with various assistants and regular accounting procedures. It was the Ordnance Office model which was followed in respect of the Navy.

The first move was the interim appointment of William Gonson's son, Benjamin, to the same sort of loosely defined treasurership which his father had held. In that capacity he accounted from 5 August to 29 November 1544, but thinking was still fluid at that point, and when a comprehensive scheme was drawn up in 1545, he was named as surveyor and rigger.[61] At the same time Robert Legge 'Fishmonger of London' was proposed as clerk controller and John Winter (a Bristol merchant) as treasurer. Discussion still seems to have been going on at that point about the size of the Council and the payment of its officers. The patents of appointment were finally issued in April 1546, more or less coinciding with the end of the French war. By then it had been decided that the new department would consist of six officers under the chairmanship of a vice admiral or lieutenant.[62] There was to be a treasurer, a surveyor and rigger, a master of the naval ordnance, a clerk controller and a clerk of the ships. Sir Thomas Clere was named as lieutenant, Robert Legge as treasurer (John Winter having died in November 1545), Benjamin Gonson as surveyor and rigger, Sir William Woodhouse as master of the ordnance, William Broke as controller, and Richard Howlett as clerk. The remuneration was generous, the

Lieutenant for example receiving £100 a year plus expenses, and the Controller £50 a year with allowances. Rather curiously, no terms of reference were drawn up for this Council, although its duties, and those of its individual officers, were well enough understood.[63] It was responsible for the maintenance and servicing of all the King's ships, for the upkeep and running of the dockyards, storehouses and other facilities, and for the recruitment and mobilisation of seamen and gunners when the fleet was required for active service. It was to be funded via the Treasurer, mainly (but not exclusively) through warrants drawn on Augmentations and the Exchequer. Each officer was to account separately to the Treasurer, and he to the Exchequer, or to commissioners specially appointed once a year. Its responsibility lay to the Privy Council through the Lord Admiral, although he was not expected to play any part in its day-by-day business.[64] Who was responsible for crafting the Marine Council in this manner is not apparent. It could have been the King, given his known interest in naval affairs, but is more likely to have been the Lord Admiral, Lord Lisle, who had learned his craft at the feet of Thomas Cromwell. It provided England with the most sophisticated naval administration anywhere in Europe. Both its maintenance arrangements and its muster provision were way ahead of either the French or the Spaniards, who were still relying on *ad hoc* systems as late as 1588.

When it came to 'front line' offices like that of Lord Admiral, Henry had by 1540 long since given up using either clergy or nobles of ancient lineage. From 1525 to 1536 that office had been held by his young son the Duke of Richmond, but thereafter it had passed to Lord John Russell, the Earl of Hertford and Viscount Lisle, all men of his own creation.[65] The Privy Seal similarly, once it had been surrendered by the Bishop of Durham in 1530, had passed to the Earl of Wiltshire, Thomas Cromwell, William Fitzwilliam, Earl of Southampton, and Lord John Russell. Even the chancellorship, following the fall of Cardinal Wolsey in 1529, had fallen to a succession of laymen: Thomas More, Thomas Audley and Thomas Wriothesley. Only the treasurership bucked this trend, remaining a Howard fiefdom throughout the reign, but then the Lord Treasurer was not expected to know anything about money, that was the function of lesser officers, such as the Chancellor of the Augmentations. Norfolk, indeed may well have had a sense of invulnerability, having survived both of the crises induced by his nieces, Anne Boleyn and Catherine Howard, and even the total eclipse of his family in the misprision proceedings of 1542. In 1546 he was still Lord Treasurer and still a leading councillor. He may well have been entertaining hopes of securing the regency when the King died, although he was Henry's senior by eighteen years, and that hope contributed to his downfall. Ostensibly it was his son, Henry Howard, Earl of Surrey, who was the cause of the problem.[66] Henry had supported the King in his desire to retain Boulogne, but he had mishandled an engagement there in the last weeks of the war and been relieved of his command. Back at court he was quickly in trouble for 'indiscreet' words about the scripture, and he seems to have been a rather chaotic evangelical, which would have put him seriously at odds with his father. However, it was not religion which brought about his downfall, but hubris. He was immensely proud of his royal ancestry, his grandmother Anne having been a daughter of Edward IV, and like the Duke of Buckingham, contemptuous of the 'foul churls' whom the King chose to favour.[67] It was alleged that he plotted to seize control of the young Prince, but his real offences seem to have been less tangible. He probably did claim to an unsympathetic audience that his father, who was closer to the blood royal than he was, would make the most suitable regent, and may even have suggested that his sister Mary (the dowager Duchess of Richmond) should strengthen the family position by becoming the royal mistress. If he made the latter suggestion, then he clearly did not understand Henry, but the whole 'charge sheet' is indicative of a thoughtless boaster, blinded by arrogance to the realities of the political situation in which he found himself. The crime which he did commit, and for which he was tried and condemned, confirms such a view. He quartered his own arms with those of Edward the Confessor.[68] This was a treasonable offence because Edward's coat armour was the ancient arms of England, and its adoption was a clear signal that its bearer claimed the blood royal.

Such a distinction could only be awarded by the College of Arms, with the express permission of the King. It was treason by implication, but it was sufficient. It may have been considered that the Duke had abetted his son's ambition, and that it was really he who aimed to control the regency. On 13 December 1546 they were both arrested and conveyed to the Tower, but once in prison, it appears from their interrogations that the Duke was a target of a rather different kind. Attempts were made to pin charges of popery upon him, involving events going back to 1541, and surreptitious dealings with the French ambassador.[69] He was a man most cordially hated, not only by opponents in the Privy Council, such as the Earl of Hertford and Viscount Lisle, but also by the many courtiers whom he had slighted or misused. He might console himself with the thought of his abiding loyalty to Henry VIII, but that, it might well have been felt, would be no safeguard against his selling out the royal supremacy if he had any controlling influence in a Regency Council. Both the Howards were dangerous men in their different ways. They were dangerous to Edward, not to Henry, but with the King on the cusp of death, it is not surprising that their enemies decided to strike while his will was still effective. They suspected that a threat to his heir would be taken more seriously by the King than any challenge to himself, and in that they were quite correct. The Earl of Surrey's title being one of honour only, he was tried by a special commission of Oyer and Terminer on 13 January 1547, and executed on the 21st.[70] The Duke was not tried. On 12 January, he confessed to treason before witnesses, begged for the King's mercy, and was condemned by Act of Attainder. One of Henry's last conscious acts was to authorise a commission, signed like his will with the drystamp, to convey to the Parliament his assent to this attainder, which had passed its third reading on the 24th. The commissioners performed their duty on the 27th, and that was the only act of the session, the others being lost when the Parliament was dissolved by the death of the monarch on the 31st.[71] Unlike his son, the Duke was not despatched, and, there being no time between his attainder and Henry's own death on the 28th, he was reprieved. He was to remain in the Tower until released on the accession of Mary in 1553.

Although he was only fifty-six years old, Henry had been a physical wreck for some years before his death. He had always eaten and drunk to excess, and as he became less active with the passing years, he became enormously fat. The best measure of just how fat is the suits of armour which were made for him after about 1535, showing a steady increase of girth. By 1530 he had given up jousting and tennis, exercise which had helped to keep his body under control, and although he still rode and walked a great deal, that was not sufficient to compensate for his appetite. By the standards of the time, his general health had been good. He had endured an attack of smallpox in 1514, but had never succumbed to the sweating sickness, to tuberculosis (which killed his brother and his son), or to the plague. The only complaint which he appears to have suffered from recurrently after 1521 was malaria, which accounts for the various 'agues' which appear in the records.[72] However, repeated falls in the lists as a young man, and later in the hunting field, had left him with ulcerated legs, and they became progressively worse as he got older. These have been diagnosed as varicose ulcers, which with inadequate treatment and insufficient rest had become thrombosed, causing him the exquisite pain which is frequently mentioned, particularly after 1540.[73] This trouble is first referred to in about 1528, and by 1537 was bad enough to contribute significantly to his decision to call off his intended progress to the North. In May 1538 the thrombosis appears to have spread to his lungs. The King became speechless, and his life was despaired of. At that stage his body was still resilient, and he made a complete recovery after a few weeks, but thereafter the attacks became more frequent. He suffered a mild recurrence in September 1540, and really bad bout in March 1541, probably as a result of ignoring symptoms while he enjoyed the renewed youth of his fifth marriage. On that occasion the ulcer closed up, and the pain became fearful until his surgeons managed to reopen it.[74] In March 1544 the old trouble flared up again, this time accompanied by fever, and although he managed to get through the French campaign, he was intermittently ill thereafter until his final collapse on 10 December 1546. Remarkably, he remained lucid throughout, and as late as 30 December was still haggling with his councillors about the details of his will. On

16 January he received both the French and Imperial ambassadors in audience, and spoke of a defensive league with the former, but he was clearly a sick man, and on the 27th he performed his last public act in commissioning the Lord Chancellor and others to give the royal assent to Norfolk's attainder. Fever had by then a firm hold, and the end was obviously approaching. The only snag was that it was high treason to predict the King's death, and it was not until Sir Anthony Denny finally summoned up the courage to tell his master the truth, on the evening of that day, that Henry made his final dispositions. He sent for Thomas Cranmer, but by the time the Archbishop arrived, he was speechless. When asked for some token of his trust in God, he wrung Cranmer's hand 'as hard as he could', and shortly after died.[75] It was the early hours of Friday, 28 January 1547. Edward Hall wrote:

> Now approached to this noble king that which is by God decreed, and appointed to all men, for at this season, in the month of January, he yielded his spirit to Almighty God and departed this world ...[76]

He died, as he had lived, confident in the assumption that all his courses had been righteous, and that God would forgive his sins 'were they greater than they be'.

12

LEGACY

Henry's formidable personality continued to overshadow England for many years after his death, but his specific legacy has to be seen in two forms, as long term and immediate. In the long term, he invented the Royal Supremacy over the Church, and although the continuous history of that jurisdiction dates from the reign of his daughter Elizabeth, her innovation would have been impossible without his precedent. In the process of bringing that about, he also transformed the authority of the Parliament, giving it effectively the sovereign powers which it still exercises – or did until the advent of the European Union. He transformed the Privy Council, changing it from a generalised body of advisers into an executive committee, in which form it survived for 200 years. The Royal Navy was also his creation, which endured in the form which he had given it at least until the later seventeenth century.[1] He converted the nobility from a lineage base to a service base, a process which had, admittedly, been initiated by his father. In spite of his enthusiasm for chivalric war games, he insisted upon licensing their retinues, and in the latter part of his reign reduced their participation in real warfare. Royal Commissions and Royal Councils increasingly centralised control over the counties, and the medieval franchises (exempt jurisdictions) were eliminated by statute, allowing the King's writ to run uniformly throughout the land.[2] Above all, perhaps, he created an image of power, and of security which did not always correspond to reality. He was the king, and personally responsible for all that happened in England during his reign, from the break with Rome to the executions of Thomas More and Anne Boleyn. This had mixed consequences, because he became for subsequent generations either the first Protestant king (which he was not) or a lecherous tyrant and serial wife-killer (which he was not either). As we have seen, historiography preserved both these myths down to the twentieth century. In the long run, Henry's reputation rested as much on what he wrote, and what was written about him, as it did upon what he actually did, but his real achievement was great enough and sufficiently long-lasting, to justify the image which he so assiduously created.[3]

In the short term, however, his legacy was practical and unavoidable. For two days his death was concealed, meals even being taken into the Privy Chamber as though for his consumption. There was nothing sinister about such secrecy; the same thing had happened on the death of Henry VII; but certain proprieties had to be observed. Above all, the heir had to be informed, and to be in the right place when the formal announcement was made. The Earl of Hertford set off at once to achieve this, Edward being at Hatfield, several miles from London, at the time. The boy was at first excited, thinking that the Earl's arrival on the morning of the 29th was in connection with his creation as Prince of Wales, a promotion which was being actively considered.[4] When he learned the truth, we are told that he wept copiously, but that was expected of him, and he cannot have known his father all that well. Elizabeth, informed at the same time, showed a similar reaction. Messengers must also have been despatched to tell the Queen and Princess Mary, neither of whom had been present at Westminster when Henry died. Rather strangely he had not chosen to send for Catherine when he knew that he was in extremis; perhaps he wanted to spare her the experience. Mary later complained that she had been kept in the dark about her father's death, but in view of the fact that she might have mounted a counter claim to the throne a delay of a few days would not be surprising.[5] Meanwhile Henry's executors had been informed, and such of them as were available gathered at Westminster on 30 January to discuss the implementation of his will. They considered issuing a general pardon straight away, but then reflected that they did not have the authority to do anything outside their specific remit until their position had been regularised by the new King. By the following day, the 31st, Edward was in London, and the Lord Chancellor formally announced the King's death to Parliament, dissolving the session.[6] At the same time the new King was proclaimed on the streets of London, amid general rejoicing. After years of niggling uncertainty, an undisputed succession was a huge relief.

In most respects Henry's will was a highly specific document, particularly in the naming of the executors and their assistants, but it did not make any provision for a minority government. Therefore, in their first recorded deliberation, on the 31st, the executors felt:

> ... that being a greate number appoyncted to be executors with equal and like charge, in should be more then necessarie aswel for the thonour, surety and gouvernment of the most royal persone of the king our Souvereigne Lorde that nowe is as for the more certaine and assured order and direction of his affayres, that somme special man of the nombre and company aforesaide should be preferred in name and place before others, to whome as to the state and head of the reste all strangers and others might have access ...[7]

They resolved to create two offices, the one Governor of the King's Person and the other Protector of the Realm, and to bestow both upon the Earl of Hertford, the King's maternal uncle. The Lord Protector was, however, appointed 'with this special and expresse condicion that he shall nat do any Acte but with thadvise and consent of the rest of the coexecutors ...', a condition which, if strictly adhered to, would have reduced his position to an honorary presidency. In taking this action the executors were using a clause in the will which empowered them to take such action as they thought necessary for the safety of the realm; a clause which indicates that the old King's thinking on the subject of the regency had been incomplete at the time of his death.[8] However, not even Henry VIII could rule from beyond the grave, and the following day the executors waited upon the young King to obtain his formal assent to their proceedings. They then reconstituted themselves as the Privy Council of King Edward VI, and proceeded to function as such.[9] The Lord Protector accepted the restraint imposed upon him in respect of important decisions, but for most purposes governed as Regent, exercising the executive powers of the Crown. Another aspect of the late King's legacy was the list of honours which, it was alleged, he had intended to bestow. This was brought to the Council's attention on 6 February, because claims were already being made, and Sir William Paget was summoned to testify to his knowledge of such intentions. The King, he declared, had been greatly concerned that he had allowed the nobility to decay, and planned to remedy that situation, partly using the lands which had recently come to the Crown through the attainder of the Howards. 'He willed me to make unto him a book,' the Secretary went on, 'of such as he did chose to advance.'[10]

The resulting document, heavily amended as the King changed his mind, is now among the Domestic State Papers. It shows that the Earl of Hertford was to be a Duke, of Hertford, Exeter or Somerset; the Earl of Essex to be a Marquis; Viscount Lisle to be Earl of Coventry; Lord Russell to be Earl of Northampton; Lord St John Earl of Winchester; Lord Wriothesley also to be Earl of Winchester; and several knights to be promoted to baronies.[11] Paget gave a long and circumstantial account of the discussions which had accompanied the compilation of this 'book', and the reasons for its various ambiguities. The Council pronounced itself to be satisfied with the genuineness of the intention, but postponed the necessary decisions until a more appropriate time. The timetable was tight, because it was important that the new dignities be conferred in time for the coronation, which was scheduled for the 19th, and in the meantime Henry's funeral had to be conducted with suitable pomp. The old King's massive body began its last journey from Westminster to Windsor on 14 February, where he was to be interred alongside his favourite wife, Jane Seymour, and his funeral took place on the 16th.[12] Edward did not attend (as was customary), nor did most of his council, and Catherine and Mary watched the ceremony from the gallery. The Chief Mourner was Henry Grey, Marquis of Dorset, the husband of Henry's niece Frances, apart from Edward the nearest thing to a male kinsman that the King had possessed. The very next day the new dignities were conferred, more or less in accordance with Paget's 'book'. The Earl of Hertford became Duke of Somerset, the Earl of Essex Marquis of Northampton, Viscount Lisle Earl of Warwick, and Lord Wriothesley Earl of Southampton.[13] Lords Russell and St John were not promoted at this time, for reasons which are now obscure. They were to become Earls of Bedford and Wiltshire respectively in January 1550. Several barons were also created, including Sir Thomas Seymour as Lord Seymour of Sudelely, a dignity which left the Protector's brother feeling seriously aggrieved. First he had been passed over for the governorship of the King's person, and now he was awarded a mere barony; his jealousy festered.[14] It has been observed that the dominant party in the Council was rewarding itself in this hand out, but there is little doubt that Henry's intention was a genuine one, and Sir William Paget, through whose mediation it came to light, himself received nothing. He was given 400 marks' worth of land, but no dignity, while those who were promoted also gained significant awards of land – £800 a year in the case of the Duke of Somerset.[15]

The structure of the minority government was thus an important aspect of Henry's legacy, as might have been expected, but it was so indirectly. It was only by second-guessing the King's intentions that a viable regency was created, and this left the way open for various disputes. There was disagreement over the exact extent of the Protector's powers, and before his office was confirmed by patent on 12 March, the principal dissident had to be removed. This was the Lord Chancellor, the Earl of Southampton, who was charged with unlawfully commissioning four civil lawyers to hear cases in Chancery on his behalf. He argued that he was entitled to do this *ex officio*, but the Council did not agree, and on 5 March removed him from office.[16] The offence, if offence it was, was minor and technical, and the punishment disproportionate; but this was a political matter, and the Protector clearly wanted rid of him. When Somerset's powers were confirmed, the clause requiring him to obtain the consent of the Council was effectively waived, and he was given the critical authority to appoint new councillors. He now had the full powers of a regent until the King came of age.[17] The other main dispute was over the nature of the Royal Supremacy. This was tested early on, because when Cranmer issued new commissions to his bishops, as was normal with royal servants on the demise of the crown, Stephen Gardiner at once objected. He was not a delegate, he argued, but an ordinary, that is one whose authority derived from his consecration, not from his appointment. The point had never been tested before, and the Council did not accept his plea; as far as they were concerned, bishops were servants of the King as Supreme Head. This, however, raised another and more important issue. Could a child exercise the full powers of that office, or was it effectively on a 'care and maintenance' basis until he came of age?[18] Both Gardiner and the Princess Mary argued strongly for the latter, but that cast doubts upon the whole validity of the minority government. For example, was the King's assent to a statute sufficient, or did it need to be repeated when he came of age? If so, what was the status of the act in the meanwhile? Henry had probably anticipated this difficulty, which was why the majority of his executors were committed evangelicals. Inevitably, the Council decided that the powers of the Supremacy were vested, whole and complete, in themselves, acting in the King's name, and this shifted the headship from a personal to an institutional basis. That was to be of crucial importance during the reigns of the two queens which followed.[19]

It was also critically important for the reform programme which the Council, under Cranmer's guidance, had in mind. This began with a royal visitation in the summer of 1547, and the imposition of a set of homilies, largely of the Archbishop's composition. Some of these Stephen Gardiner objected to on the grounds that they contravened the Act of Six Articles, but that Act was repealed towards the end of the year, and for the next two years the Church had no standard of doctrine to appeal to. An English version of the Eucharistic liturgy was issued in 1548, but not enforced, and then at Whitsun 1549 the mildly but unequivocally

Protestant *Book of Common Prayer* was imposed, and the mass was abolished.[20] These moves caused widespread consternation, and vigorous protests from Gardiner and Mary, the former finding himself imprisoned as a result. Somewhat paradoxically, what most people wanted was not Protestantism in any shape or form, but 'religion as King Henry left it'. The old King's personal and eccentric blend of jurisdiction and theology, which had not satisfied the orthodox on either wing, nevertheless spoke for the majority of his people. They liked the English Bible, and had no particular sympathy with monks, but they also liked their mass, and the traditional ceremonies of the old faith. There was much grumbling and dissatisfaction with the new order, and religion featured largely in the rebellions which convulsed Oxfordshire and the South West in the summer of 1549, but the Council imposed its will effectively, and when reform was taken a stage further in the radical Prayer Book of 1552, there was no organised resistance at all.[21] By that time the young King had made his position clear, and that may also have helped to stifle objections. The reformation was being carried out not merely in the King's name, but with his active support. So Henry, who was bitterly opposed to Protestant doctrine, nevertheless created a situation which enabled it to become established. It is highly unlikely that he, when providing for the education of his son and setting up his body of executors, could have envisaged any such outcome, but his egotism betrayed him into thinking that the Church which he had created was politically stable. He had also created precedents in the realm of ecclesiastical property. It was no longer safe to think that lands or goods given to the Church were secure in perpetuity. The property of the chantries was confiscated in 1547, and in 1552 commissioners were sent around the country to take such 'superfluous' items as ornaments, jewellery and vestments with which the piety of earlier generations had endowed their parishes, but which were no longer needed for the pared-down liturgy of the reformed Church.[22] As we have seen, rumours of such intentions had helped to trigger the Lincolnshire rising of 1536, and whether he liked it or not, the destruction of images followed Henry's desecration of the pilgrimage shires, and the removal of church plate the dissolution of the abbeys.

War with Scotland was another aspect of the old king's legacy. As we have seen, he was contemplating a further punitive expedition when he died and may (or may not) have urged upon the Earl of Hertford the need to complete that intention. Whether or not Henry willed it, such was Protector Somerset's policy from the early days of his government. He gathered forces through the summer, and in September he struck north, provoked only in the general sense that the Scots continued to be friendly with France, and refused to implement the treaty of Greenwich.[23] In spite of winning an early and striking victory at Pinkie Cleugh, near Musselborough, his policy of imposing control on Scotland by way of garrisons in such places as Haddington and Broughty Crag was an expensive failure, and invited French intervention. Evading the English fleet, a substantial force landed near Edinburgh on 18 June 1548 and turned the military situation around. The immediate result was the treaty of Haddington, signed on 10 July, which committed Mary to a marriage with the Dauphin. This finally killed off the treaty of Greenwich, and left the English policy in Scotland without a leg to stand on.[24] Mary departed for France from Ayr, on the West coast, on 13 August, and was to remain there as maid and wife for the next thirteen years. Although humiliated by this outcome, Somerset refused to give up on Scotland, and was preparing another army royal in the summer of 1549, when other preoccupations in the south forced him to desist. His obduracy on this point was undoubtedly one of the issues which forced him out of office in October 1549.

These preoccupations were the rebellions which spread across England from East Anglia to Cornwall in July and August 1549. In the South West the grievances were largely religious, and could be seen as an indirect consequence of the Royal Supremacy, or at least of the way in which it was being used.[25] Elsewhere the risings were caused more by social tensions, and by questions of land use, particularly the abuse of common land. It is very questionable whether these issues could be said to have arisen from any aspect of Henry's policies, except insofar as those policies had not been effectively enforced. The question of land use had been on the agenda since at least 1518, when Wolsey had been stimulated into initiating commissions of enquiry into alleged malpractices. The problem was caused by rising population levels imposing strains upon the tenure system, and the conversion of land from arable to pasture (which had been going on for a century) gradually became a grievance as the number of would-be tenants outnumbered the available tenements.[26] The result of Wolsey's enquiries was a number of anti-enclosure statutes, but these had been slackly enforced, and abuses had continued. Things probably came to a head in 1549, less because of any worsening of the situation than because of a campaign of agitation run by the so-called 'commonwealth men', a group of writers with no particular organisation who took it upon themselves to make representations on the part of the commons, and in the process were fiercely critical of gentry, merchants and other 'possessioners'.[27] This apportionment of blame spoke to a popular perception, and when the Duke of Somerset let it be thought that he was sympathetic to such attitudes, a series of agitations broke out. These were probably intended in the first instance as demonstrations, but they attracted other malcontents, and rapidly got out of hand. This was particularly true in areas like Norfolk and Devon where the local noble leadership had been removed by royal action. Left to their own devices, the gentlemen were unable to cope. In Sussex the Earl of Arundel was successful in defusing the situation, but in Norfolk and Devon there was nobody to try, and the 'camping movement' spread rapidly throughout East Anglia, forcing the government to take military action.[28]

The rebellions were eventually suppressed, although with considerable bloodshed and the extensive use of foreign mercenary soldiers. The Duke of Somerset was fatally compromised, and in early October his Council colleagues conspired against him and brought about his overthrow. This was achieved peacefully, largely because the Protector was unable to raise a military force to support him, and the King, who had been thoroughly frightened by the whole experience, legitimated it by giving his blessing to the victors.[29] Meanwhile King Henry II of France, who had succeeded his father in April 1547, seized the opportunity created by the confusion in England to declare war in August 1549 with the intention of recovering Boulogne. Another of Henry VIII's chickens had come home to roost, but the French found Boulogne a tough nut to crack, because the English retained the command of the sea. It was successfully defended until Somerset's successor, the Earl of Warwick, decided that it was not of sufficient strategic value to justify the cost, and sold it back to Henry II by treaty in March 1550.[30] Every aspect of Edward's reign can be seen in a sense as a part of Henry's legacy, because it was either a consequence of the minority, or a logical continuation of what had happened earlier. The ostensible return of the 'over mighty subject' is an illusion. The Duke of Somerset and the Earl of Warwick (who later became Duke of Northumberland) were men of great wealth and authority who overshadowed the boy King, but they were not powerful in the same sense that the fifteenth-century Earls of Warwick and Northumberland had been. Their strength lay in the Court and in the control of office, rather than in inherited positions and *manred*. When it came to the point, neither of them had a power base in the country to fall back on.[31] Each had great estates, but neither had any roots. The Duke of Somerset had no private army at his disposal when he was challenged in October 1549, and nor did the Duke of Northumberland in the succession crisis of 1553. In fact they were both service peers who had successfully manipulated the politics of a minority rather than princes in their own right. The Duke of Norfolk remained in the Tower, and the earldoms of Devon and Northumberland remained in abeyance. Those peers who could claim lineage, Henry Fitzalan, Earl of Arundel, Edward Stanley, Earl of Derby, and Francis Talbot, Earl of Shrewsbury, each of whom was at odds with the minority governments, survived by maintaining a low profile, as Stanley and Talbot had done under Henry VIII. Of the peers who mattered under Edward VI only Henry Grey, Marquis of Dorset and Duke of Suffolk, held a title that went back more than a single generation.[32] When it came to raising forces against the rebels in 1549, the retinues of the gentry mattered more than those of the peers, and the defence of Boulogne was managed through the levies in the same way that Henry had latterly done. The same was true of the armies launched against Scotland in 1547, each being stiffened with mercenaries, who had no interest in the politics of the country which was employing them.

Edward's reign never emerged from his father's shadow. Had he lived to achieve his majority, he might well have proved as autocratic as Henry, but he did not get the chance. The Protestant reformation which was achieved under his auspices was genuine, and not at all what Henry would have wanted, but it was only skin deep. Prevailing religious opinion supported the Royal Supremacy, but in other respects preferred the old ways, particularly the mass. The old king had died before his son's political education had properly begun, and we therefore do not know whether the regime which the Earl of Warwick instituted in 1550 would have met with his approval or not. Since it was designed to train the boy to be a decision-maker, and was intended to brief him on contemporary issues of all kinds, it probably would.[33] Edward was left in no doubt from his coronation onward that he would in due course have to assume full responsibility for the government of his realm, and for its relations with neighbouring states. Whether his betrothal to Princess Elizabeth of France meant very much to him in 1551, we do not know, but he was thrilled to receive the Order of St Michael, and entertained the Seigneur de St Andre who brought the insignia from France with every sign of enthusiasm.[34] However, he became ill, probably with tuberculosis, in the early weeks of 1553, and never recovered. He died, still a few weeks short of his sixteenth birthday, on 6 July.

This circumstance put Henry VIII's will, and the Succession Act upon which it rested, to the test. Both were quite unequivocal. If Edward died childless, then the Crown was to pass to his sister Mary, provided that she married with the advice of the Council. In the summer of 1553 Mary was still unmarried, so that condition did not apply and by the law of England she was the heir. Edward, however, had a different intention. At the beginning of the year, before he became seriously ill, the King had set down his thoughts on the succession, probably in response to the hypothetical question, what would happen if you were to die childless? It was in a sense a schoolroom exercise.[35] Thus prompted, Edward became obsessed with the male succession. He rejected both his half-sisters, and his cousin Frances Grey, settling the throne on any son who might be born to Frances, or failing that on any son who might be born to any of her three daughters. This was thinking long term, because none of the Grey girls was yet married, and only Jane was of an age to bear children. It was years since Frances had conceived, so that was a mere gesture. In fact the King's 'device' at this stage bore no relation to real politics, because it was also provided that if he should die before a son was born to any of these females, then Frances was to become 'protector' of the realm. In other words the Crown was to be held in abeyance until an eligible male appeared![36] This followed Henry's will only in rejecting the Scottish line; in other respects it ignored it completely. There are various tentative explanations for this eccentric document. Edward seems to have been convinced that no bastard should succeed, and neither of his half-sisters had been legitimated. The one was the product of an unlawful union, and the other the daughter of a convicted adulteress. There was also the additional consideration (which does not appear in the device) that Mary was a notorious religious conservative, who would undoubtedly reverse the Protestant reformation by which the King set such great store.[37] It is very doubtful whether any of the Council knew of this document, except perhaps the Clerk, William Thomas, who may have been responsible for setting it as an essay. It only became relevant when Edward's health suddenly collapsed in early June, and the prospect of his dying without direct heirs became not only real, but imminent.

As it stood, it was useless, because although Jane Grey was now married, it would be many months before her fertility could be tested, and the Duke of Northumberland, who was in control of the situation, realised that they did not have months.[38] There would not even be time to convene Parliament and get Henry's succession act repealed. It would have to be ignored on the grounds that it was *ultra vires*, because it had sought to bestow the Crown upon a bastard. The only possible course was to persuade the King to forgo his obsession with male heirs, and bequeath the Crown to his cousin Jane. Edward liked Jane, who was not much older than himself. She was a staunch Protestant and also the Duke of Northumberland's daughter-in-law. So Northumberland induced Edward to alter the relevant clause in his device to read 'the Lady Jane and her heirs male', so that Jane became the direct heir. The Crown lawyers were appalled by this exercise of the prerogative, which overturned an unrepealed statute. It was not even certain that Edward, as a minor, could make a valid will, let alone treat the law in this cavalier fashion.[39] However it would be (as Northumberland pointed out) high treason to refuse the King's direct command, and they all swore to uphold his wishes. The Council did likewise, with varying degrees of mental reservation. Even Archbishop Cranmer, whose programme stood to gain protection from the change, was deeply unhappy about his oath. About the end of June, the Imperial ambassador got wind of what was afoot, and immediately assumed that Northumberland was in communication with the French. Mary, deeply and justifiably suspicious, declined an invitation to come and see her brother, and kept herself aloof, prepared for any eventuality.[40]

As soon as Edward died on 6 July, she took herself off from Hunsdon, travelling via Sawston Hall to Kenninghall in Norfolk, in the heart of her estates. There she summoned her supporters and proclaimed herself queen. In the early months of Edward's reign Mary had been granted, in accordance with the terms of her father's will, lands to the value of nearly £4,000 a year, thus making her at a stroke not only financially independent, but one of the richest magnates in England.

Most of these estates had been in East Anglia, part of the Howard patrimony, and the Howard affinity travelled with the lands.[41] She thus had a substantial retinue to call upon, which was prepared to accept her as queen from the very beginning, and as the situation began to clarify, support from outside the region began to rally to her also. Jane had been proclaimed in London, and the Council had formally rejected Mary's counterclaim, but the new Queen's position was desperately insecure. Even Protestant London had no time for a queen who had been smuggled in through the back door. As far as they were concerned, Mary was the rightful heir. Meanwhile, the Imperial ambassadors, acting on instructions, held back from declaring an interest, and believed that Northumberland would win, because of his control of central resources.[42] On 9 July Nicholas Ridley, Bishop of London, preached in favour of Jane, but his effort was poorly received and nationally the Protestants divided, many, like the radical John Hooper, Bishop of Gloucester, declaring for Mary.[43] By the 14th the latter had moved to Framlingham in Suffolk, and her forces continued to grow. She was now a serious threat which had to be confronted, and on that day Northumberland set off from London with about 1,500 men. He was a better soldier than anyone in Mary's service, but he was heavily outnumbered, and to make matters worse, his men began to desert. As soon as he was gone, his Council support also disintegrated, and on the 19th Mary was proclaimed in London, to the astonishment of the Imperial ambassadors, who declared a miracle, and the profound satisfaction of the citizens.[44] Having reached Cambridge, and being appraised of what had happened, the Duke of Northumberland gave up, and proclaimed Mary also. There was to be no military confrontation and her victory had been bloodless.

It was almost entirely thanks to her father that Mary emerged triumphant from this crisis. Not only was she undeniably his daughter, she was also his heir both by his last Succession Act and also by his will. It was the power which Henry had given to Parliament which made this statute the decisive factor in the minds of most of Edward's subjects. Mary may have been privately convinced of her own legitimacy, but it hardly mattered in the circumstances of July 1553, and she never made any public pronouncement to that effect.[45] It had also been Henry's will which had given her the resources to mount her bid for the Crown. As it was, she had had five years to establish herself as the 'good lady' to a powerful following in East Anglia, and it had been that affinity, Robert Rochester, Edward Waldegrave and Henry Jerningham in particular, who had first rallied to her, bringing their own men to her support. This prompt backing had been critical in establishing her credibility as a potential queen, and had persuaded other sympathisers to join her, not least the captains of the warships which Northumberland had sent to the east coast to intercept any possible escape to the continent.[46] Robert Wingfield of Brantham painted a rosy picture of all the 'good men' of the region flocking to join her, but it was at first a very close-run thing, and most of the towns of the area declared initially for Jane.[47]

Once she was established on the throne, Mary applied herself energetically to undoing much of her father's achievement. She freed and restored the aged Duke of Norfolk, and the young heir of the Marquis of Exeter, Edward Courtenay. Later in her reign she also restored Sir Thomas Percy to the earldom of Northumberland, it being her declared policy to undo Henry's injustices.[48] In the first session of her first Parliament she restored the Church to the state that it had been in at January 1547, but that was only an interim stage in the abolition of the Royal Supremacy and the return of papal jurisdiction, which would surely have been the reversal to cause her father the most distress. The one thing which she did not do, however, was to abandon the sovereignty of Parliament. Every step of her retrenchment was marked by the repeal of the relevant statutes, and by the enactment of new ones. The Catholic Church which she re-established, and the heresy laws which she resurrected were all enacted in this way; and the Church was thus 'by law established' no less than her father's had been, or her sister's was to be.[49] This was contrary to the advice of Cardinal Reginald Pole, who came to England as Apostolic Legate, and who urged her to treat all such legislation as *ultra vires*. She preferred the constitutional advice of her own Council, and in that she was wise.[50] The one issue that she could not resolve, however, was that of her gender. Henry had gone to extreme lengths to beget a legitimate male heir, and although he had included Mary in the succession which he had laid down, it was not with any expectation of it happening. When she married, it was to be with the consent of the Council, otherwise her right was forfeited. The one thing that he had not envisaged was that she would come to the throne unmarried, and within half a dozen years of his own death. Mary was a spinster with no experience of men, and was probably honest when she declared that she would sooner stay that way. However, she was also a woman with a mission. Her aim was to restore all that her father and brother had marred, both in Church and State, and for that work to endure, she had to secure the succession. That meant marriage and childbearing, and little as she might relish the prospect, it was clearly her duty. So she made a mistake. Years before, when she had been under severe pressure from her father, she had appealed to the Emperor for protection, and had vowed that she would never marry without his advice. Now, as a ruling queen, she honoured that promise, and bade Charles' ambassador seek his master's guidance.[51] Charles, to whom her success in securing the throne was little short of miraculous, was quick to seize his opportunity. His health was poor, and he was contemplating abdication, so it was important that his son Philip should be secure in his inheritance. Spain was not a problem, but the Low Countries were, because the Emperor had only recently detached them from the Empire in order to settle them on his son.[52] This was a move which had caused some resentment on the part of the King of the Romans, who was his brother Ferdinand, and who now faced the diminution of his inheritance. If Philip were King of England, however, he would have a power base in the north from which to secure his interests, and Philip was available. So Charles took his chance, and suggested his son, who was twenty-seven and a widower. If Mary had been more politically astute, she would never have sought this advice, or would have rejected it once offered. Instead she seized on the idea with gratitude, and convinced herself that she was 'half in love' with the Prince of Spain. Although her councillors succeeded in negotiating a very favourable treaty, which gave Philip very little real power in England, it was nevertheless a bad move, which generated one rebellion and a great deal of resentment.[53] Spaniards were deeply unpopular in England with those that knew anything about them, and the more politically alert did not trust the marriage treaty to protect them from a Habsburg takeover. When Philip negotiated the return of the papal authority, and led England into an unnecessary war with France, their fears appeared to have been justified.

Nor did Mary find the gratification for which she was looking. Although at first very happy with her husband, the failure of her pregnancy in the summer of 1555 altered their relationship. He was convinced that she would never bear a healthy child, and went off about his other business, while she, left increasingly to her own devices, found that she was incapable of being both a sovereign and a wife.[54] The submissive dutifulness required of the latter being totally at odds with the decisive self-assertiveness of the former. Mary never found either an image or a strategy which satisfied both these requirements, and became increasingly lonely and frustrated. As England's first ruling queen, she had faced a number of problems over the nature of her authority, because of conventional ideas about the 'imbecility' of women, and their inability to cope with power. Constitutionally these problems were resolved by a statute of her second Parliament which declared her authority to be identical with that of any of her predecessors, 'kings of this realm'; in other words 'ungendered' the monarchy.[55] This however merely added to the problems caused by marriage, which thus became in a sense a union of equals, a concept which was quite alien to contemporary thought. For those with longish memories, Mary's unhappy experience served only to emphasise how wise Henry VIII had been to try so hard to avoid a female succession, and what a tragedy Edward's early death had been for England. The worst, however, did not happen. Philip knew how unpopular he was in England, and when Mary's health began to decline in 1558, he had to decide what to do in the event of her death. He could have ignored the marriage treaty and bid for the succession himself. He knew that there were noblemen in England who would have backed such a bid because he was an adult of proven competence, and because he was male.[56] But he judged that such an attempt would lead to civil war, and for that he had neither the appetite nor the resources, so he decided to back Elizabeth, who was the heir by English law.

When she learned of this, Mary was even more unhappy. She disliked her half-sister intensely, both for what she was and for the way in which she behaved. The feeling was mutual, because Elizabeth was bitterly resentful, not only at having to conform to her sister's Catholicism, but at having been imprisoned on suspicion of involvement in the Wyatt rebellion in January 1554, an imprisonment which had nearly led to her execution.[57] Nor was she particularly grateful for Philip's recognition, having narrowly fended off the King's attempt to marry her to the Duke of Savoy in 1557. She trusted, the Count of Feria observed in November 1558, entirely in the people of England for her right to the throne, and set no store by Philip's support.[58] So in the last days of her life, Mary was in a quandary. There were only three possibilities to follow her: Philip, who did not want it, Elizabeth, whom she did not want, and Margaret Clifford, the daughter of Frances Grey's younger sister, Eleanor. Margaret was acceptably Catholic, but no one knew her, and although Mary's preferred choice, she was a non-starter. Mary Stuart was too French, and nobody mentioned her, while the younger Grey girls were unacceptable for obvious reasons.[59] When it came to the point, if civil strife was no be avoided, there was no alternative, and about a week before she died, Mary reluctantly conceded Elizabeth's right to succeed. Henry's succession act thus again became the decisive factor. There was no way in which both Mary and Elizabeth could be legitimate, and Henry's first marriage had been declared good and lawful by Parliament at the beginning of Mary's reign. So Elizabeth was doubly a bastard, but she had been named both in the Act and in the old King's will as the next heir if both Edward and Mary died childless, and so it was.

Elizabeth's attitude to her father was quite different from Mary's. Mary had been correctly respectful of his memory, and the story that she had his body exhumed and burnt is probably a fabrication, but she had set herself earnestly to undo much of what he had done.[60] Not only was the Royal Supremacy repealed, but some monasteries were restored, the new financial courts were dissolved, and even the Privy Council was allowed to revert to something like its old size and lack of definition.[61] In respect of the nobility, her attitude appears to have been ambivalent. Her only major peerage creations were restorations – Howard, Courtenay and Percy – and she did not ennoble any of her more faithful servants, men such as Robert Rochester and Francis Englefield. On the other hand she did create several barons, and continued to rely upon loyal gentry to run the commissions of the peace. It is probable that she had no particular policy, and that her restorations were due rather to her sense of justice than to any particular respect for their ancestry. Her personal experience of dealing with her father had been stressful for a while, but her submission in 1536 seems to have restored amity between them, and she had distanced herself from the Emperor during the last years of Henry's life. Henry was irascible and unpredictable in his latter days, but Mary had sought haven with the Queen, and together they had endured his ill humour and black moods. It had been at a political level that their disagreements had been most profound, and that became obvious when Mary secured the throne. Elizabeth was completely different. Politically, she was at one with her father, and deliberately resurrected his crowning achievement – the Royal Supremacy.[62] She also shared his distrust of the military aristocracy, although for slightly different reasons. As a woman she could not lead armies in the field, and was suspicious of the pretensions of those who could. She did use noblemen in positions of command, but they tended to be her own personal favourites, such as the Earl of Leicester and the Earl of Essex, men whom she felt at the time that she could trust, and who would not upstage her for their own personal advantage. When it came to serious fighting, she preferred men like Sir John Norris and Lord Mountjoy, who were professional soldiers without high status. Apart from Leicester and Essex, her favourite fighting men tended to be sea captains like Hawkins and Drake, who had no social clout at all.[63] Elizabeth created peers, but they were all for service to herself, as her father's later creations had been, and the Duke of Norfolk, her premier peer (with claims to Plantagenet royal blood), went to the block for high treason in 1572. Elizabeth's policy in respect of the peerage closely followed Henry's, as did her reliance on the gentry for administrative service. Typically, her most trusted and longest-serving ally in government was William Cecil, Lord Burleigh, a third-generation gentleman whose great-grandfather had been a Herefordshire yeoman.[64] Elizabeth, we are told, gloried in her father. Even before she came to the throne the Count of Feria observed that she had learned his way of doing business, and was infinitely more feared than her sister. She was determined to 'have her way absolutely' as Henry had done.[65] Elizabeth was Henry's political and intellectual heir, even in her idiosyncratic style of piety, which might be described as conservative Protestantism, even as his had been reformed Catholicism. They shared a common interest in the Bible, and a common aptitude for music. Elizabeth shaped the conformity of the English Church, no less than her father had done, although using more subtle methods as became a woman in a man's world.[66] By never marrying, she avoided the worst of the problems which had afflicted her sister, and by developing instead the image of herself as the Virgin Queen, created a mythology to match her father's, as well as being more original. However, Elizabeth ended her reign at war in Ireland, and that was also a part of her father's legacy.

In the wake of Silken Thomas' rebellion, in 1541, when it became obvious that fresh thinking was required, he had constituted himself King of Ireland, with a view to reshaping its polity. Following the fall of Thomas Cromwell this was intended to be a policy of reconciliation through 'surrender and regrant'.[67] However, it did not work, partly because of Irish reluctance, but partly also because Henry had many other things on his mind, and did not give enough, either thought or resources, to the island. Hostility between the new English on the one hand and the old English and the Irish on the other was exacerbated by the introduction of Protestantism under Edward VI, and paradoxically that continued under the restored Catholic regime of Mary. In order to check Irish incursions into the Pale, which were becoming increasingly destructive, the King's and Queen's counties were planted with soldier-settlers in 1556, and that set a precedent for the Elizabethan government to follow.[68] By the middle of Elizabeth's reign, Ireland was a seething cauldron of discontent, with the Protestant minority in the ascendant, confronted by an increasingly militant Catholic majority, and dispossessed Irish tribesmen raiding the new plantations. Successive Lords Deputy struggled with inadequate resources to control this situation, and only the chronic divisions of the Irish allowed them a modicum of success. Then in 1595 the rebels produced a leader of stature and ability in the person of the Earl of Tyrone. Tyrone appealed for Spanish and Catholic support, and won a number of victories against the overstretched royal forces.[69] He also succeeded in uniting the Irish tribes as no leader before had managed to do. So dangerous was the situation that Elizabeth sent her military favourite, the Earl of Essex, with a large force against him, but he outmanoeuvred Essex, who was withdrawn in disgrace, and seemed likely to sweep the English into the sea. That did not happen because Spanish help did not come until it was too late, and the Queen at last sent a commander of real ability with adequate troops. Lord Mountjoy defeated Tyrone, and preserved the English ascendancy, but it was a close-run thing, and left a legacy of bitterness into the seventeenth century.[70] If Henry had not tried to rule Ireland from London, and if the Earls of Kildare had continued to run the province in their own way, it need never have become a colony, and the rebellions of the Elizabethan and Caroline periods need never have happened, so in Ireland Henry VIII's legacy was anything but benign.

In 1558 Henry's will had protected Elizabeth against the succession of Mary, Queen of Scots, because no one in England took her claim seriously. However, she did, and so did her French kindred, to the extent of quartering the arms of England with her own. Within a year, Mary was Queen of France, and not pursuing her claim, but the death of her husband, Francis II, in December 1560 brought her back to the north, and to a renewed interest in England. At this stage she accepted Elizabeth as queen, and confined her interest to claiming the succession if Elizabeth should die childless. The Queen did not respond, and there was little interest in England, except among the more extreme Catholics.[71] However in 1565 Mary married Lord Darnley and in 1566 bore him a son, who was christened James. As Elizabeth remained firmly unwed, speculation in England revived, and the succession came firmly onto the agenda.[72] Then in 1567 Darnley was murdered, and Mary was deposed for alleged complicity. At the age of one James became king, and in 1568 Mary fled across the border into England, looking for help and reinstatement. She got neither, but instead became a long-running problem to Elizabeth, as her claim to the succession began to be taken seriously, not only by Catholics, but by other Englishmen as well. As a succession of plots were woven round her, she became increasingly dangerous, and Parliament began to agitate for her execution. Eventually, with the country at war with Spain in 1587, Elizabeth yielded to the logic of the situation and had Mary beheaded, leaving her claim to England to her son, who had been brought up as a Protestant.[73] Mary was Margaret's legacy rather than Henry's, but the succession problem undoubtedly derived from the King, and by 1590 his act of 1543 was a serious embarrassment. Elizabeth was now certain to die childless, and beyond her the succession by its terms lay to the heir of Catherine Grey, that is to Edward Seymour, who would have been Earl of Hertford if it had not been for his mother's clandestine marriage. The promotion of Edward to the throne was unthinkable, and that left the King of Scots as by far the strongest contender – if it had not been for Henry's Act.[74] The simplest solution would have been to repeal it, but that would have left Elizabeth herself without a lawful claim, and that was equally unthinkable. In the end the Act was simply ignored, and in 1603, when Elizabeth died at the advanced age of seventy, James succeeded peacefully. The last tangible aspect of Henry's legacy thus fizzled out. The Act was never repealed, but rather became redundant, having done its job in 1547, 1553 and 1558, and protected Elizabeth against Mary for most of her long reign. It is difficult to assess how Henry would have regarded this outcome, but probably he would have regarded it as a good demonstration of the authority of statute, which he had done so much to promote.

Today, Henry's political legacy seems remote. The Church of England is still by law established, but that no longer matters to the great majority of Englishmen, and many Church leaders themselves favour disestablishment. Parliament traces its ascendancy to the Glorious Revolution of 1689 rather than to the Act in Restraint of Appeals, and the Privy Council is a formal body with no role in day-by-day government. Even the navy thinks of Samuel Pepys as its founder rather than Henry VIII. Yet the recovery of the *Mary Rose* has reawakened an interest in the ships of the early sixteenth century, and when an image of kingship is required, Holbein's portrait of Henry is the first to come to mind.[75] The Tudors have been recycled as an aspect of the entertainment industry, and the sex life of Henry VIII has been subjected to many imaginative reconstructions. This is useful to the historian insofar as it prompts questions about what really happened, and curiosity about Henry has been much stimulated. In the last analysis, however, much of his lasting achievement was intangible. By punching above his weight in European diplomacy, he gave his countrymen that 'good conceit' of themselves which emerged in the successes of the Elizabethan 'sea dogs' and merchants. By creating the Royal Supremacy he also gave England a sense of individuality, of distinctiveness, which Mary's reaction did not extinguish and which Elizabeth built on so fruitfully. Henry's notion of an English empire was focused on France in the true medieval fashion, and his other colonial experiment in Ireland was a failure, but he nevertheless created the mindset which made the seventeenth-century expansion and the North American empire a possibility. He stood on the cusp between medieval and modern England, and that alone makes him an intriguing subject to study.

APPENDIX OF DOCUMENTS

The spelling has been modernised.

DOCUMENT I: AN ACT CONFIRMING KING HENRY VII
Item quedam billa exhibita fuit praefato Domino Regi in presenti Parliamento per Communitates Regni Anglie in eodem Parliamento existentes, hanc seriem verborem continens.

To the pleasure of Almighty God, the wealth, prosperity and surety of this realm of England, to the singular comfort of all the king's subjects of the same, and in avoiding of all ambiguities and questions, be it ordained, established and enacted, by authority of this present parliament, that the inheritance of the crowns of the realms of England and of France, with all the pre-eminence and dignity royal to the same pertaining, and all other seignories to the king belonging beyond the sea, with the appurtenances thereto in any wise due or pertaining, be, rest, remain and abide, in the most royal person of our now sovereign lord king Harry the VIIth, and in the heirs of his body lawfully come, perpetually with the grace of God so to endure, and in none other. Qua quidem billa in Parliamento predicto lecta, audita et matura deliberatione intellecta, eidem bille, de assensu dominorum spiritualium et temporalium in dicto Parliamento existentium ad requisitionem Communitatis predicte necnon auctoritate eiusdem Parliamenti respondebatur eidem in forma sequenti: Nostre Seigneur le Roy, d l'assent des Seigneurs Espirituelx et Temporelx esteauntz en cest Parliament et a la request des Comens avanditz, le voet en totz pointz.
(*Rotuli Parliamentorum*, VI, p. 270)

DOCUMENT 2: THE CREATION OF HENRY AS DUKE OF YORK, 1494
In the year of our Lord God ml cccc iiiixx and xiiii (1494) the tenth
year of the reign of our sovereign lord King Henry VIIth, being in his
manor of Woodstock, determined at All Hallows tide then following
to hold and to keep royally and solemnly that feast in his palace of
Westminster, and at that feast to dub his iind son knight of the Bath,
and after to create him Duke of York; and thereupon directed his letters
missive and also writs according to the same to divers nobles of this his
realm to be of his son's Bath, and to receive the order of knighthood,
of which at his commandment came xxii, as shall follow after in this
book, and the remainder were pardoned, or were at their fines ...

And on St Simon and St Jude even [27 October] the Queen and my
Lady the King's Mother came from Sheen to Westminster to dinner.
And on the morrow after Simon and Jude the King sent to Eltham for
to convey the said Lord Henry, which with great honour, triumph and
of great estates, was conveyed through London, and received with the
mayor, aldermen, and all the crafts in their liveries, and so honourably
brought to Westminster. And on the Thursday, the xxx day of October
the said Lord Henry served the King of towel ...

And when it was night and that their baths were ready, first in the
King's closet was the Lord Henry's bath royally dressed, and a rich bed
well emparrelled; and the Earl of Oxford read the advertisement, and
then the King took of the water and past on his shoulder and made
a cross and kissed it, and from there went to the Queen's closet and
likewise aducted the Lord Harrington and the Lord Clifford, and from
there went into the parliament chamber where were xx baths which
hadden spaciousness, and the best endued that I have seen ... And after
that the King of his grace and benevolence had visited them all in their
baths, he departed unto his chamber; and then when they were dry in
their beds they were revested in their hermits weeds, and so departed to
the chapel where they had spices and their void, and the sergeant of the
confectionary had of every knight a noble ...

When the time was come that it was the King's pleasure that they
should arise, the Earl of Oxford, the Earl of Northumberland, the Earl

of Essex [and] the Lord Daubeney went to the said Lord Henry ...

And immediately after that they were ready they took their way secretly by Our Lady of Pew, through St Stephens Chapel on to the stairfoot of the Star Chamber ... And the Lord William Courtenay bore the said Lord Henry's sword and spurs, the pommel upwards, and when he did light off his horse Sir William Sandys bore him to the King's presence, and there the Earl of Oxford took the sword and spurs, and presented the right spur to the King, and the King commanded the Duke of Buckingham to put it on the right heel of the said Lord Henry, and likewise the left spur to the Marquis of Dorset. And then the King girt his sword about him and after dubbed him knight in manner accustomed, and then set him upon the table ...

And on the Saturday, All Hallows Day [1 November] after the King had heard matins, and was returned to his Chamber [he] did on his robes of estate royal, and, crowned, came into the parliament chamber, and there stood him under his cloth of estate, having many good estates by him, as the Cardinal of Canterbury and many other prelates, the Duke of Bedford, the Duke of Buckingham, the Earl of Oxford, the Earl of Essex, the Earl of Kent, the Earl of Wiltshire and the substance of all the barons of the realm, all in their robes, and in likewise the judges, the Master of the Rolls, the Mayor of London with his brethren the Aldermen, and great press of knights, esquires and other nobles; and out of the cloister, a gallery at the nether end of the chamber, entered divers nobles and officers of arms and proceeded towards the King's presence; and Garter, Principal King of Arms, presented his patent, and after three great estates in their robes, that is to say the Earl of Suffolk which bore a rich sword, the pommel upwards, the Earl of Northumberland bore a rod of gold, and the Earl of Derby a cap of estate, furred with ermines thickly powdered, of iiii wayes and rich coronet thereupon; and the Earl of Shrewsbury bore the said young prince. In time he entered the parliament chamber door, and then the Marquis of Dorset and the Earl of Arundel led him to the King's presence, all being in their robes of estate and doing their obeisance as appertaineth. And then the reverend Father in God, Lord Oliver King, Bishop of Exeter and the King's secretary read the patent of his creation, presented by Garter as before, and so there the King created him Duke of York, with the gift of £1,000 by year ...

And on the ix day of the said month were the jousts royal in the King's palace of Westminster, and as it was prepared and furnished, it was the most triumphant place that ever I saw ...

And out of Westminster Hall came into the field the challengers, unhelmed, and their horses richly trapped of the King's colours, accomplished with sonnets of silver and some white and some green, with other great gilt bells on the mane and also the crupper with jancils of the King's colours. That is to say the Earl of Suffolk, the Earl of Essex, Sir Richard Carlson [and] John Peche, richly accompanied with many lords, knights and esquires, marvellously well beseen, and with so great readiness ...

And then out of the King's street came the answerers, also richly accompanied, but they were helmed. There was the Earl of Shrewbury and Sir John Cheney, so well horsed and so richly beseen that it was a triumphant sight to see them, and many other, and so in like wise rode about the field. And then the Earl of Suffolk and Sir Edward A Borough ran the first six courses ...

(BL MS Cotton Julius B.XII, f.91. Printed in J. Gairdner, *Letters and Papers of the Reigns of Richard III and Henry VII*, Rolls Series, 1861-3, I, pp. 388-92)

DOCUMENT 3: THE CORONATION OF HENRY VIII, 1509

When the funerals of the late King were thus honourably finished, great preparation was made for the coronation of this new King, which was appointed on Midsummer's day next ensuing, during which preparation the King was moved by some of his council that it should be honourable and profitable to his realm to take to wife the Lady Katherine, late wife to his brother Prince Arthur deceased, lest she, having so great a dowry might marry out of the realm, which should be unprofitable to him; by reason of which motion, the King being young, and not understanding the law of God, espoused the said Lady Katherine the 3rd day of June, which marriage was dispensed with by Pope July at the request of her father King Fernando, contrary to the opinions of all the Cardinals of Rome being divines. This marriage of the brother's wife was much murmured against in the beginning, and ever more and more sounded out by learning and scripture, so that at the last by the determination of the best universities of Christendom it was adjudged detestable, and plain contrary to God's law, as you shall hear, after xx years.

If I should declare what pain, labour and diligence the tailors, embroiderers, and goldsmiths took, both to make and devise garments for Lords, Ladies, Knights and Esquires, and also for the decking, trapping and adorning of coursers, jennets and palfreys, it were too long to rehearse, but for a surety more rich nor more strange nor curious works hath not been seen than were prepared against this coronation.

On the xxi day of this month of June, the King came from Greenwich to the Tower, over London bridge, and so by Grace Church, with whom came many well equipped gentlemen, but in especial the Duke of Buckingham, which had a gown all of goldsmith's work, very costly, and there the King rested till Saturday next ensuing.

Friday the twenty and two day of June, everything being in a readiness for his coronation, his Grace with the Queen being in the Tower of London, made there Knights of the Bath, to the number of twenty and four, with all the observances and ceremonies to the same belonging.

And the morrow following, being Saturday, the xxiii of the said month, his Grace with the Queen departed from the Tower through the city of London, against whose coming the streets where his Grace should pass were hanged with tapestry and cloth of Arras. And the great part, of the south side of Cheap with cloth of Gold, and some parts of Cornhill also. And the streets railed and barred on the one side from over against Grace Church unto Breadstreet, in Cheapside, where every occupation stood in their lines in order, beginning with the base and mean occupations, and so ascending to the worshipful crafts; highest and lastly stood the Mayor and Aldermen. The Goldsmiths' stalls, unto the end of the Old Change, being replenished with Virgins in white with branches of white mace; the priests and clerks in rich copes with crosses of silver, with censing his Grace and the Queen as they passed. The features of his body, his goodly personage, his amiable visage, princely countenance, and the noble qualities of his royal estate, to every man known, needeth no rehearsal, considering that, for lack of cunning, I cannot express the gifts of grace and of nature that God hath endowed him withal.

(Edward Hall, *Chronicle*, ed. 1809, p. 502)

DOCUMENT 4: THE DOWNFALL OF EMPSON & DUDLEY, 1509–10

In the said proclamation was contained, that if any man had sustained injury, or loss of goods by the Commissioners before appointed, as appeareth in the xix year of King Henry the seventh, that he should make his humble supplication unto the King's grace, and therein express their grief, and he was ready, not only to hear them, but also to cause satisfaction to be made. When the proclamation was published and known abroad, all such from whom anything had been exacted or taken, whether it were by right or wrong, speedily came unto the Court, and every man alleged and showed just occasion that they had for complaint. But the Council examined and tried their causes, and such as they found to be openly & manifestly injured, they made due restitution ... But the rage and cry of the people was so grievous against the commissioners, whose names were Richard Empson knight and Edmund Dudley esquire, that the Council to cease and quiet the rage of the people were forced to apprehend and commit to the Tower of London the aforesaid Empson and Dudley, and being called before the council and other justices, where they (as Polydore [Vergil] saith), being both learned in the laws of England, pleaded for themselves, namely Sir Richard Empson, which was the elder, who said as followeth: I am sure, right honourable, you are not ignorant how expedient & profitable unto mans life be good and wholesome laws, without which neither private house may be maintained, nor public weal duly and orderly governed. Even those laws among us by the oversight and negligence of magistrates, partly were depraved, and now in some part abrogate and out of memory, which evil increasing daily more and more, King Henry the seventh (now deceased) a most prudent and politic prince (as ye all know) endeavoured to redress, who unto us committed the charge to see, and provide that the common and accustomed laws might be maintained and executed ... and that such persons as had violated and transgressed any of them should suffer condign and worthy punishment. We therefore as faithfully and uprightly as we could have according to our commission executed our office truly unto the great commodity of the public weal ... These their sayings, unto many that were wise, virtuous and discreet, seemed to be very good and right, but unto other, and that unto the greatest number, who supposed that the examination and execution of laws being done through avarice and covetousness and for filthy desire of gain, they judged that even they by putting in execution with extremity the laws to the loss of many an honest man's goods, should now be recompensed with the loss of their heads, who within three days after were beheaded at the Tower Hill, but their bodies with their heads were buried ...

(Richard Grafton, *A Chronicle and Mere history*, 1809 edition, pp. 235-6)

DOCUMENT 5: PROCLAMATION PROHIBITING RETAINERS, 1511

Whereas the King our sovereign lord, Henry, by the grace of God King of England and of France, and Lord of Ireland, for the defence of his most noble person, his realm and his subjects, hath now lately, by the advice of his council, by his letters under his signet and sign manual, commanded as well all the Lords as also the substance of all the nobles of this his realm forthwith to prepare such and as many able men for the war, sufficiently harnessed, as they can and may prepare of their own servants and other inhabitants within their offices and rooms, and none other, as in the said letters is more plainly expressed and specified.

Our said sovereign lord is now informed, to his great displeasure if it so be, that divers and many of the said lords and nobles, as well by colour of the said letters as of other his former and older letters and placards, prepare for the war divers and many persons not being their own tenants, nor inhabited within their offices and rooms, contrary to the king's said letters, but also retain divers persons, wheresoever they may get them, some by promises and some by badges and cognisances, and some otherwise, contrary to the mind of our said sovereign lord and his laws in that case provided.

Wherefore his highness straightly chargeth and commandeth that no manner of man, of what degree or condition he be, make no retainers otherwise than his laws will suffer, upon the dangers and peril of the same laws; nor no man bear or wear any man's badge or cognisance otherwise than the law will, upon the same peril; nor prepare no man for the war but only such as be his own servants or inhabited within his office or rooms, according to the said letters.

And that every man that hath otherwise ordered or demeaned him in that behalf forthwith purvey the remedy, so that his highness hereafter have no complaint thereof, at his utmost peril, and upon the King's great indignation and displeasure.

And as for the said former and older letters and placards, of what date and nature soever they be, or to whom or for what cause soever they were granted, the King's highness declareth them now to be void and of none effect, but utterly derogate by this his last letters which, his highness will, stand in force and effect, and none other.

(P. L. Hughes and J. F. Larkin, *Tudor Royal Proclamations*, I (1964), pp. 84-5)

DOCUMENT 6: THE WAR WITH FRANCE, 1512

While this was happening in Italy, King Henry in the meantime had already prepared an army, the hand picked flower of men in their military prime, together with a fleet of sixty great ships, complete with armament and all other equipment necessary for warlike action. He appointed Thomas, Marquis of Dorset as commander of the army and Sir Edward Howard as Admiral of the fleet; both men were well versed in the affairs of war. The King thereupon quickly sent Thomas and this fine army to Aquitaine about the 14th May (as had been agreed with the king's father-in-law, Ferdinand). Having embarked, Thomas was carried in a short term a little too far and landed in Cantabria, which adjoins Aquitaine and today is called Biscay. He disembarked his troops at the seaport of the area which is called Fuentarrabia in the vernacular, and is, both naturally and by human contrivance, a most well defended place. Here he encamped. The spot is eighteen miles from Bayonne, the nearest seaboard town in Aquitaine. High born gentlemen were sent by King Ferdinand to meet Thomas; they gave him a friendly welcome and informed him that the royal forces would be at the place very soon. This did not in fact happen, and hence nothing was done in those parts by the important English army. The English took this very badly ...

The King accordingly informed the Marquis promptly in writing and by envoys to join the Spanish army as quickly as possible. But by now winter had come and many Englishmen, unable to bear the sultry climate of the area, because they are unaccustomed to the greater heat of the sun, died of disease and fell seriously ill. The Marquis, not waiting for the King's orders, in the meantime returned home with his army, five months after he had first crossed over to the continent.

While the Marquis was immobilised in camp, Edward Howard, Admiral of the fleet, while patrolling off the French coast, turned by chance towards Brittany. Having disembarked a not very large force, he made a short incursion in full view of the French who were in garrison there; having burnt some houses, he returned safely to his ships with booty. The French did not once leave their stations ...

(Polydore Vergil, *Anglica Historia*, 1534, ed. Denys Hay, Camden Society, LXXIV, 1950, p. 175)

DOCUMENT 7: THE BATTLE OF FLODDEN, 1513
Then the English men removed their field on the water of Till, and so forth over many hills and straits, marching towards the Scots on another side, and in their sight the Scots burned certain poor villages on the other side of the marishe.

The English men always leaving the Scottish army on the left hand, took their field under a wood side, called Barmer wood, two miles from the Scots, and between the two armies was the river of Till, and there was a little hill that saved the English men from the gunshot, on which hill the Lord Admiral [Lord Thomas Howard] perfectly saw and discovered them all.

The king of Scots perceiving the Englishmen, marching towards

Scotland, thought that they would have entered into Scotland, and burn and foray the plentiful country called the March, for so he was made to believe by an Englishman named Gyles Musgrave which was familiar with the king of Scots, and did it for a policy to cause him to come down from the hill ...

Then the Lord Admiral perceived four great battles of the Scots all on foot with long spears like moorish pikes: which Scots furnished them warlike, and bent them to the forward, which was conducted by the Lord Admiral, which perceiving that, sent to his father the Earl of Surrey his *agnus dei* that hung at his breast that in all haste he would join battle even with the brunt or breast of the vanguard: for the forward alone was not able to encounter the whole battle of the Scots, the earl perceiving well the saying of his son, and seeing the Scots ready to descend the hill, advanced himself and his people forward and brought them equal in ground with the forward on the left hand, even at the brunt or breast of the same at the foot of the hill called Bramston [Branxton], the English army stretched East and West, and their backs North, and the Scots in the South before them on the foresaid hill called Bramston. Then out burst the ordnance on both sides with fire, flame and hideous noise, and the master gunner of the English part slew the master gunner of Scotland, and beat all his men from their ordnance, so that the Scottish ordnance did no harm to the Englishmen, but the Englishmen's artillery shot into the midst of the King's battle, and slew many persons, which seeing the king of Scots and his noblemen made the more haste to come to joining, & so all the four battles in manner descended the hill at once. After that the shot was done, which they defended with pavises [shield] they came to handstrokes and were encountered severally ...

All these four battles in manner fought at one time, and were determined in effect, little in distance of the beginning and ending of any of them one before the other, saving that Sir Edward Stanley, which was the last that fought, for he came up to the top of the hill, and there fought with the Scots valiantly, and chased them down the hill over that place where the king's battle joined. Besides these four Battles of the Scots were two other battles, which never came to handstokes.

Thus through the power of God on Friday, being the ix day of September in the year of our Lord 1513 was James the fourth king of Scots slain at Bramston chiefly by the power of the Earl of Surrey Lieutenant for king Henry the eight, King of England (which then lay at the siege before Tournai), and with the said king were slain; ... The Archbishop of St Andrews, the King's bastard son ... [and forty-four listed bishops, lairds and knights slain. Scots losses were estimated to total between 10,000 and 12,000. The 'Archbishop' was Alexander Stewart, the Administrator, never consecrated].

(Richard Grafton, *A Chronicle at large and Mere history of the affairs of England* (1568), ed. 1809, pp. 274-6)

DOCUMENT 8: ATTAINDER OF EDWARD, DUKE OF BUCKINGHAM, 1523

Forasmuch as Edward, late Duke of Buckingham, late of Thornbury in the county of Gloucester, the 24th day of April in the fourth year of the reign of our sovereign lord the King that now is, and at divers other times after imagined and compassed traitorously and unnaturally the destruction of the most royal person of our said sovereign lord and subversion of this his realm, and then traitorously committed and did divers and many treasons against our said sovereign lord the king, contrary to his allegiance, in the counties of Gloucester and Somerset, the City of London, the counties of Kent and Surrey, of the which treasons and offences the said late Duke was severally indicted. And afterward for and upon the same treasons the 13th day of May the 13th year of the reign of our said sovereign lord the king at Westminster in the county of Middlesex, before Thomas Duke of Norfolk, for that time only being Great Steward of England by the king's letters patent, by verdict of his peers and by judgement of the said Steward against the said late Duke then and there given after the due order of the law and custom of England, was attained of high treason, as by the records thereof more plainly appeareth. Wherefore be in ordained enacted and established by the King our sovereign lord, with the assent of the lords spiritual and temporal and the Commons in this present parliament assembled and by the authority of the same that the said late Duke for the offences above rehearsed stand and be convicted, adjudged and attainted of high treason, and forfeit to the king our sovereign lord and his heirs forever all honours, castles, manors, lordships, hundreds, franchises, liberties, privileges, advowsons, nominations, knights fees, lands, tenements, rents, services, reversions, remainders, portions, annuities, pensions, rights, possessions and other hereditaments whatsoever, in England, Ireland, Wales, Calais and the marches of the same, or elsewhere, whereof the said late duke or any other person or persons to his use were seized or possessed in fee simple, fee tail, or for term of any other man's life or lives, or any estate of inheritance or otherwise the said 24th day of April or any time since lawful cause of entry within England, Ireland, Wales, Calais, the marches of the same or elsewhere. And over that, the said Edward to forfeit unto our said sovereign lord all good and chattels, as well real as personal whatsoever, whereof the said Edward was possessed to his own use, or any other person or persons was possessed to the use of the same late Duke, the said 13th day of May, or whereof the said late Duke had lawful cause of seizure to his own proper use the said 13th day of May; and also to forfeit unto our said sovereign lord all debts which were owing by any person or persons unto the said late Duke or unto any person or persons to the use of the said late Duke the said 13th day of May. (Statute 14 & 15 Henry VIII, cap.20. *Statutes of the Realm*, III, p. 246.)

DOCUMENT 9: FESTIVITIES AT COURT, 1524

Before the feast of Christmas, the Lord Leonard Grey and the Lord John Grey, brethren to the Marquis Dorset, Sir George Cobham, son to the Lord Cobham, William Carey, Sir John Dudley, Thomas West, Francis Pointz, Francis Sidney, Sir Anthony Browne, Sir Edward Seymour, Oliver Manners, Percival Harte, Sebastian Newdigate, and Thomas Cullen, Esquires of the King's Household, enterprised a challenge of feats or arms, against the feast of Christmas. Wherefore they sent Windsor Herald, on St Thomas' day before Christmas unto the Queen's Great Chamber, the King being present, which herald had a coat of arms of red silk, beaten with a goodly castle, of four turrets silver, and in every turret a fair lady, standing gorgeously apparelled: the herald after the trumpet had blown, said where the King our sovereign lord of his bountiful goodness, hath given to four members of his court the castle of loyalty to dispose at their pleasure, the said maidens have given the custody thereof to a captain and fifteen gentlemen with him, which captain sent forth me his herald called Chateau Blanche, to declare to all kings and princes and other gentlemen of noble courage that the said captain will near to his castle raise a mount, on which shall stand an unicorn supporting four fair shields.

The first shall be White, and whosoever touch that shield shall be answered six courses at the tilt by them of the castle, with baiting harness and double pieces.

The second shield red, betokening the tourney, and whosoever toucheth that shield shall be answered ten strokes at the tourney, with sword edge and point abated.

The third shield yellow, signifying the barriers, and he that toucheth that shield shall be answered twelve strokes at the barriers with sword edge and point abated.

The fourth shield blue, touching the assault, with such weapons as the captain of the castle shall occupy, that is morris pike, sword, target, the point and edge abated.

Also the said captain and his company promised to defend the said castle against all comers, being gentlemen of name and arms; and the assaults to devise all manner of engines for the assaulting, edge tool to break the house and ground only except, and also that no other weapon shall be used but such as the parties shall be set up by the said unicorn, and that no man meddle with fire within or without but the match for guns, and every prisoner taken on either part to pay for his ransom iiii yards of right satin, and every captain xiii yards.

According to this proclamation was the Mount and all things devised sumptuously, with great craggy branches on which were hanged the shields of arms of the captain and all other of the castle. For this enterprise there was set up in the tilt yard at Greenwich a castle square every way xx foot, and fifty foot high very strong and of great trunks well fastened with iron, the embattlements, loops and every place where men should enter were set with great rolls, and turned as soon as they were touched, so that to seeming no man could enter either the houses or embattlements. On the north and south sides were two great ditches xv foot deep from the brink to the bottom, and they were very steep, and between the ditch and the castle was set a pale which was rampired with earth, so steep and thick that it was not likely to be gotten. On these ditches were two draw bridges, on the west side was great rampire or bank, very steep without and within, and like to the vamure of a fortress, by the vamure the ditches were xxiiii foot deep. When the strength of this castle was well beholden, many made dangerous to assault it, and some said it could not be won by sport but by earnest. The King minded to have it assaulted and devised engines therefore, but the carpenters were so dull that they understood not his intent and wrought all things contrary, and so for that time the assault was prolonged, and all the other parts of the challenge held, for the manner after St John Baptist's day in Christmas came out of the castle six men at arms of the castle on horseback armed at all points with their spears ready to discharge, and so came to the end of the tilt, abiding all comers. Then suddenly entered into the field two ladies on two palfreys in great robes of purple damask leading two ancient knights, with beards of silver, in the same apparel, and when they came before the Queen, they sent up a bill to her to the effect thereof that although youth had left them and age was come, and would let them to do feats of arms: yet courage, desire and good will abode with them and bad them to take upon them to break spears, which they would gladly do, if it pleased her to give them license. When the Queen and the ladies had seen the bill, they praised their courage and gave them license.

Then the knights threw away their robes, and it was known that it was the King and Duke of Suffolk ...
(Edward Hall, *Chronicle*, ed. 1809, pp. 688-9)

DOCUMENT 10: THE FAILURE OF THE AMICABLE GRANT, 1525
At the sitting if the commissioners at Otford [Watford], March 30th, [he]

obtained from the contributors the names and sums enclosed. It will be hard to raise the money, especially as other parliamentary grants are now payable. Reports for the secret ear of the Cardinal the dissatisfaction prevailing.

1. The people speak cursedly, saying they shall never have rest of payments as long as some liveth.

2. That some of commissioners, through fear of the people, will only announce the king's command, without pressing it further, leaving the obnoxious portion to the Archbishop.

3. The complaint is made that the loan is not repaid, nor will this grant be.

4. They would give, but cannot: and will not at any other than the king's appointment.

5. That too much coin of the realm is exported already into Flanders.

6. That it would be the greatest means of enriching France to have all his money spent there, out of the realm; and if the king win France, he will be obliged to spend his time and revenue there.

7. They are sorry, rather than otherwise, at the captivity of Francis I.

8. That all the sums already spent on the invasion of France have not gained the king a foot more land in it than his father had, which lacked no riches or wisdom to win the kingdom of France, if he had thought it expedient.

[He] would have been glad if the time had allowed, that this practising with the people for so great sums might have been spared to the cuckoo time, and that the hot weather (at which times mad brains be most busy) had been passed. Otford, 5th April.

(Paraphrase taken from *Letters and Papers*, IV, no. 1243)

DOCUMENT 11: HENRY FITZROY, THE ILLEGITIMATE SON, 1525

You shall understand that the king in his fresh youth was in the chains of love with a fair damsel called Elizabeth Blount, daughter to Sir John Blount, knight, which damsel in singing, dancing, and in all goodly pastimes, exceeded all other, by which goodly pastimes she won the king's heart: and she again shewed him such favour that by him she bore a goodly man child, of beauty like to the father and mother. This child was well brought up like a Prince child, and when he was six years of age, the king made him knight, and called him Lord Henry Fitzroy, and on Sunday being the xviii day of June [1525], at the manor or place of Bridewell, the said Lord, led by two Earls, was created Earl of Nottingham, and then he was brought back again by the said two Earls; then the Dukes of Norfolk and Suffolk led him into the Great Chamber again, and the king created him Duke of Richmond and Somerset ... (Richard Grafton, *A Chronicle and Mere history*, 1809 edition, pp. 382-3.)

DOCUMENT 12: HENRY'S SCRUPLE OF CONSCIENCE, 1528

Wherefore he like a prudent prince and circumspect doer in all his affairs, and willing all men to know his intent and purpose, caused all his nobility, judges and councillors, with divers other persons, to come to his palace of Bridewell on Sunday the 8th of November [1528] at afternoon in his Great Chamber, and there to them said as near as my wit could bear away, these words following.

'Our trusty and well-beloved subjects, both you of the nobility and you of the meaner sort, it is not unknown to you that we, both by God's provision and true and faithful inheritance have reigned over this realm of England almost the term of xx years, During which time we have so ordered us, thanked be God, that no outward enemy hath oppressed you or taken anything from us, nor we have invaded no realm, but we have had victory and honour, so that we think that you, nor none of your predecessors never lived more quietly, more wealthy, nor in more estimation under any of our noble progenitors: but when we remember our mortality, and that we must die, then we think that all our doings in our lifetime are clearly defaced, and worthy of no memory, if we leave you in trouble at the time of our death. For if our true heir be not known at the time of our death, see what mischief and trouble shall succeed to you and your children. The experience whereof some of you have seen after the death of our noble grandfather, king Edward the fourth, and some have heard what mischief and manslaughter continued in this realm between the houses of York and Lancaster, by the which dissention this realm was like to have been clearly destroyed. And although it hath pleased Almighty God to send us a fair daughter of a noble woman and me begotten to our great comfort and joy, yet it hath been told us by divers great clerks, that neither she is our lawful daughter, nor her mother our lawful wife, but that we live together abominably and detestably, in open adultery, insomuch that when our embassy was last in France, and motion was made that the Duke of Orleans should marry our said daughter, one of the chief councillors to the French king said, It were well done to know whether she be the king of England his lawful daughter or not, for well known it is that he begat her on his brother's wife, which is directly against God's law and his precept. Think you not my lords that these words touch not my body and soul, think you that these doings do not daily and hourly trouble my conscience and vex my spirits, yes we doubt not but and if it were your own cause every man would seek remedy, when the peril of your soul and the loss of your inheritance is openly laid to you. For this only cause I profess before God, & in the word of a prince, I have asked counsel of the greatest clerks in Christendom, and for this cause I have sent for this Legate, as a man indifferent, only to know the truth, and to settle my conscience and for none other cause as God can judge. And as touching the Queen, if it be adjudged by the law of God that she is my lawful wife, there was never thing more pleasant, nor more acceptable to me in my life, both for the discharge and clearing of my conscience, and also for the good qualities and conditions the which I know to be in her. For I assure you all that beside her noble parentage of the which she is descended (as you all know), she is a woman of most gentleness, of most humility and buxomeness, yea and of all good qualities appertaining to nobility she is without comparison as I think this xx years almost have had the true experiment, so that if I were to marry again, if the marriage might be good, I would surely chose her above all other women: But if it be determined by judgement that our marriage was against God's law & clearly void, then I shall not only sorrow the departing from so good a lady and loving companion, but much more lament and bewail my unfortunate chance, that I have so long lived in adultery to God's great displeasure, and have no true heir of my body to inherit this realm. These be the sores that vex my mind, and these be the pangs that trouble my conscience, and for these griefs I seek a remedy. Therefore I require of you all as our trust and confidence is in you, to declare to our subjects our mind and intent, according to our true meaning, and desire them to pray with us that the very truth may be known for the discharge of our conscience, and saving of our soul, and for the declaration thereof, I have assembled you together, and now you may depart.'

To see what countenance was made amongst the hearers of this oration, it was strange sight, for some sighed and said nothing, other were sorry to hear the king so troubled in his conscience. Other that favoured the Queen much sorrowed that this matter was now opened, and so every man spoke as his heart served him, but the king ever laboured to know the truth for the discharge of his conscience. (Richard Grafton, *Chronicle and Mere history*, 1809 edition, pp. 414-5)

DOCUMENT 13: ANNE BOLEYN PROCESSES TO HER CORONATION, 1533
And upon the same Saturday (31 May), being Whitsun Eve, the mayor with all the Aldermen and the crafts of the city prepared array in good order to stand and receive her Grace; and with rails for every craft to stand and lean, from the press of the people.

The Mayor met the Queen's Grace at her coming forth of the Tower. All his brethren and aldermen standing in Cheap[side] ...

She passed the streets first, with certain strangers, their horses trapped with blue silk; and themselves in blue velvet with white feathers, accompanied two and two. Likewise Squires, Knights, Barons and Baronets, Knights of the Bath clothed in violet garments, edged with ermine like judges. Then following: the Judges of the law and Abbots. All these estates were to the number of two hundred couple and more: two and two accompanied.

And then followed Bishops, two and two; and the Archbishops of York and Canterbury; the ambassadors of France and Venice; the Lord

Mayor with a mace: Master Garter the King of Heralds, and the King's coat armour upon him, with the Officers of Arms, appointing every estate in their degree.

Then followed two ancient Knights, with old fashioned hats, powdered on their heads, disguised, who did represent the Dukes of NORMANDY and of GUIENNE, after an old custom: the Lord Constable of England for the time, being the Duke of SUFFOLK; the Lord WILLIAM HOWARD, the Deputy for the time to the Lord Marshall, and the Duke of NORFOLK.

Then followed the Queen's Grace in her litter, costly and richly beseen, with a rich canopy over her: which was borne by the Lords of the Five Ports [Barons of the Cinque Ports]. After her, following the Master of the Horse with a spare white palfrey richly appointed, and led in his hand.

Then followed her noble Ladies of Estate richly clothed in crimson powdered with ermines; to the number of twelve.

Then the Master of the Guard with the guard on both sides of the streets in good array; and all the Constables well beseen in velvet and damask coats with white staves in their hand; setting every man in array and order in the streets until she came to Westminster.

Then followed four rich chariots with Ladies of Honour. After them followed thirty Ladies and gentlewomen richly garnished: and so the serving men after them.

And as she was departed from the Tower, a marvellously great shot of guns was there fired and shot off.

(*The Noble Triumphant Coronation of Queen Anne*, in A. F. Pollard, *Tudor Tracts* (1903), pp. 14-15)

DOCUMENT 14: THE ACT IN RESTRAINT OF APPEALS, 1533
Where by divers sundry old authentic histories and chronicles it is manifestly declared and expressed that this realm of England is an empire, and so hath been accepted in the world, governed by one supreme head and king having the dignity and royal estate of the Imperial Crown of the same, unto whom a body politic, compact of all sorts and degrees of people

divided in terms and by names of spirituality and temporality, be bounden and owe to bear next to God a natural and humble obedience; he being also institute and furnished by the goodness and sufferance of Almighty God with plenary whole and entire power, pre-eminence, authority, prerogative and jurisdiction to render and yield justice and final determination to all manner of folks resiants or subjects within this realm ...

II. And be it further enacted ... that if any person or persons ... do attempt, move, purchase or procure from or to the see of Rome, or from or to any other foreign court or courts out of this realm, any manner foreign process, inhibitions, appeals, sentences, summons, citations, interdictions, excommunications, restraints or judgements, of what nature, kind or quality soever they be, or execute any of the same process, or do any act or acts to the let, impediment, hindrance or derogation of any process, sentence, judgement or determination had, made, done, or hereafter to be had done or made in any courts of this realm or the King's said dominions or marches of the same for any of the causes aforesaid ... that then every person or persons so doing, and their fautors, comforters, abettors, procurers, executors and counsellors, and every of them, being convict of the same, for every such default shall incur and run in the same pains penalties and forfeitures ordained and provided by the statute of provision and praemunire made in the sixteenth year of the reign of ... King Richard II.

(Statute 24 Henry VIII, c.12. *Statutes of the Realm*, III, pp. 427-9)

Document 15: The Act of Supremacy, 1534

Albeit the King's Majesty justly and rightfully is and oweth to be the Supreme Head of the Church of England, and so is recognised by the clergy of this realm in their Convocations; yet nevertheless for corroboration and confirmation thereof, and for the increase of virtue in Christ's religion within this realm of England, and to repress and extirp all errors, heresies and other enormities and abuses heretofore used in the same, Be it enacted by authority of this present parliament that the King our sovereign Lord, his heirs and successors kings of this realm, shall be taken, accepted and reputed the only Supreme Head in earth of the Church of England called

the *Anglicana Ecclesia*, and shall have and enjoy annexed and united to
the Imperial Crown of this realm as well the title and style thereof, as all
honours, dignities, pre-eminences, jurisdictions, privileges, authorities,
immunities, profits and commodities, to the said dignity of Supreme Head
of the same church belonging and appertaining. And that our said sovereign
lord, his heirs and successors kings of this realm, shall have full power and
authority from time to time to visit, repress, redress, reform, order, correct,
restrain and amend all such errors, heresies, abuses, offences, contempts
and enormities, whatsoever they be, which by any manner spiritual
authority or jurisdiction ought or may lawfully be reformed, repressed,
ordered, redressed, corrected, restrained, or amended, most to the pleasure
of Almighty God, the increase of virtue in Christ's religion, and for the
conservation of the peace, unity and tranquillity of this realm: any usage,
custom, foreign laws, foreign authority, prescription or any other thing or
things to the contrary hereof notwithstanding.
(Statute 26 Henry VIII, c.1. *Statutes of the Realm*, III, p. 491.)

DOCUMENT 16: AN IMPERIAL VIEW OF THE PILGRIMAGE OF GRACE, 1536

Relacion de las cartas del Embaxador de Ynglaterra de 5, 14, 22 de
Noviembre de 1536.

He has heard from one of the principal gentlemen in the King's army
that the Duke of Norfolk, Talbot [George, Earl of Shrewsbury], the
Marquis [of Dorset], the Earl of Rutland and other captains had gone
to speak with the men of the north, who had risen against the King.
They never did anything so prudently, as otherwise they would have
placed the King's life and estate in great danger.

All the nobility of the Duchy of York is risen. They number 40,000
combatants and among them 10,000 horse. They are in good order and
have a crucifix as their principal banner. The Archbishop of York and
Lord Darcy are in the army. The King blames the latter more than any
man. Norfolk and his colleagues do not wish for a battle. They are all
good Christians, showing tacitly that the petitions of the insurgents are
lawful, and giving them hopes that the king will yield. It is thought that

Norfolk has come to court as much for his own justification as to assist the ambassadors from the men of the north. One of them is Sir Ralph Ellercar, one of the four knights of the King's Chamber, and the other is master Bowes, a lawyer. They are only allowed twelve days to go and return, and three days to negotiate.

The ambassadors desire that their demand and petition may be authorised by parliament, so as the better to curb the King; that henceforth parliament may be held in the ancient way; that all pensioners and officers of the Crown may be excluded. They intend to provide a remedy in parliament for the Princess' [Mary's] affairs, and other things, especially that the King shall not take money from his people except to make war on France and Scotland. The instructions to these ambassadors were signed by most of the gentlemen.

The determination of the King cannot yet be known. It is feared that his arrogance and the persuasions of those who govern him will prevent him from granting the demands, and also that he congratulates himself that the French king has offered to come and help him with 4,000 or 5,000 men.

(*Letters and Papers*, XI, no. 1143)

DOCUMENT 17: THE KILDARE REVOLT, 1534
John Alen [Vice Chancellor in Ireland] to Thomas Cromwell, 26 December 1534.

Doubts not that the Treasurer and others will write of the late journey to Waterford. Is grieved to see the expense of this army, and not such service done as ought to be. Journeyed with 300 horsemen through Kildare and Cartlagh, and by MacMaryno and O'More. The traitor and O'More dared not set upon them, but meanwhile robbed and burned Tyrone and Dunboyne. The Deputy then made a truce with them, which Alen thinks not honourable. O'Nele on the other side burnt part of the baron of Shane's lands, all Botaghe's lands and great part of Uriell. The rebel cannot be destroyed if the army stays in Dublin. He expected to be banished a month ago, but now gains in pride and strength again. The King and Council should write to the

Deputy and captains to approach to the war, and leave Dublin and Drogheda. The traitor has not more than 100 horse and 300 foot, among whom there is not one archer, nor 10 handguns, and he has no ordnance. He intends to have Trym, the Nowan, Athboy, the Nass, Kildare and other towns, and will break his own garrisons and burn his own lands lest Englishmen should profit by them. Understands that he expects an army from Spain, and has lately sent the official of Meath, the Dean of Kildare, parson Walshe, the Bishop of Killallo and other papists to Spain asking for aid against the King as an heretic.

Advises the King either to pardon him out of hand, or to send here a proclamation that he never intends to pardon him or any who take part with him thereafter. If the army would go abroad, it would not be long before he would be subdued. A marshal should be appointed who is not a Welshman, for they rob now both friend and foe. Sir Rice Manxell orders his company well. Edward FitzGerald is taken. Asks Cromwell to advertise the Deputy that he and Brooke may be justified, and the Earl of Shrewsbury that Rookes, who was taken a Wexford may be delivered to the Deputy.

The Deputy is old and cannot take pains by reason of sickness. Suggests the advisability of having 200 more northern horse.

Offers that he and the Chief Baron will go with the army if they may have 24 spearmen and six archers or gunners on horseback. Objects to the appointing of Captains as Privy Councillors. It were better they should be commanded than commanders. The Deputy, the Lord Chancellor, the Earl of Ossory, Lord Butler and the Baron of Delven know how to subdue this traitor better than all the captains of England, except the Duke of Norfolk. Desires credence for the bearer, Edward Becke. Dublin, 26th December.

Trusts the Commons of England will grant the King £100,000 for subduing this false traitor.

(*Letters and Papers*, VII, no. 1573)

DOCUMENT 18: THE ACT CURTAILING FRANCHISES, 1536
Where divers of the most ancient prerogatives and authorities of justice

appertaining to the Imperial Crown of this realm have been severed and taken from the same by sundry gifts of the king's most noble progenitors, Kings of this realm, to the great diminution and detriment of the royal estate of the same and to the hindrance and great delay of justice; For reformation whereof be it enacted by the authority of this present parliament that no person or persons of what estate or degree soever they be of, from the first day of July which shall be in the year of our Lord God 1536 shall have any power or authority to pardon or remit any treasons, murders, manslaughters or any kind of felonies ... but that the King, his heirs and successors Kings of this realm shall have the whole and sole power and authority thereof united and knit to the Imperial Crown of this realm, as of good right and equity it appertaineth, any grants, usages, prescription, act or acts of parliament or any other thing to the contrary thereof notwithstanding ...

iii. And be it further enacted ... that all original writs and judicial writs, and all manner of indictments of treason, felony or trespass, and all manner of process to be made upon the same in every county palatine and other liberty within this realm of England, Wales and marches of the same, shall from the said first day of July be made only in the name of our sovereign lord the King and his heirs kings of England ... And that in every writ and indictment that shall be made within any such county palatine or liberty, after the said first day of July next coming, whereby it shall be supposed anything to be done against the King's peace, shall be made and supposed to be done only against the King's peace, his heirs and successors, and not against the peace of any other person or persons, whatsoever they be ...

(Statute 27 Henry VIII, c.24. *Statutes of the Realm*, III, pp. 555-8)

DOCUMENT 19: THE FIRST ROYAL INJUNCTIONS, 1536
In the name of God, Amen. In the year of our Lord God 1536, and of the most noble reign of our sovereign Lord Henry VIII, King of England and of France, the twenty eighth year, and the --- day of --- , I Thomas Cromwell, knight, Lord Cromwell, Keeper of the Privy Seal of our said sovereign Lord the King, and Viceregent unto the

same, for and concerning all his jurisdiction ecclesiastical within this realm, visiting by the King's highness' supreme authority ecclesiastical the people and clergy of this deanery of --- by my trusty commissary --- lawfully deputed and constituted for this part, have to the glory of Almighty God, to the King's highness' honour, the public weal of this his realm, and increase of virtue in the same, appointed and assigned these injunctions ensuing, to be kept and observed of the dean, parsons, vicars, curates and stipendiaries, resident or having cure of souls, or any other spiritual administration within this deanery, under the pains hereafter limited and appointed.

1. The first is that the dean, parsons, vicars, and others having cure of souls anywhere within this deanery, shall faithfully keep and observe, and as far as in them may lie, shall cause to be observed and kept of other, all and singular laws and statutes of this realm made for the abolishing and extirpation of the Bishop of Rome's pretensed and usurped power and jurisdiction within this realm, and for the establishment and confirmation of the King's authority and jurisdiction within the same, as of the Supreme Head of the Church of England, and shall to the uttermost of their wit, knowledge and learning, purely, sincerely and without any colour or dissimulation, declare, manifest and open for the space of one quarter of a year now next ensuing, once every Sunday, and after that at leastwise twice every quarter, in their sermons and other collations, that the Bishop of Rome's usurped power and jurisdiction, having no establishment nor ground by the law of God, was of most just causes taken away and abolished ...

7. Item, that every parson, or proprietary of any parish church within this realm shall on this side of the feast of St Peter ad Vincula [1 August] next coming, provide a book of the whole bible, both in Latin and also in English, and lay the same in the choir, for every man that will to look on and read thereon and shall discourage no man from the reading of any part of the bible, either in Latin or in English; but rather comfort, exhort and admonish every man to read the same as the very word of God, and the spiritual food of man's soul, whereby they may the better know their duties to God, to their sovereign Lord the King, and their

neighbour; ever gently and charitably exhorting them that using a sober and modest behaviour in the reading and inquisition of the true sense of the same, they do in no wise stiffly or eagerly contend or strive one with another about the same but refer the declaration of those places that be in controversy to the judgement of them that be better learned ...

All which and singular injunctions shall be inviolably observed of the said dean, parsons, vicars, curates, stipendiaries and other clerks and beneficed men, under the pain of suspension and sequestration of the fruits of their benefices until they have done their duty according to these injunctions.

(W. H. Frere and W. M. Kennedy, *Visitation Articles and Injunctions of the Period of the Reformation* (1910), II, pp. 1-9)

DOCUMENT 20: THE DISSOLUTION OF THE MONASTERIES, 1536

20 November 1536. Instructions to the Commissioners for the suppression.

1. The Commissioners shall first repair to the monasteries, and take into their hands the common and convent seals, and cause them to be broken, or safely kept to the King's use.

2. They shall call before them the governors and officers of the said houses, and make them declare upon their oath the state and plight of the houses, and what leases, corrodies, fees etc have been granted by them before the 4th February 27 Henry VIII.

3. They shall make a true inventory of the lead, bells and superfluous buildings, and of all plate, jewels, ornaments, goods, chattels, debts, corn, stock and store of the same houses.

4. They shall survey all the possessions, spiritual and temporal of the same houses in the form heretofore used of such other like houses of religion dissolved by reason of the said Act of Parliament.

5. They shall enquire of the debts due to the house,

6. And put in safe custody to the King's use all evidences and writings.

7. They shall appoint pensions to the governors and notify them to the Chancellor and Council of the Court of Augmentations, with the total values of the pensions, then despatch the governor and other religious persons with convenient rewards.

8. They shall make letters for the capacities of the governors and religious persons to be obtained *gratis*, in the manner used in other houses heretofore suppressed.

9. They shall sell all the corn, grain, household stuff etc., except the lead, bells, plate jewels and principal ornaments in the form heretofore accustomed under the act.

10. They shall pay all servants wages and debts due for corn, cattle, victuals etc., and all other debts not exceeding £6 13s 4d.

11. They shall deliver possession to such persons as the King shall appoint.

12. They shall certify their proceedings under their seals and signs manual of the day limited.

(*Letters and Papers*, XI, Appendix no. 15)

DOCUMENT 21: THE PILGRIMAGE OF GRACE
The Pontefract articles

The first touching our faith, to have the heresies of Luther, Wycliffe, Hus, Melanchthon, Oecocolampadius, Bucer, *Confessio Germaniae* [the Augsburg confession], *Apologia Melanctionis*, the works of Tyndale, of Barnes, of Marshall, Rastell, St Germain, and other heresies of Anabaptists clearly within this realm to be annulled and destroyed.

The second to have the supreme head of the church touching our *animarum* to be reserved unto the see of Rome as before it was accustomed to be, and to have the consecrations of the bishops to be restored to the clergy from him without any first fruits or pension to him to be paid out of this realm or else a pension reasonable for the outward defence of our faith.

Item, we most humbly beseech our most dread sovereign lord that the Lady Mary may be made legitimate and the former statutes therein annulled for the danger of the title that might incur to the Crown of Scotland to this realm and other, that to be by parliament by laudable custom.

Item, to have the abbeys suppressed to be restored unto their houses, lands, and goods.

Item, to have the tenth and first fruits clearly discharged of the same, unless the clergy will of themselves grant a rent charge in generality to the augmentation of the Crown.

Item, to have the friars observants restored unto their houses again.

Item, to have the heretics, bishops, and temporal men and their sect, to have condign punishment by fire, or such otherwise, or else they and their partakers to try their quarrel with us and our part taken in battle.

Item, to have the Lord Cromwell, the Lord Chancellor [Sir Thomas Audley], and Sir Richard Rich, knight, to have condign punishment as the subvertors of the good laws of this realm and maintainers of the false sect of those heretics and the first inventors and bringers in of them.

Item, that the lands in Westmorland, Cumberland, Kendal, Dent, Sedbergh, Furness and the abbey lands in Mashamshire, Kirkbyshire and Nidderdale may be by tenant right, and the lord to have at every change 2 years rent for gressom and no more according to the grant now made by the lords to the commons there under their seal. And this to be done by Act of Parliament.

Item, the statutes of handguns and crossbows to be repealed, and the penalty thereof, unless it be in the king's forest or parks for the killing of this grace's red deer and fallow.

Item, that Dr. Leigh and Dr. Layton may have condign punishment for their extortions in their time of visitations, as in taking from religious houses £40, £20, and so to [...] sums, horses, advowsons, leases, under convent seals, bribes by them taken, and other abominable acts by them committed and done.

Item, reformation for the election of knights of the shire and burgesses, and for the uses amongst the lords in the parliament house after their ancient custom.

Item, statute for enclosures and intakes to be put in execution and that all intakes and enclosures since Anno iiii H[enry] VII to be pulled down except mountains, forest and parks.

Item, to be discharged of the quindene and taxes now granted by act of parliament.

Item, to have the parliament in a convenient place at Nottingham or

York and the same shortly summoned.

Item, the statute of the declaration of the Crown by will, that the same may be annulled and repealed.

Item, that it be enacted by authority of parliament that all recognisances, statutes, penalties new forfeit during the time of this commotion may be pardoned and discharged as well against the king as strangers.

Item, the privileges and rights of the church to be confirmed by act of parliament and priests not suffered by sword unless he be disgraced, a man to be saved by his book, sanctuary to save a man for all causes in extreme need and the church for 40 days and further according to the laws as they were used in the beginning of this king's days.

Item, the liberties of the church to have their old customs as the county palatine at Durham, Beverley, Ripon, St Peter of York, and such other by act of parliament.

Item, to have the statute that no man shall not will his lands to be repealed.

Item, that the statutes of treason for words and such like made since Anno 21 of our sovereign lord that now is to be in like wise repealed.

Item, that the common laws may have place as was used in the beginning of your grace's reign and that all injunctions may be clearly denied and not to be granted unless the matter be heard and determined in the Chancery.

Item, that no man upon subpoena is from Trent northwards to appear but at York or by attorney unless it be directed upon pain of allegiance and for like matters concerning the King.

Item, a remedy for escheators for finding of false offices and extortionate fees, taking which not be holden of the king and the promoters thereof.

(R. W. Hoyle, *The Pilgrimage of Grace and the Politics of the 1530s*, pp. 460-62. Taken from text 'A', TNA SP1/112, ff. 119-211.)

DOCUMENT 22: RELATIONS WITH ARCHBISHOP CRANMER, 1543
On the morrow, about nine of the clock before noon, the Council sent a

gentleman usher for the Archbishop, who when he came to the council chamber door, could not be let in, but of purpose, as it seemed was compelled there to wait among the pages, lackeys and serving men, all alone. Doctor Butts, the King's physician, resorting that way, and espying how my lord of Canterbury was handled, went to his highness and said: 'My Lord of Canterbury, if it please your grace, is well promoted, for now he is become a lackey or serving man, for yonder he standeth this half hour without the council chamber door amongst them.' 'It is not so,' quoth the King. 'I trow, nor the council hath so little discretion as to use the metropolitan of the realm in that sort, specially being one of their own number; but let them alone,' said the King, 'and we shall hear more soon.'

Anon the Archbishop was called into the council chamber, to whom it was alleged as before I rehearsed [the previously discussed preaching and teaching of heresy]. The Archbishop answered in like sort as the King had advised him; and in the end, when he perceived that no manner of persuasion or entreaty could serve, he delivered to them the king's ring, revoking his cause into the King's hands. The whole council being somewhat amazed, the Earl of Bedford [Lord John Russell, who did not become Earl of Bedford until 1550] with a loud voice, confirming his word with a solemn oath, said, 'When you first began this matter, my Lords, I told you what would come of it. Do you think that the King will suffer this man's finger to ache? Much more, I warrant you, he will defend his life against brabbling varlets. You do but cumber yourselves to hear tales and fables against him.' And so, incontinently upon receipt of the King's token, they all rose and carried to the King his ring, surrendering the matter ... into his own hands.

When they were all come into the King's presence, his highness with severe countenance said unto them, 'Ah my lords, I thought I had wiser men of my council than now I find you. What discretion was this in you thus to make the primate of the realm, and one of you in office, to wait at the council chamber door among serving men? You might have considered that he was a councillor as well as you, and you had no such commission of me so to handle him. I was content that you should try him as a councillor, not as mean subject. But now I well perceive that things be done against him maliciously; and if some of you might have had your minds, you would have tried him to the uttermost. But I do you all to wit, and protest, that if a prince may be beholden unto his subject' (and so solemnly laying his hand upon his breast, said) 'By the faith I owe to God, I take this man here, my lord of Canterbury, to be of all other a most faithful subject unto us, and one to whom we are much beholden,' giving him great commendation otherwise ... And with that every man caught him by the hand and made fair weather of altogethers ...

(Taken from the introduction to *The Writings and Disputations of Thomas Cranmer*, ed. J. E. Cox, 1844. Based on a narrative from John Foxe, *Acts and Monuments*.)

DOCUMENT 23: THE ACT OF SIX ARTICLES, 1539

Where the king's most excellent majesty is by God's law supreme head immediately under him of this whole church and congregation of England, intending the conservation of the same church and congregation in a true, sincere, and uniform doctrine of Christ's religion ... Hath therefore caused and commanded this his most High Court of parliament for sundry and many urgent causes and considerations to be at this time summoned, and also a synod and convocation of all archbishops, bishops and other learned men of the clergy of this his realm to be in like manner assembled; and forasmuch as in the said parliament, synod and convocation, there were certain articles, matters and questions proponed and set forth touching Christian religion ... The King's most royal majesty, most prudently pondering and considering that by occasion of variable and sundry opinions and judgements of the said articles, great discord and variance hath arisen as well among the clergy of this his realm as amongst a great number of vulgar people his loving subjects of the same, and being in a full hope and trust that a full and perfect resolution of the said articles should make a perfect concord and unity generally amongst all his loving and obedient subjects; of his most excellent goodness not only commanded that the said articles should deliberately and advisedly by his said archbishops, bishops and other learned men of his clergy be debated, argued and reasoned ...

As well by the consent of the King's highness as by the assent of the Lords spiritual and temporal and other learned men of the clergy in their convocation, and by the consent of the Commons in this present parliament assembled, it was and is finally resolved, accorded and agreed in manner and form following, that is to say:

First, that in the most blessed sacrament of the altar, by the strength and efficacy of Christ's mighty word, it being spoken by the priest, is present really, under the form of bread and wine, the natural body and blood of our Saviour Jesus Christ, conceived of the Virgin Mary, and that after the consecration there remaineth no substance of bread or wine, nor any other substance, but the substance of Christ, God and man:

Secondly, that the communion in both kinds is not necessary *ad salutem*, by the law of God to all persons, and that it is to be believed and not doubted of but in the flesh under form of bread is the very blood, and with the blood under form of wine is the very flesh, as well apart as though they were both together:

Thirdly, that priests after the order of priesthood received as afore may not marry by the law of God.

Fourthly, that vows of chastity or widowhood by man or woman made to God advisedly ought to be observed by the law of God, and that it exempteth them from other liberties of Christian people which without that they might enjoy:

Fifthly, that it is meet and necessary that private masses be continued and admitted in this the King's English Church and Congregation as whereby good Christian people ordering themselves accordingly do receive both Godly and goodly consolations and benefits, and it is agreeable also to God's law:

Sixthly, that auricular confession is expedient and necessary to be retained and continued, used and frequented, in the church of God ...

It is therefore ordained and enacted by the King our sovereign lord, the Lords spiritual and temporal and the commons in this present parliament assembled and by authority of the same ...

1. Any who after 12 July 1539 in word, writing or printing, publish, preach, teach, say, affirm, declare, dispute, argue or hold contrary to the first article, as well as their supporters, shall be guilty of heresy and burned.

2. Any who preach, teach, or affirm publicly contrary to the other five articles, or any priest, who having vowed chastity, shall marry shall be guilty of felony without benefit of clergy.

3. And any who shall otherwise maintain (in speech, writing, printing (etc.) opinions contrary to the other five articles shall forfeit all their property and be imprisoned at the King's pleasure; for a second offence they shall be guilty of felony.

(Statute 31 Henry VIII, c.14. *Statutes of the Realm*, III, pp. 739-43)

DOCUMENT 24: PROCLAMATION LIMITING THE READING OF SCRIPTURE, 1539

... And over this, his majesty straightly chargeth and commandeth that no person, except such as be curates or graduates in any of the universities of Oxford or Cambridge, or such as be, or shall be admitted to preach by the King's license or by his Vice-Regent or by any bishop of the realm, shall teach or preach the Bible or New Testament, nor expound the mysteries thereof to any other: nor that any person or persons shall openly read the Bible or New Testament in the English tongue in any churches or chapels with any loud or high voices, during the time of Divine service or of celebrating or saying of masses, and use that time in reading or praying with peace and silence, as good Christian men ought to do, upon the like pains as is afore rehearsed.

And also, his highness is pleased and contented that such as can read in the English tongue shall and may quietly and reverently read the Bible and New Testament by themselves at all times and places convenient for their own instruction and edification, to increase thereby godliness and virtuous living; and if they shall happen to stand in any doubt of any text or sentence in the reading thereof, to beware to take heed of their own presumptions and arrogant expositions of the letter, but resort humbly to such as be learned in Holy Scripture for their instruction in that behalf.

Finally his highness signifieth to all and singular his loving and obedient subjects, that his majesty was, nor is, compelled by God's word to set forth the scripture in English to all his lay subjects, but of his own liberty and goodness was and is pleased that his said loving subjects should have and read the same in convenient places and times, to the only intent to bring them from their old ignorance and blindness to virtuous living and godliness, to God's glory and honour, and not to make and take occasion of sedition or division by reason of the same.

Wherefore his majesty chargeth and commandeth all his said subjects to use the Holy Scripture in English according to his Godly purpose and gracious intent, as they would avoid his most high displeasure and indignation, beside the pains above remembered.

(P. L. Hughes and J. F. Larkin, *Tudor Royal Proclamations*, I (1964), pp. 284-6)

DOCUMENT 25: HENRY VIII AS KING OF IRELAND, 1541
Eustace Chapuys to the Emperor, 16 July 1541.

Nothing important has happened here since my last [2 July]. Some days ago the King ordered the estates of that portion of Ireland which is now under his rule to be convoked for the purpose of communicating to them, among other things, that he wishes and intends to set up under the names 'The Kingdom of Ireland' that part of the country where his lordship and rule are at present obeyed; and consequently to call and entitle himself King of Ireland; in expectation of which new title all business has for some days been suspended in the Chancery, as well as in the Exchequer court, in order that all of a sudden, and conjointly as it were, the King's name may appear decorated with his new title 'King of England and Ireland' in all Letters Patent, provisions etc., emanating from these two officers, and that by that means the news may be spread and circulated in every quarter.

(*Calendar of State Papers, Spanish*, VI, (p. 173)

DOCUMENT 26: PROCLAMATION DECLARING WAR OF FRANCE, 1543
2 August 1543

Forasmuch as by credible means it hath been declared to the king's majesty that the French King, omitting the duty and office of a good Christian prince (which is much to be lamented) hath not only by a long time and season aided the Great Turk, common enemy to Christendom, and also by sundry ways and means encouraged, procured, and incited, and daily procureth the said Turk, to arraise and assemble great armies and forces of war to enter and invade the same, which daily the said Turk attempteth and putteth in execution, to the great trouble, perturbation, and molestation of all good Christian princes and their subjects, and to the peril and danger of the state of Christian religion and imminent destruction of the universal weal and quiet of all Christendom, if good and godly kings and princes with the aid and assistance of all Christian people, should not speedily provide for the defence and relief of the same: but also the said French King, forgetting the great kindness, gratuitous and manifold benefits exhibited and ministered to him by the King's most royal majesty, our sovereign lord, by sundry ways and means in his great and extreme necessity, hath by a long season unkindly witholden and withdrawn from the King's highness his yearly pension, contrary to his liege oath and promise made for the same. The arrest whereof, besides the perpetual payment, amounteth to great sums of money. And although the King's most royal majesty hath been by a long time in good hope and trust that the said French King with gentle and friendly admonitions (which hath not lacked) would not only have desisted from intelligence with the said Turk, but also paid and satisfied the said pension. Yet nevertheless his highness now perceiving that the said French King will not be induced by any gentle means to honesty and reason, but still persist and be obstinate against his liege fidelity, oath, and honour, most especially concerning the common cause of Christendom; and next weighing his majesty's just title to the crown of France and other dukedoms and dominions unjustly withholden by the said French King, for recompense whereof the said pension was granted: hath therefore entered into a most Christian and straight league and amity with his good brother and perpetual ally the Emperor's majesty, who, joined together as well for the causes aforesaid as for other good grounds and occasions touching their private affairs, have intimated war to the same French King, he first refusing to receive their heralds which were sent to him to offer honourable and reasonable conditions of peace, which conditions have also been declared to the French King's ambassador here resident, and no convenient nor reasonable answer made to the same; by reason whereof the emperor's and King's majesties, being assuredly knit and constantly joined together. Intend jointly to proceed in the wars against the said French King, and never to cease the same until he shall be enforced, not only to desist from the Turk and all his factions but also yield and render to either of them all such rights, things, and recompenses as to honour, reason, honesty and equity shall appertain.

Wherefore like as the King's majesty our sovereign lord hath thought meet to notify the premises unto all and singular his most loving and obedient subjects, so his highness, by virtue of this his majesty's proclamation doth declare the said French King to be his highness' enemy, giving licence and authority to every his said subjects to use the said French King, and all those which depend upon him, to their most advantage and commodity, as his majesty's enemies, as hath in such like cases heretofore been used and accustomed.

(P. L. Hughes and J. F. Larkin, *Tudor Royal Proclamations*, I, pp. 320-21)

DOCUMENT 27: THE SUCCESSION ACT OF 1543

Sithens the making of the which Act [25 Henry VIII, c.22] the King's majestie hath one only issue of his body lawfully begotten betwixt his highness and his said late wife Queen Jane, the noble and excellent Prince Edward, whom Almighty God long preserve ...

Recognising and knowledging also that it is the only pleasure and will of Almighty God how long his highness or his said entirely beloved son Prince Edward shall live, and whether the said Prince shall have heirs of his body lawfully begotten or not, or whether his highness shall have heirs begotten and procreated between his majesty and his said most dear and entirely beloved wife Queen Catherine that now is, or any lawful heirs and issue of his own body begotten by any other his lawful wife ...

His majesty therefore thinketh it convenient before his departure beyond the seas that it be enacted by his highness with the assent of the Lords spiritual and temporal and the Commons in this present parliament assembled, and by authority of the same ...

That in case it shall happen the King's majesty and the said excellent prince his yet only son Prince Edward and heir apparent to decease without heirs of either of their bodies lawfully begotten (as God defend), so that there be no such heirs male or female of either of their two bodies to have and inherit the said Imperial Crown and other his dominions ... Then the said Imperial Crown and all other the premises shall be to the Lady Mary the King's highness daughter, and to the heirs of the body of the same Lady Mary lawfully begotten, with such conditions as by his highness shall be limited by his letters patent under his great seal, or by his majesties last will in writing signed with his most gracious hand: and for default of such issue the said Imperial Crown and other the premises shall be to the Lady Elizabeth, the King's second daughter, and to the heirs of the body of the said Lady Elizabeth lawfully begotten, with such conditions as shall be limited by his letters patent under his great seal, or by his highness last will in writing signed with his most gracious hand.

... that then and from thenceforth for lack of heirs of the several bodies of the King's majesty and of the said Lord Prince and of the said Lady Mary lawfully begotten, the said Imperial Crown and other the premises shall be and come to such person or persons of such estate or estates as the King's highness by his letters patent under his great seal or by his last will in writing signed with his majesties hand shall limit and appoint ...

(Statute 35 Henry VIII, c.1, *Statutes of the Realm*, III, p. 955)

DOCUMENT 28: PROVIDING THE DEATH PENALTY FOR DESERTERS, 1545
Proclamation, 24 January 1545

Forasmuch as the mariners and soldiers serving in the king's majesty's ships have in times past, and yet continually do, use not only unlawfully to depart from their ships unto the towns where they have and do arrive without any licence or leave of their admiral or captain, and tarrying a-land most ungodly and unlawfully using themselves contrary to the King's highness' laws, spending his majesty's money and victuals in vain, by means whereof his majesty's enemies have done divers exploits, enormities and hurts to divers his majesty's loving and true subjects within this his realm (in defence whereof his majesty to his great charge hath set forth his said ships), but also contrary to the most just laws of his grace's realm the said mariners and soldiers do run and steal away from the said ships, taking the King's wages, prests and conduct money to their most extreme perils; by which means, contrary to the King's majesty's expectation and trust, his said ships are constrained for want of men to lie still in the harbours and docks, neither being able to do any enterprise themselves nor yet to defend the King's majesty's people travelling in the seas, without speedy redress whereof great danger is like to ensue.

His majesty's pleasure and strait commandment is that no mariner nor soldier nor any other able person, unless he be sick or hurt, serving or pressed to serve in any of his majesty's ships, do after this present proclamation proclaimed, depart or go from their ships without testimonial signed with their captain's hands, to any place of the land, neither for victual, water, nor any other necessaries, nor for any other lawful or unlawful occasion, upon pain of death. And that no manner of person or persons shall retain into their houses, hide or succour the said mariner, soldiers, or any other person or persons pertaining or belonging to any of the King's majesty's ships upon pain of the King's highness' most grievous displeasure, loss of their goods and imprisonment of their bodies. And that all mayors, bailiffs, and constables of all towns, ports, and boroughs do see this proclamation thoroughly executed and used as they will answer to the contrary at their most extreme perils. And that no mariner or soldier so by his captain licensed to come to the land do bring with him any manner of weapon upon pain of three days imprisonment.
(P. L. Hughes and J. F. Larkin, *Tudor Royal Proclamations*, I, pp. 346-7)

DOCUMENT 29: SALVAGING THE *MARY ROSE*, 1545

The Duke of Suffolk to Sir William Paget, 1 August 1545. [Extracts]

... And as concerning the Mary Rose, we have consulted and spoken together with them that have taken upon them to recover her, who desireth to have for the saving of her such necessaries as is mentioned in a schedule herein enclosed. Not doubting, God willing, but they shall have all things ready accordingly, so that shortly she shall be saved ...

[Enclosure]

A remembrance of things necessary for the recovery, with the help of God, of the Mary Rose,

First, 2 of the greatest hulks that may be gotten.

More, the hulk that rideth within the haven.

Item, 4 of the greatest hoys within the haven.

Item, 5 of the greatest cables that may be had.

Item, 10 great hawsers.

Item, 10 new capstans with 20 pulleys.

Item, 50 pulleys bound with iron.

Item, 5 dozen ballast baskets.

Item, 40 lb of tallow.

Item, 30 Venetians, mariners, and one Venetian carpenter.

Item, 60 English mariners to attend upon them.

Item, A great quantity of cordage of all sorts.

Item, Symond, patron and master in the foist doth agree that all things must be had for the purpose abovesaid.

(*Letters and Papers*, XX, ii, no. 2. Original TNA SP1/205, ff. 1, 5.)

DOCUMENT 30: HENRY VIII's WILL, 1546

30 December 1546

Remembering the great benefits given him by Almighty God, and trusting that every Christian who dies in steadfast faith, and endeavours if he have licence to do such good deeds and charitable works as scripture commands, is ordained by Christ's passion to eternal life, Henry VIII makes such a will as he trusts shall be acceptable to God, Christ and the whole company of heaven, and satisfactory to all godly brethren on earth.

Rejecting his old life, and resolved never to return to the like, he humbly bequeaths his soul to God, who in the person of his son redeemed it ...

As to the succession of the Crown, it shall go to Prince Edward and the heirs of his body. In default to Henry's children by his present wife, Queen Catherine, or any future wife. In default to his daughter Mary and the heirs of her body, on condition that she shall not marry without the written and sealed consent of a majority of the surviving members of the privy council appointed by him to his son Prince Edward [Then to] Elizabeth on like condition In default to the heirs of the body of the Lady Frances, oldest daughter of his late sister the French Queen. In default to those of the Lady Eleanor, second daughter of the said French Queen, and in default to his right heirs. Either Mary or Elizabeth failing to observe the conditions aforesaid, shall forfeit all right to the succession ...

[Names of executors]

To his son Edward he gives the succession of his realms of England and Ireland, the title of France, and all his dominions, and also all his plate, household stuff, artillery, ordnance, ships, money and jewels, save such portions as shall satisfy this will; charging his said son to be ruled as regarding marriage and all affairs by the aforesaid councillors until he has completed his eighteenth year ...

Bequeaths to his daughters, Mary and Elizabeth, marriage to any outward potentate, £10,000 each in money, plate etc., or more at his executors' discretion; and meanwhile from the hour of his death each shall have £3,000 to live upon, at the ordering of ministers to be appointed by the foresaid councillors.

The Queen his wife shall have £3,000 in plate, jewels and stuff, besides what she shall please to take of what she has already , and further to receive in money £1,000 besides the enjoyment of her jointure ...

Westminster palace, 30th December 38 Henry VIII [signed with the stamp at the beginning and the end]

Signed by witnesses: John Gates, E. Harman, William Sandbroke, Henry Neville, Richard Coke, David Vincent, Patric, George Owen, Thomas Wendy, Robert Huyke, W. Clerk.

(*Letters and Papers*, XXI, ii, no. 634)

NOTES

INTRODUCTION: THE HISTORIOGRAPHY OF A KING

1. *Holbein and the Court of Henry VIII* (1978). A catalogue of the exhibition at the Queen's Gallery, Buckingham Palace. Paul Ganz, *The Paintings of Hans Holbein* (1950).

2. *Materials for a History of the Reign of Henry VII*, ed. William Campbell (1873-7), II, pp. 541-2.

3. S. B. Chrimes, *Henry VII* (1972), pp. 66-7.

4. *Letters and Papers ... of Henry VII*, ed. James Gairdner (1861-3), II, p. 403.

5. Chrimes, *Henry VII*, p. 93.

6. Sydney Anglo, *Spectacle, Pageantry and Early Tudor Policy* (1969), pp. 10-20.

7. Charles Cruikshank, *Henry VIII and the Invasion of France* (1990), pp. 135-6. A. Hocquet, *Tournai et l'occupation anglaise* (1900).

8. Alistair Fox, *Politics and Literature in the Reigns of Henry VII and Henry VIII* (1989), p. 237. David Starkey, *The Reign of Henry VIII: Personalities and Politics* (1985), pp. 67-81.

9. Edward Hall, *The Union of the Two Noble and Illustre Famelies of Lancastre and York* (1548), f.67v.

10. Fox, *Politics and Literature*, pp. 135-6.

11. David Starkey, *Henry: the Virtuous Prince* (2008).

12. G. R. Elton, *Policy and Police* (1972), pp. 176-80.

13. Sharon L. Jansen, *Political Protest and Prophecy under Henry VIII* (1991), pp. 39-49.

14. Thomas F. Mayer, *Reginald Pole: Prince and Prophet* (2000), pp. 13-61.

15. Ceri Sullivan, 'Oppressed by the Force of Truth', Robert Persons edits John Foxe, *John Foxe, An Historical Perspective*, ed. D. Loades (1999), pp. 154-166.

16. Philip Hughes, *The Reformation in England*, I (1956), pp. 31-85.

17. J. Scarisbrick, *The Reformation and the English People* (1984). E. Duffy, *The Stripping of the Altars* (1992).

18. D. Loades, 'John Foxe and Henry VIII', *The John Foxe Bulletin*, I, i, 2002, pp. 5-12.

19. *Holbein and the Court of Henry VIII*, p.130. 'The figure of Soloman is a portrait of King Henry VIII, the first known example of Solomon being given a contemporary likeness in such a representation'.

20. A. G. Dickens, *The English Reformation* (1964), pp. 122-38.

21. G. Bernard, *The King's Reformation* (2005).

22. Fox, *Politics and Literature*, pp. 228-32.

23. Hall, *The Union of the Two Noble and Illustre Famelies*, sig.AAa2v.

24. Ibid, ffs. Ll 12r-13r.

25. D. R. Kelley and D. H. Sacks, *The Historical Imagination in Early Modern Britain; History, Rhetoric and Fiction, 1500-1800* (1997). T. Betteridge, *Tudor Historians of the English Reformation, 1530-1583* (1999), p. 95.

26. Claire McEachern, 'Literature and National Identity', in *The Cambridge History of Early Modern English Literature*, ed. David Loewenstein and Janel Mueller (2002), p. 329.

27. J. A. Froude, *The History of England from the Fall of Wolsey to the Defeat of the Spanish Armada*, volumes 1-3 (1856).

28. A. F. Pollard, *Henry VIII* (1902).

29. G. R. Elton, *The Tudor Revolution in Government* (1953), p. 1.

30. Ibid, pp. 71-159.

31. G. R. Elton, *The Tudor Constitution* (1982), pp. 338-94.

32. J. J. Scarisbrick, *Henry VIII* (1968). D. Loades, *Henry VIII, Court, Church and Conflict* (2007).

33. Elton, *Tudor Revolution*, pp. 298-315.

34. Ibid, pp. 316-69. But see also J. A. Guy, 'The King's Council and Political Participation', in *Reassessing the Henrician Age*, ed. A. Fox and J. A. Guy (1986), pp. 59-85.

35. G. L. Harriss, 'Medieval Government and Statecraft', *Past and Present*, 24, 1963.

36. David Starkey, 'Intimacy and Innovation; the rise of the Privy Chamber, 1485-1547' in D. Starkey, ed., *The English Court from the Wars of the Roses to the Civil War* (1987), pp. 71-118.

37. Guy, 'The King's Council'.

38. Penry Williams, *The Tudor Regime* (1979), pp. 1-17.

39. G. R. Elton, *Thomas Cromwell* (1991).

40. J. Scarisbrick, *Henry VIII*, pp. 305-354, 500-02, 21-40, 424-57.

41. D. Loades, *Henry VIII*, pp. 72-3.

42. Scarisbrick, pp. 433-43. C. S. Knighton and D. Loades, 'Lord Admiral Lisle and the Invasion of Scotland, 1544' in *Naval Miscellany*, VII, ed. S. Rose, 2008, pp. 57-96.

43. H. M. Colvin, ed., *The History of the King's Works*, IV, 1485-1660, ii (1982).

44. Scarisbrick, pp. 241-304.

45. Daniel Eppley, *Defending the Royal Supremacy and Discerning God's Will in Tudor England* (2007).

46. Eric Ives, *The Life and Death of Anne Boleyn* (2004), pp. 16-17, 190-92.

47. Ibid, pp. 82-6.

48. Diarmaid MacCulloch, *Thomas Cranmer* (1996), pp. 243-53.

49. Ibid, pp. 301-2.

50. G. W. Bernard, *The King's Reformation*, pp. 228-42.

51. Ibid, pp. 445-54, 579-94.

52. L. B. Smith, *The Mask of Royalty* (1971), pp. 230-35.

53. Ibid, pp. 256-7.

54. *The Virtuous Prince*, p. 1.

55. *ODNB*.

56. L. B. Smith, *A Tudor Tragedy: the Life and Times of Catherine Howard* (1961), pp. 176-81.

57. Scarisbrick, *Henry VIII*, p. 526.

58. Denys Hay, ed., *The Anglica Historia of Polydore Vergil* (Camden Society, 74, 1950), p. 151.

1 THE PRINCE, 1491–1509

1. Margaret was fourteen when her son was born, and although she married twice more, he was to be her only child. Edmund had been created Earl of Richmond in 1452, at the age of twenty-two. He died (of natural causes) in December 1456.

2. For a full discussion of the circumstances of Owain Tudor's marriage, and of the forbidding of the succession to any children of the Swynford union, see Michael K. Jones and Malcolm Underwood, *The King's Mother* (1992) pp. 17-35. The validity of Owain Tudor's nuptials was never questioned at the time. T. Artemus Jones, 'Owen Tudor's marriage', *Bulletin of the Board of Celtic Studies*, XI, 1943, pp. 142-9.

3. S. B. Chrimes, *Henry VII*, (1972), pp. 19-22.

4. The fate of Lord Hastings served as a warning to those who questioned Richard's actions, like the Marquis of Dorset and Sir Edward Woodville. The absence of any party in favour of Edward, Earl of Warwick, the Duke of Clarence's son and Richard's nephew, is remarkable. He was later

described as a simpleton, but there is no evidence of that at the time. Charles Ross, *Richard III* (1981).

5. Buckingham may have been intending originally to put forward his own claim, derived from Thomas, Duke of Gloucester, Edward III's fourth son, but was dissuaded, perhaps by John Morton. Polydore Vergil, *Anglica Historia* (ed. Hay, 1950), p. 194.

6. Chrimes, *Henry VII*, pp. 22-3.

7. *Anglica Historia*, pp. 201-4.

8. *Rotuli Parliamentorum*, VI, cs. 3 (pp. 244-9), 5 (p. 250), 6 (pp. 250-1), 7, (p. 251). For a discussion of the significance of these acts, see Chrimes, *Henry VII*, Appendix C.

9. *Proces-verbaux des séances du Conseil de Regence du roi Charles VIII, August 1484 to January 1485*, ed. A. Bernier (1836); Collection de Documents Inedits, 128, 129, 164, 168.

10. Hall, *Chronicle*, p. 408.

11. S. B. Chrimes, 'The landing place of Henry of Richmond, 1485', *Welsh History Review*, 2, 1964, pp. 173-80.

12. Chrimes, *Henry VII*, p. 44.

13. *Anglica Historia*. Chrimes, *Henry VII*, pp. 48-9.

14. *Anglica Historia* (ed. Hay), p. 2. Edward was fifteen by this time.

15. G. Wickham Legg, *English Coronation Records* (1901), pp. 199-218.

16. P. R. Cavill, *The English Parliaments of Henry VII, 1485-1504* (2009), pp. 28-33.

17. 'The bull of Pope Innocent VIII', ed. J. Payne Collier, *Camden Miscellany*, I , 1847.

18. S. Anglo, *Spectacle, Pageantry and Early Tudor Policy* (1969), pp. 46-7.

19. *Calendar of the Patent Rolls*, 1485-1494, p.306, 24 April 1490. Grant to Katherine, 'late nurse to Arthur, the King's first born son' of an annuity of £20.

20. *Anglica Historia* (ed. Hay), pp. 12-26.

21. J. Gairdner, *Memorials of King Henry the Seventh* (Rolls Series, 1858), pp. 116, 241, 256, 260.

22. *Letters and Papers of the Reign of Henry VIII*, IV, no. 5791, 23 July 1529, but recording a conversation on 5 and 6 April 1527. TNA SP1/54, ff. 20-28.

23. *Cal. Pat.*, 1485-1494, p. 423. 5 April 1493.

24. *Cal. Pat.*, 1494-1509, p. 12. 12 September 1494.

25. Ibid, p. 26.

26. MS Cotton Julius B XII, f.91. Printed in J. Gairdner, *Letters and Papers Illustrative of the Reigns of Richard III and Henry VII* (Rolls Series, 1861-3), I, pp. 388-92.

27. Ibid. For children and their feeding, see F. G. Emmison, *Tudor Food and Pastimes* (1964), pp. 28-30.

28. The narrator added: 'How be it, hithe hathe nott ben comenly sien or els Sir Edward Darell schulde have had it …' *Letters and Papers … Henry VII*, Appendix VI, pp. 395-6.

29. David Starkey, *Henry, the Virtuous Prince* (2008).

30. Ibid. Apparently his handwriting was also very like that of his sister Mary.

31. TNA LC2/1/1, ff. 73-4. This list is for the distribution of black cloth for the funeral.

32. TNA E101 /4/6, p. 6. John Heron's Book of Payments, 1495-7.

33. J. Scarisbrick, *Henry VIII*, pp. 4-5.

34. John Skelton, *Works*, ed. Dyce (1843), I, p. 129.

35. Starkey, *Henry, the Virtuous Prince*. C. A. J. Armstrong, 'An Italian Astrologer at the court of Henry VII', in E. F. Jacob, ed., *Renaissance Studies* (1960).

36. *Letters and Papers … of Henry VII*, II, p. 57

37. Starkey, *Henry VIII*.

38. LC2/1/1, f.73.

39. W. Nelson, *John Skelton, Laureate* (1939), p. 75. Scarisbrick, *Henry VIII*, p. 5.

40. *Letters and Papers … Henry VIII*, IV, no. 5791. Testimony of Richard Fox. TNA SP1/54, ff. 20-28.

41. *The Chronicles of London*, ed. C. L. Kingsford (1905), p. 255. Chrimes, *Henry VII*, pp. 284-5.

42. *Letters and Papers … Henry VII*, Appendix B, p. 342. There was also a proposal for a match between the young Prince and the infant Eleanor, the daughter of King Philip. Thomas Lopez to

Emmanuel, King of Portugal, 10 October 1505. Ibid, p. 147.

43. *Calendar of State Papers, Spanish*, I, p. 351. T. Rymer, *Foedera, Conventiones etc.*, (1707-35), XIII, pp. 76-86.

44. From a document printed by John Leland, *De rebus Brittanicis collectanea*, ed. T. Hearne (1715), V, pp. 373-4.

45. N. H. Nicholas, *The Privy Purse Expenses of Elizabeth of York* (1830), p. 96.

46. *Memorials of King Henry VII*, ed. J. Gairdner (Rolls Series, 1858), pp. 223-39.

47. *Rotuli Parliamentorum*, VI, p. 522.

48. Charles, born 1500, later the Emperor Charles V, and Ferdinand, born 1502. For a brief sketch of the Castilian succession problem, see J. H. Elliott, *Imperial Spain, 1469-1716* (1963), pp. 127-8.

49. *Memorials of King Henry VII*, p. 260.

50. Ibid, p. 278. Chrimes, *Henry VII*, p. 288.

51. Garrett Mattingly, *Catherine of Aragon* (1963), p. 38.

52. Desiderius Erasmus, *Opus Epistolarum*, ed. P. S. and H. M. Allen (1906-58), I, no. 1. Scarisbrick, *Henry VIII*, p. 14.

53. Starkey, *Henry, the Virtuous Prince*.

54. *Opus Epistolarum*, V, no. 241. *Letters and Papers ... of Henry VIII*, IV, no. 5412.

55. *Correspondencia de Gutierre Gomez de Fuensalida*, ed. Duque de Berwick y de Alba (1907), p. 449.

56. An opinion expressed by Scarisbrick (p. 6), but for which there is no solid contemporary evidence.

57. BL Add. MS 59899. Payments made at Westminster by John Heron (1502-3), p. 16.

58. Anglo, *Spectacle, Pageantry and Early Tudor Policy*, pp. 108-9.

59. 'Here begynneth the Iustes of the moneth of maye ...' Printed in W. C. Hazlitt, *Remains of the Early Popular Poetry of England* (1864-6), II, pp. 109-30.

2. A RENAISSANCE KING, 1509–1511

1. S. Anglo, *The Great Tournament Roll of Westminster* (1968), p. 1.

2. G. R. Elton, 'Henry VII; rapacity and remorse', *Historical Journal*, I, 1958, pp. 21-39. J. P. Cooper, 'Henry VII's last years reconsidered', *HJ*, 2, 1959, pp. 103-129.

3. Edward Hall, *The Union ...* (1548), f.ii.

4. D. M. Brodie, 'Edmund Dudley: Minister of Henry VII', *Transactions of the Royal Historical Society*, 4th series, 15, 1932, pp. 133-61. M. R. Horowitz, 'Richard Empson, minister of Henry VII', *Bulletin of the Institute of Historical Research*, 55, 1982, pp. 35-49.

5. Hall, *Chronicle* (ed. 1806), p. 503.

6. Ibid, *Union*, f. vii.

7. Ibid, f. i.

8. This was the custom at all royal funerals. In fact the Lord Great Chamberlain (John de Vere, Earl of Oxford), the Treasurer of the Chamber (Sir John Heron), the Lord Steward (George Talbot, Earl of Shrewsbury), and the Treasurer of the Household (Sir Thomas Lovell) all retained their positions. Sir Richard Guildford and Giles, Lord Daubenny, were already dead.

9. Scarisbrick, *Henry VIII*, p. 23 and n. Henry commissioned a life of Henry V by Titus Livius, which was translated out of Latin into English in 1513, and edited by C. L. Kingsford in 1911.

10. *Cal. Ven.*, II, no. 1.

11. Ibid, II, no. 11.

12. *Cal. Span.*, II, no. 27, Ferdinand to Catherine, 18 November 1509. Ibid, no. 36.

13. *Cal. Ven.*, II, no. 22. 7 December 1510.

14. Scarisbrick, *Henry VIII*, pp. 24-7.

15. Luis Caroz to Ferdinand, 29 May 1510. *Cal. Span.*, II, no. 44. A failure to mention Warham suggests that his information was partial.

16. He included this information in a letter to Margaret of Savoy, dated 27 June 1509, referring to the 'old treaty' and his reluctance to disobey his father. *Letters and Papers*, I, no. 84.

17. *Correspondencia de ... Fuensalida*, 518 et seq. Garret Mattingly, *Catherine of Aragon*, pp. 93-5.

18. Mattingly, p. 98.

19. *Cal. Span.*, II, no. 27. This observation seems to have been typical of Ferdinand's devious approach to diplomacy.

20. M. A. E. Wood, *Letters of Royal and Illustrious Ladies* (1846), I, p. 158. Henry to Ferdinand (a letter of commendation for Gundisalvo Ferdinandus, the son of Dr De Puebla), *Letters and Papers*, I, no. 112.

21. Scarisbrick, *Henry VIII*, pp. 26-8.

22. In fact it mainly severed diplomatic relations between Paris and Rome, putting the French cardinals in a difficult position. Other princes largely ignored it, except when it was convenient to use it as weapon.

23. *Cal. Span.*, II, no. 56.

24. Scarisbrick, *Henry VIII*, p. 29.

25. Hall, *Union* ..., p. xxv. Poynings was Controller of the Household.

26. Ibid, p. xii.

27. Ibid.

28. F. C. Dietz, *English Government Finance, 1485-1558* (1964), pp. 86-7. Francis Bacon, writing in the early seventeenth century, believed that the surplus had been £1,800,000. Estimates nearer the time were a little more accurate – but not much. Henry went back to Parliament for a tenth and a fifteenth in 1512.

29. TNA SP1/2, f. 149. *Letters and Papers*, I, no. 1393.

30. D. M. Loades and C. S. Knighton, *Letters from the Mary Rose* (2002). Introduction.

31. N. A. M. Rodger, *The Safeguard of the Sea* (1997), p. 477.

32. Anglo, *Tournament Roll*, p. 11.

33. *The Mary Rose, Your Noblest Shippe*, ed. Peter Marsden (2009), pp. 184, 214.

34. H. Schubert, 'The first cast iron guns made in England', *Journal of the Iron and Steel Institute*, 146, 1942.

35. W. Caxton, *Book of the Order of Chivalry* (1484), ed. A. J. P. Byles (EETS, 1926), pp. 121-4.

36. Henry Stafford was the brother of the Duke of Buckingham; William Courtenay was the son of Edward Courtenay, Earl of Devon, who had been attainted on his father's death in 1509; Margaret Pole was the daughter of George, Duke of Clarence, one of whose titles had been Salisbury.

37. Alan Young, *Tudor and Jacobean Tournaments* (1987), pp. 14-5.

38. Anglo, *Tournament Roll*, pp. 40-2.

39. Ibid, p. 34.

40. Anglo, *Spectacle, Pageantry* ... p. 111.

41. Anglo, *The Tournament Roll*, p. 49. Hall, *Chronicle* (1806), p. 513.

42. *Tournament Roll*, pp. 51-8. TNA E36/217, ff. 41-5.

43. Hall, *Chronicle* (1806), p. 520.

44. Ibid, pp. 533-4. TNA E36/217, ff. 163-9.

45. Erasmus, *Opus Epistolarum*, I, p. 450.

46. Mattingly, *Catherine of Aragon*, pp. 116-7, 124-5.

47. *Cal. Ven.*, II, no. 63.

48. *De Fructu qui ex Doctina Percipitur*, by Richard Pace. Edited and translated by Frank Manley and Richard Sylvester (1967), p. 109.

49. William Roper, *The Lyfe of Sir Thomas More, knight*, ed. Hitchcock (EETS, 1935), p. 11.

50. *Letters and Papers*, II, 2401, 3455. Scarisbrick, *Henry VIII*, p. 15.

51. Mattingly, *Catherine of Aragon*, p. 99.

52. Hall, *Union* (1548), p. viii.

53. TNA E101 416/15, ff. 27-32. N. Samman, 'The Henrician Court during Cardinal Wolsey's Ascendancy, *c.*1514-1529' (University of Wales, Bangor, PhD, 1988), pp. 8-9.

54. Ibid.

55. *Cal. Span.* II, no. 43.

56. Mattingly, *Catherine of Aragon*, pp. 109-10.

57. *Letters and Papers*, I, no. 474. Luis Caroz to Almazon, 28 May 1510. TNA PRO31/11/5, f. 122.

58. Ibid.
59. Henry Ellis, *Original Letters Illustrative of English History* (1824, 1827, 1836), I, p. 88.
60. A. Kelly, 'Eleanor of Aquitaine and her courts of love', *Speculum*, 12, 1937.

3. THE KING AT WAR, 1511–1514

1. Alfred Spont, *The French War of 1512-13* (Navy Records Society, 1897), pp. 1-2. Documents taken from the *Lettres de Louis XII*, iii, pp. 149, 166.
2. Peter Gwyn, *The King's Cardinal: the rise and fall of Thomas Wolsey* (1990), p. 3. *ODNB*, Thomas Wolsey.
3. *Letters and Papers*, Volume I, preface. He had been paid £50 for 2,000 masses in conjunction with 'Master Fisher' on 25 February. Not even the industrious Wolsey could have sung 10,000 masses in less than three months.
4. Ibid.
5. George Cavendish, 'The Life and Death of Cardinal Wolsey', in *Two Early Tudor Lives*, ed. R. S. Sylvester and D. P. Harding (1962), p. 13.
6. T. Rymer, *Foedera etc.*, (1741), vi, 30b.
7. Ibid. Spont, *French War*, p. xii.
8. *Letters and Papers*, I, no. 244, dated 20 November 1509. BL Cotton Titus A xiii, f. 186. All the spears were bound to keep their 'habiliaments of war' with them at all times, and to take an oath of allegiance to the king. Spont, p. xii. The Spears were allowed to lapse in 1515.
9. Alain de Chantrezac to the Lieutenant of La Tremoille, 20 May 1512. Bibliotheque Nationale MSS fr.3925, f. 113. Spont, *French War*, pp. 17-18.
10. Ibid, p. 3.
11. R. Grafton, *Chronicle* (ed. 1809), pp. 244-5.
12. Spont, *French War*, pp. xxii-iii.
13. Grafton, *Chronicle*, p. 250. Sir Thomas Knyvett was a favourite jousting companion of the King.
14. Spont, *French War*, p. xxvii. One Rigault de Berquetot, the captain of the *Nef de Dieppe*, subsequently brought charges of cowardice against de Clermont, and he was relieved of his command. Ibid, p. 65.
15. *Letters and Papers*, I, no. 1182. Marino Sanuto, *Diarii* (Venice, 1897), XIV, p. 267. Scarisbrick, *Henry VIII*, pp. 29-30. The English were 'much encouraged' in this campaign by the issue of a special papal indulgence to those taking part.
16. Hall, *Chronicle*, p. 528.
17. Numerous attempts have been made to fathom Ferdinand's mind at this point. Scarisbrick, *Henry VIII*, p. 29.
18. *Letters and Papers*, I, no. 1458.
19. *Cal. Span.*, II, no. 72. Martin de Muxica to Ferdinand.
20. Ibid, nos 68, 70.
21. Ibid, no. 97. The original treaty had been signed on 19 November 1512. Ibid, no. 73.
22. *Letters and Papers*, I, ii, no. 1916. TNA PRO31/11/5, f. 230. Instructions from Ferdinand for a secret mission to France, in which he makes it clear that no other prince has been consulted.
23. BL Cotton MS Caligula D.VI, ff. 101-3. *Letters and Papers*, I, i, no. 1698. Information which he elaborated in a second letter on 5 April. TNA, SP1/3, ff. 149-50. *L & P*, I, ii, no. 1748.
24. Spont, *French War*, p. xxii. It was thought that he was planning to attack Falmouth. John Wilshire to Henry VIII, 20 March 1513. BL Cotton MSS, App. L. f. 40.
25. He had been appointed admiral for this voyage on 25 January 1513. *L & P*, I, ii, no. 3830. TNA SP1/3, f. 135. Clermont retained his overall title.
26. Spont, *French War*, p. xxxvi.
27. Edward Echyngham to Wolsey, 5 May 1513. BL Cotton MSS Caligula D.VI, f. 107. Spont, pp. 145-54.
28. Ibid.
29. BL Cotton MSS Caligula D.VI, ff. 104-6. Thomas, Lord Howard, to the King, 7 May 1513. D. Loades and C. S. Knighton, *Letters from the Mary Rose* (2002), pp. 36-9.

30. Polydore Vergil, *Anglica Historia*, ed. Hay, p.197. Mattingly, *Catherine of Aragon*, pp. 119-20.

31. Erasmus, *Opus Epistolarum*, IV, p. 525 etc., Henry is alleged to have said 'Let every man have his doctor. This is mine.'

32. *Statutes of the Realm*, III, pp. 43-4. Hughes and Larkin, *Tudor Royal Proclamations*, I, pp. 94-9.

33. Charles Cruickshank, *Henry VIII and the Invasion of France* (1990), pp. 6-13. *Cal. Ven.*, II, no. 225. In addition to these preparations, Henry had Edmund de la Pole summarily executed, in case he should pose a threat to the succession in the event of the King's death. Edmund had been attainted as far back as 1506, and his brother was serving in the French army. Indeed Louis contemplated recognising Richard de la Pole as the lawful King of England, which provides some justification for Henry's action.

34. 'Un breve inedito di Giulio II per la Investitura del Regno di Francia ad Enrico VIII d'Inghilterra'. *Arch. Della R. Societa Romana di Storia Patria*, xix, 1896, pp. 425 et seq.

35. Cruickshank, *Invasion of France*, p. 17.

36. Ibid, p. 27.

37. Hall, *Chronicle*, p. 542.

38. *Letters and Papers*, I, ii, no. 2053 (2). TNA E101/62/11. The King's household numbered altogether 2,039 men, of whom admittedly 600 were the guard. By way of comparison, the ordnance 'with the retinue of the same' numbered 1,173.

39. Cruickshank, *Invasion of France*, p. 77.

40. Ibid, pp. 103-5.

41. *Memoires de messier Martin du Bellay, seigneur de Langey …* (1786), p. 24.

42. Scarisbrick, *Henry VIII*, p. 36.

43. Cruickshank, *Invasion of France*, pp. 119-20.

44. *Cal. Ven.*, II, no. 316.

45. Hall, *Chronicle*, p. 566.

46. Cruickshank, *Invasion of France*, pp. 136-7. Poynings was by this time a man of vast experience, who had been at various times Lord Warden of the Cinque Ports, Lord Deputy of Ireland and Governor of Calais. The government put in place for Tournai was modelled on that of Calais.

47. Spont, *French War*, pp. xvi-xvii.

48. Gervase Phillips, *The Anglo-Scottish Wars, 1513-1550* (1999), pp. 109-32.

49. Ibid.

50. M. C. Fissel, *English Warfare, 1511-1642* (2001), pp. 21-2. *Letters and Papers*, I, ii, no. 2246. An account of the battle.

51. It was not perhaps tactful of her to add 'this battle hath been to your grace and all your realm the greatest honour that could be, and more than ye should win the crown of France …' BL Cotton Vespasian F.III, f. 15.

52. *Letters and Papers*, I, ii, no. 2366. TNA SP1/5, ff. 76-7.

53. *Letters and Papers*, I, iii, no. 5140. TNA C76/194, m.11. Peter Gwyn, *The King's Cardinal*, pp. 15-16.

54. G. E. Cockayne, *The Complete Peerage*, ed. Vicary Gibbs and others (1910-59).

55. Spont, *French War*, pp. xlv-vi. *Letters and Papers*, I, iii, no. 5021.

56. Scarisbrick, *Henry VIII*, pp. 53-4.

57. *Cal. Span.* II, no.183. Text dated 7 August. W. C. Richardson, *Mary Tudor; the White Queen* (1970).

58. *Cal. Span.*, II, no. 192. Scarisbrick, *Henry VIII*, pp. 55-6.

59. There were rumours in the diplomatic corps that Henry would repudiate his Spanish wife and marry a French princess, but they were never more than rumours. *Cal. Ven.*, II, no. 479.

60. During the whole of his period in power, from 1514 to 1529, Wolsey planned his itinerary to be close to the King – usually no more than a day's ride away – because of Henry's unpredictability in this respect. David Loades, *Cardinal Wolsey, c.1472-1530: Tudor Statesman and Chancellor* (2008), p. 7. N. Samman, 'The Henrician Court during Wolsey's Ascendancy', pp. 396-441.

61. Cruickshank, *Invasion of France*, pp. 135-6.

62. Loades, *Cardinal Wolsey*, loc. cit.

63. Bainbridge's death was suspected to be by poison, but the suspected party was Sylvestro de' Gigli, the curial official who was also Bishop of Worcester, not Wolsey. D. S. Chambers, *Cardinal Bainbridge in the Court of Rome, 1509-1514* (1965).

64. J. H. Lupton, *The Life of John Colet* (1887), pp. 293 et seq. D. Wilkins, *Concilia* (1737), iii, p. 651.

65. A. G. Dickens, *The English Reformation* (1964), pp. 90-1.

66. Ibid, pp. 93-4.

67. There are numerous accounts of the 'Hunne affair'. For a recent summary, see Gwyn, *The King's Cardinal*, pp. 34-41.

68. A. Ogle, *The Tragedy of the Lollard's Tower* (1949).

69. Ibid.

70. According to the London chronicler, Charles Wriothesley. *A Chronicle of England*, ed. W. D. Hamilton (Camden Society, new series, xi, 1875), p. 9.

71. C. S. Knighton and D. Loades, *The Anthony Roll* (2000), p. 119.

72. D. Loades, *The Tudor Navy* (1992), pp. 67-8.

73. Ibid.

74. Gwyn, *The King's Cardinal*, pp. 10-19.

4. A PRINCE AT PEACE, 1514–1522

1. *Cal. Span*, II, 192. *L & P*, I, nos 3472, 3476. Scarisbrick, *Henry VIII*, pp. 55-6.

2. *L & P*, II, preface, no. 228.

3. Ibid.

4. *L & P*, II, no. 227. Polydore Vergil, *Anglica Historia*, p. 229. W. C. Richardson, *Mary Tudor; the White Queen*, pp. 128-85. S. J. Gunn, *Charles Brandon, Duke of Suffolk, 1484-1545* (1988), pp. 35-6.

5. *L & P*, II, I, nos 224, 436. TNA C54/383, m.17, Gunn, *Brandon*, p. 38.

6. BL Galba B V, ff. 7v. *L & P*, II, no. 539.

7. Scarisbrick, *Henry VIII*, p. 58. Margaret's second husband, the Earl of Angus, accompanied her into England, but returned to Scotland ahead of her.

8. Ibid.

9. For Pace's negotiation with the Swiss, see Jervis Wegg, *Richard Pace* (1932), pp. 65 et seq. *L & P*, II, no. 1466.

10. BL, Cotton MS Vitellius B xix, f. 231. *L & P*, II, no. 1965. Scarisbrick, *Henry VIII*, p. 62 and note.

11. *L & P*, II, nos 2271, 2272.

12. Negotiations with the Emperor 'touching the friendship between the Kings of Castile and France ...' September 1516. *L & P*, II, no. 2405.

13. Thomas Spinelly to Wolsey, 15 August 1515. *L & P*, II, no. 2279. Tunstall to Wolsey, 13 September. Ibid, no. 2358.

14. Negotiations with the Emperor, *L & P*, II, no. 2405.

15. Scarisbrick, *Henry VIII*, p. 69. The Emperor's scheme involved the Emperor of Abyssinia, the King of Georgia and the Shah of Persia. Henry mocked it.

16. BL Cotton MS Vitellius B iii, f. 245. *L & P*, II, no. 4034.

17. The original draft of this scheme, dated January 1518, can be found in TNA SP1/17, f. 13. *L & P*, II, no. 4357.

18. *L & P*, II, nos 4356, 4401, 4440-1, 4462.

19. T. Rymer, *Foedera, Conventiones etc.*, XIII, pp. 624 et seq.

20. *Cal. Ven.*, II, nos 1085, 1088.

21. For a full consideration of this aspect of Wolsey's work, see J. A. Guy, *The Cardinal's Court* (1977).

22. Samman, 'The Henrician Court', p. 342.

23. David Starkey, 'Intimacy and innovation', in *The English Court from the Wars of the Roses to the Civil War*, ed. D. Starkey (1987), p. 102.

24. Richard Grafton, *Chronicle* (1809), p. 290.

25. Ibid, p. 291.
26. Sebastian Guistiniani to the Doge and Senate, 5 May 1517. *L & P*, II, no. 3204. According to this report, 5,000 armed men were put into the City.
27. Ibid. According to Polydore Vergil 'John Lincoln and four of his associates were put to death', the rest being pardoned. *Anglica Historia*, p. 245.
28. *Cal. Ven.*, II, no. 887.
29. Garrett Mattingly, *Catherine of Aragon*, p. 132.
30. Ibid, p. 127.
31. Samman, 'Henrician Court', p. 147. B. Murphy, *Bastard Prince* (2001), pp. 24-6.
32. Ibid, pp. 26-7.
33. Ibid, p. 31. Mattingly, *Catherine of Aragon*, p. 132.
34. Statute 15 Henry VIII, c.34. *Statutes of the Realm*, III, p. 280, 'An Act concerning Elizabeth Tailboys'.
35. E. W. Ives, *The Life and Death of Anne Boleyn* (2004), pp. 15-16.
36. This news was conveyed in a letter to Cardinal Campeggio, which arrived on 19 February. Guasti, 'I manoscritti Torrigiani donati al R. Archivo di Stato di Firenze', *Archivo Storico Italiano*, 3rd series, xxv (1887), p. 383. Scarisbrick, *Henry VIII*, p. 99 and note.
37. Ibid, p. 102.
38. *L & P*, III, no. 432.
39. Jocelyne G. Russell, *The Field of Cloth of Gold* (1969), p. 16.
40. Ibid, pp. 18-19.
41. One Venetian observed, 'These sovereigns are not at peace … they hate each other cordially'. *Cal. Ven.*, III, no. 108.
42. For a full description of these preparations, see Russell, *Field of Cloth of Gold*, pp. 22-47.
43. The score sheets which survive from the jousts are hard to decipher in terms of results, and this must surely have been deliberate. Bodleian Ashmole MS 1116, f. 108.
44. *Cal. Ven.*, III, no. 95.
45. TNA SP1 /21, f. 23. *L & P*, III, 936.
46. Scarisbrick, *Henry VIII*, pp. 81-3.
47. *L & P*, III, nos 1876, 1877, 1884, 3389.
48. P. Gwyn, *The King's Cardinal* (1990), pp. 156, 551.
49. BL Cotton MS Vitellius B xx, f. 98. *L & P*, II, no. 4257. Scarisbrick, *Henry VIII*, p. 110.
50. Thomas More and Cuthbert Tunstall have both been suggested as 'ghost' writers for this work, but it is unlikely that either of them would have made the errors which it actually contains. Scarisbrick, *Henry VIII*, p. 111.
51. Gwyn, *King's Cardinal*, p. 157. See also below, pp. 119-213.
52. Sebastian Guistanini to the Signory. *Cal. Ven.*, II, no. 1220.
53. Greg Walker, 'The "expulsion of the minions" of 1519 reconsidered', *Historical Journal*, 32, 1989, p. 1.
54. Ibid.
55. *L & P*, III, no. 1. Scarisbrick dates it later.
56. Report of Guistianini, July 1519, ibid, no. 402.
57. Gwyn, *King's Cardinal*, pp. 159-72.
58. Carole Rawcliffe, *The Staffords' Earls of Stafford and Dukes of Buckingham, 1394-1521* (1978), pp. 41-5. 'Instructions given by Buckingham to his Chancellor, Robert Gilbert', *L & P*, III, no. 1070.
59. *L & P*, III, nos 412, 497.
60. It had been another servant, Charles Knyvet, who had provided Wolsey with his original information. Rawcliffe, *The Staffords*, pp. 42-3.
61. Indictments against the Duke of Buckingham, 13th May 1521. *L & P*, III, no. 1284.
62. Rawcliffe, *The Staffords*, p. 44
63. David Loades, *Henry VIII. Court, church and conflict* (2007), pp. 135-6.
64. Helen Miller, *Henry VIII and the English Nobility* (1986), p. 221. This arrangement was confirmed by Act of Parliament, 27 Henry VIII, cap.47.

65. Scarisbrick, *Henry VIII*, pp. 125-6.
66. The particulars of the treaty are contained in a brief dated 25 August 1521. *Cal. Span., 1509-1525*, no. 355.
67. Ibid.
68. *L & P*, III, no. 1994. Francis I to La Batie and Poillot in England, January 1522.

5. THE COURT OF KING HENRY

1. For a fuller structural analysis of the court, see David Loades, *The Tudor Court* (1992), pp. 25-54.
2. There was an established definition of the verge for the palaces of Westminster and Whitehall, which took in some of the surrounding streets. In the cases of the Tower and Windsor, the verge was defined by the castle itself. When the court was on the move, the verge was defined *ad hoc* at each resting place. Jurisdictional disputes were consequently frequent.
3. Henry was not necessarily ignorant of what went on 'below stairs'. For example, Richard Hill, the Sergeant of the Cellar, was a frequent gambling companion of the King between 1527 and 1533. *The Tudor Court*, p. 39.
4. D. Starkey, 'The age of the Household: politics, society and the arts, *c.*1350-1500' in S. Medcalf, *The Later Middle Ages* (1981).
5. Entitlement to bouge depended upon rank as well as residence. Councillors, for example, were entitled although not resident. Part-timers, such as Gentlemen Ushers 'Quarter Waiters', were only entitled when on duty. In practice the rules were not very strictly enforced.
6. D. Starkey, 'Intimacy and Innovation; the Rise of the Privy Chamber, 1485-1547', in *The English Court*, ed. D. Starkey (1987).
7. So called because his original function had been to empty the royal close stool, or privy. By this time that actual task was performed by a menial servant.
8. Greg Walker, 'The expulsion of the minions of 1519 reconsidered', *Historical Journal*, 32, 1989.
9. George Cavendish, *The Life and Death of Cardinal Wolsey*, ed. R. S. Sylvester and Davis P. Harding (1962), p. 122.
10. For a detailed account of these purges, see E. W. Ives, *The Life and Death of Anne Boleyn* (2004), pp. 148-62 and 319-38.
11. Anne Boleyn was unique in that her endowment went with her creation as Marquis of Pembroke, the others were endowed as queens, with lands worth between £3,000 and £4,000 per annum.
12. *Tudor Court*, p. 32.
13. H. M. Colvin, *The History of the Kings Works*, Vol. IV (1982), pt.ii, pp. 1-367.
14. For an early example of the use of the Treasury of the Chamber (1512), see *Letters and Papers*, II, pp. 1441-1480.
15. This is an average. In the course of the reign ordinary revenue rose (roughly in line with inflation) from about £100,000 to about £150,000. A single Fifteenth and Tenth was worth about £15,000, and a subsidy around £50,000. These are approximate figures, because the actually yield depended upon circumstances.
16. D. E. Hoak, 'The Secret History of the Tudor Court; the King's Coffers and the King's Purse, 1542-1553', *Journal of British Studies*, 26, 1987.
17. Ibid.
18. There is a vivid and unflattering account of a skirmish at the court gate during that rebellion in the narrative of Edward Underhill, who was a Gentleman at Arms. This is BL Harleian MS 425, and is printed in A. F. Pollard, *Tudor Tracts* (1903), pp. 170-98.
19. W. J. Tighe, 'Gentlemen Pensioners in the Reign of Elizabeth' (Cambridge Ph.D, 1984) has a good historical introduction.
20. *Tudor Court*, pp. 54-5. For a fuller account, albeit of a later period, see Lawrence Stone, *The Crisis of the Aristocracy, 1558-1641* (1965), pp. 223-234.
21. Catherine of Aragon's most famous intercession was for the rioters of the Evil May Day in 1517. *Cal. Ven.*, ii, p. 887. The ladies of later queens tended to concentrate on smaller and more specific requests.

22. Sometimes these were issued as public proclamations, as was done in 1533. *Tudor Royal Proclamations*, I, 141. 'The King's royal majesty straightly chargeth and commandeth that all vagabonds, masterless folk, rascals and other idle persons which have used to hang on, haunt, and follow the court, do depart from thence within 24 hours of this proclamation made, upon such pains as in his laws therefore is appointed.'

23. *Tudor Court*, p. 56.

24. E. W. Ives, 'Faction at the court of Henry VIII; the fall of Anne Boleyn', *History*, 57, 1972. Ives' various works on Anne Boleyn contain the best general discussion of the nature of faction during Henry's reign. See also Joseph S. Block, *Factional Politics and the English Reformation, 1520-1540* (London, Royal Historical Society, 1993).

6. WAR & POVERTY, 1522–1525

1. C. S. Knighton and David Loades, *Letters from the Mary Rose* (2002), p. 80.

2. Lord Admiral Surrey to the King, 21 June 1522. TNA SP1 /24, f.325. *L & P*, III, ii, no. 2337.

3. Surrey to Wolsey, 3 July 1522. TNA SP1 /25, f.22. *L & P*, III, ii, no. 2362.

4. Grafton, *Chronicle*, p. 324.

5. 'Which verses were also written in other Tables in Golden letters, as ensueth.

Long prosperitie	The one of fayth
To Charles and Henry	The other of the Church
Princes most puyssaunt	Chosen defendant'

Ibid, p. 323.

6. *L & P*, III, ii, no. 3346. G. W. Bernard, *War, Taxation and Rebellion in Early Tudor England* (1986), pp. 53-4.

7. *L & P*, III, ii, no. 2537. Scarisbrick, *Henry VIII*, p. 126.

8. Grafton, *Chronicle*, pp. 328-9.

9. Ibid, p. 331.

10. A. Levey, *Le Connetable de Bourbon* (Paris, 1904), livre ii. Scarisbrick, *Henry VIII*, p. 127.

11. *L & P*, III, ii, nos 3123, 3225.

12. S. J. Gunn, 'The Duke of Suffolk's March on Paris in 1523', *EHR*, 101, 1986, pp. 596-634.

13. F. C. Dietz, *English Government Finance, 1485-1558* (1964), p. 91. R. W. Hoyle, ed., *The Military Survey of Gloucestershire, 1522* (Gloucester Record Series, 6, 1993), pp. xii-xiii.

14. Dietz, *English Government Finance*, pp. 92-3.

15. *L & P*, III, ii, 3082. Dietz, p. 94. Grafton, *Chronicle*, p. 338.

16. *L & P*, III, ii, nos 3123, 3154.

17. Gunn, 'The Duke of Suffolk's March on Paris …'.

18. Ibid.

19. S. J. Gunn, *Charles Brandon, Duke of Suffolk, 1484-1545* (1988), pp. 75-6.

20. Grafton, *Chronicle*, p. 354, which also includes a full account of the taking of Montidier.

21. Ibid, p. 355.

22. TNA SP1/32, f. 39. *L & P*, IV, I, no. 619. Gunn, *Charles Brandon*, pp. 76-7.

23. Edward Hall, *Chronicle* (1809), p. 664. Grafton, *Chronicle*, p. 348.

24. 'When the Duke of Albany and the Lordes of Scotlande knew that the Erle of Surrey approached with his puissant army, they thought it not convenient to jeopard all the nobilitie of Scotland in one field, considering their chaunce ten yeares before, and therefore they concluded to returne, and so on the second day of November in the night, the Duke and all his army retreated, more for his suretie than honor …' Grafton, *Chronicle*, p. 349.

25. *L & P*, III, ii, no. 2537.

26. Scarisbrick, *Henry VIII*, pp. 131-2. Bernard, *War, Taxation and Rebellion*, pp. 10-11.

27. *State Papers of Henry VIII*, VI, pp. 242, 261, 278.

28. Ibid, p. 288.

29. *L & P*, IV, no. 384. There is some evidence that the King and the Cardinal were at odds over this matter. Scarisbrick, *Henry VIII*, p. 132.

30. *L & P*, IV, no. 724.

31. The story of Henry's reception of the news is told from R. Macquereau, *Histoire Generale de*

l'Europe (Louvain, 1765), p. 231. No source is given.

32. Grafton, *Chronicle*, p. 373.

33. Hall, *Chronicle*, p. 694.

34. Bernard, *War, Taxation and Rebellion*, pp. 55-6. Grafton, *Chronicle*, p. 376.

35. Bernard, p. 57, citing Coventry Record Office, A 79 I, p. 55.

36. BL Cotton MS Cleopatra F.VI, f. 341. *L & P*, IV, I , no. 1332. Hall, *Chronicle*, pp. 700-01.

37. *L & P*, IV, no. 1212. Scarisbrick, *Henry VIII*, p. 137.

38. *State Papers*, I, p. 160. *L & P*, IV, no. 1371.

39. He had had a letter of the Imperial ambassador seized, and then denounced the ambassador before the Council because the letter contained unflattering remarks about himself. *Cal. Span.*, III, nos 51, 62.

40. For the story of their precipitate flight see, Jacqueton, *La Politique Exterieure de Louise de Savoie* (Paris, 1892), p. 46. Scarisbrick, *Henry VIII*, p. 140.

41. By the terms of this treaty, Francis bound himself to pay Henry the princely sum of 2,052,631 crowns (about £650,000), made up of various arrearages from previous treaties. Rymer, *Foedera*, XIV, pp. 58-68.

42. Scarisbrick, *Henry VIII*, p. 141.

43. For Francis' observations upon the treaty of Madrid, see *L & P*, IV, no. 2079.

44. Mattingly, *Catherine of Aragon*, pp. 174-5.

45. Ibid, p. 170.

46. G. R. Elton, *The Tudor Constitution* (1982), p. 200.

47. Loades, *Mary Tudor*, p. 39. Hazel Pierce, *Margaret Pole, Countess of Salisbury, 1473-1541* (2003), p. 43.

48. Eric Ives, *The Life and Death of Anne Boleyn* (2004), pp. 16-17.

49. Ibid.

50. For reactions when this problem actually arose in 1554, see Judith. M. Richards, 'Mary Tudor as "Sole Quene"? Gendering Tudor Monarchy', *Historical Journal*, 40, 1997, pp. 895-924; and Glyn Redworth, '"Matters impertinent to women"; male and female monarchy under Philip and Mary', *EHR*, 112, 1997, pp. 597-613.

51. When representatives from Francis I came to inspect her with a view to matrimony in 1527, they reported that she was 'so thin, spare and small as to make it impossible to be married for the next three years'. She was then eleven. Loades, *Mary Tudor*, p. 45.

52. Mattingly, *Catherine of Aragon*, pp. 50-4.

53. It was Richard Wakefield who suggested to Henry that the true reading of the Hebrew should be 'they shall be without sons', an interpretation which the King eagerly accepted.

54. Ives, *Life and Death*, p. 90.

55. Ibid, pp. 18-25.

56. Lancelot de Carles, 'De la royne d'Angleterre', in G. Ascoli, *La Grande-Bretagne devant l'Opinion Francaise* (Paris, 1927).

57. George Wyatt, 'The Life of Queen Anne Boleigne' in S. W. Singer, ed., *The Life of Cardinal Wolsie* by George Cavendish (1827).

58. Ives, *Life and Death*, pp. 30-31.

59. Ibid, pp.xxi, 34-5.

60. 'The Life and Death of Cardinal Wolsey by George Cavendish', in R. S. Sylvester and D. P. Harding, *Two Early Tudor Lives* (1962), p. 36.

61. Ives, *Life and Death*, p. 79.

62. BL Add. MS 28585, f. 45. *Cal. Span.*, 1531-33, p. 473.

63. Nicholas Sander, *The Rise and Growth of the Anglican Schism*, ed. D. Lewis (1877), p. 25.

64. Hall, *Chronicle*, p. 633.

65. Ibid. This was exceedingly fortunate, bearing in mind the manner of the death of Henry II of France in 1559.

66. When they jousted again in December, they challenged together. Gunn, *Charles Brandon*, p. 97. The Marquis of Exeter replaced Suffolk as the King's main opponent over the next two or three years.

67. Dietz, *English Government Finance*, p. 92.

7. THE ORIGIN OF THE 'GREAT MATTER', 1525–1529
1. Eric Ives dates it to later in 1526, and connects it with Wyatt's decision to go to Italy in early January 1527. The evidence is not conclusive. Ives, *Life and Death*, p. 76.
2. *The Love Letters of Henry VIII*, ed. H. Savage (1949), pp. 38-9, 32-4. *L & P*, IV, nos 3219, 3218.
3. Ives, *Life and Death*, pp. 88-9.
4. TNA SP2/C i. *L & P*, IV, no. 3140.
5. Scarisbrick, *Henry VIII*, p. 155.
6. Judith Hook, *The Sack of Rome* (1972).
7. *L & P*, IV, nos 3247, 3311. Gwyn, The *King's Cardinal*, pp. 537-8.
8. *State Papers*, I, p. 198. *L & P*, IV, no. 3231.
9. Nicholas Pocock, *Records of the Reformation; the divorce 1527-1533* (2 vols., 1870), I, p. 11.
10. Knight to Wolsey, 14 July 1527. *State Papers*, I, p. 215. *L & P*, IV, no. 3265.
11. *State Papers*, I, p. 267. *L & P*, IV, no. 3400. Scarisbrick, *Henry VIII*, p. 158.
12. TNA SP1 /42, f.255. *L & P*, IV, no. 3318.
13. Pocock, *Records of the Reformation*, I, p. 22.
14. *Cal. Span*, III, ii, p. 277.
15. Scarisbrick, *Henry VIII*, p. 158.
16. L. von Pastor, *History of the Popes*, trs, F. I. Antrobus and R. F. Kerr (23 vols., 1891-1933), X, p. 29.
17. *L & P*, IV, nos 3827, 4564. Knighton and Loades, *Letters from the Mary Rose*, pp. 95-105.
18. TNA 31/3/3, f. 237. *L & P*, IV, nos 4269, 4637, 4802, 4909-11.
19. Scarisbrick, *Henry VIII*, pp. 208-9.
20. The effective agent in this demolition was Cardinal Lorenzo Pucci, who was notoriously hostile to the divorce. *L & P*, IV, nos 3751, 3756.
21. Ibid, no. 3802.
22. Pocock, *Records of the Reformation*, I, p. 128. *L & P*, IV, no. 4167.
23. Scarisbrick, *Henry VIII*, p. 208.
24. Brian Tuke, the master of the Posts, expressed the view that the missing letter had been intercepted somewhere in France – which added to the annoyance. *L & P*, IV, nos 4358, 4359, 4361, 4390.
25. Ibid, nos 4391, 4398, 4440, 4542, 4409. Grafton, *Chronicle*, p. 412.
26. Ibid, pp. 413-14.
27. *L & P*, IV, nos 5604, 4721, 4736-7, 4857. Scarisbrick, *Henry VIII*, p. 216.
28. Stefan Ehses, *Romische Dokumente zur Geschichte der Ehescheidung Heinrichs VIII von England*, 1527-1534 (Paderborn, 1893), p. 58.
29. Hall, *Chronicle*, p. 754.
30. Ibid, p. 755.
31. *State Papers*, VII, p. 102. *L & P*, IV, no. 4897.
32. Hall, *Chronicle*, p. 756.
33. Deuteronomy 25:5. 'When brothers live together and one of them dies without leaving a son, his widow shall not marry outside the family. Her husband's brother shall take her ...'.
34. Edward Surtz SJ and Virginia Murphy, *The Divorce Tracts of Henry VIII* (Angers, 1988), pp. ii-iii. Scarisbrick, *Henry VIII*, pp. 198-241.
35. Patrick Le Gal, 'Le cas canonique et le probleme exegetique' in Guy Bedouelle and Patrick Le Gal, *Le 'Divorce' du Roi Henry VIII* (Geneva, 1987), pp. 29-46.
36. Ibid.
37. Scarisbrick, *Henry VIII*, pp. 194-5.
38. *Cal. Span*., III, ii, no. 845. *L & P*, IV, no. 3844.
39. Inigo de Mendoza, Bishop of Burgos, arrived in England in December 1526, and was still in post in 1529, so the 'declaration of war' does not seem to have been taken very seriously by either side.

40. Hall, *Chronicle*, p. 724.

41. Ives, *Life and Death of Anne Boleyn*, pp. 111-13.

42. This was the so-called 'black salt' tax, which was commuted for 10,000 crowns a year. *L & P*, IV, nos 6755, 6775. Dietz, *English Government Finance*, p. 101.

43. Hall, *Chronicle*, p. 707.

44. Statute 1 Henry VIII, c.16. Dietz, *English Government Finance*, p. 89. For the text of the Eltham Ordinances, see *Household Ordinances* (1790) pp. 137-47.

45. Scarisbrick, *Henry VIII*, p. 218.

46. *L & P*, IV nos 5375, 5423, 5471. *Cal. Span.*, III, ii, no. 662.

47. *L & P*, IV, nos 4977-9. Scarisbrick, *Henry VIII*, p. 220.

48. *L & P*, IV, nos 5368-72.

49. *Cal. Span.*, III, ii, nos 652, 676-7.

50. *L & P*, IV, nos 5604, 5602, 5611, 5613.

51. Grafton, *Chronicle*, p. 417.

52. B. Bradshaw and E. Duffy, *Humanism, Reform and the Reformation; the career of Bishop John Fisher* (1989), p. 9.

53. *Cal. Span.*, IV, nos 97, 121.

54. *State Papers*, VII, p. 193. *L & P*, IV, no. 5797.

55. Scarisbrick, *Henry VIII*, p. 227.

56. R. J. Knecht, *Francis I* (1982), p. 218.

57. *L & P*, IV, nos 5636, 5713.

58. Knecht, *Francis I*, pp. 219-20.

59. *Cal. Span.*, IV, nos 189, 195. *State Papers*, I, pp. 343 et seq.

60. Cecily Willoughby, the Abbess of Wilton, died in April 1528, and Henry promised Anne that her sister-in-law Eleanor Carey should have the position, ahead of the obvious candidate, the prioress Isabel Jordayne. However, investigation showed that Eleanor had a past which made her most unsuitable, and the King declared that neither of these ladies was to be appointed. Wolsey, who seems to have believed that the patronage belonged to him, nevertheless went ahead and named Isabel Jordayne – to Henry's great anger.

61. Cavendish, *Life and Death of Cardinal Wolsey* (ed. Singer), pp. 92 et seq.

62. Ibid, p. 101.

63. Gwyn, *The King's Cardinal*, pp. 612-13.

64. Ibid, pp. 615-7.

8. CRISIS & CHANGE, 1529–1536

1. For the ambiguities in Henry's attitude to Wolsey at the time of his fall, see P. Gwyn, *The King's Cardinal*, pp. 634-5.

2. *L & P*, IV, no. 3361. *State Papers*, I, p. 261.

3. For a discussion of Henry's attitude towards the Church, see Scarisbrick, *Henry VIII*, pp. 241-5.

4. Robert Keilwey, *Reports*, ed. John Croke (1688), cited by A. Ogle, *The Lollards' Tower* (1949), p. 140.

5. *Cal. Span.*, IV, no. 224.

6. Ibid, no. 160. Campeggio had protested to the King about some of the literature circulating in the court, calling upon the King to strip the clergy of their property.

7. Hall, *Chronicle*, p. 764.

8. *The Earliest English Life of St John Fisher*, ed. P. Hughes (1935), p. 109.

9. *RSTC* 10883.

10. 21 Henry VIII, c.2; c.5; c.6; c.13. *Statutes of the Realm*, III, pp. 284, 285, 288, 292.

11. *L & P*, IV, no. 6385.

12. Graham Nicholson, 'The Act of Appeals and the English Reformation', in *Law and Government under the Tudors*, ed. C. Cross etc. (1988), pp. 19-30.

13. *L & P*, IV, no. 6667.

14. TNA KB29/162, ro.12. J. Scarisbrick, 'The Pardon of the Clergy, 1531', *Cambridge Historical*

Journal, 12, 1956, p. 25.

15. Scarisbrick, *Henry VIII*, pp. 274-5.

16. D. Wilkins, *Concilia Magnae Britanniae et Hiberniae* (4 vols., 1737), III, p. 725.

17. Statute 21 Henry VIII, c.24. 'An Acte for the returning unto the Kinges Highness of such somes of money as was to be required of him by any of his subjects for any loan ...' *Statutes of the Realm*, III, p. 315.

18. Scarisbrick, 'The Pardon of the Clergy', p. 31.

19. Wilkins, *Concilia*, III, p. 745. Tunstall's original letter is not extant, and must be reconstructed from Henry's response.

20. Ibid, p. 762.

21. Statute 22 Henry VIII, c.15. *Statutes of the Realm*, III, pp. 334-8.

22. *State Papers*, VII, p. 281. *L & P*, V, nos 102, 256. *Cal. Span.*, IV, nos 630, 659. Scarisbrick, *Henry VIII*, pp. 281-2.

23. *L & P*, V, no. 908.

24. Ibid, nos 1157, 1159, 1194.

25. Ibid, nos 352, 355, *State Papers*, VII, p. 305.

26. Scarisbrick, *Henry VIII*, p. 286.

27. For some discussion of Warham's attitude, and his long record of service, see Gwyn, *The King's Cardinal*, p. 310.

28. *Cal. Span.*, IV, no. 134.

29. Ibid, no. 224. Ives, *Life and Death*, p. 128.

30. Ibid, p. 130.

31. Cavendish, *Life of Wolsey* (ed. Singer), p. 132.

32. *L & P*, IV, nos 6720, 6733. *Cal. Span.*, IV, no. 492. L. R. Gardiner, 'Further news of Cardinal Wolsey's end', *Bulletin of the Institute of Historical Research*, 57, 1984, pp. 99-107.

33. Ralph Morice, in *Narratives of the Days of the Reformation*, ed. J. G. Nicholas (1879), p. 242. E. Surtz and V. Murphy, eds., *The Divorce Tracts of Henry VIII* (1988), p. xx.

34. Diarmaid MacCulloch, *Thomas Cranmer* (1996), pp. 45-8.

35. Simon Fish, *The Supplication of the Beggars*, in *English Historical Documents, 1485-1558*, ed. C. H. Williams (1967), p. 673.

36. *Cal. Span.*, IV, nos 354, 366.

37. Ibid, no. 460.

38. *RSTC* 11918, 21563.

39. Gunn, *Charles Brandon*, pp. 117-21. Loades, *Mary Tudor*, p. 63.

40. Ives, *Life and Death*, pp. 139-41.

41. BL Add. MS 48044, f. 13.

42. They were considered to be mainly anti-Boleyn utterances at this time. *L & P*, V, no. 216; VI, nos 1464-6, 1468, 1470.

43. A. Neame, *The Holy Maid of Kent: the Life of Elizabeth Barton, 1506-1534* (1971).

44. G. R. Elton, *Thomas Cromwell*, ed. D. Loades (2008).

45. G. R. Elton, *The Tudor Constitution*, pp. 333-5.

46. *RSTC* 11584. G. Redworth, *In Defence of the Church Catholic*, pp. 190-1.

47. Statute 23 Henry VIII, c.20. *Statutes of the Realm*, III, pp. 385-8.

48. The next woman to be so honoured was Elizabeth Heneage, created Countess of Winchelsea in 1628. There were several similar creations in and after 1660.

49. *The manner of the triumph at Calais and Boulogne* (*RSTC* 4350), in A. F. Pollard, *Tudor Tracts* (1903), pp. 1-19. Ives, *Life and Death*, pp. 157-62.

50. Ibid, p. 160.

51. *The manner of the triumph* ..., p. 7.

52. MacCulloch, *Cranmer*, pp. 75-6.

53. *The Miscellaneous Writings and Letters of Thomas Cranmer*, ed. J. E. Cox (Parker Society, 1846), p. 246. Ives, *Life and Death*, p. 162.

54. MacCulloch, *Cranmer*, pp. 88-9.

55. Statute 24 Henry VIII, c.12. *Statutes of the Realm*, III, pp. 427-9.

56. *Cal. Span.*, IV, no. 619. S. Lehmberg, *The Reformation Parliament* (1970), pp. 174-8. MacCulloch, *Cranmer*, pp. 84-9.

57. *The noble triumphant Coronation of Queen Anne, Wife unto the most noble King Henry the VIIIth*. In Pollard, *Tudor Tracts*, pp. 11-19.

58. *RSTC* 656.

59. TNA PRO31/8, f. 51. *L & P*, VI, no. 585.

60. Lehmberg, *The Reformation Parliament*, pp. 155-6.

61. Elton, *The Tudor Constitition*, pp. 245-9.

62. Statute 24 Henry VIII, c.12. *Statutes of the Realm*, III, pp. 427-9.

63. Ibid.

64. *L & P*. VI, no. 807, and Appendix, no. 3.

65. *Cal. Ven.*, IV, no. 923.

66. Ibid.

67. *Cal. Span.*, 1531-3, p. 788, Ives, *Life and Death*, p. 185.

68. Hall, *Chronicle*, pp. 803 & *L & P*, VI, no. 1111.

69. Ives, *Life and Death*, pp. 195-6.

70. *Cal. Span.*, V, no. 12. Loades, *Mary Tudor*, pp. 82-3.

71. Ibid.

72. For Bonner's account of this mission, see G. Burnet, *History of the Reformation of the Church of England* (1679), III, ii, pp. 37-46.

73. *L & P*, VI, nos 1426, 1427.

74. Scarisbrick, *Henry VIII*, p. 322.

75. Henry was personally responsible for handling this case, and Chapuys was convinced of his role. *L & P*, VI, no. 887, *Cal. Span.*, IV, no. 1153. Cromwell noted that he needed to know 'what the king will have done with the nun and her accomplices'. *L & P*, VII, no. 52.

76. Statute 25 Henry VIII, c.21. *Statutes of the Realm*, III, pp. 464-71.

77. E. F. Jacob, *The Fifteenth Century, 1399-1485* (1961), pp. 520-22.

78. Statute 26 Henry VIII, c.1. *Statutes of the Realm*, III, p. 492.

79. *L & P*, VII, nos 1255, 1262, 1298. It was generally assumed in Imperial circles that Henry would do a deal, now that his personal enmity to the Pope was no longer a factor.

80. *State Papers*, VII, no. 565; *L & P*, VII, no. 958. *Cal. Span.*, V, no. 75.

81. Ives, *Life and Death*, pp. 195-6.

82. Ibid, p. 203.

83. *L & P*, VIII, no. 174.

84. Mattingly, *Catherine of Aragon*, p. 269.

85. Ibid, p. 271.

86. *L & P*, VII, no. 1208. Loades, *Mary Tudor*, p. 79.

87. J. A. Guy, *The Public Career of Sir Thomas More* (1980), p. 203.

88. *L & P*, IX, no. 207. The bull of deprivation was not finally approved in Consistory until January 1536.

9. THE LORDSHIP & KINGDOM OF IRELAND

1. G. O. Sayles, *The Administration of Ireland, 1172-1377* (1963).

2. S. G. Ellis, *Tudor Ireland* (1985), pp. 19-32.

3. S. J. Gunn, *Early Tudor Government* (1995), pp. 62-70.

4. S. G. Ellis, 'Tudor policy and the Kildare ascendancy in the Lordship of Ireland, 1496-1534', *Irish Historical Studies*, 20, 1976-7.

5. His son and heir married in England, to Elizabeth Zouche, while two of his daughters were married to Irish chieftains.

6. Brendan Bradshaw, *The Irish Constitutional Revolution of the Sixteenth Century* (1979), p. 9.

7. H. G. Richardson and G. O. Sayles, *The Irish Parliament in the Middle Ages* (1952), p. 274.

8. Appointed in 1513. William Rokeby, the Archbishop of Dublin, who had held the office before Compton, continued as his deputy, and regained the office in 1516.

9. Ellis, *Tudor Ireland*, p. 102.

10. S. G. Ellis, *Reform and Revival; English Government in Ireland, 1470-1534* (1984), pp. 157-8.

11. Ibid, pp. 13, 16, 27. TNA SP60/3/162. *Letters and Papers*, III, 670, 899.

12. Ellis, 'Tudor Policy and the Kildare Ascendancy', p. 239.

13. *State Papers*, Henry VIII (1830-52) II, 60.

14. Ellis, *Tudor Ireland*, p. 115.

15. R. J. Knecht, *Francis I* (1982), p. 147.

16. *Letters and Papers*, IV, 3698. Ellis, *Tudor Ireland*, pp. 118-9.

17. See B. Murphy, *Bastard Prince* (2001), pp. 107-148 for a full account of Fitzroy's role (or lack of it) in this capacity.

18. D. B. Quinn, 'Henry VIII and Ireland', *Irish Historical Studies*, XII, 1960-2001, pp. 338-9.

19. Ellis, *Tudor Ireland*, pp. 124-5. Ellis, 'The Kildare rebellion and the early Henrician Reformation', *Historical Journal*, XIX, 1976.

20. S. G. Ellis, *Tudor Frontiers and Noble Power* (1995), p. 176.

21. Both Francis I and Charles V were arming early in 1535 in preparation for a fresh round in their confrontation. Whenever this happened, it took the pressure off Henry. Knecht, *Francis I*, pp. 274-6.

22. The ninth Earl had died in London in September 1534.

23. Bradshaw, *The Irish Constitutional Revolution*, pp. 154-159. Ibid, 'The opposition to the ecclesiastical legislation in the Irish reformation Parliament', *Irish Historical Studies*, 16, 1969.

24. Ellis, *Tudor Ireland*, pp. 135-6.

25. Bradshaw, *Irish Constitutional Revolution*, pp. 193-196.

26. *State Papers*, III, p. 326. Ellis, *Tudor Ireland*, pp. 139-40.

27. Bradshaw, *Irish Constitutional Revolution*, pp. 196-200.

28. For a discussion of the complexities of the Gaelic tenurial system, see K. Nicholls, *Gaelic and Gaelicised Ireland* (1972), pp. 37-9, 57-67.

29. *Handbook of British Chronology*, ed., E. B. Fryde, D. E. Greeway, S. Porter and I. Roy (1986), pp. 323-377.

30. B. Bradshaw, *The Dissolution of the Religious Orders in Ireland* (1974).

31. Ellis, *Tudor Ireland*, pp. 200-204.

32. R. D. Edwards, 'The Irish bishops and the Anglican schism', *Irish Ecclesiastical Record*, 45, 1935.

33. R. D. Edwards, *Ireland in the Age of the Tudors: the destruction of Hiberno-Norman civilisation* (1977)

34. *State Papers*, II, p. 122.

35. Bradshaw, *The Dissolution of the Religious Orders in Ireland*.

36. Ibid, pp. 36-7. Ellis, *Tudor Ireland*, pp. 200-203.

37. Nicholls, *Gaelic and Gaelicised Ireland*, pp. 107-9.

38. C. Conway, 'Decline and attempted reform of the Irish Cistercians, 1445-1531', *Collectanea Ordinis Cisterciensium Reformatorum*, XIX, 1957, pp. 146-62, 371-84.

39. Ellis, *Tudor Ireland*, p. 190.

40. Bradshaw, *Dissolution of the Religious Orders*, pp. 32-3, 47-77.

41. Ibid, pp. 206-7.

42. Ibid, Appendix I. Ellis, *Tudor Ireland*, pp. 2-4.

10. A KING IN HIS SPLENDOUR, 1536–1542

1. Tracey A. Sowerby, *Renaissance and Reform in Tudor England: the career of Sir Richard Morison, c.1513-1556* (2010), pp. 2-13. Surtz and Murphy, *Divorce Tracts*, pp. viii-x.

2. Ibid, p. ix. TNA SP1/94, f. 98. *L & P*, VIII, no. 1054.

3. *RSTC* 14286, 14287.

4. Guy Bedouelle, 'Le recours aux Universites et ses implications', in Bedouelle and Le Gal, *Le Divorce du Roi Henry VIII*, pp. 49-57.

5. Ibid, p. 52.

6. Surtz and Murphy, pp. ix-xix.

7. Sowerby, *Renaissance and Reform*, pp. 104-7.

8. D. Loades, *Mary Tudor: the tragical history of the first Queen of England* (2006), p. 33.

9. Ives, *Life and Death of Anne Boleyn*, pp. 199-202.

10. R. M. Warnicke, *The Rise and Fall of Anne Boleyn* (1989), pp. 196-8. Charles Wriothesley, *A Chronicle of England, 1485-1559*, ed., W. D. Hamilton (Camden Society, 2nd Series, 1875, 1877) i, p. 33.

11. Nicholas Sander, *The Rise and Growth of the Anglican Schism*, ed., D. Lewis (1877), p. 132.

12. *Cal. Span.*, 1536-8, pp. 39-40.

13. Wriothesley, *Chronicle*, I, pp. 189-91.

14. *State Papers*, VII, pp. 683-6. *L & P*, X, no. 726. Ives, *Life and Death*, p. 321.

15. Ibid, p. 325.

16. Alexander Ales, letter to Queen Elizabeth, 1 September 1559. TNA SP70/7, ff. 1-11. Translated and Calendared in *The Calendar of State Papers, Foreign, 1558-9*, no. 1303.

17. Hall, *Chronicle*, p. 819.

18. Ives, *Life and Death*, pp. 343-7.

19. *Cal. Span.*, V, ii, pp. 124-5, 127. *L & P*, X, no. 908.

20. Cavendish, *Wolsey*, ed. Singer, pp. 458-9.

21. Ives, *Life and Death*, pp. 338-9.

22. Loades, *Mary Tudor*, p. 98.

23. Hall, *Chronicle*, p. 819.

24. *The Reports of Sir John Spelman*, ed. J. A. Baker, Selden Society, 93, 94 (1977-8), I, p. 59.

25. *L & P*, X, no. 896. H. A. Kelly, *The Matrimonial Trials of Henry VIII* (1976), pp. 250-59.

26. Hall, *Chronicle*, p. 819.

27. D. Loades, *Henry VIII and his Queens* (1997), pp. 95-6.

28. BL Cotton MS Otho C. X, f. 283. *L & P*, X, no. 968.

29. Loades, *Mary Tudor*, pp. 99-103.

30. *L & P*, XIII, I, no. 1198.

31. None of the documents connected with this crisis are dated, but circumstantial evidence points to the 15th as being the date of this visitation. BL Cotton MS Otho C.X, f. 289. *L & P*, X, no. 1136. Loades, *Mary Tudor*, p. 101.

32. Chapuys to the Emperor, 1 July 1536. *L & P*, XI, no. 7.

33. Chapuys wisely advised Lady Shelton to accept no such applicants without the King's express permission. Loades, *Mary Tudor*, p. 99.

34. BL Cotton MS Vespasian C.xiv, f. 246.

35. Loades, *Mary Tudor*, Appendix I (c).

36. Frere and Kennedy, *Visitation Articles*, II, pp.1-11.

37. For a discussion see G. W. Bernard, *The King's Reformation* (2005), p. 245. For the text, *Valor Ecclesiasticus temp. Henry VIII. Auctoritate Regis institutus*, ed. J. Caley and J. Hunter (1810-34).

38. V. Murphy, 'The literature and propaganda of Henry VIII's first divorce' in D. MacCulloch, ed., *The Reign of Henry VIII; politics, policy and piety* (1995), p. 139.

39. Bernard, *The King's Reformation*, pp. 249-55.

40. M. D. Knowles, *The Religious Orders in England*, Vol. III, *The Tudor Age* (1959).

41. Ibid. Dietz, *English Government Finance*, pp. 118-36.

42. W. C. Richardson, *A History of the Court of Augmentations* (1962). Joyce Youings, *Devon Monastic Lands; Calendar of Particulars for Grants, 1536-58* (1955), p. xiv.

43. Hall, *Chronicle*, p. 818.

44. Hughes, *Reformation in England*, I, Appendix 1.

45. P. Cunich, 'The Dissolution', in D. Rees, ed, *Monks of England; the Benedictines in England from Augustine to the Present Day* (1997), pp. 148-66.

46. R. W. Hoyle, *The Pilgrimage of Grace and the Politics of the 1530s* (2001), p. 109.

47. Ibid, pp. 11-12.

48. Gunn, *Charles Brandon, Duke of Suffolk*, pp. 144-52.

49. TNA SP1/110, ff. 149-58. *L & P*, XI, no. 971.

50. Ibid, no. 694.

51. These articles are printed by Hoyle from the only surviving text. *Pilgrimage of Grace*, pp. 455-6.

52. G. R. Elton, *Policy and Police* (1972), p. 387. A breakdown of the fate of those accused of treason during the reign.

53. *L & P*, XII, nos 201 (iv), 202 (v). Hoyle, *Pilgrimage of Grace*, pp. 188-208.

54. Ibid, p. 460-63. The text of the Articles.

55. M. E. James, 'Obedience and Dissent in Henrician England; the Lincolnshire Revolt, 1536', in James, *Society, Politics and Culture, Studies in Early Modern England* (1986), pp. 188-269.

56. Hoyle, *Pilgrimage of Grace*, p. 461.

57. T. N. Toller, ed., 'Correspondence of Edward, third Earl of Derby during the years 24 to 31 Henry VIII, preserved in a MS in the possession of Miss ffaringdon of Worden Hall', *Chetham Society*, ns 19 (1890), pp. 28-36.

58. M. H. and R. Dodds, *The Pilgrimage of Grace, 1536-7, and The Exeter Conspiracy, 1538*, (2 vols., 1915), I, pp. 283-6.

59. Hoyle, *Pilgrimage of Grace*, pp. 298-305.

60. *L & P*, XI, no. 1410 (i).

61. *L & P*, XII, no. 369. Hoyle, *Pilgrimage of Grace*, pp. 378-85.

62. Elton, *Policy and Police*, p. 387.

63. Scarisbrick, *Henry VIII*, pp. 336, 366-7.

64. Sowerby, *Renaissance and Reformation*, pp. 66, 171-3.

65. Hall, *Chronicle*, p. 825.

66. Ibid.

67. *L & P*, XII, I, no. 779. Scarisbrick, *Henry VIII*, pp. 346-7.

68. T. F. Mayer, *Reginald Pole, Prince and Prophet* (2000), pp. 19-21.

69. *L & P*, XIII, ii, no. 818 (19). Pierce, *Margaret Pole*, pp. 107-11.

70. Ibid, pp. 115-16.

71. Montague's claim was derived from his mother, who was the daughter of George, Duke of Clarence, brother to Edward IV, Exeter's also through his mother, Katherine, a daughter of Edward IV, who had married William Courtenay, Earl of Devon.

72. Pierce, *Margaret Pole*, pp. 176-7.

73. *L & P*, XIV, I, nos 62, 345, 365.

74. Scarisbrick, *Henry VIII*, pp. 362-3. For an analysis of the fortifications, see H. M. Colvin, *The History of the King's Works*, IV, ii (1976).

75. *L & P*, XIV, I, nos 723, 724, 1110, 1237.

76. For the options which Henry was considering at this point, see Scarisbrick, *Henry VIII*, pp. 356-8. They included Francis' daughter, Margaret, and Marie de Guise.

77. Loades, *Henry VIII and his Queens*, pp. 114-5.

78. Bernard, *The King's Reformation*, pp. 282-5.

79. Statute 31 Henry VIII, c.14. *Statutes of the Realm*, III, pp. 739-43. Bernard, pp. 498-505.

80. Act Abolishing Diversity in Opinions, clauses 1-4.

81. One of the main reasons for the misunderstanding of English religious history in this period has been the desire to make Henry conform to later models of orthodoxy. John Foxe was a prime offender in this respect. D. Loades, 'John Foxe and Henry VIII', *John Foxe Bulletin*, I, i, 2002, pp. 5-12.

82. Antonia Fraser, *The Six Wives of Henry VIII* (1993), p. 303. R. M. Warnicke, *The Marrying of Anne of Cleves* (2000).

83. J. Strype, *Ecclesiastical Memorials* (1822), I, p. 459.

84. Henry Ellis, *Original Letters illustrative of English History* (1824), II, pp. 122 et seq.

85. Strype, *Ecclesiastical Memorials*, II, p. 462.

86. Loades, *Henry VIII and His Queens*, p. 125.

87. Ibid, p. 124.

88. G. R. Elton, 'Thomas Cromwell's decline and fall', in Elton, *Studies*, I, pp. 189-230, Susan Brigden, 'Thomas Cromwell and the "brethren"', in *Law and Government under the Tudors*, pp. 51-66.

89. Bernard, *King's Reformation*, pp. 527-33.

90. Statute 32 Henry VIII, c.60. House of Lords, Original Acts.

91. Statute 27 Henry VIII, c.24. *Statutes of the Realm*, III, pp. 555-8.

92. G. R. Elton, *The Tudor Revolution in Government* (1953). J. A. Guy, 'The Privy Council; revolution or evolution', in *Revolution Reassessed*, ed. D. Starkey and C. Coleman (1986).

93. Dietz, *English Government Finance*, pp. 202-14.

94. S. G. Ellis, *Tudor Ireland* (1985), pp. 122-35.

95. The most constructive was the 'surrender and re-grant' policy, aimed at reconciling the Irish Chieftains to English rule. The intention was that a chieftain would surrender his tribal lands to the King and receive them back as a fief, to be held in chief of the Crown. He would then be given a peerage title and a seat in the Irish House of Lords. This policy was associated particularly with the deputyship of Anthony St Leger, which began in 1540. Unfortunately only a minority of chieftains took up the offer, and the policy was abandoned in 1556. Ellis, *Tudor Ireland*.

96. Ralph Morice, *Narratives of the Days of the Reformation*, ed. J. G. Nichols, Camden Society, 1859, p. 259. Loades, *Henry VIII and his Queens*, pp. 124-5.

97. Ibid, p. 125.

98. Lacey Baldwin Smith, *A Tudor Tragedy* (1961), pp. 162-70.

99. TNA SP1/167, f. 138. *L & P*, XVI, no. 1321. The girl's name was Joan Bulmer.

100. *L & P*, XVI. no. 766, in which he endeavoured to persuade James that the clergy would aim to set up a 'realm of their own'.

101. Loades, *Henry VIII and his Queens*, p. 127.

102. Sir H. Nicholas, *Proceedings and Ordinances of the Privy Council of England* (1837), VII, pp. 352-4.

103. Smith, *Tudor Tragedy*, pp. 181-2.

104. Loades, *Henry VIII and his Queens*, p. 129.

105. *Historical Manuscripts Commission, Bath Papers*, II, pp. 8-9.

106. *State Papers*, I, ii, nos 163, 164. Catherine's confession is among the Bath Papers.

107. Loades, *Henry VIII and his Queens*, p. 131.

108. Ellis, *Original Letters*, First Series, II, pp. 128-9.

109. *L & P*, XVII, no. 862.

11. THE RETURN TO WAR, 1542–1547

1. It was alleged that the King of Scots had sworn homage to the King of England on more than thirty occasions. John Morrill, 'The British Problem, *c.*1534-1707', in Brendan Bradshaw and John Morrill, eds., *The British Problem, c.1534-1707* (1996), p. 5. For a review of this issue, see D. M. Head, 'Henry VIII's Scottish Policy' in *Scottish History Review*, 61, 1982, pp. 1-24. Henry set out his own case in his *Declaration, Conteyning the just causes and consyderations of this present warre* (1542 RSTC 9179), reprinted in J. A. H. Murray, ed., *The Complaynte of Scotland* (1550, RSTC 22009) (EETS, 1872).

2. *L & P*, XVII, no. 862. Scarisbrick, *Henry VIII*, p. 435.

3. *L & P*, XVII, no. 1016.

4. Gervase Phillips, *The Anglo Scottish Wars: A Military History* (1999) pp. 150-53. HMC, Papers of the Duke of Hamilton (1932), p. 240.

5. *L & P*, XVIII, nos 7, 22, 44.

6. Ibid, no. 22. Scarisbrick, *Henry VIII*, p. 437.

7. *L & P*, XVIII, no. 270.

8. Arran had secretly placed Scotland under papal protection, in spite of his professions to wish for reform of the Kirk. G. Donaldson, *Scotland, James V to James VII* (1965).

9. Sir Rhys Mansell to Lord Lisle, 9 July 1543. TNA SP1/180, f. 46. *L & P*, XVIII, no. 849. Loades and Knighton, 'Lord Lisle and Invasion of Scotland, 1544' in *Naval Miscellany*, VII, pp. 70-72.

10. *L & P*, XVIII, ii, nos 128, 132.

11. Ibid, nos 164, 189, 256. Scarisbrick, *Henry VIII*, p. 442.

12. His bullying tactics had effectively driven Scotland into the arms of France, and the 'sworn Englishmen' had turned out to be broken reeds. Ibid.

13. *L & P*, XVIII, i, nos 36, 100 (27). The Earl of Hertford is recorded as Lord Admiral in December 1542, but his appointment does not seem to have been effective. D. Loades, *John Dudley, Duke of Northumberland* (1996), p. 55.

14. Hughes and Larkin, *Tudor Royal Proclamations*, I, pp. 345-6.

15. Loades and Knighton, 'Lord Admiral Lisle and the Invasion of Scotland, 1544', pp. 57-65.

16. Paget to Hertford, 21 March 1544. Ibid. p. 77.

17. Gardiner and St John to Hertford, ibid, p. 78.

18. Ibid, pp. 85-6.

19. *The late Expedition into Scotland*, (1544, RSTC 22270) reprinted in Pollard, *Tudor Tracts*, pp. 39-51; at p. 40

20. Hertford, Lisle and Sadler to the King, 18 May 1544. BL Add. MS 32654, ff. 198-200. Hamilton Papers, II, pp. 379-82.

21. Scarisbrick, *Henry VIII*, p. 444.

22. TNA E351/2, i, *L & P*, XIX, I, no. 619.

23. M. C. Fissel, *English Warfare, 1511-1642* (2001), pp. 13-19.

24. *L & P*, XIX, i, no. 932.

25. Ibid, ii, nos 35, 174, 424.

26. Scarisbrick, *Henry VIII*, p. 449.

27. Loades, *John Dudley*, pp. 66-8. Logistically, the campaign was a mess from beginning to end.

28. For a full examination of this financial plight, see Dietz, *English Government Finance*, pp. 149, 169-74.

29. Fissel, *English Warfare*, p. 29. For the German negotiations, see *L & P*, XX, i, nos 677, 715, 808, 1047, 1135, 1207; ii, nos 46, 67-9, 102.

30. Loades and Knighton, *Letters from the Mary Rose*, pp. 96-7.

31. Loades, *Tudor Navy*, pp. 131-5.

32. *Letters from the Mary Rose*, p. 109.

33. It has been deduced from the archaeological evidence that the ship had become somewhat top-heavy as a result of its rebuild, and that made it more vulnerable to a sudden gust. Margaret Rule, *The Mary Rose* (1982), pp. 19-28. Peter Marsden, ed. *Mary Rose: Your Noblest Shippe* (2009), pp. 380-85.

34. Ibid, p. 392.

35. J. A. Muller, *The Letters of Stephen Gardiner* (1933), p. 185.

36. Another General Council had been mooted as early as 1542, but it was 1544 before the Bull of Summons was issued. It was called on 30 November to meet at Trent, on the borders of the Tyrole on 15 March 1545. It was actually 13 December before enough bishops had assembled to enable it to be opened.

37. Scarisbrick, *Henry VIII*, p. 458.

38. *L & P*, XX, ii, nos 455, 738.

39. Scarisbrick, *Henry VIII*, pp. 459-60,

40. *L & P*, XXI, i, nos 85, 91, 122, 124, 218, 221, 251-2, 272.

41. Scotland was included in the treaty, but only to the extent that Henry agreed not to attack again unless he was provoked. As provocation was in the eye of the beholder, this did not mean very much. Rymer, *Foedera*, XV, p. 98.

42. Grafton, *Chronicle*, p. 500.

43. Catherine had been born in about 1512, and was consequently thirty-one at this time. Susan James, *Katheryn Parr: the making of a Queen* (1999).

44. Four years later, when the King's death had freed her for a fourth marriage, she wrote to Seymour, '... as truly as God is God my mind was fully bent, the other time I was at liberty, to marry you before any man I know. However, God withstood my will therein most vehemently for a time ...' Loades, *Henry VIII and his Queens*, p. 138.

45. *Lords Journals*, I, p. 171.

46. Loades, *Henry VIII and his Queens*, loc. cit.

47. Bernard, *The King's Reformation*, pp. 475-90.

48. *The King's Book, or A necessary doctrine and erudition for any Christian man* (1543 RSTC

5168) ed. T. A. Lacey (1932), p. 3.

49. Foxe, *Acts and Monuments* (1583), pp. 1242-9.

50. For the 'Prebendaries plot' and its successor, see MacCulloch, *Thomas Cranmer*, pp. 297-323.

51. Ibid, p. 315.

52. Scarisbrick, *Henry VIII*, p. 478. John Bale, *Select Works* (Parker Society, 1849), pp. 1-136.

53. Loades, *Mary Tudor*, p. 117.

54. Jennifer Loach, *Edward VI*, edited by George Bernard and Penry Williams (1999), pp. 9-17.

55. Statute 35 Henry VIII, c.1. *Statutes of the Realm*, III, p. 955.

56. D. E. Hoak, *The King's Council in the Reign of Edward VI* (1976), pp. 34-46. E. W. Ives, 'Henry VIII's Will: a forensic conundrum', *Historical Journal*, 37, 1994, pp. 779-804. The will itself is TNA E214/1, printed in Rymer, *Foedera* (1741), VI, iii, pp. 142-5.

57. *L & P*, XX, ii, no. 1031. He thanked them particularly for the Act dissolving the Chantries, (which was not implemented) and promised that the ministry of the Church would not suffer in any way.

58. H. Schubert, 'The first cast iron cannon made in England', *Journal of the Iron and Steel Institute*, 146, 1942. pp. 131-40. Alexandra Hildred, 'The Fighting Ship', in *The Mary Rose*, ed. Marsden, pp. 297-346.

59. Loades, *Tudor Navy*, pp. 72-3.

60. Ibid, p. 76.

61. C. S. L. Davies, 'The Administration of the Navy under Henry VIII: the Origins of the Navy Board', *EHR*, 80, 1965, pp. 268-88.

62. D. Loades, *The Making of the Elizabethan Navy, 1540-1590* (2009), pp. 39-55.

63. TNA C66/788, mm 27-30. Loades, *Tudor Navy*, pp. 82-3.

64. The Lord Admiral remained in overall charge, until that responsibility was given to the Lord Treasurer in 1557.

65. Helen Miller, *Henry VIII and the English Nobility* (1986).

66. Scarisbrick, *Henry VIII*, pp. 482-3.

67. *L & P*, XXI, ii, no. 555.

68. Ibid.

69. L. B. Smith, 'Henry VIII and the Protestant triumph', *American Historical Review*, 71, 1966, pp. 1237-64.

70. *L & P*, XXI, ii, no. 697.

71. *L & P*, XXI, ii, no. 696. *Lords Journals*, I, pp. 287, 289.

72. Scarisbrick, *Henry VIII*, pp. 484-6.

73. A. MacNalty, *Henry VIII, a difficult patient* (1952), pp. 159 et seq.

74. *L & P*, XVI, nos 558, 589.

75. MacCulloch, *Thomas Cranmer*, p. 360.

76. Hall, *Chronicle*, p. 900.

12. LEGACY

1. The Navy Board was reconstituted on 4 July 1660, to consist of a Treasurer, Comptroller, Surveyor, and Clerk of the Acts, together with three extra commissioners. C. S. Knighton, *Pepys and the Navy* (2003), pp. 12-14, 18.

2. As long as these franchises continued, the King's writ ran only indirectly, through the franchise holders. The courts of the franchises continued after the dissolution, but acting in the King's name only. Elton, *Tudor Constitution*, pp. 155-6.

3. Kevin Sharpe, *Selling the Tudor Monarchy* (2009), pp. 159-65.

4. *L & P*, XXI, ii, no. 694. William, Lord Grey to Paget, 11 January 1547.

5. The Emperor refrained from exchanging greetings with the new king until it was clear that Mary was not going to mount a challenge. Loades, *John Dudley*, p. 89.

6. *Lords Journals*, I, p. 291.

7. *Acts of the Privy Council*, ed. J. Dasent et al. (1890-1907), ii, p. 17.

8. Ives, 'Henry VIII's will'.

9. W. K. Jordan, *Edward VI, the Young King* (1968), p. 60.

10. *Acts of the Privy Council*, ii, p. 16.

11. TNA SP10/1, no. 11

12. Ibid, no. 17. Strype, *Ecclesiastical Memorials*, II, ii, pp. 289-311.

13. *Calendar of the Patent Rolls, Edward VI*, ed. R.H. Brodie (1924-29), i, pp. 45-6.

14. G. W. Bernard, 'The Downfall of Sir Thomas Seymour' in Bernard, ed., *The Tudor Nobility* (1992), pp. 212-40.

15. *Cal. Pat.*, Edward VI, i, pp. 45-6.

16. A. J. Slavin, 'The Fall of Lord Chancellor Wriothesley; a Study in the Politics of Conspiracy', *Albion*, 7, 1975, pp. 265-85.

17. *APC*, ii, pp. 522-33. *Cal. Pat.*, Edward VI, i, p. 97.

18. Stephen Gardiner to Protector Somerset, 6 June 1547. Muller, *Letters of Stephen Gardiner*, pp. 286-95.

19. Mary never had any intention of using the title of Supreme Head, and Elizabeth reduced it to Supreme Governor precisely because of the episcopal implications of 'Head'. No woman could be a bishop.

20. *The Book of Common Prayer* was largely a translation of the Sarum rite, but omitted such key doctrines as transubstantiation and penance. MacCulloch, *Thomas Cranmer*, pp. 410-20.

21. This was partly due to the fact that it did not come into official use until November 1552, at which point the King had only seven months to live. Enforcement was therefore patchy, it not being usual to hold visitations during the winter. W. K. Jordan, *Edward VI; the Threshold of Power* (1970), pp. 348-9.

22. Ibid, pp. 386-401.

23. M. L. Bush, *The Government Policy of Protector Somerset* (1975), pp. 7-13. W. Patten, *The Expedition into Scotland of the most worthily fortunate Prince Edward, Duke of Somerset*, (*RSTC* 19476.5). Pollard, *Tudor Tracts*, pp. 53-157.

24. *State Papers, Scotland*, I, nos 345-6.

25. Frances Rose-Troup, *The Western Rebellion of 1549* (1913), Appendix K.

26. E. Kerridge, *The Agrarian Problem in the Sixteenth Century and After* (1969).

27. E. H. Shagan, *Popular Politics and the English Reformation* (2003), pp. 275-8.

28. J. Cornwall, *The Revolt of the Peasantry, 1549* (1977). D. MacCulloch, *Suffolk and the Tudors* (1986), pp. 303-7.

29. TNA SP10/9, no. 42. *APC*, ii, p. 342.

30. Loades, *John Dudley*, pp. 151-6. The text of the treaty of Boulogne is in Rymer, *Foedera*, XV, pp. 212-15.

31. Dudley in particular shifted his landed estate several times, selling off lands as he received grants or made purchases elsewhere. Loades, *John Dudley*, Appendix I.

32. *Handbook of British Chronology*, pp. 447-89.

33. Jordan, *Edward VI; the Threshold of Power*, pp. 402-419.

34. W. K. Jordan. *The Chronicle and Political Papers of Edward VI* (1966), pp. 69-73. John Hayward, *The Life and Raigne of King Edward VI* (*RSTC* 12998), ed. Barrett L. Beer (1993), pp. 135-6.

35. Loades, *John Dudley*, pp. 231-3. The text of the 'Device' is Inner Temple MS Petyt xlvii, f. 316. It was printed by J. G. Nichols in *Literary Remains of King Edward VI* (1857), ii, pp. 571-2.

36. Nichols, *Literary Remains*, p. 571.

37. Jennifer Loach, *Edward VI* (1999), p. 176.

38. Ibid, pp. 165-6.

39. The situation was unprecedented, and it was not clear whether the law as it applied to normal minors also applied to the King. It is noteworthy that when the conspirators were tried for the offence of seeking to divert the succession, none was charged with any offence prior to 6 July. Loades, *John Dudley*, p. 256.

40. Ibid, pp. 254-6.

41. Loades, *Mary Tudor*, pp. xi, 135-70.

42. Ambassadors to the Emperor, 12 July 1553. *Cal. Span.*, XI, p. 85.

43. D. G. Newcombe, *John Hooper: Tudor Bishop and Martyr* (2009), pp. 205-6.

44. *Cal. Span.*, XI, p. 95.

45. The proclamation announcing her accession simply referred to the Crown as 'rightfully and lawfully belong[ing] unto us'. Hughes and Larkin, *Tudor Royal Proclamations*, II, p. 3.

46. J. D. Alsop, 'A regime at sea; the navy and the succession crisis of 1553', *Albion*, 24, 1992, pp. 577-90.

47. R. Tittler and S. L. Battley, 'The Local Community and the Crown in 1553: the accession of Mary Tudor Revisited', *Bulletin of the Institute of Historical Research*, 136, 1984, pp. 131-40.

48. P. G. Boscher, 'Politics, Administration and Diplomacy: the Anglo-Scottish Border, 1550-1560' (Ph.D., University of Durham, 1985).

49. D. Loades, *The Religious Culture of Marian England* (2010), p. 1-16.

50. *Cal. Ven.*, V, p. 421. Jennifer Loach, *Parliament and the Crown in the Reign of Mary Tudor* (1986), pp. 75-6.

51. E. H. Harbison, *Rival ambassadors at the Court of Queen Mary* (1940), pp. 57-65. *Cal. Span.*, XI, pp. 198-207. Ambassadors to the Emperor, 4 September 1553.

52. In 1543, Charles had created the Burgundian Circle of the Empire, which emancipated the Netherlands from Imperial law. He had then settled the succession of each of the seventeen provinces on Philip, thus detaching the area from the Empire altogether. M-J. Rodriguez-Salgado, *The Changing Face of Empire; Charles V, Philip II and Habsburg Authority, 1551-1559* (1988), pp. 37-9.

53. D. Loades, *Two Tudor Conspiracies* (1965). The text of the treaty is printed in Rymer, *Foedera*, XV, p. 377. See also Hughes and Larkin, *Tudor Royal Proclamations*, II, pp. 21-6.

54. Loades, *Mary Tudor*, pp. 223-73.

55. Statute 1 Mary, sess. 3, c.1. *Statutes of the Realm*, IV, I.

56. Glyn Redworth, '"Matters impertinent to women"; male and female monarchy under Philip and Mary'. *EHR*, 112, 1997, pp. 597-613. Loades, *Mary Tudor: the tragical history of England's first ruling Queen* (2006), p. 129.

57. John Foxe, *Acts and Monuments* (1583), pp. 2091-5.

58. J. Rodriguez-Salgado and S. Adams, 'The Count of Feria's dispatch to Philip II of 14th November 1558', in *Camden Miscellany*, XXVIII, 1984, pp. 228-38.

59. Mary Stuart had been in France since 1548, and was betrothed to the Dauphin. Margaret Clifford was married to the Earl of Lennox and was the mother of Henry, Lord Darnley.

60. The story of the burning, based on 'persistent whispering', can be found in Thomas Fuller, *Church History of Britain* (1665), V, p. 255. Henry's tomb was never finished. The empty sarcophagus was eventually used for Nelson, and is now in the crypt at St Paul's.

61. A. Weikel, 'The Marian Council Revisited' in J. Loach and R. Tittler, *The Mid-Tudor Polity, 1540-1560* (1980).

62. By the Acts of Supremacy and Uniformity of 1559. Statutes 1 Elizabeth, c.1 and 2. *Statutes of the Realm*, IV, I, pp. 350-55 and 355-8. Elizabeth, however, governed the Church by means of an Ecclesiastical Commission, rather than directly.

63. Harry Kelsey, *Sir John Hawkins: Queen Elizabeth's Slave Trader* (2003). Kelsey, *Sir Francis Drake: the Queen's Pirate* (1998).

64. D. Loades, *The Cecils: privilege and power behind the throne* (2007), pp. 10-29.

65. 'The Count of Feria's dispatch …'.

66. Sharpe, *Selling the Tudor Monarchy*, pp. 348-51.

67. S. G. Ellis, *Tudor Frontiers and Noble Power* (1995), pp. 121, 232, 266.

68. Ellis, *Tudor Ireland*, pp. 242-4.

69. Most notably at Yellow Ford in August 1598. Ibid, pp. 305-6.

70. Ibid, pp. 310-12.

71. D. Loades, *Elizabeth I* (2003), p. 175. J. Wormald, *Mary, Queen of Scots, a Study in Failure* (1988).

72. Wallace T. MacCaffrey, *Elizabeth I: War and Politics, 1588-1603* (1992), p. 545.

73. J. Wormald, 'James VI, James I and the identity of Britain', in Bradshaw and Morrill, eds., *The British Problem c.1534-1707*, pp. 148-72.

74. Loades, *The Cecils*, pp. 250-5.

75. Sharpe, *Selling the Tudor Monarchy*, pp. 135-7.

BIBLIOGRAPHY:
PRINCIPALLY OF WORKS CITED

MANUSCRIPTS
The British Library:
Add. 28585
Add. 48044
Add. 59899
Cotton Julius B.XII
Cotton Caligula D.VI
Cotton Vespasian F.III, C.XIV
Cotton Galba B.V
Cotton Vitellius B.III, B.XIX, B.XX
Cotton Cleopatra F.VI
Cotton Otho C.X

The National Archives:
C66/788
E101 /16/15
KB29/162
PRO.31/3/3, 31/8
SP1 /2, /3, /17, /21, /24, /32, /42, /94, /110
SP2/Ci
SP10/1, /9

Bodleian Library:
MS Ashmole 1116

CALENDARS, GUIDES, & PRINTED DOCUMENTS
Acts of the Privy Council, ed. J. Dasent et al. (1890-1907)
Anglo, S., *The Great Tournament Roll of Westminster* (1968)
Ascoli, G., *La Grande Bretagne devant l'Opinion Francaise* (1927)
Baker, J. A., ed., *The Reports of Sir John Spelman* (Selden Society, 93-4, 1977-8)
Bedouelle, Guy, and Patrick Le Gal, *Le 'Divorce' du roi Henry VIII* (1987)
Calendar of the Patent Rolls, 1485-1494, 1494-1509 (1914-16)
Calendar of the Patent Rolls, Edward VI (1924-1929)
Calendar of State Papers, Foreign, ed. W. B. Turnbull et al. (1861-1950)
Calendar of State Papers relating to Scotland, ed. J. Bain et al. (1898-1952)
Calendar of State Papers, Spanish, ed. G. A. Bergenroth, Royall Tyler et al. (1862-1954)

Calendar of State Papers, Venetian, ed. Rawdon Brown et al. (1864-98)

Campbell, W., ed., *Materials for a History of the Reign of Henry VII* (1873-7)

Cockayne, G. E., *The Complete Peerage*, ed. V. Gibbs et al., (1910-1959)

Correspondencia de Gutierre Gomez de Fuensalida, ed. Duque de Berwick y de Alba (1907)

Cranmer, Thomas, *The Miscellaneous Writings of Thomas Cranmer*, ed. J. E. Cox (Parker Society, 1846)

Ehses, Stefan, *Romische Dokumente sur Geschichte der Ehescheidung Heinrich VIII von England, 1527-1534* (1893)

Ellis, Henry, *Original Letters Illustrative of English History* (1824-1836)

Elton, G. R., *The Tudor Constitution* (1982)

Erasmus, D., *Opus Epistelorum*, ed. P. S. and H. M. Allen (1906-1958)

Frere, W. H. and Kennedy, W. M. *Visitation Articles and Injunctions of the Period of the Reformation* (Alcuin Club, 1910)

Gairdner, J., ed., *Memorials of King Henry VII* (Rolls Series, 1858)

Gairdner, J., ed. *Letters and Papers of the Reign of Henry VII* (1861-3)

Handbook of British Chronology (3rd edition) (1986)

Historical Manuscripts Commission, Bath Papers (1904, 1907, 1908)

Holbein and the Court of Henry VIII (Exhibition catalogue, 1978)

Household Ordinances (1790)

Hoyle, R. W., *The Military Survey of Gloucestershire*, 1522 (1993)

Hughes, P. L. and Larkin, J. F., *Tudor Royal Proclamations* (1964-69)

Knighton, C. S. and Loades, D., *The Anthony Roll of Henry VIII* (2000)

Knighton, C. S. and Loades, D., *Letters from the Mary Rose* (2002)

Knighton, C. S. and Loades, D., eds., 'Lord Admiral Lisle and the Invasion of Scotland, 1544' in S. Rose, ed., *Naval Miscellany*, VII (Navy Records Society, 2008)

Letters and Papers, Foreign and Domestic, of the Reign of Henry VIII, ed. J. S. Brewer et al. (1862-1910)

Memoires de messier Martin du Bellay, seigneur de Langey (1786)

Muller, J. A., *The Letters of Stephen Gardiner* (1933)

Nicholas, Sir H., *Proceedings and Ordinances of the Privy Council of England* (1837)

Nicholas, N. H., *The Privy Purse Expenses of Elizabeth of York* (1830)

Nicholas, N. H., *The Privy Purse Expenses of Henry VIII* (1827)

Nichols, J. G. *Narratives of the Days of the Reformation* (Camden Society, LXXVII, 1879)

Nichols, J. G. *The Literary Remains of King Edward VI* (Roxburgh Club, 1857)

Pocock, Nicholas, *Records of the Reformation; the Divorce 1527-1533* (1870)

Rodriguez Salgado, M-J., and Adams, S., 'The Count of Feria's dispatch to Philip II of 14th November 1558', in *Camden Miscellany*, XXVIII, 1984, pp.228-38.

Rotuli Parliamentorum (1278-1504) (1832)

Rymer, T., *Foedera, conventiones etc.*, (1707-35)

Savage, H., ed., *The Love Letters of Henry VIII* (1949)

Spont, Alfred, ed., *The French War of 1512-13* (Navy Records Society, 1897)

State Papers of Henry VIII (1830-1852)

Statutes of the Realm, ed. A. Luders et al. (1810-28)

Strype, J., *Ecclesiastical Memorials* (1820-40)

Surtz, Edward, SJ and Murphy, V., *The Divorce Tracts of Henry VIII* (1988)

Valor Ecclesiasticus temp. Henry VIII. Auctoritate Regis institutio, ed. J. Carey and J. Hunter (1810-1834)

Wickham Legg, G., *English Coronation Records* (1901)

Wilkins, D., *Concilia Magnae Britanniae et Hiberniae* (1737)

Wood, M. A. E., *Letters of Royal and Illustrious Ladies* (1846)

Youings, J., *Devon Monastic Lands: Calendar of Particulars for Grants, 1536-1558* (1955)

EDITIONS OF CONTEMPORARY WORKS

Cavendish, George, 'The Life and Death of Cardinal Wolsey', in *Two Early Tudor Lives*, ed. R. S.

Bibliography

Sylvester and D. P. Harding (1962). Also edited by S. W. Singer (1827)

Caxton, W., *The Book of the Order of Chivalry*, ed. A. J. P. Byles (Early English Text Society, 1926)

Fish, Simon, *The Supplication of the Beggars* in *English Historical Documents 1485-1558*, ed., C. H. Williams (1967)

Grafton, Richard, *Chronicle* (1809) [*A Chronicle at Large*, 1569]

Hall, Edward, *Chronicle* (1809) [*The Union of the Two noble and Illustre Houses of Lancaster and York* 1548]

Hayward, J., *The Life and Raigne of King Edward VI*, ed. B. L. Beer (1993)

Hazlitt, W. C., *Remains of Early Popular Poetry of England* (1864-6)

Jordan, W. K., ed., *The Chronicle and Political Papers of Edward VI* (1966)

Lacey, T. A. ed. *The King's Book, or A Necessary Doctrine and Erudition for any Christian Man* (1932)

Pace, Richard, *De Fructu qui ex Doctrina Percipitur*, ed. F. Manley and R. S. Sylvester (1967)

Pollard, A. F., *Tudor Tracts* (1903) [*The manner of the triumph at Calais and Boulogne* (1532): *The Noble Triumphant Coronation of Queen Anne* (1533): *The late Expedition into Scotland* (1544): *The expedition into Scotland of the most worthily fortunate Prince Edward, Duke of Somerset*, by William Patten (1548)]

Sander, Nicholas, *The Rise and Growth of the Anglican Schism*, ed. D. Lewis (1877)

Skelton, J., *Works*, ed. A. Dyce (1843)

Vergil, Polydore, *The Anglica Historia of Polydore Vergil*, ed. D. Hay (Camden Society, LXXIV, 1950)

The Complaynt of Scotland, ed. J. A. Murray (Early English Text Society, 1872)

The Earliest English Life of St John Fisher, ed. P. Hughes (1935)

Wriothesley, Charles, *A Chronicle of England*, ed. W. D. Hamilton (Camden Society, new series XI, 1875)

SECONDARY WORKS: BOOKS

Anglo, S., *Spectacle, Pageantry and Early Tudor Policy* (1969)

Bernard, G., *War, Taxation and Rebellion in Early Tudor England* (1986)

Bernard, G., *The King's Reformation* (2005)

Betteridge, T., *Historians of the English Reformation, 1530-1583* (1999)

Bradshaw, B., and Duffy, E., *Humanism, Reform and Reformation: the career of Bishop John Fisher* (1989)

Burnet, Gilbert, *The History of the Reformation of the Church of England* (1679)

Bush, M. L., *The Government Policy of Protector Somerset* (1975)

Cavill, P. R., *The English Parliaments of Henry VII, 1485-1504* (2009)

Chambers, D. S., *Cardinal Bainbridge in the Court of Rome, 1509-1514* (1965)

Chrimes, S. B., *Henry VII* (1972)

Colvin, H. M., *The History of the King's Works; IV, 1485-1660* (1982)

Cornwall, J., *The Revolt of the Peasantry, 1549* (1977)

Cruickshank, C., *Henry VIII and the Invasion of France, 1513* (1990)

Dickens, A. G., *The English Reformation* (1964, 1989)

Dietz, F. C., *English Government Finance, 1485-1558* (1921, 1964)

Dodds, M. H. and R., *The Pilgrimage of Grace, 1536-7 and the Exeter Conspiracy 1538* (1915)

Donaldson, G., *Scotland: James V to James VII* (1965)

Duffy, E., *The Stripping of the Altars* (1992)

Ellis, S. G., *Tudor Ireland* (1985)

Ellis, S. G., *Tudor Frontiers and Noble Power* (1995)

Elton, G. R., *The Tudor Revolution in Government* (1953)

Elton, G. R., *Policy and Police* (1972)

Elton, G. R., *Thomas Cromwell* (1991; second edition ed. D. Loades 2008)

Emmison, F. G., *Tudor Food and Pastimes* (1964)

Eppley, D., *Defending the Royal Supremacy and Discerning God's Will in Tudor England* (2007)

Fissell, M. C., *English Warfare, 1511-1642* (2001)

Fox, A., *Politics and Literature in the Reigns of Henry VII and Henry VIII* (1989)
Fraser, Antonia, *The Six Wives of Henry VIII* (1993)
Froude, J. A., *The History of England from the fall of Wolsey to the defeat of the Spanish Armada* (1856)
Gunn, S. J., *Charles Brandon, Duke of Suffolk, 1484-1545* (1988)
Gunn, S. J. and Lindley, P. G., eds., *Cardinal Wolsey: Church, State and Art* (1991)
Guy, J. A., *The Cardinal's Court* (1977)
Guy, J. A., *The Public Career of Sir Thomas More* (1980)
Gwyn, Peter, *The King's Cardinal: the rise and Fall of Thomas Wolsey* (1990)
Harbison, E. H., *Rival Ambassadors at the Court of Queen Mary* (1940)
Hoak, D. E., *The King's Council in the Reign of Edward VI* (1976)
Hook, Judith, *The Sack of Rome, 1527* (1972)
Hoyle, R. W., *The Pilgrimage of Grace and the Politics of the 1530s* (2001)
Hughes, P., *The Reformation in England* (1956)
Ives, E. W., *The Life and Death of Anne Boleyn* (2004)
Jacob, E. F., *The Fifteenth Century, 1399-1485* (1961)
Jacqueton, G., *La Politique Exterieure de Louise de Savoie* (1892)
James, Susan, *Katheryn Parr: the Making of a Queen* (1999)
Jensen, Sharon L., *Political Protest and Prophecy under Henry VIII* (1991)
Jones, M. K., and Underwood, M., *The King's Mother* (1992)
Jordan, W. K., *Edward VI: the Young King* (1968)
Jordan, W. K., *Edward VI: the Threshold of Power* (1970)
Kelly, D. R. and Sachs, D. H., *The Historical Imagination in Early Modern Britain; History, Rhetoric and Fiction, 1500-1800* (1997)
Kelly, H. A., *The Matrimonial Trials of Henry VIII* (1976)
Kelsey, Harry, *Sir Francis Drake: the Queen's Pirate* (1998)
Kelsey, Harry, *Sir John Hawkins: Queen Elizabeth's Slave Trader* (2003)
Kerridge, E., *The Agrarian Problem in the Sixteenth Century and After* (1969)
Knecht, R. J. *Francis I* (1982)
Knighton, C. S., *Pepys and the Navy* (2003)
Knowles, M. C., *The Religious Orders in England, III, The Tudor Age* (1959)
Lehmberg, S., *The Reformation Parliament* (1970)
Levey, A., *Le Connetable de Bourbon* (1904)
Loach, Jennifer, *Parliament and the Crown in the Reign of Mary Tudor* (1986)
Loach, Jennifer, ed. G. Bernard and P. Williams, *Edward VI* (1999)
Loades, D., *Two Tudor Conspiracies* (1965)
Loades, D., *Mary Tudor* (1989)
Loades, D., *The Tudor Navy* (1992)
Loades, D., *Henry VIII and his Queens* (1997)
Loades, D., *Elizabeth I* (2003)
Loades, D., *Henry VIII: Court, Church and Conflict* (2007)
Loades, D., *The Cecils: Privilege and Power behind the Throne* (2007)
Loades, D., *Cardinal Wolsey, c.1472-1530; Tudor Statesman and Chancellor* (2008)
Loades, D., *The Making of the Elizabethan Navy, 1540-1590* (2009)
Loades, D., *The Religious Culture of Marian England* (2010)
Lupton, J. H., *The Life of John Colet* (1887)
MacCaffrey, W. T., *Elizabeth I: War and Politics, 1588-1603* (1992)
MacCulloch, D., *Suffolk and the Tudors* (1986)
MacCulloch, D., *Thomas Cranmer* (1996)
MacCulloch, D., ed., *The Reign of Henry VIII: Politics, Policy and Piety* (1995)
MacNalty, A., *Henry VIII, a Difficult Patient* (1952)
Marsden, Peter, ed., *The Mary Rose: your Noblest Shippe* (2009)
Mattingly, Garrett, *Catherine of Aragon* (1942, 1963)
Mayer, T. F., *Reginald Pole: Prince and Prophet* (2000)

Bibliography

Miller, Helen, *Henry VIII and the English Nobility* (1986)
Murphy, B., *Bastard Prince: Henry VIII's lost son* (2001)
Neame, A., *The Holy Maid of Kent; the Life of Elizabeth Barton, 1506-1534* (1971)
Nelson, W., *John Skelton, Laureate* (1939)
Newcombe, D. G., *John Hooper, Tudor Bishop and Martyr* (2009)
Ogle, A., *The Tragedy of the Lollards' Tower* (1949)
Oxford Dictionary of National Biography (2005)
Phillips, Gervase, *The Anglo-Scottish Wars, 1513-1550* (1999)
Pierce, Helen, *Margaret Pole, Countess of Salisbury, 1473-1541* (2003)
Pollard, A. F., *Henry VIII* (1902)
Rawcliffe, Carole, *The Staffords, Earls of Stafford and Dukes of Buckingham, 1394-1521* (1978)
Redworth, Glyn, *In Defence of the Church Catholic: a Life of Stephen Gardiner* (1990)
Richardson, W. C., *A History of the Court of Augmentations* (1962)
Richardson, W. C., *Mary Tudor, The White Queen* (1970)
Rodger, N. A. M., *The Safeguard of the Sea* (1997)
Rodriguez Salgado, M-J., *The Changing Face of Empire: Charles V Philip II and Habsburg Authority. 1551-1559* (1988)
Rose-Troup, F., *The Western Rebellion of 1549* (1913)
Ross, Charles, *Richard III* (1981)
Russell, J. G., *The Field of Cloth of Gold* (1969)
Scarisbrick, J., *Henry VIII* (1968)
Scarisbrick, J., *The Reformation and the English People* (1984)
Sharpe, Kevin, *Selling the Tudor Monarchy* (2009)
Smith, L. B., *The Mask of Royalty* (1971)
Smith, L. B., *A Tudor Tragedy: the Life and Times of Catherine Howard* (1961)
Sowerby, Tracey A., *Renaissance and Reform in Tudor England; the career of Sir Richard Morison, c.1513-1556* (2010)
Starkey, D., *The Reign of Henry VIII; Personalities and Politics* (1985)
Starkey, D., *Henry: the Virtuous Prince* (2008)
Warnicke, R. M., *The Rise and Fall of Anne Boleyn* (1989)
Warnicke, R. M., *The Marrying of Anne of Cleves* (2000)
Wegg, Jervis, *Richard Pace* (1932)
Williams, Penry, *The Tudor Regime* (1979)
Wormald, J., *Mary Queen of Scots: a study in failure* (1988)
Young, Alan, *Tudor and Jacobean Tournaments* (1987)

ARTICLES, PAPERS & THESES
Alsop, J. D., 'A regime at sea; the navy and the succession crisis of 1553', *Albion*, 24, 1992.
Armstrong, C. A. J., 'An Italian astrologer at the court of Henry VII', in *Renaissance Studies*, ed. E. F. Jacob (1960).
Bernard, G., 'The Downfall of Sir Thomas Seymour', in Bernard *The Tudor Nobility* (1992).
Boscher, P. G., 'Politics, Administration and Diplomacy: the Anglo-Scottish Border, 1550-1560', University of Durham Ph.D, 1985.
Brigden, Susan, 'Thomas Cromwell and the Brethren', in *Law and Government under the Tudors*, ed. C. Cross et al., 1988.
Brodie, D. M., 'Edmund Dudley; minister of Henry VII', *Transactions of the Royal Historical Society*, 4th series, 15, 1932.
Cooper, J. P., 'Henry VII's last years reconsidered', *Historical Journal*, 2, 1959.
Cunich, P., 'The dissolution' in *Monks of England; the Benedictines in England from Augustine to the Present Day*, ed. D. Rees (1997).
Davies, C. S. L., 'The Administration of the navy under Henry VIII; the origins of the Navy Board', *English Historical Review*, 80, 1965.
Elton, G. R., 'Henry VII; Rapacity and Remorse', *Historical Journal*, 1, 1958.
Elton, G. R., 'Thomas Cromwell's Decline and Fall', in Elton, *Studies in Tudor and Stuart*

Government and Politics, I, 1974.

Gardiner, L. R., 'Further news of Cardinal Wolsey's end', *Bulletin of the Institute of Historical Research*, 57, 1984.

Gunn, S. J. 'The Duke of Suffolk's march on Paris in 1523', *English Historical Review*, 101, 1986.

Guy, J. A., 'The King's Council and Political Participation' in *Reassessing the Henrician Age*, ed. J. A. Guy and A. Fox (1986).

Guy, J. A., 'The Privy Council; revolution or evolution?' in *Revolution Reassessed*, ed. D. Starkey and C. Coleman (1986).

Harriss, G. L., 'Medieval Government and Statecraft', *Past and Present*, 24, 1963.

Head, D. M., 'Henry VIII's Scottish policy', *Scottish History Review*, 61, 1982.

Horowitz, M. R., 'Richard Empson; minister of Henry VII', *Bulletin of the Institute of Historical Research*, 55, 1982.

Ives, E. W., 'Henry VIII's will: a forensic conundrum', *Historical Journal*, 37, 1994.

James, M. E., 'Obedience and dissent in Henrician England; the Lincolnshire revolt of 1536', in James, *Society, Politics and Culture: Studies in Early Modern England* (1980).

Kelly, A., 'Eleanor of Aquitaine and her Courts of Love', *Speculum*, 12, 1937.

Loades, D., 'John Foxe and Henry VIII', *John Foxe Bulletin*, 1, i, 2002.

McEachean, Claire, 'Literature and National Identity' in *The Cambridge History of Early Modern English Literature*, ed. D. Loewnestien and J. Mueller (2002).

Morrill, John, 'The British Problem, c.1534-1707' in *The British Problem, c.1534-1707*, ed., J. Morrill and B. Bradshaw (1996).

Murphy, V., 'The Literature and Propaganda of Henry VIII's first divorce', in *The Reign of Henry VIII; Politics, Policy and Piety*, ed. D. MacCulloch (1995).

Nicholson, Graham, 'The Act of Appeals and the English Reformation', in *Law and Government under the Tudors*, ed. C. Cross et al., 1988.

Redworth, Glyn, '"Matters impertinent to women"; male and female monarchy under Philip and Mary', *English Historical Review*, 112, 1997.

Richards, Judith M., 'Mary Tudor as "Sole Quene"? Gendering Tudor Monarchy', *Historical Journal*, 40, 1997.

Samman, Neil, 'The Henrician Court during Cardinal Wolsey's Ascendancy, 1514-1529', University of Wales Ph.D, 1988.

Schubert, H., 'The first cast iron guns made in England', *Journal of the Iron and Steel Institute*, 146, 1942.

Slavin, A. J., 'The fall of Lord Chancellor Wriothesley: a study in the politics of conspiracy', *Albion*, 7, 1975.

Smith, L. B., 'Henry VIII and the Protestant Triumph', *American Historical Review*, 71, 1966.

Starkey, D., 'Intimacy and Innovation; the rise of the Privy Chamber, 1485-1547' in *The English Court from the Wars of the Roses to the Civil War*, ed. D. Starkey (1987).

Sullivan, Ceri, '"Oppressed by the force of truth"; Robert Parsons edits John Foxe' in *John Foxe, an Historical Perspective*, ed. D. Loades (1999).

Tittler, R., and Battley, S. L., 'The local community and the Crown in 1553: the accession of Mary Tudor revisited', *Bulletin of the Institute of Historical Research*, 57, 1984.

Walker, Greg, 'The expulsion of the minions of 1519 reconsidered', *Historical Journal*, 32, 1989.

Weikel, A., 'The Marian Council revisited', in *The Mid-Tudor Polity, 1540-1560*, ed. J. Loach and R. Tittler (1980).

Wormald, J., 'James VI, James I and the identity of Britain', in *The British Problem c.1534-1707*, ed. J. Morrill and B. Bradshaw (1996).

LIST OF ILLUSTRATIONS

1. & 2. Two views of the Tudor Palace at Greenwich, massively and expensively rebuilt by Henry VII. Henry VIII was born there, and it remained his favourite residence. Nothing of the Tudor building now survives above ground. © Jonathan Reeve JR1882b46fp186 14501500. © Jonathan Reeve JR944b46fp180 14501500.
3. Richmond Palace, otherwise known as Sheen, rebuilt by Henry VII after a fire. It was home to Henry VIII for much of his childhood. © Jonathan Reeve JR1112b67plviii 16001650.
4. Henry VII as a young man. Attributed to Jacques Le Boucq, mid-sixteenth century. The original is in the Library of Arras. © Jonathan Reeve JRCD2b20p764 14501500.
5. Perkin Warbeck, the pretender whose claim to be Richard of York, the younger son of Edward IV, afflicted Henry VII from 1492 to 1497. This drawing, attributed to Jacques Le Boucq, shows the strong physical resemblance to Edward which first drew attention to him. © Jonathan Reeve JRCD3b20p795 14501500.
6. Henry VII's chantry in Westminster Abbey. Completed by Henry VIII after his father's death, with funeral effigies by Pietro Torrigiano. © Jonathan Reeve JR1188b67plivB 16001650.
7. Margaret Tudor, elder daughter of Henry VII, and Henry VIII's sister. She married in 1503 James IV of Scotland, and became by him the grandmother of Mary, Queen of Scots. © Jonathan Reeve JR982b20p837 15001600.
8. Plan of the palaces of Westminster and Whitehall, formerly known as York Place. From a later version of the 1578 map known as Ralph Agas' map, although not in fact by him. The Thames was the main highway connecting London, Westminster, Lambeth, Hampton Court, Southwark and Greenwich. © Jonathan Reeve JRCD2b20p769 15501600.
9. A view of Westminster, c. 1550, by Anthony van Wyngaerde. Westminster was the seat of the royal courts of justice, the meeting place of the parliament, and the nearest thing to a fixed capital that England possessed. © Jonathan Reeve JR1872b46fp16 13001350.
10. Whitehall palace, c. 1550, also by van Wyngaerde. As York Place this had been the traditional Westminster residence of the Archbishops of York, and had been extensively rebuilt by Cardinal Wolsey. It came into the King's hands on the fall of Wolsey in 1529, and was further rebuilt. It was used as a principal royal residence until largely destroyed by fire in the 1690s. © Jonathan Reeve JR1884b46fp192 15001550.
11. & 12. London from Westminster through the Strand (top) and St Paul's (bottom), c. 1550 by Anthony van Wyngaerde. These views show the closely packed nature of the City. © Jonathan Reeve JR1873b46fp22 15001550 & © Jonathan Reeve JR1874b46fp28 15001550.
13. & 14. London bridge (top) and the Tower of London (bottom), c. 1550 by Anthony van Wyngaerde. The Tower was a fortress, prison, royal residence, and the home of the royal archives. © Jonathan Reeve JR1875b46fp34 15001550 & © Jonathan Reeve JRCD3b20p1025 15501600.
15. From a later copy of the parliament roll of 1512. The young king is shown going in procession to the opening of parliament, walking beneath a ceremonial canopy of blue and gold, blazoned with a Tudor rose. The canopy is borne by monks, and followed by peers of the realm bearing his train. © Jonathan Reeve JR971b54p363 15001600.
16. The coronation of Henry VIII, taken from an illuminated initial in the mortuary roll of John Islip, Abbot of Westminster (1500–1532). In this perspective the abbey is cut open to give a view of the coronation itself (24 June 1509), which was probably the highlight of Islip's incumbency. © Jonathan Reeve JR1161b4p604 15001550.
17. An iron lock-plate, temp. Henry VIII. © Jonathan Reeve JR976b61p709 15001600.
18. 19. & 20. Henry VIII's Great Seals. The Great Seal, which was normally held by the Lord Chancellor, or Lord Keeper, was the ultimate authentication for acts of royal power. It was affixed (for example) to international treaties and to charters of grant. The Seal was changed periodically to express developing ideas of kingship – for example the Royal Supremacy over the Church. © Jonathan Reeve JR1170b2p11 15001550, © Jonathan Reeve JR1172b2p57T 15001550 & © Jonathan Reeve

JR1173b2p57B 15001550.

21. The *Henry Grace à Dieu*, taken from the Anthony Roll of 1545. When Henry's capital ship, the *Regent*, was lost in battle in 1512, Henry caused a replacement to be built '... such another as was never seen before in England, and called it the Henry Grace de Dieu ...' It was launched on 15 October 1515, and displaced about 1,500 tons, making it by far the largest ship in the navy. Rebuilt in the late 1530s, it was reduced in size, and destroyed by fire in 1553. It was launched by Queen Catherine (then visibly pregnant), and the King, Queen and court enjoyed a splendid banquet on board. © Jonathan Reeve JR1180b20p814 15001550.

22. Letter from Catherine of Aragon to Thomas Wolsey, as the King's Almoner. Dated from Richmond, 2 September 1513, and signed 'Katherine the Qwene', it recommends that Louis d'Orléans, Duke of Longueville, who had been taken prisoner at the battle of the Spurs (17 August), and sent to Catherine as a 'trophy', should be conveyed to the Tower 'as sone as he commethe' for 'it shuld be a grete combraunce to me to have this prisoner here'. Henry was still in France, and Catherine was ruling as Regent in his absence. The battle of Flodden was fought a week later. © Jonathan Reeve JR962b20p895 15001600.

23. Letter from Henry VIII to Cardinal Wolsey, March 1518. This letter, which is a holograph, shows the affable side of Henry's character. The King addresses Wolsey as 'Myne Awne good cardinall' and continues in the same vein to thank him for the 'grette payne and labour' that he has taken in the King's affairs. Henry sends the Queen's good wishes ('most harty recommendations'), and concludes 'Wrytten with the hand off your loving master, Henry R.' © Jonathan Reeve JRCD2b20p88? 15001550.

24. 'Pastyme with good companye', Henry VIII's most famous composition. Henry had a good singing voice and was a (moderately) talented composer. Taken from 'Henry VIII's song book', in the British Library. © Jonathan Reeve JR1176b2p149 15001550.

25. Illuminated capital from a plea roll of 1514. It was normal for these formal legal records to be decorated with initial letters depicting the kings on his throne., sometimes in black and white, and sometimes (as here) in colour. © Jonathan Reeve JR1183b20p885 15001550.

26. & 27. The meeting of the kings at the Field of Cloth of Gold, taken from plaster casts of the bas-reliefs in the Galerie d'Aumale at the Hotel de Bourgtheroulde, a noble townhouse in Rouen. Above, Henry VIII's party sets out from Guisnes. Below, the meeting of the Kings; Henry VIII is on the left, and Francis I on the right, a positioning reflecting French priorities. © Jonathan Reeve JR1177b2p167B 15001550 & © Jonathan Reeve JR1177b2p167T 15001550.

28. Henry VIII in the House of Lords, 1523 or 1529, taken from a later copy of a contemporary drawing 'ordered by the then Garter [King of Arms]'. © Jonathan Reeve JRCD2b20p948 15001550.

29. Title page of the 1523 edition of Henry VIII's *Assertio Septem Sacramentorum* against Martin Luther. This work was written and originally printed in 1521, but that edition was circulated only to a limited number of recipients (including the Pope). This title page describes the King as 'regiam maiestatem' (his royal majesty) a usage unusual before the break with Rome. © Jonathan Reeve JRCD2b20p868 15001550.

30. A drawing for the painting of Sir Thomas More and his family, by Hans Holbein, *c.* 1527. The painting itself was copied by Rowland Lockey in 1593, and the original does not survive. © Elizabeth Norton and the Amberley Archive.

31. Golden Bull of Pope Leo X confirming the grant of the title 'Fidei Defensor' to King Henry VIII in 1521. The papal 'bull' or seal was usually cast in lead, but on special occasions (as here) might be cast in gold. This one, designed by Benvenuto Cellini, shows as usual the twin founders of the Church of Rome, SS Peter and Paul. © Jonathan Reeve JR1184b20p888 15001550.

32. Letter from Anne Boleyn to Cardinal Wolsey, *c.* 1528, when she was still hopeful that Wolsey would be able to clear a path for her marriage to the King. She thanks him for his services to her cause and promises me that, after the attainment of her hopes, if there is anything that she can do for him 'you shall fynd me the gladdyst woman in the woreld to do yt.© Jonathan Reeve JRCD3b20p899 15001550.

33. Letter from Anne Boleyn to 'Master Stephyns' (i.e. Stephen Gardiner, the King's secretary, in Rome, 4 April 1529. Dated at Greenwich and signed 'Anne Boleyn', the letter expresses the hope 'that the ende of this jorney shall be more pleasant' to her than its beginning. Gardiner was in Italy for a second time endeavouring to persuade Pope Clement VII to convert Wolsey and Campeggio's commission (then in England) into a decretal commission – from which there could be no appeal. © Jonathan Reeve JR964b20p900 15001600.

34. Holbein's design for a jewelled pendant, intended as a gift for Princess Mary, probably executed during his first visit to England (1526–28). At that time Mary was representing the king in the Marches of Wales, and was still in favour as the heir to the throne. © Elizabeth Norton and the Amberley Archive.

35. Anne Boleyn's clock. One of many artefacts given to her by the king as tokens of his affection. It has the initials H and A engraved on its weights. © Jonathan Reeve JR1162b4p648 15001550.

36. A carving in wood from Canterbury cathedral, perhaps from a series caricaturing Henry's opponents. This shows Catherine of Aragon flanked by Cardinals Wolsey and Campeggio, in a clear reference to the failure of the Blackfriars court in the summer of 1529, when Catherine had aroused the King's anger by appealing directly to Rome, and Pope Clement had revoked the case. Wolsey's failure to prevent this led directly to his fall.© Jonathan Reeve JR977oldpc 15001600.

37. The Anglo-French treaty of Amiens, 18 August 1527, whereby Henry joined the League of Cognac against the Emperor. © Jonathan Reeve JR1182b20p881 15001550.

38. A grovelling letter from Cardinal Wolsey to the King, dated 8 October 1529, begging for forgiveness. It is signed 'Your Graces moste prostrat poore chapleyn, creature and bedisman'. In terms reminiscent of a prayer to God, the letter states that he, the king's 'poore hevy and wrechyd prest', daily calls upon his royal majesty 'for grace, mercy remyssyon, and pardon'. The King ignored him. © Jonathan Reeve JRCD3b20p902.

39. Letter from Wolsey to Stephen Gardiner, the King's Secretary in February or March 1530. The Cardinal never abandoned his hope for a recall to favour. Here he writes with reference to arrangements respecting appointments in the Province of York, to which he had been instructed to withdraw. He trusts 'yt wole now please hys maiste to shewe hys pety ... without sufferyng me any leynger to lye langwyshyng and consuming awey ...' © Jonathan Reeve JRCD3b20p905.

List of Illustrations

40. Windsor Castle – a royal palace and fortress, and home of the Knights of the Garter. It was at Windsor on 11 July 1531 that Henry saw Catherine of Aragon for the last time. © Jonathan Reeve JR1189b67plixB 16001650.

41. Calais and its harbour from a sixteenth-century drawing. It was to Calais that Henry and Anne crossed in October 1532, for their meeting with Francis I, which occurred there and at Boulogne. Henry believed that he had secured Francis's diplomatic backing for his 'divorce' from Catherine, and while at Calais slept with Anne Boleyn for the first time. © Jonathan Reeve JR1186b20p1009 15001550.

42. A copy of Pope Clement VII's 'definitive sentence' in favour of Catherine of Aragon and against Henry VIII. Issued on the 23 March 1534, after vain calls to Henry to give up Anne and return to his first wife. It was ignored in England. © Jonathan Reeve JR1171b2p45 15001550.

43. The Act in Restraint of Appeals (25 Henry VIII, c.20) of 1533. The preamble opens with the portentous claim 'that this Realme of Englond is an Impire', and goes on to state that it is governed by one supreme head and king, whose jurisdiction is competent to adjudge all spiritual cases which may arise within the realm. All appeals to the pope, and to any 'foreign princes and potentates' are absolutely forbidden. In passing this act, the parliament claimed jurisdiction over spiritual causes in a manner which had never hitherto been thought possible. Before it was passed, Archbishop Cranmer had received from Rome the pallium which confirmed his metropolitan authority, and this Act enabled his decision to be definitive. © Jonathan Reeve JRCD2b20p912 15001550.

44. Letter from Cranmer to the king, dated from Dunstable 17 May 1533. The Archbishop informs Henry, with apologies, that his great matter cannot be resolved until Friday, because of the liturgical calendar. © Jonathan Reeve JR894b7p53 15001550.

45. Extract from the Treasons Act of 1534 (26 Henry VIII, c. 13). This provides that 'everie offendour....hereafter laufully convicte of any maner of high treasons shall lose & forfayte to the kynges highnes his heirs and successours all suche landes tenements and heriditaments whiche any suche offendour....shall have of any estate of inheritaunce yn use or possession by any right title or menes within this realme of Englonde'. Its innovation lay in the fact that it extended the definition of treason to include the Royal Supremacy over the Church, which many contemporaries saw as making treason out of mere words. © Jonathan Reeve JRCD2b20p918 15001550.

46. The Act of Supremacy, 1534 (26 Henry VIII, c.1). This act declared that 'the kynges maiestie iustley and ryghtfully is & oweth to be the supreme heed of the churche of England...' It was carefully phrased to make it clear that parliament was recognising a title which the king already possessed, not conferring it upon him. By Letters Patent of 15 June 1535, Henry formally added the phrase 'in terra supremum caput Anglicane Ecclesie' to his royal style and title. © Jonathan Reeve JRCD2b20p915 15001550.

47. An imaginative nineteenth-century portrayal of Queen Catherine before the Blackfriars court in 1529. This shows the proceedings of the second session on 21 June, when the king was also present. © Jonathan Reeve JR95ab7p49 15001600.

48. A nineteenth-century representation of the death of Catherine of Aragon at Kimbolton in January 1536. Although allegedly very much afraid of poison, it is almost certain that she died of coronary thrombosis. © Jonathan Reeve JR958b61p693 15001600.

49. The coronation procession of Anne Boleyn approaches Westminster Abbey, June 1533. A published account shortly after did its best to portray spontaneous rejoicings, but in fact a number of prominent individuals boycotted the proceedings, including the King's sister, Mary, his daughter and the Imperial ambassador. © Jonathan Reeve JR968b42p404 15001600.

50. A nineteenth century representation of the execution of Anne Boleyn. The Calais executioner, with his sword, stands waiting on the right. © Jonathan Reeve JR965b20p921 15001600.

51. Henry VIII in council. This appears to be a formal session, with the King seated under his 'cloth of estate'. In practice the council normally met without the King, and attendance was usually about a dozen. © Jonathan Reeve JRCD3b20p913 15001550.

52. Page from the original manuscript of 'The Institution of a Christian Man' (The King's Book), showing the extensive corrections made in the King's own hand. Henry lost no opportunity to emphasise, clearly and in detail, his repudiation of the Roman jurisdiction. © Jonathan Reeve JRCD2b20p925 15001550.

53. The barn at Wolf Hall, near Marlborough, the seat of Sir John Seymour. Jane Seymour was allegedly born in the house, which was long ago demolished. The barn, however, survived until it was burned down in the early twentieth century. Local legend has it that Henry and Jane were married in the barn, but in fact that happened at Whitehall (originally York place) on 30 May 1536. © Elizabeth Norton and the Amberley Archive.

54. Monumental brass of Thomas Boleyn, Earl of Wiltshire. Following the executions of his daughter Anne and son George in 1536, Thomas lost the Privy Seal, but was allowed to withdraw to his estates, and not otherwise penalised. He died at Hever Castle on the 13 March 1539. © Jonathan Reeve JR1174b2p87 15001550.

55. Declaration by the bishops, probably of 1536, explaining that two disputed scriptural texts (John 20:21 and Acts 20:28) confer spiritual but not political power upon the episcopate. © Jonathan Reeve JR1158b7p73 15001550.

56. Title page from the Great Bible, printed by Richard Grafton and Edward Whitchurch, 1539. Enthroned as God's vicar, Henry symbolically hands out the Word of God to the spiritual and temporal hierarchies of his realm, headed by Thomas Cranmer on his right, and Thomas Cromwell on his left. © Jonathan Reeve JRCD2b20p929 15001550.

57. The Act of Six Articles (31 Henry VIII, c.14). This conservative measure enforced all the traditional doctrines of the mass, including transubstantiation – the conversion of the bread and wine in the Eucharist into the physical body and blood of Christ. © Jonathan Reeve JR159b7p169 15001550.

58. Henry VIII as King David. One of several beautiful illuminations decorating a manuscript book of the psalms produced for the King's personal use in 1540. © Jonathan Reeve JR1164b4p663 15001550.

59. Henry VIII's new palace of Nonsuch, built (roughly) in imitation of Francis I's chateau of Chambord. It was never finished in Henry's lifetime and was demolished in the late seventeenth century. It was allegedly constructed partly using materials looted from the dissolved monasteries. © Jonathan Reeve JR1018b5fp204 15001550.

60. Oatlands in Surrey, another of Henry's palaces, which was upgraded from a hunting lodge. It was here that the King

married his fifth Queen, Catherine Howard, on 28 July 1540. The palace was subsequently demolished and archaeological investigations were carried out in the 1950s. © Jonathan Reeve JR1149pc 15001550.

61. Third Succession Act (35 Henry VIII, *c.*1), 1544. This was the act which designated Mary and Elizabeth to follow Edward if he should die without heirs, and broke new ground in that it authorised the succession of illegitimate children.© Jonathan Reeve JR1185b20p920 15001550.

62. Design for a timepiece by Hans Holbein. This was made by Nicholas Kratzer for Sir Anthony Denny, and presented by him to the King for a New Year's gift in 1545. © Elizabeth Norton and the Amberley Archive.

63. Henry VIII's will, dated 30 December 1546. It was signed with a dry stamp, not with the King's own hand, which was a cause of later disputes. © Jonathan Reeve JRCD2b20p961 15501600.

64. St George's Chapel, Windsor, which was the home of the Garter Knights, and which Henry chose for his last resting place in preference to his father's chapel at Westminster. This was probably because he wanted to be beside Jane Seymour, who had been interred there in 1537.© Jonathan Reeve JR1190b67plx 16001650.

66. Henry VII by an unknown artist *c.* 1500. © Ripon Cathedral.

67. Henry VII's Queen, and Henry VIII's mother, Elizabeth of York. She holds a Tudor rose, as a symbol of her dynastic significance.I. By kind permission of Ripon Cathedral Chapter.

68. Westminster Abbey. The site of Anne Boleyn's greatest triumph when she was crowned queen of England. © Elizabeth Norton.

69. Lady Margaret Beaufort. The matriarch of the Tudor dynasty, through whom Henry VII derived his tenuous claim to the throne. Lady Margaret narrowly outlived her son, to die early in her grandson's reign. Like her son, she is buried in what is in effect the Tudor mausoleum, the Lady Chapel he built at the back of Westminster Abbey. By kind permission of Ripon Cathedral Chapter.

70. Henry VIII portrayed in all his magnificence at King's College, Cambridge. © Elizabeth Norton.

71. Cartoon of Henry VIII with his father by Hans Holbein, 1536-37. Drawn in black ink with watercolour washes. Paper, mounted on canvas. © Elizabeth Norton and the Amberley Archive.

72. Catherine of Aragon as a slightly younger woman (c.1520?). By kind permission of Ripon Cathedral Chapter.

73. Henry VIII tilting before Queen Catherine, celebrating the birth of his short-lived son, February 1511. From the Great Tournament Roll of Westminster. © Jonathan Reeve JR1098b2fp204 15001550.

74. The tomb of Henry Fitzroy, Duke of Richmond, Henry VIII's bastard son. At St Michael's church, Framlingham, Suffolk. Courtesy of Elizabeth Norton and the Amberley Archive.

75. Elizabeth (Bessie) Blount, Henry's mistress and the mother of Henry Fitzroy. From her funeral effigy. © Elizabeth Norton and the Amberley Archive.

76. Cardinal Thomas Wolsey (1471 or 1475-1530). From a drawing by Jacques le Boucq. © Jonathan Reeve JR1169b2p7 15001550.

77. Thomas Cranmer (1489-1556). He was appointed Archbishop of Canterbury following the death of William Warham. From a painting by Gerhard. © Elizabeth Norton and the Amberley Archive.

78. The Field of Cloth of Gold, 1520, depicting the temporary palace built at Henry's orders especially for the occasion. The King takes centre stage. © Jonathan Reeve JR1151b66p1 15001550.

79. Design for a pageant tableau, probably intended for use by the merchants of the Steelyard at the coronation of Anne Boleyn in 1533. Anne was apparently upset by the fact that it was surmounted by an Imperial eagle rather than her own badge of a white falcon. © Elizabeth Norton and the Amberley Archive.

80. Thomas Wyatt the elder, by Hans Holbein. Wyatt was a royal servant and diplomat who had, allegedly, been one of Anne Boleyn's 'lovers' in the 1520s. © Elizabeth Norton.

81. Anne Boleyn. Her relationship with Henry VIII from 1525 to 1532 was fraught with consequences, because of her insistance of marriage as a condition of sharing his bed. She failed to adapt to the role of Queen after 1533, and was executed in 1536. By kind permission of Ripon Cathedral Chapter.

82. Stained glass from Wolfhall. The glass showing Jane Seymour's phoenix badge and other royal images was moved to Great Bedwyn Church following the destruction of Wolfhall. The feathers under Jane's Phoenix badge show her to have been the mother of the prince of Wales. © Elizabeth Norton.

83. Jane Seymour, who was generally reckoned to be a comfortable creature rather than a great beauty. Drawing by Hans Holbein. © Jonathan Reeve.

84. A depiction of Henry VIII in a stained-glass window at Canterbury cathedral. The dependence of the design on Holbein's original is obvious. © Elizabeth Norton and the Amberley Archive.

85. Henry VIII, from a window in the chapel at Sudeley Castle. © Elizabeth Norton and the Amberley Archive.

86. Henry VIII and his family, artist unknown, but about 1545. The Queen depicted is Jane Seymour. On the King's right is Prince Edward. Mary is further out on his right, and the twelve-year-old Elizabeth on his left. The figure on the extreme right is alleged to represent Will Somers, the King's jester. © Jonathan Reeve JR997b66fp40 15001550.

87. Drawing of Sir Thomas More by Hans Holbein, *c.* 1527. This drawing is pricked for transfer to canvas, and is the original of the painting by Holbein now in the Frick gallery in New York. © Elizabeth Norton and the Amberley Archive.

88. Drawing of Archbishop William Warham by Hans Holbein, c. 1527–8, which is the original of the painting now in the Louvre. Paris. © Elizabeth Norton.

89. Thomas Howard, 3rd Duke of Norfolk, Henry's Lord Treasurer until his fall in December 1546, and uncle to both Anne Boleyn and Catherine Howard. By Hans Holbein. © Jonathan Reeve JR949b2p110 15001550.

90. Anne of Cleves, Henry's fourth wife. This is the portrait by Hans Holbein that misled theKing into thinking that he was marrying a beauty. The marriage was dissolved after three months on the grounds of non-consummation. Amberley Archive.

91. Catherine Howard, Henry's fifth wife, as the Queen of Sheba. From a window at King's College Chapel, Cambridge. © Elizabeth Norton and the Amberley Archive.

92. The meeting of the Emperor Maximilian I and Henry VIII during his campaign against Boulogne in 1544. Artist unknown. © Jonathan Reeve JR1154b66p29 15001550.

Also available from Amberley Publishing

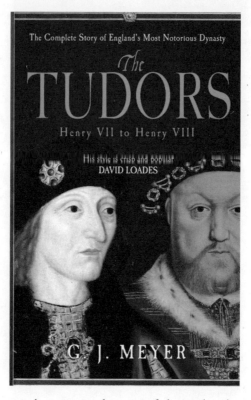

A superb narrative history of the Tudor dynasty

In 1485, young Henry Tudor, whose claim to the throne was so weak as to be almost laughable, crossed the English Channel from France at the head of a ragtag little army and took the crown from the family that had ruled England for almost four hundred years. Half a century later his son, Henry VIII, desperate to rid himself of his first wife in order to marry a second, launched a reign of terror aimed at taking powers no previous monarch had even dreamed of possessing. In the process he plunged his kingdom into generations of division and disorder, creating a legacy of blood and betrayal that would blight the lives of his children and the destiny of his country.

£12.99 Paperback
72 illustrations (54 colour)
384 pages
978-1-4456-0143-4

Available from all good bookshops or to order direct
Please call **01453-847-800**
www.amberleybooks.com

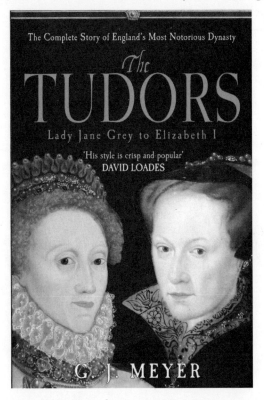

Also available from Amberley Publishing

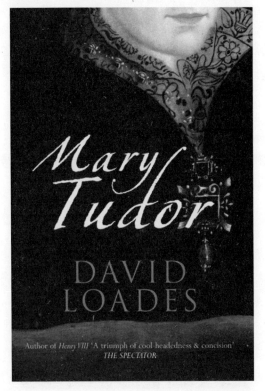

The dramatic story of the first woman to rule England - and the cruel fate of those who opposed her iron will

David Loades explores the twisting path whereby Princess Mary, daughter of a rejected wife, Catherine of Aragon, and a capricious father - Henry VIII - endured disfavour, personal crisis and house arrest to emerge as Queen of England with huge popular support. Loades' probing yet sympathetic account reveals an intriguing personality, impelled by deep-set beliefs and principles yet uncertain how to behave in a 'man's' role.

Also available from Amberley Publishing

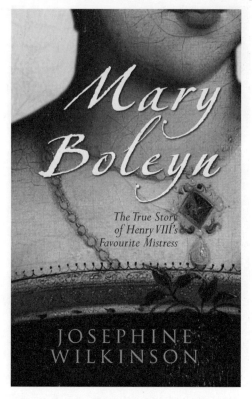

The scandalous true story of Mary Boleyn, infamous sister of Anne, and mistress of Henry VIII

Mary Boleyn, 'the infamous other Boleyn girl', began her court career as the mistress of the king of France. François I of France would later call her 'The Great Prostitute' and the slur stuck. The bête-noir of her family, Mary was married off to a minor courtier but it was not long before she caught the eye of Henry VIII and a new affair began.

Mary would emerge the sole survivor of a family torn apart by lust and ambition, and it is in Mary and her progeny that the Boleyn legacy rests.

£9.99 Paperback
22 illustrations (10 colour)
224 pages
978-1-84868-525-3

Available from all good bookshops or to order direct
Please call **01453-847-800**
www.amberleybooks.com

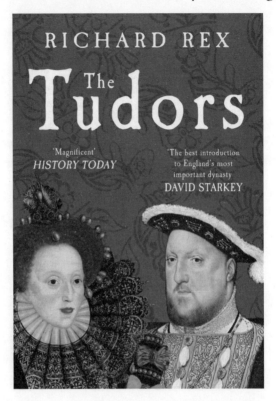

Also available from Amberley Publishing

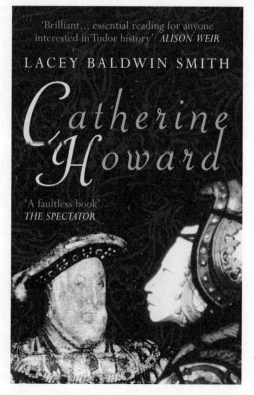

A biography of Henry VIII's fifth wife, beheaded for playing Henry at his own game – adultery

'Brilliant... essential reading for anyone interested in Tudor history' ALISON WEIR

'A faultless book' THE SPECTATOR

'Lacey Baldwin Smith has so excellently caught the atmosphere of the Tudor age' THE OBSERVER

£9.99 Paperback
25 colour illustrations
288 pages
978-1-84868-521-5

Available from all good bookshops or to order direct
Please call **01453-847-800**
www.amberleybooks.com

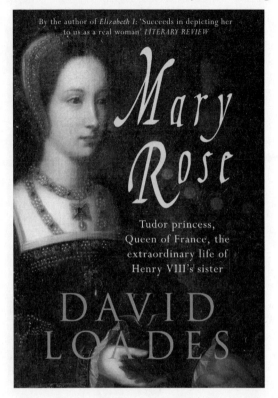

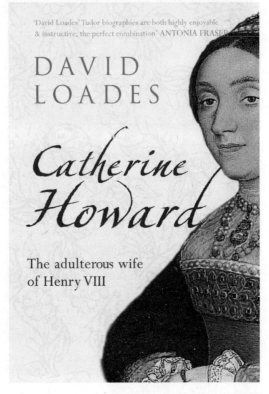

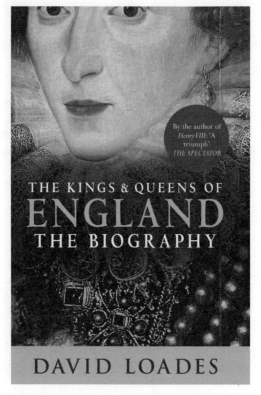

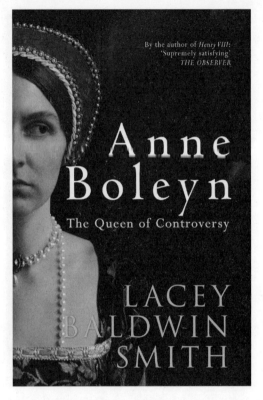

Also available from Amberley Publishing

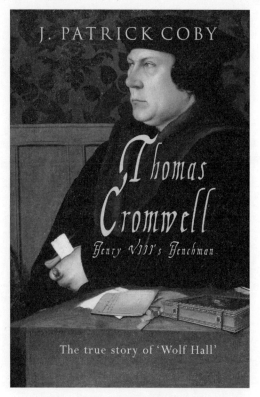

The real story of 'Wolf Hall'

Thomas Cromwell, chief architect of the English Reformation served as chief minister of Henry VIII from 1531 to 1540, the most tumultuous period in Henry's thirty-seven-year reign. Many of the momentous events of the 1530s are attributed to Cromwell's agency, the Reformation, the dissolution of the monasteries and the fall of Henry's second wife, the bewitching Anne Boleyn.

Cromwell has been the subject of close and continuous attention for the last half century, with positive appraisal of his work and achievements by historians, this new biography shows the true face of a Machiavellian Tudor statesmans of no equal.

£20 Hardback
30 illustrations (10 col)
292 pages
978-1-4456-0775-7

Available from all good bookshops or to order direct
Please call **01453-847-800**
www.amberleybooks.com

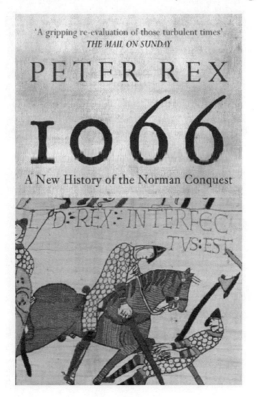

Tudor History from Amberley Publishing

THE TUDORS
Richard Rex

'The best introduction to England's most important dynasty'
DAVID STARKEY

'Gripping and told with enviable narrative skill... a delight'
TLLS

'Vivid, entertaining and carrying its learning lightly'
EAMON DUFFY

'A lively overview' **THE GUARDIAN**

£9.99   978-1-4456-0700-9   256 pages PB 143 illus., 66 col

CATHERINE HOWARD
Lacey Baldwin Smith

'A brilliant, compelling account' **ALISON WEIR**

'A faultless book' **THE SPECTATOR**

'Lacey Baldwin Smith has so excellently caught the
atmosphere of the Tudor age' **THE OBSERVER**

£9.99   978-1-84868-521-5   256 pages PB 25 col illus

MARGARET OF YORK
Christine Weightman

'A pioneering biography of the Tudor dynasty's most
dangerous enemy'
PROFESSOR MICHAEL HICKS

'Christine Weightman brings Margaret alive once more'
THE YORKSHIRE POST

'A fascinating account of a remarkable woman'
THE BIRMINGHAM POST

£10.99   978-1-4456-0819-8   256 pages PB 51 illus

THE SIX WIVES OF HENRY VIII
David Loades

'Neither Starkey nor Weir has the assurance and command
of Loades' **SIMON HEFFER, LITERARY REVIEW**

'Incisive and profound. I warmly recommend this book'
ALISON WEIR

£9.99   978-1-4456-0049-9   256 pages PB 55 illus, 31 col

MARY ROSE
David Loades

£20.00 978-1-4456-0622-4
272 pages HB 17 col illus

MARY BOLEYN
Josephine Wilkinson

£9.99 978-1-84868-525-3
208 pages PB 22 illus, 10 col

JANE SEYMOUR
Elizabeth Norton

£9.99 978-1-84868-527-7
224 pages PB 53 illus, 26 col

HENRY VIII
Richard Rex

£9.99 978-1-84868-098-2
192 pages PB 81 illus, 48 col

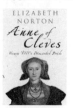

THOMAS CROMWELL
Patrick Coby

£20.00 978-1-4456-0775-7
272 pages HB 30 illus (20 col)

ANNE BOLEYN THE
YOUNG QUEEN TO BE
Josephine Wilkinson

£9.99 978-1-4456-0395-7
208 pages PB 34 illus (19 col)

ELIZABETH I
Richard Rex

£9.99 978-1-84868-423-2
192 pages PB 75 illus

ANNE OF CLEVES
Elizabeth Norton

£9.99 978-1-4456-0183-0
224 pages HB 54 illus, 27 col

Available from all good bookshops or to order direct
Please call **01453-847-800 www.amberleybooks.com**

More Tudor History from Amberley Publishing

Forthcoming February 2013 from Amberley Publishing

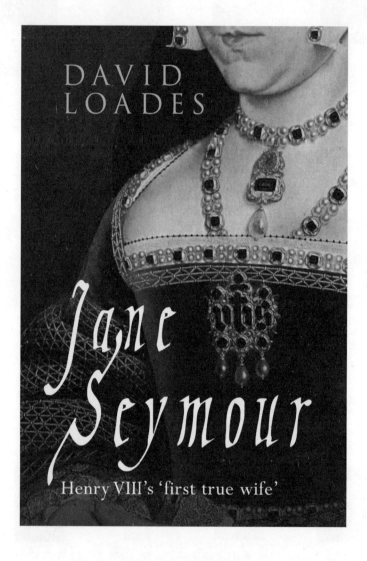

DAVID
LOADES

Jane
Seymour

Henry VIII's 'first true wife'

Available from all good bookshops or to order direct
Please call **01453-847-800**
www.amberleybooks.com

INDEX